MW00718919

ROME THE COSMOPOLIS

Rome stands today for an empire and for a city. The essays gathered in this volume explore some of the many ways in which the two were interwoven. Rome was fed, beautified and enriched by empire just as it was swollen, polluted, infected and occupied by it. Empire was paraded in the streets of Rome, and exhibited in the city's buildings. Empire also made the city ineradicably foreign, polyglot, an alien capital, and a focus for un-Roman activities. The city was where the Roman cosmos was most concentrated, and so was most contested. Deploying a range of methodologies on materials ranging from Egyptian obelisks to human skeletal remains, via Christian art and Latin poetry, the contributors to this volume weave a series of pathways through the World City, exploring the different kinds of centrality Rome had in the empire. The result is a startlingly original picture of both empire and city.

CATHARINE EDWARDS is Lecturer in Ancient History at Birkbeck College, University of London, having previously taught at the University of Bristol. Her publications include *The politics of immorality in ancient Rome* (1993), *Writing Rome: textual approaches to the city* (1996), an edited volume *Roman presences: receptions of Rome in European culture 1789–1945* (1999) and an annotated translation of Suetonius' *Lives of the Caesars* for the Oxford World's Classics (2000). She is currently working on Seneca and Roman attitudes to death.

GREG WOOLF is Professor of Ancient History at the University of St Andrews, having previously taught at the University of Oxford. His publications include *Literacy and power in the ancient world* (1994) and *Becoming Roman* (1998). He is currently writing a book on *The imperial culture of the Romans* and engaged in research into the local cults of the Roman Empire and on the letters of the Younger Pliny.

ROME THE COSMOPOLIS

EDITED BY

CATHARINE EDWARDS

AND

GREG WOOLF

CAMBRIDGE
UNIVERSITY PRESS

CAMBRIDGE UNIVERSITY PRESS
Cambridge, New York, Melbourne, Madrid, Cape Town, Singapore, São Paulo

Cambridge University Press
The Edinburgh Building, Cambridge CB2 2RU, UK

Published in the United States of America by Cambridge University Press, New York

www.cambridge.org
Information on this title: www.cambridge.org/9780521800051

First published 2003
Reprinted 2004
This digitally printed first paperback version 2006

A catalogue record for this publication is available from the British Library

ISBN-13 978-0-521-80005-1 hardback
ISBN-10 0-521-80005-6 hardback

ISBN-13 978-0-521-03011-3 paperback
ISBN-10 0-521-03011-0 paperback

Contents

Figures

Contributors

MARY BEARD is Reader in Classics at the University of Cambridge and Fellow of Newnham College. Her recent publications include *The invention of Jane Harrison* (Harvard University Press 2000), *The Parthenon* (Profile Books 2002) and *Classical art: from Greece to Rome* (Oxford University Press 2001), (with John Henderson).

CATHARINE EDWARDS teaches Ancient History at Birkbeck College, University of London. Her first book, *The politics of immorality in ancient Rome* (Cambridge University Press 1993) was based on a PhD thesis supervised by Keith Hopkins. Her publications also include *Writing Rome: textual approaches to the city* (Cambridge University Press 1996). She is currently working on Seneca and Roman attitudes to death.

JAŚ ELSNER is Humfry Payne Senior Research Fellow at Corpus Christi College, Oxford, but he was educated in Cambridge and – in the last year of his doctoral research – was supervised by Keith Hopkins. His most recent book is *Imperial Rome and Christian triumph: the art of the Roman Empire AD 100–450* (Oxford University Press 1998), and in addition to Classical art he works on the interface of literature, history and material culture in the Roman world.

WILLEM JONGMAN teaches Ancient History at Groningen University. He is currently an overseas fellow at Churchill College, Cambridge. He has published widely on Roman economic history, including *The economy and society of Pompeii* (1988). His current work is on Roman consumption. He is preparing a book on *The political economy of the Roman Empire*. Keith Hopkins taught him to shed his Teutonic style.

RICHARD MILES is a Research Fellow in Classical Studies at the Open University and a Teaching Fellow at Churchill College, Cambridge. He is the editor of *Constructing identities in late antiquity* (Routledge 1999) and author of *Message and authority in the age of Augustine* (Routledge forthcoming). Keith Hopkins had the grave misfortune of supervising Richard for the first year of his PhD thesis.

NEVILLE MORLEY is Senior Lecturer in Ancient History at the University of Bristol. Although he was supervised by Keith for only a single term as a graduate student, his work on economic history and historical theory shows an indelible Hopkins influence. His publications include *Metropolis and hinterland: the city of Rome and the Italian economy 200 BC – AD 200* (Cambridge University Press 1996) and *Writing ancient history* (London, 1999); he is currently writing books on trade and on social theory for ancient historians.

WALTER SCHEIDEL is Associate Professor in the Department of Classics at Stanford University. His latest book is *Death on the Nile: disease and the demography of Roman Egypt* (Brill 2001).

CAROLINE VOUT is Lecturer in Classics at the University of Nottingham. She has published on various aspects of Roman imperial culture and art. Her doctoral thesis *Eroticised political discourse in imperial Rome* was supervised in part by Keith Hopkins.

GREG WOOLF is Professor of Ancient History at the University of St Andrews. Like all of those who experienced Keith Hopkins' supervision, he has never been able to remove Keith from the ranks of his imagined readers. He has published on the Roman economy, ancient literacy and Roman religion, and is the author of *Becoming Roman. The origins of provincial civilization in Gaul* (Cambridge University Press 1998).

Keith Hopkins passed away on 8th March 2004. As well as the many obituaries, a memoir by W. V. Harris was published in the Proceedings of the British Academy 130 (2005) pp. 81–105. Keith's last book, The Colosseum, was completed by Mary Beard and published in 2005 by Profile Books. It is a reminder of how clever, funny and original he could be. The contributors to this volume are only a few of all those who will miss him.

Preface

This book is for Keith Hopkins.

As contributors, we do not comprise a complete line-up of his past students, nor even a representative sample of those who have, over the years, benefited from Keith's generous and trenchant criticism. Our decision to offer Keith a 'real book' made that impossible. The subject was chosen because it interested us, and because we hoped it might interest Keith. Slavish adherence to the dedicatee's views would have been no tribute. We are sure he will find much to disagree with here, and look forward to debating it with him on many future occasions. We share a sense of how much we learned from Keith's teaching, and continue to learn from his practice as one of the world's premier historians of antiquity. For most of us that experience began between 1985 and 2001, when, as Professor of Ancient History in the Faculty of Classics of the University of Cambridge, he held the chair formerly occupied by his own teachers, Sir Moses Finley and A. H. M. Jones. He was, he used to assure us in his unforgettable graduate seminars, a gentler critic than either of them, though we remain unconvinced.

Cosmopolis was not built in a day. During the period of construction, the editors have incurred numerous (other) debts of gratitude. Among those who lent support at various stages, we would like to thank Sue Alcock, Tamsyn Barton, Graham Burton, Valérie Huet, Christopher Kelly, Rebecca Preston and Seth Schwartz. Pauline Hire and Michael Sharp at the Press have been enthusiastic, as well as patient, supporters of the project. Susan Moore has been an heroic copy editor. Our thanks to all.

Birkbeck College, London　　　　　　　　　　CATHARINE EDWARDS
University of St Andrews　　　　　　　　　　　　GREG WOOLF

Abbreviations

AC	L'Antiquité classique
AE	L'Année épigraphique
AJA	American Journal of Archaeology
ANRW	Aufstieg und Niedergang der römischen Welt
AJA	American Journal of Archaeology
BASP	Bulletin of the American Society of Papyrologists
CCL	Corpus Christianorum, series Latina
CIL	Corpus Inscriptionum Latinarum
CEFR	Collections de l'Ecole française de Rome
CQ	Classical Quarterly
DdA	Dialoghi di archeologia
G&R	Greece and Rome
HSCP	Harvard Studies in Classical Philology
IG	Inscriptiones Graecae
IGUR	Inscriptiones Graecae Urbis Romae
ILS	Inscriptiones Latinae Selectae
JbAC	Jahrbuch für Antike und Christentum
JECS	Journal of Early Christian Studies
JHS	Journal of Hellenic Studies
JRA	Journal of Roman Archaeology
JRS	Journal of Roman Studies
JTS	Journal of Theological Studies
LIMC	Lexicon Iconographicum Mythologiae Classicae
MAAR	Memoirs of the American Academy in Rome
MDAI(R)	Mitteilungen des deutschen archäologischen Instituts (Römische Abteilung)
MGH	Monumenta Germaniae Historica
OCD³	Oxford Classical Dictionary, 3rd edition
P&P	Past and Present
PBSR	Papers of the British School at Rome

PCPS	*Proceedings of the Cambridge Philological Society*
P.Oxy.	*Oxyrhynchus papyri*
RAC	*Reallexicon für Antike und Christentum*
RE	*Pauly–Wissowa, Real-Encyclopädie der klassischen Altertumswissenschaft*
REL	*Revue des études latines*
RhM	*Rheinisches Museum für Philologie*
RIB	*Roman Inscriptions of Britain*
RIC	*Roman Imperial Coinage*
SMSR	*Studi e materiali di storia delle religioni*
TAPA	*Transactions of the American Philological Association*
VC	*Vigiliae Christianae*
ZPE	*Zeitschrift für Papyrologie und Epigraphik*

CHAPTER I

Cosmopolis: Rome as World City

Catharine Edwards and Greg Woolf

> What race is so remote, what so barbarous, Caesar, from which there
> is no spectator in your city?[1]

This book begins in the Colosseum – that site of so many deaths, human
and animal – which is perhaps the most potent emblem of the all-
encompassing, all-consuming city of Rome. Our epigraph is the opening of
the third poem in Martial's short collection *De spectaculis*, 'On the games',
written to commemorate the Colosseum's inauguration in the reign of the
emperor Titus. The spectacles produced in the vast arena paraded the city's
mastery of the world.[2] Gladiators themselves were often drawn from distant parts of the empire.[3] Lions and elephants from Africa, bears from
Dalmatia, tigers from India were brought to Rome to meet violent deaths
in the arena.[4] However, not only were the spectacles themselves sumptuous and awesome demonstrations of the extent of Rome's power, but, as
Martial's poem emphasizes, those who watched them could also function as
symbols of the empire's reach. Martial lists Thracians, Sarmatians (from the
region of the Danube), Sygambrians (a German tribe), Arabs, Ethiopians.
Marked out by their exotic clothing and hair arrangements, their incomprehensible speech, these people embodied the vastness and diversity of
Roman territory, their presence in the heart of the city underlining Rome's
power to draw people to itself over distances almost unimaginable, from
cultures thrillingly alien.

Other writers, too, remark on the diversity of the city's population as one
of its hallmarks – and not always in such positive terms. For some ancient
writers, notoriously, the multifarious population of Rome was a threat to

---

[1] *quae tam seposita est, quae gens tam barbara, Caesar, | ex qua spectator non sit in urbe tua?*
[2] As Hopkins so vividly emphasises (1983b) ch. 1, esp. 11–12.
[3] See Noy (2000) 117–18 on the origins of entertainers in Rome.
[4] On the range of animals put on show in Rome, see e.g. Pliny, *NH* 8.64–71.

its Romanness – the perennial paradox of the imperial metropolis.[5] Martial himself marvels at his exotic fellow spectators; as always at the games in Rome, the audience was itself an intrinsic part of the show. But we shall also be considering how these diverse spectators would themselves have responded to what was on view in the Colosseum – and in the city around it. One of the principal concerns of this book is the experiences of those millions of people who came to Rome from all over the empire, often over vast distances, to visit or to live (and all too frequently to die).[6]

There was much for them to wonder at in the metropolis of the emperors. Its enormous size was unparalleled; no human eye could comprehend it. The splendour of its buildings, constructed from gleaming marbles brought from distant lands, was incomparable. The marketplaces of the city were crammed with more transitory reminders of Rome's dominance over the world. Rome's appetite was often conceived as insatiable. The Younger Seneca's complaint that Romans scour the globe to load their tables (*Ad Helv.* 10.3) is echoed by countless other Roman writers.[7] Those who had travelled vast distances to the city might be disconcerted to see familiar products on sale in the markets – or even familiar monuments on display. In the Campus Martius, for instance, Augustus re-erected an obelisk from Heliopolis, taken as part of the spoils of his victory at Actium, with the inscription on its base: *AEGVPTO IN POTESTATEM POPVLI ROMANI REDACTA* – 'Egypt having been brought under the dominion of the Roman people'.[8] Everywhere in the city elements of the conquered world had been appropriated and recontextualized; the city had absorbed the world.

ROME THE COSMOPOLIS?

Rome itself is sometimes referred to in antiquity as 'cosmotrophos', 'nurturer of the world' (e.g. in *IG* XIV 1108).[9] The term 'cosmopolis', however, derived from the Greek words for 'world' and 'city', occurs only as the title

---

[5] Juvenal's third satire is perhaps the most notoriously negative characterization. On diversity see Herodian 1.12.1; still impressive in 357 CE, according to Ammianus (26.61). And, of course, even hostile accounts of the diversity of Rome's population such as Juvenal's third satire at the same time celebrate the extent of the city's power.

[6] As Hopkins emphasizes, 'Rome was a huge death-trap' (1995/6) 60. See further Scheidel in this volume.

[7] As Gowers comments: 'Like the spoils heaped up in a Roman triumphal procession lists of food, verbal "heaps" which challenged the reader's or listener's bodily capacity graphically reproduced the amassing of goods in Rome, whether on the tables of the rich or in the city's cookshops, where the wealth of conquered nations was translated into ingestible matter' (1993) 18–19.

[8] See Steinby (1993–9) s.v. horologium.   [9] Discussed by Purcell (1999) 141.

of a magistrate in a handful of Greek city-states.[10] Stoic philosophers used the term 'cosmopolites' to refer to the position aspired to by the would-be wise man, transcending local attachments to identify with all of humanity as a 'citizen of the world'.[11] Yet Romans from the time of Cicero onwards – and Greeks, too – liked to play on the idea of Rome as a city in some ways equivalent to the world; *Romanae spatium est urbis et orbis idem*, 'The world and the city of Rome occupy the same space', in Ovid's words (*Fasti* 2.684). There is no part of the world which is not also Rome. To be a citizen of Rome was thus to be a citizen of the world.[12]

This is a familiar and enduring trope but one which bears closer examination, for this volume takes as its central concern the nature of the relationship between the city and the world; the terms in which that relationship was articulated are of crucial importance. What were the implications of likening Rome to the world – or the world to Rome? The Greek aristocrat Aelius Aristides' oration *To Rome* (written in the mid second century) praises the Romans for extending the security associated with urban life throughout the empire (100). The Romans manage the world as if it were one *polis* (36).[13] Written centuries later just after the sack of the city in 416 CE, Rutilius Namatianus' nostalgic address to Rome (which he is leaving to return to his native Gaul), also evokes this aspect of the city/world equation:

By offering to the vanquished a share in your own justice, you have made a city out of what was once a world.[14] (*De red. suo* 65–6)

Rutilius emphasizes the extension of Roman law throughout the Roman world; citizenship is the mechanism through which *urbs* and *orbis* are equated (though, since by this time Rome had long ceased to be a centre of government, the force of the term 'city' is to some extent metaphorical). Here, too, the emphasis is primarily on the city's impact on the empire – not surprisingly so, perhaps, given the perspective from which these men were writing.

Other ancient discussions are more preoccupied with the manifestations of empire within and through the city itself. At least from the time of Augustus (when the fabric of the city underwent a major overhaul), Roman

---

[10] According to Liddell, Scott and Jones.

[11] On Stoic cosmopolitanism, see Schofield (1991).

[12] The trope and its deployment are further explored by Nicolet (1991) 98–114; Griffin (1991); Gowers (1995); Edwards (1996) 99–100.

[13] Swain (1996) 274–84 argues that Aristides is rather lukewarm in his praise of the advantages Rome brings to provincial subjects.

[14] *Dumque offers victis proprii consortia iuris, | urbem fecisti quod prius orbis erat.*

writers express concern that the city's appearance should be commensurate with its power over the world.[15] The architect Vitruvius praises Augustus for the care he has taken: 'that the splendour of public buildings should bear witness to the majesty of the empire', *ut maiestas imperii publicorum aedificiorum egregias haberet auctoritates* (1 pr. 2). For the Elder Pliny writing under Vespasian (like Augustus, responsible for initiating extensive public building projects) the buildings of Rome, which he terms *miracula*, 'marvels', were another demonstration that the rest of the world was *victum*, 'outdone', of course, but also 'conquered'; *sic quoque terrarum orbem victum ostendere* (*NH* 36.101). And Aristides, too, in an earlier section of his oration, uses the vocabulary of wonder; the extent of the city's power initially inspires amazement:

If one looks at the whole empire and reflects how small a fraction rules the whole world, he may be amazed at the city, but when he has beheld the city herself and the boundaries of the city, he can no longer be amazed that the entire civilized world is ruled by one so great. (*To Rome* 9)

The physical fabric of the city gives plausibility – authority even – to Rome's claim to rule the world. The greatness of the city at the same time serves to render comprehensible the extent of its vast empire. And thus the huge expenditure of resources in the capital (not least on successive emperors' building projects) is justified.

Other approaches to characterizing Rome's relationship to the world deployed by Greek authors include the notion of Rome as an epitome or summary of the world. The medical writer Galen invokes it (attributing it to the sophist Polemo), in emphasizing the huge number of types of limb dislocation he has had the opportunity to see while working in the city (one consequence, then, of the varied nature of the city's population).[16] Athenaeus, in the *Deipnosophists* (written in the final years of the second century CE), comments: 'it would not be far off the mark to call the city of Rome an epitome of the civilized world, for within it every city may be seen to have planted a colony' (1.20.b–c). The availability within the city of the produce of every region could be similarly interpreted. Aristides notes:

Here is brought from every land and sea all the crops of the seasons and the produce of each land, river, lake, as well as of the arts of the Greeks and barbarians, so that if someone should wish to view all these things, he must either see them by travelling over the whole world or be in this city. (*To Rome* 10)

---

[15] According to Livy (also writing under Augustus), Rome's shabbiness in comparison with the capitals of the Greek East had been mocked in the middle and late republic (40.5.7).

[16] Galen 18a.347. On this see Swain (1996) 363–5.

All the world is to be found in Rome. This point is reinforced a few paragraphs later, as Aristides comments: 'And whatever one does not see here neither did nor does exist' (13).

The slippery rhetoric of comparisons between the city and the world could lend itself to negative readings. In the course of his description of the Temple of Peace (which immediately follows his account of the triumph of Titus and Vespasian, celebrating their victory over the Jews) the Jewish writer Josephus comments that in Rome one could see the treasures of the world brought together; the convenient assembly of these spectacular objects thus saves the seeker after marvels from touring around all those different cities (*Jewish War* 7.5.7).[17] But the remark (from one who had witnessed the Romans' devastating victory over his own people) is double-edged. Rome creams off the best of everything. The city draws to itself from the rest of the world the most valuable and beautiful of its possessions, as well as the most gifted of its inhabitants (including Josephus himself, of course). The city, then, could be figured as dominating the world but also as representing or summing up the world – in terms of synecdoche constituting its head (*caput mundi*), in terms of metonymy standing for its totality (every region is represented within it), in terms of epitome gathering together its most precious contents.

In this sense, at least from the perspective of those within the city, Rome had not merely taken over the world but eclipsed it completely. The city's relative indifference to its vast territories is perhaps reflected in a comment the geographer Strabo makes about Rome's architectural splendour. In his account of Rome, he praises the structures of the Campus Martius in detail, lists the monuments of the rest of the city and then concludes that, if you saw all these: 'you would easily become oblivious to everything else outside. Such is Rome' (*Geography* 5.3.8). The world as it is represented within the city displaces the actual world beyond it.

More specific evocations of the interrelationship between *urbs* and *orbis* were also to be found incorporated into Rome's built environment.[18] Pompey celebrated his great victories in the east with the construction of a magnificent theatre complex in 52 BCE, in which was set up a statue of Pompey himself holding a globe, thus signifying Rome's dominance over the *orbis terrarum*. Among the honours decreed to Julius Caesar in association with his triumphs of 46 BCE was a statue set up on the Capitoline hill, of Caesar with his foot on a bronze image of the *oikoumene* – the

[17] On Rome as a city of wonders, see Purcell (2000) 405–7.
[18] These monuments have been suggestively discussed in Nicolet (1991).

inhabited world.[19] According to the Elder Pliny, the map of the world set up by Augustus' associate Agrippa in the northern Campus Martius aimed to 'show the entire world to the city', *orbem terrarum urbi spectandum propositurus* (*NH* 3.17).[20] The notion of display is foregrounded here, the city itself personified as the viewer. Agrippa's map and the inscription bearing Augustus' achievements, his *Res gestae* (with its long list of territories incorporated into the empire) can thus be seen as a development of the 'cosmocratic tradition' of Rome's triumphant generals.[21]

The city's physical fabric more generally has been a particular focus of scholars' attention in recent decades. Several of the essays offered in this volume (those by Edwards, Elsner and Vout) pursue specific aspects of the impact of empire on the fabric of the city (though we do not aim to offer a comprehensive account of this vast issue). Some of the most influential recent work in this area has tended to simplify the impact of Rome's public monuments.[22] A common concern of our essays is to emphasize the multivalent and shifting significance of monuments in the city and in particular the varied perspectives of viewers. Vout, for instance, explores the potential meanings of Egyptian imagery, as it was used in a number of contexts in the city of Rome. Was the pyramid (constructed around 12 BCE) which served as the funeral monument of Gaius Cestius perceived as a gesture of sympathy with the Egyptianizing Mark Antony, Augustus' arch rival in the civil wars so recently concluded? Or perhaps as an appropriation of Egypt in homage to those undertaken by the emperor himself? Can such allusions to and explorations of the 'alien' cultures included within the empire ever have been straightforward? Vout's paper highlights the importance of examining the specific contexts in which particular cultures are evoked.

The problem of representing empire in the city is an issue also explored in Beard's discussion of the ritual of the triumph. This spectacular procession, staged only to celebrate the greatest Roman victories, was centred on the person of the triumphant general. It regularly included campaign spoils, as well as the most distinguished of the conquered enemy and sometimes representations of battles fought or territories acquired; the triumph served

---

[19] The significance of these statues is discussed by Nicolet (1991) 37–41.
[20] The symbolic significance of this has been discussed by Nicolet (1991) 98–114.
[21] Nicolet (1991) 11.
[22] Zanker (1989). For criticisms of his position see Wallace-Hadrill, 'Rome's cultural revolution', *JRS* 79 (1989) 157–64. While Zanker's more recent work (e.g. 1997) has focused more closely on the experience of the viewers of ancient monuments, he has been concerned rather with change over time, arguing that viewers were more interested in the political symbolism of images in the early principate than they were later. The differing perspectives of individual viewers as conditioned by e.g. their own place of origin are not discussed.

to put Rome's increasingly exotic conquests on display before the people of Rome. But to what extent could its meaning be controlled? The crowds in the Roman streets were to a significant degree composed of conquered people themselves, or at least their descendants. How did they respond to these spectacles? What was the relationship between the spectacle and what had happened on the empire's frontiers? Some triumphs were presented in written accounts as substitutes for rather than representations of conquest. And the triumphant general's symbolically charged yet problematic status (he was dressed in the same costume as the statue of Jupiter on the Capitol) may itself have served, as Beard emphasizes, to raise questions about the credibility of the whole show.

Prominent among the spoils paraded through the city in triumphs of the middle years of the republic were artworks, particularly statues, taken from the Greek East. Edwards' paper explores a variety of responses, Roman and Greek, to these 'foreign bodies', many of which found a permanent home in Rome's public spaces. Here they might function as symbols of Rome's conquest over the Greek world; but they could also be read as highlighting Rome's artistic inferiority or the disruptive personal ambitions of the generals who had captured them and put them on display. Commissioned statues might also play a part in representing empire within the city. Pompey's theatre complex, mentioned above, included statues personifying the territories he had conquered. But these, too (and others like them), did not function simply as reassuring indices of the empire's vast extent.

The city of imperial splendour was full of reminders of the violence of conquest. This violence might be translated into the arena, where gladiatorial fights and wild beast hunts were staged to celebrate great victories. It might be frozen in the defeated stance of a marble barbarian, displayed on a triumphal monument. It might be reconfigured in the brutality of a master beating a slave, captured, brought to Rome and sold in the aftermath of another imperial victory. The bustling metropolis may have seemed largely ordered but how confident could its inhabitants be that this violence would always be contained?

SUSTAINING COSMOPOLIS

Rome, the Cosmopolis, was made to stand against change. As the power of the Roman people grew so the roots of the City were dug deeper into antiquity, down beneath Romulean Rome and Evander's settlement, to the scene of Hercules' battle with the monster Cacus, and ultimately back to Troy. At the same time Rome's posterity was extended forwards. The monuments

created by Republican dynasts, Caesar's and Augustus' calendrical manip-
ulations and the latter's monumentalization of the Fasti pointed the way to
the slogan Roma Aeterna.[23] The City became a fixed point in the Cosmos, a
cityscape layered and relayered with myth and history, a theatre of memory
and at the same time a stage on which all future generations of Romans
were destined to play a part... or else have their absence noted. Ammianus'
Constantius II, visiting Rome for the first time in 357 in the twentieth year
of his reign, is prepared for his *adventus* to play the part of an impassive
and colossal statue, but he is transformed from spectacle to spectator by
the sights of the City.[24] His inadequacy as an emperor is underlined by his
ignorance of what lies at the heart of his empire, the 'glories of the eternal
city'.

In reality, naturally, the Cosmopolis was not built once and for all time.
The City had to be constantly rebuilt and repaired, both at the mundane
and at the cosmic level. Roads needed periodic repaving, the embankments
along the Tiber and the bridges that crossed it needed maintenance, the
insulae of the city needed to be reconstructed after fire damage, flood-
ing and the collapses caused by their often poor construction: the cost of
this enterprise was phenomenal.[25] As Frontinus' treatise, along with a vast
body of recent epigraphic and archaeological research, makes very clear,
the complex water supply of the city required constant expert attention.[26]
The monumental fabric too could not be static. If Rome was to remain
central to the Cosmos, to persist as a faithful epitome of the world, it had
to keep pace with the changes in that greater whole. New imperial *fora* had
to be added, bigger and better amphitheatres and *basilicae*, more splendid *thermae* furnished with artworks appropriate to their theme. Earlier
programmes might be slighted or plundered in the endless recalibration
of Urbs and Orbis. The Arch of Constantine points us back to the early
second-century monuments it reuses at the same time as it marks a new
stage in the endless renegotiations of the Senate's tortuous relationship with
the emperors.

Perhaps the most obvious feature of this homeostatic process is seen in the
evolving sacred topography of the city.[27] The Flavians brought their patron

---

[23] Wallace-Hadrill (1987), Griffin (1991) and Hardie (1992) on the Augustan manipulation of time.
Matthews (1986) on Roma Aeterna, and Constantius' *adventus*.

[24] Ammianus Marcellinus 16.10.14–15.

[25] DeLaine (2000) on the constant need for rebuilding and maintenance of the urban fabric.

[26] Bruun (1991), Dodge (2000) offer excellent accounts.

[27] Beard, North and Price (1998), vol. 1 maps 2–4 give a vivid impression of the ubiquity of new cults
in Rome. For a succinct account of developments in the cults of the City cf. chapter 5 of the same
volume.

Isis to Rome and established her in a splendid sanctuary on the Campus Martius. Successive emperors made their own marks with immense temples to their chosen divinities, Domitian to Minerva, Hadrian to Venus, Severus to Liber and Hercules, Caracalla to Sarapis, Aurelian to Sol, Constantine to Christ and so on. The cults of the Cosmopolis were notionally regulated by the Senate, although the emperors' interventions were never challenged even when, as in the case of the fourth-century Christian emperors, they were often resented.

Change was not always managed from above. The monuments of imperial Rome show shifts of religious topography that were not co-ordinated from the centre. Immigrants brought with them to Rome a bewildering variety of cults from all over the empire.[28] Shrines to Palmyrene and Syrian deities are prominent in Trastevere but there was little religious zoning and new cults appear all over the City. Some forty sanctuaries and monuments to Mithras are known from all parts of the City: most must be dated between the early second century and 376–7, when a Mithraeum was destroyed by a Christian urban prefect Furius Maecius Gracchus in a *cause célèbre* related gleefully by Jerome.[29] The destruction of shrines too was a necessary recalibration of City to Empire, the process Elsner describes in this volume as the invention of Christian Rome. Changing patterns of private cult seem generally to set the pace, until specific cults attained the prominence that led to prohibitions, expulsions or incorporation into the *sacra publica*, and sometimes all of these in turn. Cult illustrates the limits in the capacity of Senate and emperors to orchestrate the performance of Empire in the City.

Rome's evolution as Cosmopolis was never wholly planned: at times the process evidently generated considerable anxiety. Much of what passes for testimony to Rome's cosmopolitanism is in fact generated by attempts to police, limit and control the influx of people and traditions on which the physical and demographic survival of the city depended. Some Romans sought to reject the Cosmos. Umbricius' condemnation of the 'Greek City' in Juvenal's third satire is the most quoted example of this.[30] The satire does not attack an innovation but a perennial concern: Greek Rome was as old as all the other Romes.[31] By presenting Rome as an alien capital, Juvenal's speaker attacks a series of fundamental culture myths that opposed the heterogeneous roots of Rome – her great families above all – to the myth of Athenian autochthony. Trojan and Arcadian refugees provide the

---

[28] Noy (2000) on immigration and its consequences.
[29] Epistle 107.2, with discussion in Matthews (1975) 22–3.   [30] Edwards (1996) ch. 5.
[31] A theme of Cornell (1995).

chronologically earliest layer of these myths, but the theme is taken up in Romulus' establishment of the asylum, in the kidnap of Sabine women, in the Etruscan and Greek ancestry claimed by various of the older houses, a series of legends brought together by Cato in his *Origines*, by Livy in his archaeology of the Roman people and by Claudius in his speech on the admission of Gauls to a Senate in part resistant to the move. At no period in Roman history is it possible to detect a consensus about the most desirable rate at which the aliens should be admitted into the city.

Modern accounts stress migration to Rome as the main means by which it grew – perhaps doubling in size twice a century over the course of the middle and late Republic to an Augustan peak of 1 million – and then as the precondition for its survival as the greatest city of the Mediterranean world for the first three centuries CE. The argument is familiar. Death rates exceeded birth rates so dramatically in all pre-industrial cities for which we have figures, that any ancient megalopolis must have needed constant replenishment from without.[32] Recent research has further strengthened this inference. Scheidel shows in this volume how the City gathered to itself all the most noxious germs of the empire and set them loose on a population as densely packed as any, and which included many whom systematic malnutrition had rendered especially vulnerable. At a lesser scale similar processes of high mortality, and even higher immigration, must lie behind the survival of other great regional hubs, Carthage – discussed by Miles in this volume – and also Alexandria and Antioch, Pergamum, Athens and Ephesus. As Jongman shows in his chapter, the first three centuries of the empire saw large cities grow at the expense of smaller ones, and the global urban population of the empire approach an apogee in absolute terms and as a proportion of the total population. If Rome was swollen by imperialism, she was sustained at that level as the peak of a settlement hierarchy generated by empire.

Yet this demographic picture is too simple. Or rather this model illustrates the *minimum* levels of immigration needed to sustain the megalopolis. As Morley's chapter makes clear, these mass movements are in fact aggregates of many different kinds of journeys to Rome. And there were journeys away as well. Rutilius Namatianus' *envoi* and Umbricius' bitter leave-taking have already been mentioned. And others left only to return and leave again.[33] These trajectories can be imagined at different

---

[32] A case made brilliantly for the Republic by Hopkins (1978a) chapter 1 and for the early empire in Hopkins (1995/6) 58–60. For late imperial Rome see Purcell (1999) 140–4.

[33] Parkin (1992) 5 noting the potential demographic complications introduced once movement back and forth from Rome are taken into account.

levels of society. At its summit Constantius was not the only emperor to visit the World City rarely: after the first century CE few emperors ruled mainly from Rome. Senators were required by law to spend much of their lives in the City, but in their first two or three decades after admission to the Senate many spent quite long periods in the provinces. The imperial Senate when it met lacked the current commanders of the legions, those away governing provinces and a few others deputed on special missions for the emperor as well as those over 60 (or 65) who exercised the option of not attending meetings. If part of the shared experience of senators in Rome was service abroad, past and anticipated, so senators in the provinces looked back and forward to Rome. Equally as provincials entered the Senate in greater and greater numbers they retained strong links with their ancestral homes.[34] Provincial wealth flowed to Rome as they purchased their houses on the Esquiline and in other fashionable areas and set up their considerable establishments. Many senators also continued to patronise their compatriots and monumentalise their home cities. On visits home they and their relatives brought experience of the capital with them. Rome thus became part of the mental furniture of the empire's elite.

The journeys of others took them back and forth between the metropole and the provinces. Equestrians are less epigraphically visible but some examples of provincial recruits to the procuratorial service are known and many served in the City for part of their careers.[35] Imperial patronage, and that of the senators, brought poets, teachers, orators and other performers to the City.[36] Other visitors included scholars, missionaries and, when the emperors were in Rome, ambassadors. One way Rome became a Cosmopolis was as a place much visited, a common point through which many of the empire's most prominent inhabitants passed at least once in their lifetimes, a secular Mecca and so a shared cityscape of memory and the imagination.

The transient, temporary and occasional population of the City was much more diverse than the xenophobic rant of Juvenal's third satire

---

[34] Eck (1997). On the changing character of the senatorial elite cf. Hopkins (1983b) 120–200. On the Senate itself Talbert (1984).

[35] Sablayrolles (1999) for a recent survey of the grandest posts in the equestrian service. At 378–9 he notes the relative slowness of the order to recruit from provincials, except to the highest levels, and Eck (1997) 76 notes how few equestrian as opposed to senatorial names appear on the lead water pipes that provided private water supplies, by imperial permission, for mansions in Rome. For Eck, the latter indicates 'the marked difference in the strength of the ties that bound the two *ordines* to Rome'. Yet even if fewer equestrians were granted the right to abstract water from the public aqueducts, it is difficult to believe that provincial recruitment of senators did not rest on the recruitment of equestrians.

[36] For Lucian's satire on this see Woolf in this volume.

pretends. Umbricius' tirade pictures the immigrants as opportunistic economic migrants, adventurers trading on their lack of moral constancy or
scruple to insinuate themselves into every possible role offered by the imperial city. Some of the rhetoric is all too familiar to us today: just as today
migration into ancient Rome must have been much more complex than
it suggests.[37] Many, after all, were involuntary migrants, slaves arriving by
sea from the trading markets of the east, or marched by land from Roman
Europe or beyond.[38] A significant section of the population – numbering
over 30,000 by the Severan period – were soldiers: the majority were recruited from Italy, but there was also a unit of German cavalry and there
were some troops detached from provincial armies.[39] Many of the demands
for labour in Rome's evolving ports and transport structure, and on the
building sites – private and public – that dotted the City, were seasonal
or casual.[40] Slave workforces are less plausible in these contexts and so we
must imagine the Italian poor moving to the City when work was likely to
be had, and leaving it again for their homes in the slack season.

What were the mechanisms that sustained this labour? Recent studies have concentrated on the best-attested activities, those funded by the
emperors and so, indirectly, by the empire. The great dispersals of grain,
followed by oil and meat, to the Roman masses are well documented.[41]
The greatest building projects too – aqueducts and the thermae they fed as
well as temples, entertainment structures and palaces – were imperial, both
because of their cost, and because no-one dared rival the emperors.[42] There
is no question that the emperors used wealth extracted from the provincials
to maintain the City and its population – the permanent part of it, that is,
as far as they could distinguish – in a privileged condition. The City was a
showpiece of imperial munificence to all who passed through it.[43]

There were other sources of wealth too. First the senatorial elite, who may
have spent less on public monuments than their republican predecessors
but spent more on their own houses and establishments. Generation by
generation they seem to have had more to spend, as their failure to reproduce
led to the concentration of fortunes into fewer and fewer families and as
their numbers were swollen by new senators bringing provincial wealth

---

[37] For a suggestive modern parallel see Hopkins (1971) on Hong Kong.
[38] Harris (1999a) 72–3 for the continued import of slaves from outside the empire.
[39] Coulston (2000).   [40] Whittaker (1993).
[41] Rickman (1980), Garnsey (1988), Morley (1996). Note also several of the contributions to part II of
Moatti (1998).
[42] DeLaine (1997) is a path-breaking study in costing imperial building. For the decline of senatorial
building in Rome cf. Eck (1984).
[43] Griffin (1991).

with them. The process is difficult to trace in detail, but the Senate of the late empire collectively controlled much more land than had its first-century CE predecessors and at least some senatorial families were sustained by landholding in many different provinces. Even before then, the super-wealthy appear celebrated in Statius' *Silvae* and Gellius' anecdotes and satirized by Lucian and Galen among others. Collectively the spending power of an imperial elite resident in Rome, for at least part of their lives, represented an alternative route through which provincial production was channelled into expenditure in the capital. Rome's many visitors brought more wealth to the city. Tourists have already been mentioned. Traders also swelled the population (for at least for part of the year). Philo writes of traders from everywhere leaving Rome for their home ports at the beginning of autumn rather than over-winter in a foreign land.[44] Rome was not just a good place to sell produce but also an excellent place to buy it, as the shipping routes and harbour facilities stimulated by the needs of the capital made it the regional hub of the western Mediterranean. The wealth of senators and the centrality of Rome in the market-oriented network of exchanges that bound together the cities of the Mediterranean world, and through them their more productive hinterlands, together help explain why the City thrived in the second century even as emperors began to spend less and less of their time and money at Rome. The notion of Rome as a cultural and economic – and not just an administrative – capital is central to the notion of it as a World City.

CULTURE AND IMPERIALISM

The most powerful and glamorous of Hellenistic rulers, the Attalids of Pergamum, the Ptolemies of Egypt in particular, were famed not only for the exquisite artworks they possessed and the imposing buildings they commissioned but also for their extensive libraries, in which the greatest scholars of their day conducted their labours. Books figured among the spoils brought back to Rome by the conquering generals of the late republic, men who were coming to see themselves as the equals, indeed the superiors, of those Hellenistic kings.[45] Lucius Aemilius Paullus took nothing but books from among all the royal treasures of Macedon after his great victory of 167 BCE (Plut. *Aem.* 28.6). This was, it seems, the first Greek library to come to Rome. In 86 BCE, Sulla's trophies from conquered Athens apparently

[44] Philo, *Legatio ad Gaium* 14.
[45] On the monarchical pretensions of the generals of the late republic, see Rawson (1975).

included the remains of Aristotle's library (Strabo 13.1.54). Lucius Licinius Lucullus also appears to have acquired much of his famous collection of books in the aftermath of his great eastern victories; Plutarch comments that 'his use of them was more honourable than the way he acquired them' (Plut. *Luc.* 42).[46]

The libraries acquired by the great men of the republic were, it seems, often located in their villas (where they had more leisure for scholarly pursuits – and their pretensions to Hellenistic grandeur were less conspicuous than would have been the case in the city itself).[47] That of Lucullus, for instance, was housed at Tusculum. After the civil wars between Pompey and Caesar, however, libraries came to be included among the monumental amenities of the city – as efforts were made to transform Rome into a capital worthy of an empire. Caesar himself planned a library for the city (Suet. *Jul.* 44.2). To mark his triumph over the Illyrians in 39 BCE, Asinius Pollio founded a library in his Atrium Libertatis; Pliny terms it 'the earliest public library in the world funded out of the spoils of war', *bibliotheca quae prima in orbe... ex manubiis publicata* (Pliny, *NH* 7.115) – a graphic example of the conquest of culture.[48] A few years later, Augustus set up a library in the Porticus Octaviae and another attached to the Temple of Apollo on the Palatine (each with one section for Greek works and one for Latin).[49] Later emperors followed his example, most notably Trajan, who incorporated a vast library into his Forum complex. All the learning of the civilized world was brought together in Rome.[50]

Scholars, too, flocked to the city from all over the Greek world (some perhaps following their relocated libraries). Plutarch writes that for Greek scholars in Rome Lucullus' library had functioned as a home from home (*Luc.* 42). Rome offered opportunities for the learned to study – and to earn a living through teaching. In attempting to estimate the number of scholars in Tarsus, Strabo comments paradoxically, 'But it is Rome that is best able to tell us the number of learned men from this city; for it is full of Tarsians and Alexandrians' (14.5.15). Strabo himself had come to Rome from Pontus, one of many Greek intellectuals to do so in the aftermath of Actium.[51] Seneca, writing in the time of Nero, lists the desire for study among the many possible motives of those who leave their native lands to

---

[46] On libraries in the late republic, see Marshall (1976); Rawson (1985) ch. 3; Casson (2001).
[47] As Zanker has suggested (1988) ch. 1.   [48] See also Isidore, *Orig.* 6.5.2.
[49] Suet. *Aug.* 29.3; Plut. *Marc.* 30.6; Dio 49.43.8.
[50] Though emperors might choose to exclude some volumes from their libraries. Some of Ovid's works were, it seems, banned from the libraries of Augustus (Ovid, *Tristia* 3.1.59–72).
[51] Bowersock (1965) 123–8.

come to the city (*Ad Helv.* 6.2–3).[52] The medical writer Galen, originally from Pergamon, was one of many scholars drawn to Rome in the second century CE. Morley's piece, later in this volume, emphasizes the continuing attraction of Rome for scholars from all over the empire.

Rome gathered to itself the world's greatest books and greatest scholars. Already in the second century BCE the ever-expanding Roman empire was spawning books which themselves sought to comprehend the world; Polybius' *Histories*, written in Rome, adapted Greek historiographical traditions to give an account of the history of the entire inhabited world, which focused on the rise of Rome as a world-power.[53] A few decades later, Posidonius' highly influential history (which survives only in fragments) also focused on the Roman empire, recording the habits and customs of many peoples within it (fr. 15). Ancient readers perceived his account as consistent with a Stoic view of the cosmos. Thus the Roman empire, embracing as it did all the peoples of the world, could perhaps be seen as reflecting the unified, living universe.[54] Strabo's *Geography*, written in the time of Augustus (when, as we have seen, a variety of strategies were being deployed to represent the world in and for the city), also gives an account of the Roman world, an account profoundly informed by earlier Greek literary models, from Homer on. Indeed, it has been suggested that the Roman world could not be conceptualized and depicted except through recourse to Greek historiographical and geographical traditions.[55]

Rome, then, took possession of Greek literary culture, which, in some contexts, became a medium, if a somewhat slippery one, for the expression of Roman power. But Greek culture – *paideia* – had notoriously taken possession of Rome. By the late republic, familiarity with the great works of Greek literature was, it seems, a requirement for Romans with aspirations to refinement; to be educated meant reading Homer and Plato. For some, at least, knowing Greek was part of what it was to be Roman.[56] At the same time, the rapidly developing Latin literary tradition was itself self-consciously modelled on and informed by Greek literature.[57] Roman culture bore striking traces of the conquered.

---

[52] As the Greek world became more prosperous from the mid first century CE Greek scholars became less dependent on the opportunities in Rome and intellectual life in the Greek east focused rather on Athens, as Swain emphasises (1996) 3. Rome nevertheless remained a major draw.

[53] Henderson (2001a).   [54] Clarke (1999) 188–9.

[55] Clarke (1999) 334. Numerous later Roman works can also be seen as attempts to comprehend the world, most particularly the Elder Pliny's *Naturalis historia*.

[56] See Wallace-Hadrill (1998).   [57] For a suggestive discussion of this see Hinds (1998), esp. ch. 3.

To a significant degree generated and informed by imperial expansion in the East, Latin literature had a crucial part to play in the continuing development of empire in the West in particular. Latin literary culture quickly became an index of Roman identity.[58] And it was to remain so for centuries. Ausonius' *Ordo nobilium urbium* written in the late fourth century CE parades the author's participation in the world of literature which marked him out as a true Roman (as Miles emphasizes later in this volume). Ausonius' birth in Bordeaux was no more a disqualification for this than had been Cicero's in Arpinum.[59] The responses of provincial elites to their own localities were filtered through a central Roman perspective. Miles writes of the elite of Roman Carthage approaching their own city's past through reading Virgil. Similarly, Woolf, in his discussion of Rome as cultural capital, explores the Spanish-born Martial's use of Latin literary tradition to denigrate the primitive level of culture in his native Bilbilis.

Ausonius' poem also celebrates, if defensively, the continuing pre-eminence of the city of Rome over all other cities. It was perhaps precisely provincial writers such as Ausonius who had the most intense cultural in-vestment in Rome. Miles explores a number of texts of the third and fourth centuries CE which highlight the uniqueness of Rome in comparison with other cities of the empire, albeit for rather different reasons. SHA and Herodian's accounts of the revolt of the Gordians in the third century CE illustrate a wider discourse of power which sought to explain and justify the position of Rome as head of the empire – a project which continued even when (as Woolf emphasizes) the empire was actually governed from wherever the emperor (or emperors) happened to be.

Also focusing on perceptions of Rome from the provinces, Woolf's essay is principally concerned to analyse the image of Rome as 'the city of letters' – a city filled with elite littérateurs perpetually engaged in reading, writing and discussing literary texts to the exclusion of more mundane activities. This implausible world, he suggests, was very much a literary creation. And while this version of Rome may be seen as initially the product of struggles for distinction within the central Roman elite, it was an image of 'Rome' which must have dominated the perceptions of the increasing numbers in the provinces whose own Romanness was primarily generated through their relative competence in reading Latin texts. Indeed, as Woolf suggests, the link between literary texts and Roman identity was almost certainly stronger outside the capital than within it. Literary achievement became an

---

[58] See Woolf (1998) 72–5, 126.
[59] As Miles emphasizes, below, the final lines of *Ordo nobilium urbium* echo Cicero's articulation in *De leg.* 2.5 of the idea that every Roman has two *patriae*.

avenue through which some provincials at least could stake their claim to full participation in Roman identity. Yet for most, he argues, even – indeed especially – for those who had acquired a modest degree of familiarity with Virgil and Cicero, the allusive complexity of literary Latin was such that a little learning only made them more aware of their own ignorance.

The notion of Rome as cultural capital may be traced in some Greek literature of the principate, too. Rome's centrality is also celebrated in Athenaeus' compendious *Deipnosophistae*. Athenaeus, Egyptian-born, lived in Rome in the late second and early third centuries CE. Writing in Greek, he adapts a symposiastic setting of the kind sometimes used in Plato's dialogues but with an eclectic mix of subject matter which perhaps has more in common with the Roman genre of satire.[60] The *Deipnosophistae* is set in the home of a Roman man of letters, Larensis, who has had a distinguished career, culminating in a period as procurator of Moesia. The table-talk of the participants in the *Deipnosophistae* ranges over the Roman empire, east and west, as well as parading an erudite familiarity with all the central texts of Latin and Greek literature. At one point, the host Larensis asks his guests if they know what a *tetrax* is (9.398e–399a). After much discussion, an actual *tetrax* – a bird, as it turns out – is carried in in a cage; it has been brought all the way from its native habitat in Moesia, the province where Larensis himself was stationed. Larensis impresses his guests with his knowledge of birdlife, gleaned through both observation and reading the proper authorities (above all, of course, Aristotle). This is also an opportunity to offer further evidence of his refined table; the *tetrax* is taken away, to return later, cooked, as a part of the feast.[61] The refined and sophisticated elite of the Roman empire demonstrate their power, classifying, appraising and ultimately consuming the products of the world.

Athenaeus has recently been invoked to paint a seductive picture of Rome as a city of culture around the turn of the second and third centuries. Among his refined interlocutors there is little sign of friction between Greek and Roman. Larensis makes all his guests feel at home in Rome (1.3c). The Roman empire, on this view, ethnically diverse even – or especially – at its heart, may be seen as held together by culture.[62] But whose culture is this? Larensis, we might pause to remember, does not invite just anyone to dinner. Perhaps we need to keep our distance a little more from the attractions of Larensis' table, to resist what is part of the continuing lure of

---

[60] On the relationship of satire to Roman imperialism, see Gowers (1993) 124–6.
[61] This incident is suggestively discussed by Braund (2000).   [62] Purcell (1994) at 443.

Graeco-Roman culture, that insidious feeling that you only need to read
the books to belong – even if, as Woolf emphasizes, such feelings are rarely
uncomplicated by doubts about one's own competence as a reader.

COSMOPOLIS – SO WHAT?

As Keith Hopkins' students we learned early the importance of being able
to justify our labours and always to have ready an answer, ideally both elegant and plausible, to the implied question So what? It is appropriate, then,
to end this introduction by asking: What gains are to be had in looking at
Rome as a Cosmopolis? Do the chapters that follow simply explore and
document a trope, a commonplace metaphor of the kind that we might
expect to have existed in any world empire? Is Cosmopolis merely a conveniently inclusive rubric under which to assemble chapters and authors that
in fact testify to the breadth and diversity of Keith's interests and influence?

Cosmopolis is indeed an inclusive rubric, and some such inclusive rubric
was indeed a necessity to draw together even an unrepresentative sample of
Keith's students.[63] It would be disingenuous to deny this. Yet it is perhaps
not by chance that in different ways we have all picked up from Keith
Hopkins an inclination to look at the bigger pictures, at issues cast on an
imperial – if not always cosmic – scale. We make no apologies for this.
For us too the Cosmopolis of Rome has been a convenient microcosm of
empire, a good stage on which to deploy arguments about imperial culture
and religion, about the economics and epidemics of the Roman world,
about the visual and textual fabric of imperial Roman life (and much else).

And yet there are other justifications for focusing attention on the Cosmopolitanism of Rome. Other imperial capitals have resembled Rome, but
not all have become epitomes of empire. Many early empires made the
body of the emperor, and the rituals that surrounded it, the point at which
the cosmos was collapsed into the contingent.[64] Elements of this strategy
are evident in the Roman case too. An early component of Roman court
rituals that might take place anywhere would be the receptions given to
the ambassadors wherever they managed to track emperors down in their
travels around the empire: the account of Wei-lio is justly famous.[65] An

---

[63] An appropriate point to register how many more would have liked to contribute to this volume had
other commitments allowed. The risk of omitting names makes us reluctant to list any.
[64] No book in honour of Keith would be complete without a reference to China. Here it is Yates
(2001).
[65] Conveniently reproduced in Hopkins (1978b), 181–2. On the principal function of footnotes see
Hopkins (1990), 624.

important theme of many of the chapters that follow is the transformation of the Cosmopolis as emperors first appeared on the scene, and then gradually disappeared from it. Constantius' *adventus* has already been discussed. Rituals like this and *osculatio*, combined with a court staffed with eunuchs and bureaucrats, were used by the emperors to gradually convert the image of their power from that of the *civilis princeps*, a first citizen-cum-senior senator, a *privatus* with extraordinary personal rights and privileges, to that of a full-blown itinerant monarchy. Always gods in some parts of the empire, and always able to absent themselves from the capital if they wished, from the mid-second century on it was residence in Rome, rather than absence from it, that became an option. *Senatus consulta* were eclipsed by *edicta*, embassies rarely approached the City, senators ceased to hold the chief military commands or to govern provinces ... and yet Rome survived, indeed flourished. How? Several chapters try to answer that question. Here we limit ourselves to pointing to the vast investment of symbolic capital in the City from the middle republic on. Edwards and Vout show the way the alien was appropriated and incorporated into the fabric of the City, until it became a permanent mnemonic of empire. Beard offers the spectacle of ritual performances that drew the urban plebs into a pageant of empire. Jongman, Morley and Scheidel explore some of the unintended consequences of empire and how they too contributed to fixing Rome at the centre. Elsner and Woolf focus on the work done by interested groups to refurbish Cosmopolis, to suit *urbs* to *orbis* in times of change. Late antique Rome was no mere relic or fossil of an earlier imperialism. Rome remained the Cosmopolis because the power invested in it was still of use, because its claims to epitomise the empire were still worth defending to groups with the power to do so. Another way of envisaging this is to say that Rome the City was so deeply inscribed in the master texts of empire that it could never safely be erased. New Rome on the Hellespont indicates the power of empires, but the survival of Old Rome on the Tiber shows the limits of that power.[66]

Finally, Rome is our Cosmopolis too. Latinists and Roman historians as well as classical archaeologists of every kind have, from Winckelmann on, passed back and forth through the Eternal City on trajectories that mirror those of ancient senators and sophists. Back in our libraries and lecture halls we summon up images of the *fora* and other monuments just as Cicero did in Cilicia or Ausonius in Bordeaux. This is not (just) a matter of romance. For classical archaeologists the monuments of Rome have proved

---

[66] Harris (1999c) collects a rich variety of papers that illustrate this theme.

the essential reference collection in relation to which all imperial art and architecture is to be assessed. Long study visits to the foreign schools and academies play formative roles in the training and subsequent 'networking' of classicists from all those countries where the study of ancient Rome is now strong. The long succession of patrons that have ruled from and endowed Rome makes its museums and libraries unavoidable (not that many in the profession make much effort to avoid them). And even for the most literary of scholars the City is so central in Latin literature that it must be imagined if it is not visited and remembered. This is not to say that Romanists must study the City of Rome above all else: indeed several chapters here emphasize the difficulty of understanding the City without the Empire. Rather, we argue, the creation of Rome as Cosmopolis has bound empire and city together into an indissoluble complex. It is that nexus that these chapters set out to explore.

CHAPTER 2

*The triumph of the absurd: Roman street theatre**

Mary Beard

'MEET ME IN ST LOUIS, LOUIS'[1]

In 1904 the world went to St Louis, Missouri. Just as it had gone to the Crystal Palace in 1851, Vienna in 1873, Barcelona in 1888, Paris in 1889, Chicago in 1893, Nashville in 1897, Buffalo in 1901; and would turn up again in Seattle in 1909, San Francisco in 1915, and (albeit in a rather tamer form) in New York in 1939. The craze for 'World's Fairs' which dominated the cultural politics and diplomacy of the late nineteenth and early twentieth centuries quite literally brought the different nations of the planet together in one spot.[2] Simultaneously imperialist parades and self-interested trading ventures, these fairs hosted elaborate displays of ethnic diversity and proud national traditions – not to mention all the state-of-the-art manufactured goods and consumer trinkets that the proud nations wanted to flog. It was *spectacle* on the grandest scale: not just the temporary museums stuffed full of the world's art treasures, or at least copies of them (Britain sent more than 100 paintings to St Louis;[3] the Nashville Parthenon is a striking

---

* This chapter has done the rounds, and has been improved in seminar discussion with (especially) Marcel Benabou, Florence Dupont and Margaret Malamud; and later under the eagle eye of the editors. It owes its inspiration, I think, to a memorable lecture for sixth-formers by John Henderson – on Plautus' *Amphitruo* (with props). In the course of writing this final version, I have enjoyed discussing a whole variety of triumphal problems with Keith Hopkins, who (with an uncharacteristic lapse of curiosity) never once inquired about the destination, purpose or honorand of the finished essay.

[1] '. . . Meet me at the fair, | Don't tell me the lights are shining | Any place but there; | We will dance the Hoochee-Koochee | I will be your tootsie wootsie | If you will meet me in St Louis, Louis, | Meet me at the fair' (words by Andrew B. Sterling, music by Kerry Mills). As most of us have forgotten, this classic ditty was written as a celebration of the 1904 World's Fair in St Louis; see Geller (1931) 241–4.

[2] The best guides to these occasions are Benedict et al. (1983), Rydell (1984), Greenhalgh (1988) and Rydell et al. (1994). There are genealogical links between these fairs and later world fairs, but what I describe here is a pre-Second World War phenomenon (in fact, in its most flamboyantly distinctive form, pre-First World War).

[3] Carefully selected to represent the best of late Victorian art, these included such (respectable) favourites as Waterhouse's 'Hylas and the Nymphs', Leighton's 'Clytemnestra' and Burne-Jones's

remnant of the 1897 'Exposition'); but also the human zoos that were
the highspot for many visitors. By the end of the nineteenth century, no
decent World's Fair could do without its living specimens of the 'primitive
nations', preferably to be seen going about their day-to-day tasks in a series
of specially faked-up 'primitive villages'. At St Louis, for example, 'about
2000 natives of the various races' marched in the opening parade;[4] and
the stars of the whole event were the notorious dog-eating Igorots, who
entertained anthropologists and tourists alike by consuming their native
dish in a look-alike Igorot village.[5] Even the old world was drawn into the
show. A number of fairs were graced by stage-set Irish villages, complete
with fresh-faced girls in green dresses; still others by the thatched cottages
and maypoles that reproduced the 'English village'.[6]

Inevitably, things went wrong as well as right. It was at Buffalo in 1901
that President McKinley was shot, while touring the 'Temple of Music';
the fact that the assassin was a discontented Polish immigrant cut dramatically across the utopian vision of international and Pan-American harmony
otherwise extolled by the fair.[7] At St Louis controversy clustered around
the Igorot. From the very start there was the question of whether the fair's
commitment to ethnographic realism should allow them to wander round
naked. Despite outcries from the anthropologists (and ridicule from the
local and national press), President Taft advised against: 'President still
thinks' ran a telegram to one of the exhibit's organisers, 'that where the
Igorot has a mere G string that it might be well to add a short trunk
to cover the buttocks and front.'[8] But worse trouble threatened, when

'Dream of Launcelot'; they were backed up by even more etchings, architectural drawings, sculptures
and highpoints of British craftsmanship (from typography to textiles). For the full, jingoistic account,
see Spielmann (1906).

[4] *St Louis World*, 21 April 1904, 2; see Rydell (1984) 178–82 for a description of 'The Pike', the street
in the fair where many of the ethnological exhibits were concentrated. 'The Pike is a living color
page of the world' puffed one of the exhibition's promoters; it included, alongside such exotica as
a 'Cairo Street', 'Moorish Palace' and 'Old Plantation', an extraordinary 'Boer War Exhibit', where
(according to Rydell) 'twice daily, British and Boer troops, including several wartime heroes from
both sides, reenacted battles of the recently ended war against a backdrop of "a village of Zulus,
Swazies and other South African tribes" that also formed part of the concession'.

[5] Rydell (1984) 171–8; the presence of these Filipinos was all the more pointed as the United States had
only recently acquired the Philippines, as its first overseas colonial territory.

[6] These are well discussed by Greenhalgh (1988) 105–7, who explores the (British) political dimension of
some of these displays. One notable Irish 'village' ('Bally Maclinton') was 'conceived at a time when the
high Tories Bonar-Law and Carson were stirring Ulster to revolt, against a Liberal government despe-
rately attempting to find a solution to the Irish issue. Bally Maclinton presented Ireland as ancient
and rural, with thatched cottages, peat burners, traditional dancing and the Gaelic language; all was
wrapped in a self-sufficiency scarcely less complete than that of the Senegalese village next to it.'

[7] Rydell (1984) 151–3.

[8] Quoted in Rydell (1984) 172. The cartoon in the *St Louis Post-Dispatch* (3 July 1904), showing Taft
carrying a pair of trousers, chasing an Igorot man wearing a G-string, catches the mood.

the local dog-owners came to reflect on the likely source of the Igorots' favourite meal, and a profitable alliance was exposed between the 'savages' and the boys on the block. For the greatest journalistic scoop of the fair was the revelation that the dogmeat did indeed come from the pet dogs of St Louis citizens, supplied to the Igorot – at a price – by a gang of local youths.[9]

These fairs and their controversies highlight many of the tensions that you find in almost any cultural performance or staged display. How do you draw the boundaries between the watchers and the watched? Where does the 'show' end and 'real life' start? How far does the *mimesis* always risk seeping out into the world outside the 'performance' as narrowly defined – and vice versa? The Igorot, for example, were actors in a staged display, and in a real-life drama too; the assassination of McKinley, far from dampening enthusiasm for the Buffalo fair, was soon puffed into its greatest spectacle – in the process, sending the price of any souvenir of the Temple of Music soaring.[10] And how many levels of representation are we dealing with? Picture, for example, a group of young Englishwomen, kitted out in fancy dress in front of a make-believe thatched cottage, pretending to be the kind of Englishwomen who once upon a time (if you can believe it) did dance around maypoles wearing such silly clothes; and they are being ogled, and written up, as if they really were that kind of woman ... It is hard (as my title hints) not to feel the *absurdity* inscribed in the display: the richest industrial nations of a century ago choosing to represent themselves as poor-but-honest, homespun peasants, apparently happy to share the stage with 'real savages'.[11] As always the bigger the claims for the show, the more they risked toppling into bathos.

It is with these issues in mind that I shall be exploring in this chapter the ceremony of the Roman triumph: the victory-parade-cum-thank-offering to the gods which brought the conquered world to Rome and put it on show in an often extravagant procession, winding through the streets of the city up to the temple of Jupiter on the Capitoline hill. Performed in the wake of all the bloodiest Roman massacres, from the beginning of the city's myth-history to the fifth century CE (and imitated by every self-respecting monarch or power-crazed autocrat in the West ever since[12]), the

---

[9] Greenhalgh (1988) 101.   [10] Rydell (1984) 153.

[11] Predictably the layout of some fairs attempted to separate the Old World exhibits from the 'savages', and indeed to grade the colonial exhibits according to their supposed level of evolutionary development (Benedict et al. (1983) 43–50).

[12] For a vast bibliography of triumphal *Nachleben*, see Wisch and Munshower (1990) Part 1. As late as 1899 the victory of US Admiral Dewey over the Spanish fleet in Manila Bay (which was to bring

triumph was a complex choreography of the victorious Roman army and their defeated enemy. The general himself rode in a chariot, followed by his soldiers on foot, singing – so convention had it – ribald songs at their leader's expense: 'Romans keep an eye on your wives, we're bringing the bald-headed adulterer home' were among the lyrics that Julius Caesar's soldiers chanted in his triumph over Gaul in 46 BCE.[13] In front of the general went the animal victims to be sacrificed on the Capitol, the human captives and their spoils. By the second century BCE at least, when Roman conquests had reached the rich and sometimes exotic kingdoms of the eastern Mediterranean, this part of the show could amount to a dazzling display of treasure, wealth and strange ethnicities: captured kings in their native regalia, relics of the conquered gods, piles of gold, silver and foreign coin, whole troupes of precious statues, paintings depicting the action of far distant battles, as well as placards blazoning the unpronounceable names of cities that had fallen to the Romans. At his triumph over the kingdom of Pontus, also in 46 BCE, Caesar notoriously turned these placards into a celebration of the speed of his conquest (and simultaneously, of course, into a display of his own rhetorical dexterity): the words *Veni. Vidi. Vici* were carried as a slogan in the procession.[14]

The triumph was the one ceremony, more than any other, that extolled Rome's status as a military power – and, in due course, as a World City. Dio wrote of one of the trophies displayed in Pompey's extraordinary procession in 61 BCE: '[it was] huge, decorated at great expense and with an inscription attached to say "this is a trophy of the whole inhabited world" '; just as, for Plutarch, Pompey's three triumphal celebrations ('over Libya, Europe and Asia') made it seem that the 'whole inhabited world had been included in his triumphs'.[15] Along the route the crowds of Roman onlookers (many

the Philippines into American control; see above n. 6) was commemorated by a vast triumphal procession, including a triumphal arch modelled on the arch of Titus in Rome; this event is well analysed by Malamud (forthcoming).

[13] *Urbani, servate uxores: moechum calvom adducimus* (Suet. *Iul*. 51); they went on *Aurum in Gallia effutuisti, hic sumpsisti mutuum* ('You fucked away in Gaul the money you borrowed here'). Caesar, one imagines, would have felt quite comfortably ambivalent about this treatment.

[14] Suet. *Iul*. 37: *Pontico triumpho inter pompae fercula trium verborum praetulit titulum 'Veni. Vidi. Vici.' non acta belli significantem sicut ceteris, sed celeriter confecti notam.* ('At his triumph over Pontus, among the floats in the procession he paraded an inscription of three words "Came, Saw, Conquered", not conveying the achievements of the war as in the other displays, but an indication of the speed at which it had been finished.')

[15] Dio Cass. 37. 21 (. . . μέγα πολυτελῶς τε κεκοσμημένον καὶ γραφὴν ἔχον ὅτι τῆς οἰκουμένης ἐστίν). Plut. *Pomp*. 45 (τρόπον τινα τήν οἰκουμένην ἐδόκει τοῖς τρισὶν ὑπῆχθαι θριάμβοις); cf. Plin. *HN* 7.99, who writes in the context of this triumph that Pompey boasted of having found Asia the remotest of places (*ultima*) and making her central (*media*) to the Roman state. It is very hard to resist the idea that Pompey was punning on 'media' (= central) and 'Media' (= a part

of whom traced their 'Roman' origins to some earlier war of conquest that had been celebrated in just such a parade) witnessed the beginning of that *rite de passage* that would now turn these conquered enemies and abject foreign prisoners into regular citizens. This, in fact, is exactly what Plutarch hints at when, in his account of the triumph of Aemilius Paullus in 167 BCE, he flashes forward to tell 'what happened next' to one of the sons of the vanquished King Perseus: at Rome the boy became an expert metal worker, learnt Latin and was known as a first-rate secretary to Roman magistrates.[16] A perfect story of foreign enmity transformed into Roman service.

THE TRIUMPH OF HISTORY

The ceremony of triumph has been used and abused in modern history-writing. Many historians pay it lip-service as a colourful symbol of Rome's commitment to militarism and of the Roman elite's investment in the glory of victory. They stress the vote of the Senate that was necessary for a triumph to take place (in the Republic at least, the Roman oligarchy was careful to ration such ostentatious display) and the sheer numbers of people involved, combined with the wealth and variety of the spoils on show (how, after all, did the first masterpieces of Greek art end up in Rome if not via some triumphal procession?).[17] They linger too on the figure of the general in his chariot, enjoying his greatest moment of glory ever:

The general's cheeks were daubed with red; he was clothed like Jupiter himself, in a purple cloak over a toga sown with golden stars. In one hand, he carried a sceptre crowned with an eagle, in the other a laurel branch. Above his head, a slave held a heavy gold crown. Each time the crowd cheered, the slave ritualistically murmured: 'Remember you are only a man.' The triumphal procession dramatized the splendour of Roman victories, reinforced public pride in the value of conquest, at once elevated the successful leader and yet fitted him into a well-worn slot, so that with luck his popularity would not subvert the power-sharing oligarchy.[18]

---

of Asia) – notwithstanding the mismatch of quantities (short 'e' for the adjective, long 'e' for the country).

[16] Plut. *Aem.* 37. There are similar narratives for young Juba, who moves via Caesar's triumph of 46 to the status of historian, albeit Greek (Plut. *Caes.* 55) and Zenobia, who follows her appearance in Aurelian's triumph by Roman matronhood (SHA, *Thirty pretenders*, 30, 27).

[17] See, for example, Harris (1979) 25–6; Patterson (2000b) 31–3; Pollitt (1983) 24–5, 42–8; Wiseman (1985) 4.

[18] The last sentence gives the author of this passage away: Hopkins (1978a) 27. It is a classic example of old-style Hopkins argument, some evocative empathy (not entirely trammelled by the most rigorous reading of ancient texts: see below, n. 22) paving the way for a striking insight into the structures of Roman *Realpolitik*.

All of which produces a tidy account, relatively undisturbed by the questions and problems that a few minutes' reflection must bring to mind. How on earth, for example, was it all organized? What mechanisms of control allowed the Romans to parade thousands of soldiers and prisoners through the streets, watched by at least as many spectators, and then disperse them safely afterwards? Could they really have carted all that bric-à-brac and money through the city ('... 118,000 Athenian *tetradrachmae*, 12,322 coins called Philippics...'[19]) without losing a good bit *en route*? And if the whole show was an elaborate choreography, who do we imagine acted as the choreographer, got it moving and ensured that nothing went badly wrong? And what, moreover, of the changes over time? The only serious rupture that is regularly signalled in modern discussions comes as part and parcel of the Augustan monarchy, when the honour of a triumph became restricted, *de facto*, to members of the imperial family.[20] But, that apart, did the ceremony really remain to all intents and purposes 'the same' over a thousand years of Roman history, varying only in the fluctuating scale of its ostentation?[21] Add this kind of uncertainty to the uncomfortable fragility of many of our favourite 'facts' about the triumph (the famous words of the slave, for example, muttered into the general's ear, are most clearly documented in a passage of Christian polemic from Tertullian, railing against the divinity of the Roman emperor[22]); and you will soon realize that we know considerably less than we think we do about what went on at a Roman triumph.

True, a number of historians have dug a lot more deeply into the ceremony, its background and its origins. But their interests have largely concentrated on very specific aspects of the ritual.[23] For Roman topographers, the key question has been what was the exact route of the triumphal

---

[19] Hopkins (1978a) 26 (quoting Livy 39.5, on 187 BCE).

[20] See Syme (1939) 404 (a classically cynical formulation); Eck (1984) 138–41. Warren (1970) objects to the general '"unitarian" view of the triumph as something permanent and immutable, untouched by history', though her own historical changes are largely located deep in the murky prehistory of the institution. Weinstock's learned attempt to argue for a major break at the time of Julius Caesar (legitimated through the mythical precedent of Camillus) has not convinced many readers; see Weinstock (1971) 71–5.

[21] For a powerful statement of the increasing lavishness of the ceremony (and with it, as is also regularly claimed, increasing emphasis on the glory of the general rather than the gods), see Nicolet (1980) 352–6.

[22] Tert. *Apol*. 33.4. Other writers (e.g. Arr. *Epict. diss.* 3, 25, 85) offer evidence compatible with Tertullian, but by no means so explicit. Dio (in Zonar. 7.21.9) suggests a moral for the words of the slave quite different from that drawn by all modern commentators: the point is, he writes, that the general should take care lest disaster is waiting for him in the future. For a visual representation of the figure behind the general, see the famous Boscoreale silver cup (illustrated in Beard, North and Price (1998) 147).

[23] The best detailed accounts of the institution *as a whole* are *RE* VIIA 493–511, 'Triumphus' (W. Ehlers) and Künzl (1988).

procession, and where was the so-called *porta triumphalis* through which the general was supposed to pass?[24] Historians of earliest Rome have treated the ceremony as a rare window onto the politics, religion and culture of the archaic city; wondering in the process whether the triumph is to be seen as 'native Roman' or Etruscan in origin, and what links there might be between its procession (*pompa*) and the processions that accompanied the *ludi Romani* and the traditional aristocratic Roman funeral.[25] Others have explored at enormous length the constitutional complexities of the *ius triumphandi*: who had the right to triumph under what circumstances, and how that changed over time.[26] More than anything else, however, it has been the figure of the triumphing general himself (*triumphator*[27]) and his distinctive costume that have attracted attention and controversy. Dressed, more or less, in the costume of the cult image of Jupiter Optimus Maximus, his face painted red just like the statue, decked out with a series of regal and/or divine attributes, while constantly being reminded – if we believe Tertullian – that he was (only) a man: it is hardly surprising that the question of what this figure was meant to represent has been high on the agenda.

Historians of religion, from James Frazer to John Scheid, have offered plenty of answers. Frazer, predictably enough, found in the *triumphator* a brilliant argument for his view of divine kingship: all you needed to do was to recognise that the general was the direct descendant of the early Italic kings, and then it became perfectly obvious (to Frazer at least) that those kings had been, in Frazerian terms, 'gods'.[28] Equally true to type, Scheid attempted to see the problem in terms of much wider conflicts about religious representation as a whole, and the conceptualization and 'embodiment' of deities at Rome. Setting the figure of the *triumphator* alongside the Flamen Dialis and the Vestal Virgins (who each, in their different ways, 'stood for' or 'stood proxy for' a deity), Scheid stressed the 'oscillation during the course of the triumphal procession between, on the

---

[24] For example, Pfanner (1980); Coarelli (1968), (1988) 363–414. A surfeit of earlier bibliography can be found in Versnel (1970) 132–63.

[25] That the triumph can act as a 'window' onto early Rome is the basic premise of Versnel (1970) and Warren (1970). The classic statement of the links between the *pompa* of the *ludi Romani* and that of the triumph, is Mommsen (1859); and between the funeral procession and the triumph, Brelich (1938). See further, Versnel (1970) 94–131.

[26] The historic dispute on the *ius triumphandi* between Mommsen (1887) 126–36 and Laqueur (1909) is re-examined by Versnel (1970) 164–95. Richardson (1975) suggests changes in the period of the Hannibalic War, further discussed in Gruen (1990) 129–33.

[27] This convenient term (which I shall use throughout this chapter) is not, strictly speaking, a modern coinage; but it is not far off. It is found in a few late imperial inscriptions (e.g. *CIL* VI.1158, 1189, 31395 etc.), a couple of times in Apuleius (e.g. *Apol.* 17) and in Minucius Felix (*Oct.* 37); its sphere of reference is as much divine or religious triumph as human victory in war.

[28] Frazer (1911) 175–8.

one hand, a living image of the god, almost immovable and identical to his model [viz. the statue] on the Capitoline; and, on the other, the negation of this divine presence [through the words of the slave]'.[29]

Between these two positions (and beyond) all kinds of options have been canvassed, most of which were summed up, ordered and neatly categorized by Henk Versnel in his 1960s doctoral thesis: the now classic, if misleadingly entitled, *Triumphus: an inquiry into the origin, development and meaning of the Roman triumph*.[30] For all their many superficial differences, opinions could be divided into two basic camps.[31] On the one hand, were those who interpreted the costume and attributes of the general as divine: the *triumphator* was indeed Jupiter for a day – so god-like, in fact, that he needed the slave to remind him of his mortality; and the triumph itself, as an institution and as a cultural category, provided a traditional Roman background (and legitimation) for the later deification of emperors and members of the imperial family. On the other hand, were those who held that the general's costume was not divine at all, but derived from that of the early Etruscan kings and was a reflection of the specifically Etruscan origin of the ceremony; in fact, the Etruscan connection was, as they regularly insisted, a much stronger theme in ancient discussions of the triumph than any links with Jupiter. Versnel's own solution to the problem was to have it both ways (a typically late 1960s intellectual tactic, with hints of modish 'ambivalence' and 'interstitiality'): for him the *triumphator* was *both* god *and* king; the iconography of Jupiter being, in any case, inextricable from (and partly derived from) the insignia of Etruscan monarchy – and vice versa.[32]

Most of this chapter is concerned not with the puzzling figure of the *triumphator*, but more widely with the procession in which he figured and the extravagant forms of *mimesis* that were associated with it. My main focus of interest is the *written* triumph – not so much the noisy, messy, probably rowdy and almost entirely irrecoverable events of the ceremony 'as it really happened'; but the written accounts of triumphal processions, largely in Graeco-Roman writers of the first two centuries of the common era (Plutarch, Ovid, Josephus, Appian). After all, apart from a handful

---

[29] Scheid (1986) 224; for an English summary of his position, see Scheid (1993) 82–4.

[30] Misleading, because it doesn't actually like poking its nose much beyond the sixth century BCE; hence its (surprising) absence from n. 23.

[31] Versnel (1970) 56–93. You will find a much more succinct summary of the two basic positions in Warren (1970) and Weinstock (1971) 66–8.

[32] See, especially, Versnel (1970) 84–93. A slightly later example of this modish fascination with inter-stitiality is Beard (1980), which was duly cut down to size in the index of Hopkins (1983b): 'Vestal virgins, honorary men'.

of visual images,[33] this is all that survives of Roman triumphal culture. I hope to show that these (written) processions involved a whole series of mimetic strategies, extending far beyond the general himself; and that the written accounts of the ceremony repeatedly emphasize the modes of representation, the artifice and contrivance which constitute the ritual. This will ultimately lead to a new look at the *triumphator*, attempting to integrate his role into the representational games of the procession as a whole. With the help, in particular, of one Plautine comedy, the *Amphitruo*, and its brilliant (meta-)theatrical parody of the *triumphator*, I shall present a victorious general who is as much a performance artist as a religious symbol; who is caught as much between glory and absurdity, as between man and god.[34]

PERFORMANCE ART

In September 61 BCE Pompey the Great celebrated a lavish triumph for his victories in the Eastern Mediterranean; it took place over two days, the 28th and the 29th, which was also (it can hardly have been a coincidence) his forty-fifth birthday. For many modern historians, this moment marks the highspot of Pompey's whole career: from then on he would be increasingly outmanoeuvred by Julius Caesar, never quite regaining his magic touch with the Roman people; but in 61, fresh from Rome's greatest conquests ever, in a triumphal procession which outdid all predecessors for its sheer array of captured kings and princelings, he must have seemed unassailable – the Roman Alexander, an emperor in all but name.[35]

We can only guess 'what it was like to be there'[36] on those two days of September 61. The main written accounts that we have (dating from between one and two hundred years after the event) may, or may not, have drawn on closely contemporary or even eyewitness descriptions;[37] even

---

[33] I hope to return to the relationship between visual and textual representations of the triumph in a longer study. Brilliant (1999) is a stimulating analysis of the visual images; see also Favro (1994), for the triumph's impact on urban space.

[34] You will find that this chapter plays on the impact of juxtaposing triumphal texts written at different dates, in different circumstances, for different purposes and in different languages. The results are, I hope, worth the price of blurring some of those potentially important distinctions – which I shall be examining more closely in a longer study of the topic.

[35] See, for example, Greenhalgh (1980) 168–96; Seager (1979) 72–84.

[36] Hopkins (1999) 2: 'What was it like to be there? We don't and cannot know.' Hopkins' fascination with the (im)possibility of historical autopsy reaches its highpoint (or *mise en abîme*) in this book, with his description of a pair of clever, if irritatingly over-enthusiastic, modern 'time-travellers' returning to Pompeii and other notorious ancient sites.

[37] Eyewitness accounts are a tempting possibility. Anyone who thinks Asinius Pollio's history lies not far below the surface of Appian (see, for example, Gabba (1956) 79–88) may flirt with the idea that we

if they did, their authors were certainly pursuing their own agendas when they chose to dwell on the wealth and extravagance of the display, and they could hardly fail to be as 'unreliable' (in the narrowest sense) as any account of any Roman spectacle. Nevertheless, taken together, these accounts succeed in writing into Roman history a kaleidoscopic vision of triumphal grandeur, as they conjure into permanence the extraordinary two-day, fleeting extravaganza that was paraded past the watching crowd on the way to the Capitol.

Plutarch starts his procession with the forest of placards that carried the names of the (fifteen) foreign nations conquered: 'Pontus, Armenia, Cappadocia, Paphlagonia, Media, Colchis, Iberia, Albania...' and so on; quickly followed by the roster of 1,000 fortresses taken, almost 900 enemy cities and 800 pirate ships, plus the list of profits that the victories had brought to Rome (not only the coin, and the gold and silver treasure, but inscriptions also celebrated the names of thirty-nine new cities founded by Pompey in the East).[38] It is the star items of plunder, on the other hand, that launch Appian's account: the carriages full of precious metal, the piles of silver drachmae, the 'countless' wagons that carried the enemy armour and ships' beaks, Mithridates' throne and sceptre, plus a colossal statue of the king in solid gold. Next comes the exotic list of defeated generals and royal captives who walked in front of Pompey himself – 324 in all, whose very names must have evoked any number of Graeco-Roman conflicts with oriental barbarity ('Tigranes son of Tigranes... Artaphernes, Cyrus, Oxathres, Darius and Xerxes, the sons of Mithridates, with his daughters Orsabaris and Eupatra; Olthaces ruler of Colchis; Aristobulus, king of the Jews...'). Statues and paintings followed, depicting those unavoidably absent (Mithridates himself, already dead; the elder Tigranes, already re-installed as vassal ruler), as well as the critical moments of conflict and the 'barbarian gods' with their distinctive costume.[39] Add to this Dio's trophy of 'the whole inhabited world'[40] and Pliny's sour fascination with the gems, jewels and 'natural history' on parade: the huge and precious royal gaming board, golden dining

---

may be just one remove from an eyewitness account of Pompey's triumph: Pollio could well have been there; if his *Histories* began in 60 a backward glance at the previous year is plausible enough; and besides he had a personal investment in triumphs, having celebrated one himself. But probably the temptation is better resisted.

[38] *Pomp.* 45.1–3.

[39] *Mith.* 116–17. The idea that the booty included the couch of the Darius who more than 200 years earlier had been defeated by Alexander will have reinforced the impression of the whole history of oriental enemies stretching back behind those on parade.

[40] Above, n. 15.

couches, wood and trees from the distant east, golden statues of Minerva, Mars and Apollo, and to cap it all a portrait-head of Pompey in *pearls* ('the triumph of luxury', carped Pliny, while gleefully identifying it as a nasty omen of Pompey's ultimate decapitation).[41] It is all a powerful mixture of the fear and wonder, admiration and disgust that made up the story of *triumph*.

But it is more than that. For the written accounts of triumphal processions do not only harp on the elaborate spectacle of the occasion and the impact of what was on display; they also repeatedly return to how that display was staged, as if *representation itself* – its conventions, contrivances and paradoxes – was a central part of the show. For author after author, in other words, the triumph is construed as a performance of performance itself; as much about image-*making* as about images. Look a little closer, for example, at Appian's account of Pompey's triumph in 61, and you will find that his apparently straightforward narrative of the procession leads the reader through a series of reflections on what is to count as an image, on the contested boundaries between reality and representation, and on where the limits of representation lie.

As we have noted, Appian moves from the real-life collection of 324 illustrious eastern captives to the images (εἰκόνες) of Mithridates and Tigranes, one already dead, the other safely absent on his vassal throne back home. His account has already referred to one version of Mithridates that had starred in the triumphal show: the colossal solid gold statue brought back from the East, plus the symbols of his royal office (throne and sceptre). Here, by contrast, the skills of Roman artistic 'realism' are deployed to cast both of these rulers as they appeared in the conflict, 'fighting, losing and running away (μαχομένων τε καὶ νικωμένων καὶ φευγόντων)'.[42] For Mithridates himself, Appian's claims of mimetic likeness go one step further: 'The besieging of Mithridates was represented, and the night when he fled, and the silence. Finally, there was also a display of how he died, and a painting of the daughters who opted to die with him.'[43] Here realistic representation reaches its limits. An image of the final siege (or the dark night, or the pitiful daughters) is one thing; an image of 'silence' is quite another. By casually introducing this ecphrastic paradox (only in writing can a painting show sound or its absence) Appian is not only pointing to the inevitable mismatch of the visual images and his own written description, he is also

---

[41] *HN* 37.14–16 (. . . *severitate victa et veriore luxuriae triumpho*).   [42] *Mith.* 117.

[43] Ibid: Μιθριδάτου δὲ καὶ ἡ πολιορκία, καὶ ἡ νὺξ ὅτε ἔφυγεν, εἴκαστο καὶ ἡ σιωπή etc. Translations, such as the Loeb, erode the peculiarity of the Greek by recognizing it as a trope: 'Even the besieging of Mithridates and *his silent flight by night* were represented.'

prompting us to consider where the triumph's mimetic games plunge into implausibility.[44]

A different aspect of representational paradox follows almost instantly. After paintings (γραφαί) of the sons and daughters of Mithridates who had died before him, come 'images of the barbarian gods and their native costume (θεῶν τε βαρβαρικῶν εἰκόνες καὶ κόσμοι πάτριοι).' I shall be returning at the end of this chapter to the complex role of all 'images of gods' in a triumphal procession (if, for example, we see the *triumphator* as a double of the statue of Jupiter, what difference would that make to the way we approach *these* images...?). For the moment, notice only how elusive the very idea of 'representation' or 'image' is in this case. With Tigranes, Mithridates and his family, the images in the procession stood for human beings who, in other circumstances, might well have been present in the flesh: if Mithridates had not been killed he too would have walked in front of Pompey. These gods, by contrast, could appear in no form other than εἰκόνες – whether we read that term to indicate the cult images themselves (and there was no divine form more 'real' than that), or to indicate εἰκόνες of those εἰκόνες, a second order of representation on painted canvas. *Statues* and *paintings of statues* are here impossible to distinguish.[45]

The other written accounts of this triumph raise similar issues. They foreground, for example, the role of writing as representation: whether as an object of display itself, inscribed on placards that proclaimed cities conquered and founded; or as a caption – a decoding device, to make some required sense of the strange visual icons on parade ('this is a trophy of the whole inhabited world'[46]). Scratch the surface of Pliny's story also, look beyond his huffing and puffing over luxury and extravagance, and you will find there too image-making and its interpretation on the line. The pearly head of Pompey is not only an omen to presage his violent end; nor to be read just as a sign that, as always, excess has made a woman of our manly hero ('to think that it was out of pearls, such a wasteful material and one meant for women, things that it would not be right for you to wear, that you had your features fashioned'[47]). At the same time we must see it in loaded juxtaposition with the other face of (the real) Pompey on display,

---

[44] Hölscher (1987) 29 is one of the few scholars to have spotted this striking passage, though he incautiously leaps to the conclusion that it is good evidence for the 'mehr und mehr rührende und sensationelle Effekte' sought by art in the late Republic. For the theme of sound in ecphrasis, see Laird (1993).

[45] The best discussion of the complex problems of divine imaging in antiquity is still Gordon (1979).

[46] Above, n. 15.

[47] *HN* 37.15: *e margaritis, Magne, tam prodiga re et feminis reperta, quas gerere te fas non sit, fieri tuos voltus?*

laurel crowned and red-painted – just like, we should not forget, that statue in the Capitoline temple.

So too in the pages and pages of Graeco-Roman literature that called to mind other triumphs of the late Republic and early Empire. Ancient writers repeatedly revel in the multifarious tactics of *mimesis* that a triumph stages: from the sacred books of the Jewish Law that according to Josephus did duty for the εἰκόνες of the defeated gods in the triumph of Vespasian and Titus in 71 CE (and, in the process, putting another representational spin on the written word);[48] through the elaborate model rivers and mountains which, like Pliny's trees, stood as metonymic trophies of their conquered lands or the piles of weapons elaborately arranged to appear to be lying at random;[49] to the gory tableaux of death, re-enacting for all to see the destruction of Rome's enemies. Appian, for example, reports that in his triumph of 46 BCE Julius Caesar did not stoop (or dare) to display in writing the names of fellow Romans, crushed in his civil wars; he was, however, quite prepared to orchestrate visual images that replayed some very nasty suicides (L. Scipio thowing himself into the sea, Petreius shafting himself at dinner, Cato disembowelling himself 'like a wild animal' ὡς θηρίον) – at which the audience groaned, before settling down to applaud or mock some less tragic final moments.[50] This was famously matched by one of the star turns in the story of Octavian's mammoth triumph for his victory at Actium and the conquest of Egypt. He could not, as he had hoped, have the parade of a walking-talking Cleopatra amongst his captives; so instead a (model) queen appeared on a couch in a notable *tableau mourant*, complete with an asp or two. As Dio implies, it meant that 'in a kind of way' (τρόπον τινά) she was there with the other prisoners, (and) ogled as a triumphal ornament.[51]

Perhaps the most striking passage of all is part of Appian's account of Scipio's triumph over Carthage in 201 BCE, a ceremony which in his narrative also serves as a blue-print for the future ('this is the way they still do it . . .').[52] After listing the wagon loads of spoils, the 'towers' (πύργοι) standing for conquered cities, the 'pictures and plans' (γραφαὶ καὶ σχήματα) of the campaigns, the piles of coin and bullion, the elephants and the prisoners, Appian turns to the musicians accompanying the procession:

And there is a chorus of lyre-players and pipers, in imitation of an Etruscan procession (ἐς μίμημα Τυρρηνικῆς πομπῆς), clad in waistcloths and with golden diadems on their heads. They move in regular time, keeping step with their singing

---

[48] *BJ* 7.150.   [49] For example, Tac. *Ann.* 2.41; Plut. *Aem.* 32.   [50] App. *B.Civ.* 2.101.
[51] Dio Cass. 51.21; the lifelike effigy of Cleopatra serves also to highlight the ambivalence more generally of the prisoners in the procession: as both (artistic) ornament and living captives.
[52] *Pun.* 66, opening: καὶ ὁ τρόπος, ᾧ καὶ νῦν ἔτι χρώμενοι διατελοῦσιν, ἐστὶ τοιόσδε.

and dancing. 'Lydians' is their usual title, because (or this is what I believe) the
Etruscans were colonists from Lydia. One of these in the middle of the procession,
wearing a purple robe down to his feet, with armlets and necklace of gold, raises a
laugh by gesticulating (σχηματίζεται) in all kinds of ways as if he is dancing in
triumph (ὡς ἐπορχούμενος) over the enemy.

Striking enough in the context of triumphal performance is Appian's
emphasis here on the role of one of these musicians as mime-actor:
σχηματίζω/'gesticulate' is a term that can be used of stage movement
and gesture (while resonating also in this context, of course, with the
'pictures and plans' / γραφαὶ καὶ σχήματα of the procession);[53] the man's
actions here cast the celebration of victory as comic parody ('*as if* he is
dancing in triumph over the enemy'). But notice also how Appian chooses
to describe the whole group of musicians and their role in the procession.
These lyre-players and pipers, he writes, *acted out* (ἐς μίμημα) an Etruscan
procession; they were putting on a show of *imitating* an Etruscan *pompa*.
As we have already noted, modern historians have debated at great length
the (real) ethnic origins of the ceremony, whether it was a native Roman
or native Etruscan institution. Appian here, by implication at least, under-
mines much of this debate. For he is presenting triumphal origins as already
part of the *mimesis* (or pretence) of the show; he is presenting the triumph,
in other words, as a ceremony which itself stages a myth of its own origins.

BELIEVING YOUR EYES?

Performance implies spectators; and, indeed, the engagement of the triumphal audience is one significant theme in the descriptions of the procession. Here what repeatedly counts is πίστις, how much of all this are the
onlookers going to believe? or rather, how much disbelief will they be prepared to suspend? For Josephus, describing the elaborate tableaux mounted
on portable stages at the triumph of Vespasian and Titus in 71 CE, the representational effects worked just as intended (except for a certain reported
anxiety amongst the crowd that, in the real-time of the show, these feats
of engineering might actually collapse). The events of the war, he claims,
were shown 'in a series of representations' (διὰ πολλῶν δὲ μιμημάτων):
the devastation of the countryside, whole battalions of the enemy wiped
out, the storming of forts and cities, a deluge of blood, temples razed and

---

[53] See, for example, Xen. *Symp.* 1.9. Professional mimics, of course, had a role in another of Rome's
   major civic celebrations: the funeral procession, where actors played the part of dead ancestors (see,
   for example, Suet. *Vesp.* 19).

houses too ('on top of their inhabitants'), rivers flowing through land completely ablaze. 'The skill and magnificent workmanship of the structures now portrayed the events to those who had not witnessed them, as if they were there in person.' Part of the success of this triumph, then, was to have offered to its audience something closely equivalent to *presence* at the victories; a replay of reality.[54] But other writers, describing other occasions, frame the conditions for (dis)belief in the spectacular representations in a much trickier way.

Appian, for one, explicitly raises the possibility that the onlookers are being taken for a ride. In the final section of his account of Pompey's triumph he turns to the figure of the *triumphator* himself, impersonating not so much the god Jupiter, but the conquering hero Alexander the Great – whose mantle he has inherited. Quite literally, it seems.

> Pompey himself was in a chariot, one studded with gems, and he was wearing the cloak, it is said (ὥς φασιν), of Alexander the Macedonian, if anyone can believe it (εἴ τῳ πιστόν ἐστιν). He seems (ἔοικε) to have found it among the possessions of Mithridates, the people of Cos having previously acquired it from Cleopatra [i.e. Alexander's sister].[55]

Appian here directly confronts the problem of πίστις. His first move is almost to insist that the claims of the cloak could not possibly be true; if 'anyone' were to believe that, they would be gullible indeed. But he then offers a plausibly implausible genealogy for the object. If you did choose to believe that Pompey really was wearing Alexander's cloak (and εἴ τῳ πιστόν ἐστιν must allow for that possibility), then this tale stretching back to Alexander's sister could explain exactly how he had got his hands on it; or so the logic of πίστις would go. It is a neat encapsulation of the ambivalence that 'belief' in triumphal spectacle entails.

Ovid spins the problem of belief and interpretation in a different way. In the first book of the *Ars amatoria* he presents a triumphal procession as a good place for his learner-lover to pick up a girl, the licensed transgression of the ceremony signalling fun and games in the audience too:

> Watching will be fun for boys and girls together; and it's a day that will let everyone's heart off the leash. When one of the girls asks what the names of the kings are, what places, mountains or rivers are being carried past, have an answer for everything – and don't just wait to be asked. And anything you don't know, reply as if you did. Here is Euphrates, with the reeds around his forehead. The one with the blue locks

---

hanging down will be Tigris. Have these as the Armenians; she is Persia, sprung
from Danae; this one was a city in the Achaemenian valleys. That one there or
there, they're chieftains. And you'll have names to give them, correct if you can
manage it; if not, then at least sounding right (*apta*).[56]

The series of jokes in this passage turns on the slipperiness of triumphal
imagery. Ovid's girl (being a girl) cannot work out for herself who or what
on earth the personifications of conquered places and peoples are meant to
be; the boy is advised to play the interpreter and (with confident, if entirely
spurious learning) to produce a set of plausible names to identify the figures
as they pass. The joke is, of course, partly on the girl, who cannot make
sense of what she sees. But we must suspect that it is on the boy and the
narrator too, as well as on the conventions of the whole charade – and
so also on the reader. After all, how plausible *are* the confidently spurious
identifications that the boy and narrator between them devise? They may
seem *apta* enough to start with, but a moment's thought (from reader,
or girl for that matter) should hint otherwise. Was it not, for example, a
dumb decision to pretend to distinguish so easily the two rivers that, more
then any other, are the natural twins of the world's waterways? Has not
the boy been misled by the narrator into revealing the very superficiality
of his own patronizing bravura? Maybe. But any readers who were to take
pleasure in their own superiority in this interpretative game would risk
falling into exactly the same trap as the learner-lover.[57] For part of the
point of the passage is cleverly to insinuate the sheer under-determinacy
of the images that pass in a triumph: kings, rivers, mountains, chieftains
here and there; put a name on them yourself (just as the narrator tells you).
Besides, the chances are that the victory we're celebrating is just another
of those diplomatic stitch-ups passing as heroics that characterized most
Augustan encounters with the Parthians and their neighbours;[58] and who

---

[56] *Ars am.* 1.217–28 *spectabunt laeti iuvenes mixtaeque puellae,* | *diffundetque animos omnibus ista dies.* |
atque aliqua ex illis cum regum nomina quaeret, | *quae loca, qui montes, quaeve ferantur aquae,* | *omnia*
responde, nec tantum siqua rogabit; | *et quae nescieris, ut bene nota refer.* | *hic est Euphrates, praecinctus*
arundine frontem; | *cui coma dependet caerula, Tigris erit.* | *hos facito Armenios; haec est Danaeia Persis;* |
urbs in Achaemeniis vallibus ista fuit. | *ille vel ille, duces; et erunt quae nomina dicas,* | *si poteris, vere,*
si minus, apta tamen.
[57] A classic trap set by this tricky text. See Sharrock (1994) 1–20 for the complex question of who is
being instructed, addressed or seduced by the *Ars amatoria*.
[58] Predictably, this is no straightforwardly historical triumphal procession. Ovid's description follows
his heralding of Gaius Caesar's departure from Rome to sort out another round of long-standing
Parthian troubles (in 1 BCE). In foretelling Gaius' success, he also foretells his triumph. At the time
of writing, Ovid did not yet know for sure (though readers cannot fail to – and he probably could
have guessed) that Gaius' heroism would amount to nothing much more than some well-massaged
dinner-table diplomacy; what is more, with the typical luck of an Augustan heir, a lingering wound

cares about getting it right anyway, if the real 'conquest' is the girl standing next to you?

In the end, as usual, it is the poet who has the last laugh, insinuating also a subversively sinister agenda into the mimetic fun, and turning on its head the conventional distinction between representation and reality. Banish, for a moment, any suspicion that these processional images are overblown symbols to bolster bogus heroics, tricks to impress the crowd back home, and take them straight – as memorials of Roman military might and of a successful series of massacres out East. At first sight, the mixture of tenses in Ovid's description seems tied to the perspective of the boy and girl – as the present tense of what they see *now* ('she *is* Persia...') gives way to the past tense of what has just passed by ('this one *was*...'). But, as we might expect from Ovid, there is more hanging on the verbs than that. 'This one *was* a city in the Achaemenian valleys' (*Urbs in Achaemeniis vallibus ista fuit*) is literally true in quite another sense. Whatever this nameless town used to be, the chances are that following our glorious Roman victory it existed no more: it had only a past. All that is 'real' about it now is the brilliant cardboard cut-out or gaudy painting carried along in the spectacle.[59] Representation, in other words, has become the only reality there is – apart from memory.

THE *SIMULACRA* OF AUTOCRACY

How far you can believe your eyes, or whether things are as they seem, are questions central to political debate almost everywhere. In the Roman empire, in particular, accusations of dissembling and pretence were major weapons wielded against uncongenial emperors or imperial power in general. It should come as no surprise, then, that ancient discussion of the strategies of representation employed in the triumph are often closely linked to discussions of political image-making and dissimulation more widely. A taste of this can be found in Plutarch's lengthy account of the triumph of Aemilius Paullus over King Perseus in 167 BCE, where the theme of *mimesis* versus reality is embedded not only in the account of the procession itself, but also in the heated discussions that lead up to it.[60] The account opens

---

from a dissident Parthian dagger was to finish the boy off in 4 CE. A funeral then was actually in the offing, not a triumph. For the chronological and (non-)military details, see Hollis (1977) 65–73. For the idea of (sham) triumphal representations signalling sham victories, see below, pp. 38–9.

[59] We should not fail to spot the playfully loaded reference here to Virg. *Aen.* 1.12 *urbs antiqua fuit* (that is Carthage, a city very definitely in the past tense. Austin (1971) *ad loc.* will have none of it ('The nuance in *fuit* ... can hardly be pressed'), despite producing a further telling parallel (*Aen.* 2.325 *fuit Ilium*).

[60] *Aem.* 30–2 (cf. Livy 45.35.5–39).

with Paullus' own troops opposing the proposal that he be awarded a triumph; they are angry because, amongst other things, they had not received
what they thought to be a fair share of the booty. The main spokesman
on Paullus' behalf is the elderly military hero M. Servilius Geminus, who
is given a speech that picks up the contrast between truth and pretence:
Paullus, he emphasizes, had won a 'real victory' (ἀληθινὴ νίκη); it was not
just an insubstantial rumour; and he himself was a trustworthy witness to
this fact – as he demonstrates by opening his clothes and showing off the
'unbelievable' (ἄπιστοι) wounds on his chest, suffered in the campaign,
and the lacerations on his bottom, sustained by riding continually night
and day. The vote for a triumph (with all its games of representation) then
goes through, validated by real scars on a real bottom thrust in the face of
the voting assembly.

At the same period as Plutarch was writing (and the thematic similarity
can hardly be coincidental), other historians were using the perversion of
triumphal imagery as a way of pointing up the corruption and hypocrisy
of imperial power. Tacitus, predictably, found in the 'mimic mountains,
rivers and battles' (*simulacra montium, fluminum, proeliorum*) that were
carried in the triumphal procession of Germanicus in 17 CE a metaphor for
the entirely mimic victory that the triumph was celebrating. Germanicus
had, in fact, been forbidden to complete the war against the Germans;
his grand triumph put the seal on the pretence that he really had done
the job ('. . . and the war, because he had been forbidden to finish it, was
treated as finished', *bellumque, quia conficere prohibitus erat, pro confecto
accipiebatur*).[61] In the lives of two classic despots of Roman historiography,
Caligula and Domitian, this manipulation of the conventions of triumphal
mimesis is pushed one step further: both of them turn *mimesis* to outright
deception by acquiring men to act out the role of the native prisoners
in their celebrations of sham victories. Caligula, according to Suetonius,
staged his triumph over the Germans with the help of some Gauls, whom
he forced 'not only to dye their hair red and let it grow long, but also to
learn the German language and adopt barbarian names'. In this triumph
the walking-talking 'captives' were just as 'fake' as the usual tableaux of the
absent dead or the model rivers and mountains.[62] A fake victory meant
a(n even more) fake procession.

---

[61] *Ann.* 2.41.
[62] Suet. *Calig.* 47 (*coegitque non tantum rutilare et summittere comam, sed et sermonem Germanicum
addiscere et nomina barbarica ferre*), possibly also the *cause célèbre* targeted by Pers. 6.46–7. For
Domitian's similar trick, see Tac. *Agr.* 39.1; Plin. *Pan.* 16.3.

In Roman imperial ideology one of the characteristics of monstrous despots is that they *literalize* the metaphors of cultural politics – to disastrous effect: Elagabalus responded to the religious metaphors of ambivalent gendering in his eastern cult by 'really' attempting to give himself a vagina; Commodus sought the charisma of the arena by literally jumping over the barrier to make himself a gladiator.[63] In the stories of despotic triumphs, we find an elegant twist. Here transgressive rulers play out 'for real' the mimetic games of the procession by faking the human captives who validated the whole show. Despots' triumphs, in other words, literalize triumphal *mimesis* into sheer pretence; the culture of representation becomes (or is exposed as) the culture of sham.

PLAYING GOD (OR ACTING UP)

It was in the midst of this extraordinary mimetic performance that the *triumphator* took his place on the chariot that carried him up to the Capitoline temple – looking just like, and simultaneously not quite like, the cult statue of Jupiter Optimus Maximus. Strikingly, most modern debates on the (divine, human, regal) status of the victorious general choose to allow the rest of the procession into the picture only at its margins. They are intent instead on pinning down the diagnostic signs in the attributes of the *triumphator* himself and in his immediate entourage: the red face, the sceptre, the purple toga and that (in modern accounts) ubiquitous slave. My question is: what happens to our understanding of this puzzling figure if we do re-integrate him into the procession as a whole, and its whole array of representational games?

The first thing that happens is that we find the *triumphator*, inevitably, in competition with the other elements of the procession for the gaze and attention of the audience. All complex performances make their actors rivals: who is the star? can the bit-part steal the show? who commands our attention the most? No less than other spectacles, the triumph entailed a competition for the eyes of the audience. Of course, the general could claim a formal centrality; and there are numerous ancient accounts where he is given centre stage, or is made the culmination of the show (as, for example, in Appian's account of 61 BCE, which climaxes in Pompey's chariot, cloak, progress to the Capitol and clemency to the prisoners). But as Plutarch repeatedly emphasizes in his account of Aemilius Paullus' triumph of 167 BCE,

[63] Dio Cass. 80.16; 73.17–20.

there was always a risk that other actors would usurp the stardom. In Plutarch's tale, in fact, it was the pathos of the victims on display that outbid the victor; and all eyes were turned on the children of the defeated. Though Paullus was 'gazed upon from all sides' (περίβλεπτος) and 'admired by all' (ζηλωτὸς ὑπὸ πάντων), and though he had been struck by tragedies of his own (one of his sons died a few days before the procession, the other just afterwards), it was the three children of King Perseus who evoked the pity and so found the limelight: 'out of compassion the Romans held their eyes on the innocents, and many of them ended up shedding tears, and all of them found the spectacle a mixture of pain and pleasure until the children had gone by'.[64] An object lesson in the rhetoric of pathos.

But more radically, the extravagant mimetics that we have explored through the procession as a whole must prompt us to think differently about the status of the general as image and representation; and to reflect on how our understanding of the other divine images on parade must 'rub off' on our attempts to make sense of the *triumphator*. Think back, for example, to Appian's teasing account of the εἰκόνες of the barbarian gods in Pompey's parade: statues of gods and/or (at a second order of representation) paintings of statues of gods.[65] Are these perilously like our general (dressed up as if he was the statue of Jupiter)? Or not like him at all?

In these terms, our question will be not only *what the general represents*, but *how religious representation itself is to be interpreted*. The *triumphator* is not merely an exercise in religious hermeneutics; as part of a parade of the processes of representation and its interpretation, he puts religious hermeneutics *on display*. The bottom line is not whether he is to be seen either as a god or a king (nor even the judicious compromise of *both* god *and* king); but how he parades precisely those dilemmas. It is central to the culture of the triumph, in other words, that the audience (whether enthusiastic spectators along the route or canny commentators, then and now) be engaged in a debate around the margins of their own credibility and/or suspicion – whether that is in reading the *tableaux vivants* as replications of reality, brilliant artifice or treacherous sham, or in seeing the general as the god's double, a living statue or a ludicrous actor in fancy dress.

I mean 'ludicrous actor' quite literally. For one of the most powerful ancient explorations of the figure of the *triumphator* is to be found in a

---

[64] *Aem.* 34.4 (Paullus); 33. 4 (the children: οὕτως ὑπ' οἴκτου τοῖς νηπίοις προσεῖχον τὰς ὄψεις οἱ ‘Ρωμαῖοι καὶ δάκρυα πολλοῖς ἐκβάλλειν συνέβη, πᾶσι δὲ μεμιγμένην ἀλγηδόνι καὶ χάριτι τὴν θέαν εἶναι μέχρι οὗ τὰ παιδία παρῆλθεν). There was pity for Arsinoe too, in Caesar's triumph of 46 (Dio 43.19.3).

[65] Above, p. 32.

play written for the comic stage, Plautus' *Amphitruo*.[66] Some two centuries earlier than any of the texts I have so far considered, it was probably first staged in the early second century BCE – possibly (we do not know; but, as you will see, it would be hugely significant if so) at the *ludi Romani*, where the presiding magistrate was famously dressed in the costume of a *triumphator*.[67] This play has hardly ever been brought into mainstream discussion of the Roman triumph. But I hope to show, by way of conclusion, that its title role is explicitly cast in terms of a Roman triumphing general (albeit within a Hellenizing, mythic context), and that it simultaneously parodies and problematizes his divine mimicry. It is, I shall suggest, a piece of theatre that frames, is framed by and exposes the mimetic conventions of the triumph, and of its god-general.

The action of the play leads up to the birth of Hercules – by way of an intricate tale of adultery, disguise and mistaken identity. Amphitruo himself is a Theban general, just returned from a heroically successful campaign against the 'Teloboans' (a people of Acarnania if you like spurious geographic precision, but most of all 'a far cry' from wherever we are[68]). While he has been away, Jupiter has taken a fancy to Amphitruo's wife, Alcmena, and he has been making love to her cunningly disguised as her husband. In fact, the disguise is almost seamless, for the play insists that the only difference between the two is the gold tassel hanging down from Jupiter's hat.[69] The return of the real Amphitruo causes the predictable confusion, archly complicated by Mercury – also in (almost seamless) disguise, as Amphitruo's slave Sosia. The ensuing slapstick and carnival sadism (part of which is lost in a break in our text) finally ends with a resolution in which divine unction is poured on the proceedings: Alcmena bears twins, Hercules son of Jupiter and Iphicles son of Amphitruo; and for the rest of Roman time cuckold Amphitruo will glory in his role as Joseph to Hercules' Jesus.

Apart from the well known mythical tradition of Hercules' birth (Plautus' baby has, in fact, strangled his required snakes before the end of the play), we know, and can conjecture, even less than usual about the exact source

---

[66] Christenson (2000) offers a clear overview of the play in its literary, political and theatrical context, plus ample bibliography.

[67] This is just one of the links between those games and the triumphal ceremony, and has been the cause of much debate (which I have carefully skirted in this chapter): were these *ludi* a direct offshoot of the early triumph? If not, how do you explain their shared features? The answers are lost in what we optimistically call early Roman 'history'. See above, n. 25.

[68] τῆλε/τηλοῦ = 'far'; βοή = 'cry/shout'.

[69] Lines 144–5, Mercury speaking: *tum meo patri autem torulus inerit aureus | sub petaso*. Though, as John Henderson points out, the Latin leaves the visible difference between Jupiter and Amphitruo more open than my paraphrase would suggest; it could equally be teasing the audience with the idea that Jupiter is recognizable by the 'gold bun [hidden] under his hat'.

and dramatic antecedents of Plautus' plot.[70] What is clear, however, is
the extent to which any putative Greek model has been 'Romanized', so
comprehensively that much of the story as we have it would scarcely make
sense outside Rome or Rome's cultural orbit. A good deal of this exclusively
Roman flavour is delivered through the role of Amphitruo himself and the
clear hints in the text that we should see him in terms of a victorious and
triumphant Roman general. So, for example, his trouncing of the Teloboans
is accomplished under a specifically Roman rubric (*suo auspicio* and *suo
imperio*).[71] And the long account by (the real) Sosia giving the details of
(the real) Amphitruo's victory almost certainly depends on the standard
Roman general's formulation of his achievements when he was seeking
nomination for a triumph.[72] These echoes have prompted in turn a whole
series of suggestions about which particular recent victory, or *triumphator*,
Plautus might have had mind when he adapted his source. Are we dealing,
for example, with a comic glance at the triumph of M. Fulvius Nobilior
over the Ambracians in 186 BCE? Or how about the campaigns of Livius
Salinator or Lucius Scipio?[73]

This desperate search for a specific historical referent for Amphitruo's
victory has tended to occlude many more important aspects of the play.
Those critics who have taken care to lift their eyes above the geo-politics
of the early second century have seen the *Amphitruo* as a play where the
representational games of the stage are aggressively on parade: the divine
doubling, mistaken identities and impersonations offer a reflection on the
very nature of theatre and its rules; and beyond that on human subjectivity
and the idea of the unitary personality.[74] Even so, the central (Roman) joke
around which the play is structured is almost always lost. For *Amphitruo* is an
in-your-face parody of triumphal *mimesis*. The triumph staged the general
as a perfect look-alike Jupiter, dressed up (or disguised) in the distinctive
purple toga plus wreath, red face and sceptre; he 'acted' Jupiter for the day.
Here Plautus simply, but cunningly, reverses those mimetic conventions to
stage the god disguised almost indistinguishably as the victorious general,
acting human for the day (or, mimetically, for the one night that the play's
action takes).

---

[70] See, for example, Hunter (1987).   [71] Line 192.

[72] Lines 186–261. Halkin (1948) lays out the similarities between this speech and formal triumphal
language. The levels of parody are, of course, more complicated than that: other critics have detected
echoes of tragic messenger speeches and Roman epic (see Christenson (2000) *ad loc.*).

[73] For discussion of various suggested models among the Roman elite for the character of Amphitruo
(none very plausible), see Galinsky (1966); Harvey (1981).

[74] The most notable contribution is Dupont (1976); but even she stops short of directly exposing the
triumphal parody.

The temptation to fix on the *Ludi Romani* as the original context for the play's performance is almost irresistible. The idea of the impresario, the presiding magistrate in his triumphal costume, being turned into the object, or target, of the spectacle on stage is too good to be true – and deliciously reminisicent of all the blurring of the boundaries between performance and real life that prompted such dilemmas for the citizens of St Louis, not to mention President Taft. But even if we must leave that case as unproven (for there is no external evidence on the play's original context) the cultural politics of this drama should still claim our attention. For what could be more appropriate in Roman religious terms than to set the triumph, and the general-as-actor, at the heart of a play which broaches such major problems of representation? Or, to put it the other way round, what could be more appropriate than using the conventions of the triumph as a peg and a prompt for debating those problems? The hermeneutic question that is at stake here (both in the drama and the procession) is: how *can* you ever tell the difference between 'being', 'playing', or 'acting', god?

Is it more than a question of the tassel on the hat?

CHAPTER 3

Incorporating the alien: the art of conquest*

Catharine Edwards

Huge numbers of statues thronged the city of Rome in antiquity. The Elder Pliny in his *Natural histories* emphasizes the vast quantity of them, commenting, for instance, of bronze statuary, that it:

has flourished without limit ... When Marcus Scaurus was aedile, there were 3,000 statues on the stage of what was merely a temporary theatre. Mummius after conquering Achaea filled the city with statues ... A great many were also brought in by the Luculli.[1] (*NH* 34.36)

Rome's 'second population', as it was to be termed by Cassiodorus in the sixth century,[2] included, of course, innumerable images of emperors and other prominent citizens – an honorific statue soon came to substitute for the volatile splendour of a triumph (for those who were not members of the imperial family, at least). But also prominent among Rome's statues were images of quite un-Roman bodies.

Rome's population of statues was as cosmopolitan as its human population. As Pirro Ligorio commented in the sixteenth century, developing Cassiodorus' metaphor of Rome's two populations, the city's stone and bronze inhabitants, like those of flesh, comprised both Romans and foreigners 'transported from all the various parts of the world.'[3] It is these bodies of stone and bronze I wish to concentrate on here, looking both at

---

* I am very grateful to Peter Stewart, who kindly allowed me to read part of his unpublished dissertation on Roman statuary, and to Caroline Vout and Greg Woolf for their perceptive comments on an earlier draft, as well as their bibliographic suggestions. I also learned much from audiences in Stanford in February 1998, at UCL in May 2000 and at Birkbeck in November 2000.

[1] Translations are my own unless otherwise indicated.

[2] In his *Formula Comitivae Romanae* he marvelled at the huge number of statues in the city of Rome, describing them as Rome's second population: 'It is said that the Etruscans were first in Italy to discover this art, which an ample posterity so developed as to provide almost another population for the city of Rome to match the one created by nature' – *quas amplexa posteritas paene parum populum urbi dedit quam natura procreavit* (*Variae* 7.15).

[3] This passage is cited by Leonard Barkan (1999) 63. As Barkan comments in his note, though Ligorio attributes the metaphor to Pliny it does not appear in Pliny, *NH* and Ligorio probably took it from the Cassiodorus passage quoted above.

the many masterpieces of Greek art, such as those brought by Mummius and the Luculli, which found their place in Rome (particularly in the mid and late republic), and also at statues specifically intended to represent defeated enemies and conquered peoples.[4] My focus will be Rome from the first century BCE to the second century CE, though earlier material will also be considered, especially where it is discussed in later texts such as Livy or Pliny's *Natural histories*.

This essay aims to raise a range of questions in relation to these statues. How comfortably, we might wonder, did they fit into the city's topography? Were they invariably viewed as emblems of Rome's power? Or might they sometimes seem more problematic, evidence perhaps of Rome's artistic inferiority, or of attempts on the part of individuals to promote themselves in quite un-Roman ways? What did such monuments say about the conquered? Might, for instance, the colossal statues of brooding Dacians which decorated Trajan's Forum ever seem a menacing rather than a reassuring presence? We could consider, too, whether Rome's diverse human population might have responded in equally diverse ways to the city's statues.

Statues in modern western cityscapes may often appear somewhat inert; perhaps the majority of those who live and work in London (to take the example of another imperial capital) rush daily past many statues on display in public places without giving them a second glance.[5] How far were Romans alert to such elements of their material environment? We might note a comment made by Pliny:

At Rome, indeed, the great quantity of works of art and their resulting obliteration from our memory, and, particularly, the multitude of official functions and business activities must . . . deter anyone from serious study, since the appreciation involved requires leisure and an atmosphere of profound silence.[6] (*NH* 36.27)

Statues in the city, Pliny suggests, cannot be fully appreciated (thus parading his own sensitivity as a connoisseur, while also excusing himself from providing detailed responses to the mass of statues in Rome). Yet there are reasons for supposing that statues in the city did not go unnoticed. They served, for instance, as useful markers in the cityscape; individuals wanting to meet in the Forum of Augustus, for example, might agree on a particular

---

[4] I shall restrict my discussion to statues partly for reasons of space but also because of the particular potency (discussed below) of statues as compared with e.g. reliefs. For an account of representations of barbarians in reliefs and coinage, as well as statues, see Ferris (2000). He also considers material from outside the city of Rome.

[5] Though I shall consider an interesting exception to this below.

[6] *Romae quidem multitudo operum et iam obliteratio ac magis officiorum negotiorumque acervi omnes a contemplatione tamen abducunt, quoniam otiosorum et in magno loci silentio talis admiratio est.*

sculpture as a meeting point.[7] More significantly we can sometimes find statues provoking highly emotional responses – desire, fear, wonder, grief, rage – as we shall see below.[8]

In Graeco-Roman antiquity the relationship between a statue and what it represented was a particularly potent one. Statues of specific individuals were reminders of their achievements and qualities. Plutarch comments in passing that Cineas had been a pupil of Demosthenes and his skill as a public speaker reminded people of Demosthenes' own power and ability as a speaker, 'just as a statue might recall them' (*Pyrrhus* 14).[9] While statues of deities will not be considered in detail in this essay, some aspects of their role are relevant to the status of statues more generally. In the Roman world (as in the Greek) statues of gods were, in an important sense, viewed as gods.[10] In the processions preceding the games given as part of religious festivals, statues of the gods were carried from their temples to the theatre or circus where they were positioned to witness the entertainment.[11] Later, statues of Roman emperors also functioned as powerful bearers of meaning, venerated as substitutes for the emperor himself; slaves, for instance, could gain protection against their masters by appealing to the emperor's statue.[12] Even after the Christianization of the Roman empire, there was a 'deep sense of divine charisma immanent in such objects', as Jaś Elsner puts it.[13] This has implications for perceptions of statues in general.

Statues were regularly praised for their lifelike qualities;[14] the topos had a force we might not expect.[15] Classical literature includes some striking stories of statues coming to life, most famously the image of a woman crafted by the sculptor Pygmalion (as recounted in Ovid's *Metamorphoses* 10.243–92).[16] As we shall see, the statues associated with at least one Roman monument were imagined stepping off their pedestals and terrorizing a nervous emperor.

---

[7] See Zanker (1997) 186 and n. 28.

[8] On the importance (and dangers) of the historian's quest for empathy, see Hopkins (1983b) xiv–xv.

[9] Cf. Plutarch, *Titus Flamininus* 1; *Marius* 2. On the associations of portrait statues in Rome see Gregory (1994) and Tanner (2000).

[10] See Gordon (1979), esp. 16, 'People believed simultaneously that statues were gods and that they were not.' These issues are further explored by Elsner (1996).

[11] Dionysius of Halicarnassus 7.72.13.   [12] As Hopkins has emphasized (1978a) 222–4.

[13] Elsner (1998) 54–63, at 57.   [14] See Spivey (1995).

[15] Elsner (1996) argues that in pagan writings there was a distinction between aesthetic (admiring a statue's lifelike qualities) and religious (feeling awe at the presence of the god) modes of apprehension and that they did not operate simultaneously. However, he points to authors (and indeed individual texts) where both attitudes seem to operate.

[16] See Elsner and Sharrock (1991).

HONORIFIC STATUES

Statues of non-Romans are the focus of this essay. But to appreciate their impact we should perhaps first consider briefly the statues of Romans with which the city abounded.[17] These included figures from the very distant past; statues of Rome's kings stood near the temple of Jupiter on the Capitoline, along with a statue of the Brutus who had driven them out (Plutarch, *Brutus* 1). These may perhaps be dated to the late fourth century BCE.[18] The regal age and its termination were thus simultaneously commemorated. Other figures from the early days of Rome were also represented, such as Horatius Cocles, famous for defending Rome single-handed (Pliny, *NH* 34.22).

The Elder Pliny has much to say on the subject of commemorative statuary, commenting that it originated in Greece, as an honour to Olympic victors, then spread to other places:

Thereafter this custom was adopted across the known world in a very civilized rivalry, and the squares in all towns came to be decorated with statues. People should live on in the memory and their titles should be read for ever inscribed on the base of statues, not only on their tombs.[19] (*NH* 34.17)

Both the people and the Senate might vote statues to particular individuals (cf. Pliny, *NH* 34.21–4).[20] Some Romans erected statues commemorating themselves; Cicero jokes about Scipio's squadron of gilded equestrian statues (*Ad Att.* 6.1.7). The degree of state control exercised over this varied; in 158 BCE, for instance, the censors removed from the forum all statues of magistrates, except those voted by Senate and people (Pliny, *NH* 34.30). The prestige brought by a statue depended on its form (equestrian statues afforded particular honour), its materials (a gilded statue reflected especially well on the honorand) and its location.

While statues were probably not awarded to triumphant generals under the republic, Augustus provided for all who were granted a triumph to

---

[17] This is itself a huge topic. See Lahusen (1983), Wallace-Hadrill (1990), Anderson (1984), Gregory (1994) and Tanner (2000).

[18] See Evans (1990).

[19] *Excepta deinde res est a toto orbe terrarum humanissima ambitione, et in omnium municipiorum foris statuae ornamentum esse coepere propagarique memoria hominum et honores legendi aevo basibus inscribi, ne in sepulchris tantum legerentur.*

[20] It remains unclear how widespread this practice was under the republic. See Lahusen (1983). Wallace-Hadrill argues it is probably unhelpful to seek for a 'rule' (see 1990 appendix for detailed critique of Lahusen). As Tanner (2000) 28 emphasizes, there is significant evidence for statuary in this category dating back to the fourth century BCE.

receive a bronze statue in his own Forum Augustum (Dio 55.10.3). The
glory these brought individual generals was thus controlled by – and reflected on – the emperor (at the same time, statues of the great Romans
of earlier days – led by Romulus on one side and Aeneas on the other –
positioned in the main niches, cast a different kind of glory on the princeps
whose image stood in the centre of the forum).[21] Later, statues of triumphant generals found their place in Trajan's Forum, the largest of all the
imperial fora.[22] With the emperor's permission, members of the elite could
also erect statues of prominent individuals in prominent public places.[23]
The profusion of honorific statuary in the Roman forum and elsewhere
was such that measures were periodically introduced to clear them away, in
order to make room for the next generation – though the clearances undertaken by Augustus and later by Caligula and Claudius may have been as
much motivated by a desire to play down the honour thereby conferred on
members of the elite and their families.[24] Yet there was still a perception –
reflected in Pliny's comment at *NH* 34.17, quoted above – that through
their statues great Romans were represented in perpetuity in Rome's public
places.

Honorific portraits can be seen as standing for the relationship between
the giver of the portrait and the portrayed.[25] In the civil-war-torn decades
of the first century BCE, statues might well be given out of fear of force,
to placate powerful generals prepared to use their troops against the state.
The gift of such honours might be hoped to create moral obligations on
the part of the honorand.[26] Under the principate, honorific statues of the
emperor proliferated, undoubtedly forming the most conspicuous category
of statues in the city.

Pliny, praising the emperor Trajan, contrasts his images (few, made of
bronze and positioned with proper deference to the gods) with the excessive
statuary of Domitian. He goes on to describe the destruction of Domitian's
statues in the wake of his assassination in 96 CE:

What pleasure it gave to smash those proud faces to the ground, to strike them with
swords and savage them with axes, as if blood and pain might follow each wound.
No-one was so restrained in his joy and deferred happiness as not to consider it a
form of vengeance to witness those bodies mutilated, limbs hacked to pieces, and
finally those gloomy, fearsome faces thrown into the fire and melted down, so that

---

[21] See Zanker (1988) 201–3.   [22] Anderson (1984) ch. v.   [23] See e.g. Pliny, *Letters* 1.17.
[24] Suet. *Cal*. 34; Dio 60.25.2–3. Emperors might also be criticized for putting up too many statues
(Pliny, *Pan*. 52.3 on Domitian).
[25] As Tanner has emphasized (2000) 34.   [26] As Tanner suggests (2000) 28.

the fire might transform this source of terror and threat into something for the use and pleasure of humankind.[27] (*Pan.* 52.4–5)

The statues' destruction is given a thrilling resonance – and is indeed provoked by – an intense identification between them and the person they represent. Such moments of symbolic destruction were relatively rare. And statues of emperors were in a category of their own. Yet this passage conveys the passion statues might evoke on the part of the Roman people, even including – if we believe Pliny – an otherwise very restrained senator.

SPOILS

The middle and late republic saw a horde of statues making their way to the city as spoils from successful campaigns, particularly in the eastern Mediterranean. This was especially concentrated in the period from 211, when Marcellus captured Syracuse, to the capture of Corinth in 146 BCE by Mummius. Strabo, writing in the time of Augustus, comments in relation to the activities of Mummius' soldiers in Corinth: 'In fact, I might almost say that out of all the other offerings in Rome, the majority (and the better examples) came from there' (8.6.23). These statues were paraded through the city in triumphal processions, like human prisoners of war. Livy writes of Flamininus' triumph of 194 BCE: 'On the first day were carried in procession the arms, weapons and statues of bronze and marble' (34.52.4). Many were subsequently put on display in the city's temples and porticoes; inscriptions reminded the curious viewer by what process they had found their way to Rome.[28]

Cicero, in his indictment of Verres of 70 BCE, contrasts the governor of Sicily's private passion for stolen art with the public generosity of the conquerors of the Greek world in earlier days:

What should I say about Marcus Marcellus, who captured Syracuse, the city most adorned with art? What about Lucius Scipio, who waged war in Asia and defeated that most mighty king Antiochus? What about Flamininus, who conquered King Philip and Macedonia? What about Lucius Paullus, who overcame King Perseus by his strength and bravery? Or what about Lucius Mummius, who destroyed Corinth, a city of the greatest beauty and every kind of artistic richness, and who

---

[27] *Iuvabat illidere solo superbissimos vultus, instare ferro, saevire securibus, ut si singulos ictus sanguis dolorque sequeretur. nemo tam temperans gaudii seraeque laetitiae, quin instar ultionis videretur cernere laceros artus truncata membra, postremo truces horrendasque imagines obiectas excoctasque flammis, ut ex illo terrore et minis in usum hominum ac voluptates ignibus mutarentur.* This incident is helpfully discussed by Gregory (1994) 95–6.

[28] For a full account, see Pape (1975).

brought many cities of Boeotia and Achaea under the power and dominion of the Roman people? These men were of the greatest standing and character, but their homes were empty of statues and paintings.[29] Yet we see the entire city and the temples of the gods, and similarly all the other parts of Italy ornamented with the gifts and monuments they brought.[30] (*Verr.* 2.1.55)

One might add to Cicero's list Fabius Maximus, who brought quantities of statues back as spoils from Tarentum in 209, and Marcus Fulvius Nobilior, who returned triumphant from Aetolia in 187.[31] The display of these art-works celebrates the achievement of Rome. They offer a means to honour Rome's gods and ornament the city. The quantity as well of the quality of the works brought to Rome is repeatedly stressed by other authors, too.[32]

Sometimes these Greek statues might take on the role of cult statues in Roman temples (for instance, the statue of Hercules Victor, in the temple dedicated by Mummius, commemorating his defeat of Corinth in 146 BCE).[33] More often they appear to have been put on display as votive offerings in public sanctuaries, though as Richard Gordon comments: 'In the process of cultural borrowing between Greece and Rome in which Romans ransacked the Hellenistic world for art objects there occurred an important reclassification of Greek religious art: it became "art" not an "offering".'[34] The Romans were not the first to alienate statues, to deprive them of their 'indigenous cultural significance',[35] while endowing them with a whole host of new meanings. Concerning Augustus' removal of the ancient image of Athena Alea (from the Arcadians who had sided with

---

[29] Similar remarks on the private restraint and public generosity of these generals are articulated in *De off.* 2.76. In *De rep.* 1.21, however, Cicero makes one of his characters refer to a celestial globe as the only item from Syracuse Marcellus kept for himself.

[30] *quid ego de M. Marcello loquar, qui Syracusas urbem ornatissimam cepit? quid de Scipione, qui bellum in Asia gessit Antiochumque regem potentissimum vicit? quid de Flaminino, qui regem Philippum et Macedoniam subegit? quid de L. Paulo, qui regem Persen vi ac virtute superavit? quid de L. Mummio, qui urbem pulcherrimam atque ornatissimam Corinthum, plenissimam rerum omnium, sustulit, urbesque Achaiae Boeotiaeque multas sub imperium populi Romani dictionemque subiunxit? quorum domus, cum honore et virtute florerent, signis et tabulis pictis erant vacuae; at vero urbem totam templaque deorum omnesque Italiae partes illorum donis ac monumentis exornatas videmus.*

[31] The victory of Scipio was in 186 BCE, that of Flamininus in 194 BCE and that of Paullus in 168 BCE.

[32] For instance, Plutarch, *Marcellus* 21; Pliny, *NH* 34.36, quoted above.

[33] *CIL* 1.2 626. Note, too the example of the statue of Apollo, brought to Rome from Seleucia by Gaius Sosius in the late first century BCE, which seems to have been the cult statue in the temple of Apollo Sosianus (Pliny, *NH* 3.53). Cf. Kleiner (1992) 84–5. The temple pediment was also filled with classical Greek statuary depicting conflict between Greeks and Amazons (see La Rocca (1985)). NB Cicero on statue of Jupiter brought to its 'rightful home' on the Capitoline, *In Verr.*, discussed below. The display of booty is discussed in detail in Pape (1975).

[34] Gordon (1979) 11. According to Livy, in the aftermath of the siege of Capua, the college of *pontifices* was given the task of determining which of the captured statues were sacred and which profane (26.34.12).

[35] In Barkan's words (1999) 129.

Antony during the civil war), Pausanias comments that he 'only followed a custom observed by the Greeks and barbarians from ancient times' (8.46.4). But Roman depredations were on a scale which put all previous plunderers in the shade.[36]

Rome in some ways came to function as a museum city, where one might see masterpieces by the most acclaimed artists of the Greek world. After Quintus Metellus plundered Macedonia in 148 BCE he had built the Porticus Metelli in the lower Campus Martius – probably the first building in Rome constructed to house Greek art brought as *spolia*. This included a group of bronze statues by Lysippus representing Alexander with twenty-five companions.[37] Writing in the time of Tiberius, Velleius Paterculus refers to 'the group of equestrian statues which even now are the principal ornament of the place' – *hanc turmam statuarum equestrium... hodieque maximum ornamentum eius loci* (1.11.4).[38] Later the Jewish writer Josephus saw the mass of works of art decorating Vespasian's Temple of Peace as symbolic of Rome's dominion over the rest of the world: 'In that sanctuary were gathered together and deposited all those works of art which before, if he wished to see them, a tourist had had to visit each in a different place' (*Jewish War* 7.5.7).[39] Rome was so full of art that Pliny comments in relation to a naked Venus by Scopas, located in the circus, that it 'would have brought fame to any locality but Rome', *quemcumque alium locum nobilitatura* (*NH* 36.26).

Not all plundered statues were honoured, however:

A statue which cannot be accorded any honour (*inhonorus*) and which has been without a temple is that of Hercules, to whom the Carthaginians annually sacrificed humans. It stands on the ground at the entrance to the Portico of the Nations. (*NH* 36.39)

Presumably this was part of the spoils from the sack of Carthage in 146 BCE; for Pliny at least, the statue served as a perpetual reminder of the

---

[36] Pausanias comments further on plundering by Greeks (9.40.4 – on this see Pape (1975) 87–8). At least some of the Hellenistic rulers the Romans defeated had themselves very probably amassed statue collections from other cities in Greece – so suggests Pape with regard to the treasures of Ambracia, which had been the home of King Pyrrhus (1975) 12. Scipio Aemilianus was praised for, after the defeat of Carthage, returning to their cities of origin statues which had been taken by the Carthaginians from Sicily (Cic. *Verr.* 2.2.86). Of course, as Cicero points out, the restored statues are themselves celebrated as perpetual reminders of Scipio's generosity – *monumenta Africani* (2.2.87). Appian notes that Scipio also brought many statues back to Rome (*Pun.* 135).

[37] The Granikos monument (*NH* 34.6). This was replaced by the Porticus Octaviae in 33 BCE. For other examples, see Pliny, *NH* 36.34–6.

[38] Pollitt lists numerous other statues, known to have been on display in the city, and their locations (1978) 170–4. See also Pape (1975).

[39] Many of these had been appropriated by Nero.

barbarousness of Rome's arch enemy (and one which might give the viewer a voyeuristic frisson). But the effect of the haul from the Greek East is perhaps harder to determine.

A range of different – and sometimes conflicting – responses can be traced in Roman texts.[40] Cicero's treatment of Roman plunder in his attack on Verres is certainly ambivalent. He praises the generals of earlier periods, yet writes of 'Lucius Mummius, who destroyed Corinth, a city of the greatest beauty and every kind of artistic richness.' The removal of the statues of the gods was a particularly complex issue.[41] Elsewhere in his attack on Verres, Cicero attempts to emphasise the importance of the statue of Jupiter which Verres had allegedly taken from Syracuse by comparing it with a much venerated image of Jupiter on the Capitoline in Rome. But he also makes clear that the statue in Rome had been taken by Titus Flamininus from Macedonia: *illud Flamininus ita ex aede sua sustulit ut in Capitolio, hoc est in terrestri domicilio Iovis, poneret*, 'He took it out of its own temple in order to set it up on the Capitoline which is the terrestrial home of Jupiter' (*Verr.* 2.4.129). The distinction Cicero draws between these two statues is inevitably an uneasy one, even if conquering generals had, in theory, every right to plunder defeated cities.[42] Writing a few decades later, Livy specifically praises Fabius for not taking statues of the gods when Tarentum was conquered in 209 BCE: 'Fabius showed greater nobility in refraining from that kind of plunder than did Marcellus. When a scribe asked him what he wanted done with the statues of colossal size (gods represented in the dress of warriors, each different) Fabius ordered that their angry gods should be left to the Tarentines' (27.16.8).[43]

Livy is generally complimentary about the arrangements Marcellus made in Syracuse after his capture of the city. But he is critical of his treatment of artworks:

The ornaments of the city, the statues and pictures which were so numerous in Syracuse, he had transported to Rome. They were certainly spoils of the enemy and the rightful fruit of war. Yet it was this which first introduced admiration

---

[40] For modern discussions see particularly Pollitt (1978) and Gruen (1992) chs. 3 and 4.

[41] In earlier centuries, Roman generals would attempt to deprive their enemies of divine protection by offering their patron deity a cult in Rome through the ritual of *evocatio*. It remains unclear how long this ritual continued in use. Even if it was practised to draw Juno out of Carthage in 146 BCE, it seems no temple for the goddess was built in Rome (see Beard, North and Price (1998) vol. 1, 133).

[42] The law governing the taking of booty and its distribution is discussed in detail by Pape (1975) 27–40.

[43] *sed maiore animo generis eius praeda abstinuit Fabius quam Marcellus; qui interrogante scriba quid fieri signis vellet ingentis magnitudinis – di sunt, suo quisque habitu in modum pugnantium formati – deos iratos Tarentinis relinqui iussit.* Gruen has some helpful comments on the political infighting back in Rome which may well have affected subsequent accounts of these generals' activities (1992) 100–2.

for the creations of Greek art and began the licentiousness with which all places everywhere, sacred and profane, were plundered. Eventually, this licentiousness was turned against the Roman gods and first of all against the very temple Marcellus had so splendidly adorned; for the temples outside the Porta Capena, dedicated by Marcellus, used to be frequented by foreigners because of the splendour of their ornaments, of which now only the smallest part may be seen.[44] (25.40.1–3)

Livy refers here to the temples of Honos and Virtus (Honour and Virtue), which Marcellus had adorned with numerous spoils from Syracuse and planned to rededicate. The Roman despoliation of temples in Sicily has helped to make acceptable the removal of artworks from temples more generally, Livy alleges, suggesting that this trend eventually led to the despoliation of the temples adorned by Marcellus.[45] Livy's disapproval of this *licentia* is marked. The passage also (unusually) draws attention to the function of Rome's treasures as tourist attractions – *visebantur enim ab externis*.

The possible impact of these artworks on the 'innocent' Roman public of the second century BCE seems also to have been seen as problematic, at least in retrospect.[46] Many texts express anxiety about the seductive nature both of statues themselves and of the precious materials from which they were made. This is a persistent theme in Pliny's treatment of marble in his *Natural histories*. He comments, for instance, 'It seems to me strange that although statues have been so long present in Italy, the images of the gods dedicated in shrines were usually of wood or terracotta down to the time of the conquest of Asia, whence came luxury'[47] (34.34). Even marble images of the gods, then, are conceived of as manifestations of luxury.

Plutarch offers a more detailed account of Roman responses to Greek art in his biography of Marcellus the conqueror of Syracuse:

---

[44] *ornamenta urbis, signa tabulasque quibus abundabant Syracusae, Romam devexit, hostium quidem illa spolia et parta belli iure; ceterum inde primum initium mirandi Graecarum artium operae licentiaeque huius sacra profanaque omnia vulgo spoliandi factum est, quae postremo in Romanos deos, templum id ipsum primum quod a Marcello eximie ornatum est, vertit. visebantur enim ab externis ad portam Capenam dedicata a M. Marcello templa propter excellentia eius generis ornamenta, quorum perexigua pars comparet.*

[45] The removal of artworks from the temples presumably occurred during the civil conflicts of the first century BCE, as Pape suggests (1975) 6 n. 6.

[46] Gruen (1992) emphasizes that Romans had been incorporating spoils into their city long before Marcellus' sack of Syracuse and we may not be able to infer a great deal about responses to Greek art in the third and second centuries from the accounts, Roman and Greek, written considerably later. My main focus here, however, is principally on the period when Cicero, Livy, Pliny and Plutarch (the principal sources) were writing.

[47] *mirumque mihi videtur, cum statuarum origo tam vetus Italiae sit, lignea potius aut fictilia deorum simulacra in delubris dicata usque ad devictam Asiam, unde luxuria.*

With the common people Marcellus secured greater favour because he adorned
the city with objects that had Hellenic grace, charm and persuasiveness (*hedone*,
charis, *pithanotes*).... [The elders] blamed Marcellus first of all because he made
the city an object of envy, not only by men but also by the gods whom he had led
into the city like slaves in his triumphal procession, and second because he filled
the Roman people (who had previously been accustomed to fighting or farming
and had no experience of a life of softness and ease but were rather ... 'vulgar,
uncultured but good in things which are important') with a taste for leisure and
idle talk, affecting urbane opinions about the arts and about artists, even to the
point of wasting the better part of the day on such things. (*Marcellus* ch. 21)

Roman generals were enslaving artworks – yet the artworks might well
have their revenge, transforming manly Romans into idle, soft easterners
(no doubt we might detect a note of irony in the words put into the mouths
of Roman elders by the Greek Plutarch). Somewhat similar comments are
attributed to the Elder Cato by Livy (in the context of a debate about repeal-
ing the sumptuary *lex Oppia* in 195 BCE). Rome, Cato argues, is increasingly
afflicted with *avaritia* and *luxuria*, which have been the destruction of every
great empire.

The better and the happier becomes the fortune of our commonwealth day by day
and the greater the empire grows – and already we have crossed into Greece and
Asia, places filled with the seductions of vice, and we are handling the treasure of
kings – the more I fear that these things will capture us rather than we them. Like
an enemy horde were statues brought from Syracuse to this city. For now I hear
far too many people praising and admiring the ornaments of Corinth and Athens
and laughing at our terracotta antefixes of the Roman gods.[48] (34.4.3–4)

These captured artworks were tokens of Rome's military might but could
also be seen as offering, with their fine workmanship, embarrassing demonstrations of Roman artistic inferiority. Their beauty threatened to undermine Roman attachment to the traditional trappings of their ancestral
religion. Like a Trojan Horse these artworks had the power to attack Rome
from within.[49] The 'capture' of the Romans – Cato is made to use the verb
ceperint – is, of course, a metaphorical one and one with a sexual dimension,
for the manliness of the Romans is at risk.

---

[48] *haec ego quo melior laetior in dies fortuna rei publicae est imperiumque crescit – et iam in Graeciam
    Asiamque transcendimus omnibus libidinum illecebris repletas et regias etiam attrectamus gazas – eo plus
    horreo, ne illae magis res nos ceperint quam nos illas. infesta, mihi credite, signa ab Syracusis illata sunt
    huic urbi. iam nimis multos audio Corinthi et Athenarum ornamenta laudantes mirantesque et antefixa
    fictilia deorum Romanorum ridentes.*
[49] Cf. too the comments offered by Velleius Paterculus with reference to the sack of Corinth in 146
    BCE: 'I do not think, Vinicius, that you would hesitate to admit that it would have been better for
    the state if the appreciation of Corinthian art should remain undeveloped to the present day rather
    than that it should be appreciated as much as it is now' (1.13.5).

Maybe Scopas' naked Venus did not receive the attention she merited, as Pliny suggests. It is nevertheless tempting to suppose that at least some of the anxiety which seems to have been aroused by the influx of Greek statuary is to be associated with the sexiness of many of the images, languid Apollos, effete Castors and voluptuous Venuses. Scholars puzzle over how to interpret the gestures of the naked Venuses attributed to Pheidias and Praxiteles – and debate whether ancient viewers would have found them desirable (see fig. 1).[50] The story recounted by Ps.-Lucian in his *Amores* (13–16) of the young man whose amorous obsession with the original Knidian Venus left a permanent stain on the statue suggests an erotic response to such images of the gods was at least conceivable.[51] Much, of course, depended on the viewer; Augustus' wife Livia famously remarked, when some men had been condemned to death for having encountered her when they were naked, that 'to chaste women such men were in no respect different from statues' – thus saving their lives (Dio 58.2.4).

Imported statues posed a further danger, as Livy's Cato emphasizes: those who handled the treasures of kings might also come to covet regal power. One issue which numerous ancient texts foreground is the distinction between public and private displays of works of art. Cicero, as we saw in the passage from his attack on Verres, contrasts the public generosity of earlier generals (whose own homes remained unadorned) with Verres' private indulgence of his own passion for art objects. Private collections served to align conquering generals (such as Lucullus in the first century BCE, described by Plutarch, *Luc.* 39) with the Hellenistic rulers they had defeated. This kind of private splendour might be represented as particularly un-Roman. Augustus' associate Agrippa is reported by Pliny to have made a speech arguing that all statues and painting should be made public property (*NH* 35.26).[52] The issue of whether art should be publicly or privately displayed was a particularly live one in the time of Augustus, who was

---

[50] On this issue, see Stewart's discussion of Aphrodite Knidia (1997) 97–107; also Osborne (1994) and (1998). On the 'sexiness' of some imperial statuary in particular see also Vout (2000).

[51] Similar stories are to be found in Lucian, *Imagines* ch. 4; Athenaeus, *Deipnosophistae* 13.606. A visitor to Rome in the twelfth century (Magister Gregorius) describes his own response to an ancient statue (which has been identified by some scholars as the Capitoline Venus, a statue of the Knidian Venus type): 'The image is made from Parian marble with such wonderful and intricate skill, that she seems more like a living creature than a statue; indeed she seems to blush in her nakedness . . . Because of this wonderful image and perhaps some magic spell that I'm unaware of, I was drawn back three times to look at it despite the fact that it was two stades distant from my inn' (*Marvels of Rome*, trs. J. Osborne, Toronto 1987, ch. 12).

[52] The fact that Livy's Cato complains specifically about art from Corinth and Athens (not conquered by Rome until well after this speech is supposed to have been delivered) is all the more reason for seeing the speech as Livy's invention (as Pape notes (1975) 83–4).

Figure 1. Capitoline Venus (a statue of the Knidian Venus type).

seeking to moderate the troubling grandeur of the great magnates of the late republic.[53]

The incorporation of all these works of art into the city of Rome could be viewed as serving to demonstrate the achievements of the Roman people in general. But of course these displays could also serve to celebrate the victories of individual generals. We can assume that many statues were displayed on bases which made clear exactly how they had come to be in Rome. For example, Pliny writes of the statue of Hercules *tunicatus* next to the rostra:

There are three inscriptions on the statue: one says that it is 'from the booty taken by the general L. Lucullus'; another says that Lucullus' ward and son dedicated it after authorization from the Senate, and the third that T. Septimius Sabinus, the curule aedile, restored it from private to public ownership. So many were the rivalries over this statue and so great the value attached to it. (*NH* 34.93)

Lucullus' connection with the statue was still being publicly asserted more than a century after he had seized it.

Similarly, Metellus' portico was a monument to Metellus as well as a gift to Rome. And what was the relationship between Metellus and Alexander whose splendid image so impressed visitors? Was Metellus to be seen as a Roman successor to that great conqueror? Or even as his superior? Another image of Alexander allegedly created by Lysippus also found a new resting-place in Rome – in the Forum Julium; its head, was, however, apparently replaced – with that of Julius Caesar (Statius, *Silvae* 1.1.84–8). Works of art which on one level served to represent the extent of Rome's power over other cultures could also work to convey the position of particular individuals drawing on new languages of power – indeed actually filling the shoes of the greatest of Greek rulers.

UN-ROMAN EYES?

It was not only Romans themselves who saw and responded to the statues which decorated their city. Livy, as we saw, comments on the *externis* who visit the temples dedicated by Marcellus specifically to wonder at their decorations (25.40.1–3). And admiration might not be the only response. Underlining Verres' depredations of Rome's subject peoples, Cicero comments:

---

[53] As Pollitt plausibly argues (1978), with reference also to the reign of Vespasian, when Pliny himself was writing. That emperor made capital out of putting on public display the looted artworks Nero had used to decorate his Golden House (as Pliny emphasizes, *NH* 36.84).

And it was then . . . that the allied and foreign peoples cast away their last hope of prosperity and happiness; for a large number of individuals from Asia and Achaea, who happened to be in Rome serving on deputations at the time, saw in our Forum the revered images of their gods that had been carried away from their own sanctuaries, and recognizing also other statues and works of art, some here and some there, would stand gazing at them, tears flowing from their eyes. What we then heard all these people saying was this, that no-one could doubt the impending ruin of our allies and friends; for there in the Forum of Rome, in the place where once those who had wronged our allies used to be prosecuted and found guilty, now stood, openly displayed, the objects seized from those allies through theft and robbery.[54] (*Verr.* 2.1.59)

Verres, of course, had taken these statues not as the spoils of war but as the spoils of provincial government. Yet we might wonder how far newly conquered peoples would see this as an important distinction.

It is interesting to compare the response articulated by the Greek Polybius (normally well disposed towards the Romans) writing a century earlier about Marcellus' 'legitimate' activities in Syracuse in 211 (9.10). Like some Roman writers, he suggests the presence of Greek statues in Rome may have served to undermine with superfluous magnificence the simplicity and strength of the traditional Roman way of life; it is surely a mistake to abandon the habits of the victors and imitate those of the conquered. He suggests, too, that taking the statues might attract the hostility of the gods. Polybius also mentions as disadvantageous to the Romans the pity people will feel for the original owners when they look at the statues in their new setting. We may perhaps sense a shift of focalization as the Greek Polybius expatiates on the responses of those whose statues have been taken. Familiar and venerated works of art, alienated, torn from their proper contexts and put on display in the city of the conquerors could be a shocking reminder of the real extent of Roman power. He imagines the future, when Rome shall not only have accumulated all the possessions of the rest of the world but those treasures will induce the plundered to view the spectacle: then 'it is no longer a case of the spectators pitying their neighbours, but themselves as they remember the ruin of their own country'. The sight of these statues adorning the city of Rome, Polybius warns, will provoke blazing hatred of

---

[54] *socii vero nationesque exterae spem omnem tum primum abiecerunt rerum ac fortunarum suarum, propterea quod casu legati ex Asia atque Achaia plurimi Romae tunc fuerunt, qui deorum simulacra ex suis fanis sublata in foro venerabantur, itemque cetera signa et ornamenta cum cognoscerent, alia alio in loco lacrimantes intuebantur. quorum omnium hunc sermonem tum esse audiebamus, nihil esse quod quisquam dubitaret de exitio sociorum atque amicorum, cum quidem viderent in foro populi Romani, quo in loco antea qui sociis iniurias fecerant accusari et condemnari solebant, ibi esse palam posita ea quae ab sociis per scelus ablata ereptaque essent.*

the Romans among those they have conquered. For some viewers, Rome's Greek statues might be no more than attractive ornaments, for others, their symbolism was arrestingly potent.

ROMAN READINGS

The Augustan period has been seen as a high point in harnessing the significance of artworks displayed in Rome (though some of these were not strictly spoils).[55] Augustus himself celebrated numerous military victories, in commemoration of which, according to Dio:

Caesar dedicated the temple of Minerva (also called the Chalcidicum) and the Curia Julia, which had been built in honour of his father. In the latter he set up the statue of Victory which still exists today, thus making clear (it seems) that it was from her that he had received the empire. It had belonged to the people of Tarentum. From there it was now brought to Rome, placed in the Senate chamber and adorned with the spoils of Egypt.[56] (51.22.1)

The Nike from Tarentum, set up by Octavian as his *Victoria* in the new *Curia*,[57] was centuries later to be celebrated as an essential part of Rome's identity by the urban prefect Symmachus, whose third *Relatio* pleads for the restoration of the altar of Victory which had been removed by the Christian emperor Gratian.[58]

At what point Greek spoils were effectively domesticated, no longer identified as 'Greek' rather than 'Roman', it is hard to determine. By the latter half of the first century BCE fewer statues were reaching Rome as spoils. Statues tended rather to be purchased or commissioned.[59] This shift must inevitably have blurred the distinction between Greek and Roman. Yet many spoils were still on display in the city – and were labelled precisely as spoils, as is clear from Pliny's comment on the statue of Hercules *tunicatus*. And it is texts written in Augustan Rome and later which emphasise the

[55] See Zanker (1979). For the impact of these 'acts of symbolic violence' on particular Greek communities, for whom such statues were emblems of history and identity, see Alcock (1993) 175–80.
[56] Augustus (like Scipio Africanus in the incident referred to in n. 36 above) no doubt also derived prestige from returning artworks taken by Mark Antony from the cities of the province of Asia; he lists this among his achievements, *Res gestae* 24.
[57] It is not clear whether this had come to Rome as part of the booty from Tarentum back in the third century BCE.
[58] Symmachus makes a personified Rome ask permission to continue to practise her ancient ceremonies (3.9) before going on to request peace for *diis patriis* 'the gods of our fathers', of which the originally Tarentine Victory has, it seems, become the symbol.
[59] On the art trade, see Crawford (1977). The Romans' creative adaptation of Greek models has recently been the subject of several studies. See for instance Gazda (1995).

corrupting power of imported art.[60] These texts surely reflect the way at least some Romans (and Greeks too perhaps) perceived the statues that decorated their city.

Statues from the Greek east might raise other problematic issues. I have already speculated on the relationship between Metellus and Alexander, whose statue he displayed in his portico. A highly resonant context has recently been suggested for some of the most striking statues to have survived from ancient Rome – the Dying Gaul (now in the Capitoline collection) and the statue group of a Gallic chieftain stabbing himself after killing his woman (now in Palazzo Altemps; see fig. 2).[61] These statues were probably marble copies of a bronze group created for Attalus I of Pergamon to decorate the sanctuary of Athena Nikephoros in celebration of his victory over the Gauls.[62] Coarelli, noting that Julius Caesar was for a while the occupant of the Horti Sallustiani (where the statues were found), suggests that these copies may have been commissioned by Caesar for his own Gallic triumph in 46 BCE, their imagery being, of course, singularly appropriate for that event.[63] Caesar could thus be seen as aligning himself with the monarchical Attalus of Pergamon.[64] The exact context in which they were subsequently displayed is also unclear, though the display of such symbolically potent statues in the semi-private setting of a suburban villa would presumably have been somewhat less provocative than a more public position in the centre of the city.

In recent years, scholars have offered some very different readings of these statues. These images, by magnifying the ferocity, power and even the dignity of the defeated enemy could be seen as enhancing the effect of the victor's triumph, as Pollitt comments with reference to the original context of these statues as part of the Attalid victory monument.[65] Such meanings could be readily appropriated in a new Roman context. At the same time, he allows that these statues may also have evoked empathy for the defeated. Stewart, by contrast, suggests that in their original Pergamene context, at least, the bodies of these Celts would have reinforced the perception that they were sociopaths, savage men (and women), wholly without fear

---

[60] Though Gruen dismisses the links made by ancient texts between the appropriation of Greek statues and the arrival of luxury in Rome as 'hackneyed' and 'devoid of historical value' (1992) 116.

[61] Coarelli (1978), further discussed by Zecchini (1990).

[62] Though the date remains unclear as the reference in Pausanias (1.25.2) does not specify which Attalus. Cf. Pollitt (1986) 85–97.

[63] Coarelli (1978) 234.

[64] The bronzes themselves later came to Rome (appropriated from Pergamon) to adorn Nero's golden house. Subsequently they were transferred by Vespasian to the Temple of Peace (*NH* 34.84).

[65] Pollitt (1986) 96.

Figure 2. Statue group of suicidal Gaul and woman.

and bent on the complete destruction of their enemies. Once defeat was inevitable, the Celts would take the cowardly option of suicide.[66] These figures, he argues, are represented as wholly alien.

Yet for Roman viewers, at least, these vivid images of the barbarian enemy may not have seemed so Other. The Gallic chieftain prepares to plunge the dagger into his own breast after first killing his wife – presumably to preserve her from falling into the hands of the enemy. This was surely just the kind of deed attributed to the Romans of old (think of the story of Virginius, who, according to Livy 3.44–8, kills his daughter in order to preserve her chastity).[67] Empathy for the defeated might be tinged with identification. But what did it mean when sophisticated, Hellenized Romans defeated such people? In 46 BCE, however, at the time of Caesar's triumph, another and far more chilling parallel would surely have struck Roman viewers. Earlier that year, as the civil war between Caesar and his enemies drew to a close, the Younger Cato, unable to bear the imminent and inevitable prospect of Caesar's domination, had stabbed himself, his suicide rapidly coming to symbolize, for many, the end of the Roman republic. Caesar himself gloated over his enemy's suicide; other Romans might find his choice of statuary no less disturbing than his decision to include in his triumphal procession an image of Cato killing himself.[68] Though suicide was not seen by Romans as always justifiable, few saw Cato as having taken a 'cowardly option'.[69]

HONOURING THE ENEMY?

It was not only those statues brought from conquered countries which reminded Romans of their past victories and the extent of their empire. Occasionally Rome's enemies were themselves explicitly commemorated. According to Plutarch, the African ruler Bocchus

to flatter the Roman people and to please Sulla, set up images of Victory bearing trophies on the Capitoline and, next to them, a gold image of Jugurtha being handed over for justice to Sulla himself. (Plut. *Sulla* 6)

Images of the enemy might also appear in a triumphal procession.[70] According to Appian, Pompey's triumph in 61 BCE included portraits of

---

[66] Stewart (1997) 217–20.

[67] Roman texts may also be found portraying barbarian enemies in ways which make them potently similar to earlier Romans (at least as later generations liked to imagine them). Cf. O'Gorman (1993).

[68] According to Appian, *BC* 2.101, Caesar chose to parade an image of Cato's suicide in his triumph, provoking anger among the onlookers.

[69] Cato rapidly became a symbol of Stoic *constantia*. On Roman attitudes to suicide see Griffin (1986) and Edwards (2002).

[70] It was common for defeated enemy leaders themselves to form part of the triumphal procession (see Beard in this volume). These individuals might be kept on in Rome (rather than being executed)

those enemies who were not actually present (i.e. Mithridates and Tigranes, App. *Mith.* 117). These may have been part of the spoils or else were commissioned for the occasion. It is not clear if they were put on more permanent display. Other enemies of Rome, however, do seem to have found a lasting home in the city. Pliny indeed complains, 'All discrimination was so completely abandoned that in three places in Rome there may be seen statues of Hannibal, the only enemy ever to have thrown a spear inside the very walls of Rome' (34.32).[71]

What did it mean for Romans to see statues of Hannibal in the heart of their city? Was it an illustration of Roman victory, like the statue of Jugurtha – a visible demonstration of the incorporation of the conquered? Or did it perhaps reflect a sense that, for some at least, Rome's greatest enemy was great enough to deserve his own statue in the city (his greatness of course reflecting well on those who had eventually succeeded in defeating him)?[72] One might argue that Hannibal's role in constituting Roman identity was so crucial that statues of him were a necessity.[73] We might wonder whether these images were commissioned for Rome or whether they were taken as booty from Spain or from North Africa, a change of location here too effecting a dramatic shift in the meaning of the statues.[74]

And Hannibal and Jugurtha were not the only ones among Rome's conquered enemies to secure such a position in the city. Dio, writing on Rome under Augustus, refers to the emperor's display of a statue of the defeated queen of Egypt after his Actian victory of 31 BCE:

Thus Cleopatra, though defeated and captured, was still glorified, inasmuch as her adornments lie as dedications in our temples and she herself is seen in gold in the shrine of Venus. (51.22.3)

For Dio, the statue of Cleopatra is paradoxical in its impact. Her statue's presence in Rome parades her status as a conquered enemy. But the gold image in the shrine of the goddess of love also serves to celebrate the

as living reminders of victory; Tacitus makes the defeated British king Caratacus say to Claudius 'If you spare me, I shall be an everlasting token of your clemency' (*Ann.* 12.37). Statues, of course, might prove more convenient as well as more lasting than the real thing.
[71] *et adeo discrimen omne sublatum, ut Hannibalis etiam statuae tribus locis visantur in ea urbe, cuius intra muros solus hostium emisit hastam.*
[72] Perhaps there is a parallel here with the world of Roman declamation and moralistic anecdote, as Greg Woolf has suggested to me. Trainee Roman orators were given the task of devising speeches offering advice to famous figures from history such as Scipio or Hannibal. Beard comments: 'history was recaptured for the Roman present' (1993) 62. Thus might Hannibal take his place amid the statues which kept Rome's past perpetually before the eyes of its citizens.
[73] On the continuing significance of Carthage as Rome's archetypal enemy even in late antiquity, see Miles in this volume.
[74] Cf. from a much later period the repositioning of Canova's heroic nude statue of Napoleon in the Duke of Wellington's front hall at Apsley House (discussed by Huet (1999) esp. 58–61).

power – and confirm the undying fame – of an Egyptian queen who seduced more than one of Rome's greatest generals.[75]

We might wonder, too, what a North African visiting Rome might make of a statue of Hannibal or what Rome's many Egyptian inhabitants thought when they looked at Cleopatra's image.[76] Their views have not survived but perhaps a modern parallel may give some substance to our speculative reconstructions. In a recent collection of essays, *London: the lives of the city*, Ferdinand Dennis explores his own shifting perceptions of the iconographic programme of the Albert Memorial, particularly its representations of Europe, Africa, Asia and America, as he became increasingly aware of his own Afro-Caribbean heritage.[77] As a child guided by his teachers he had found it an inspirational celebration of all kinds of human achievement. But as he grew older he was increasingly puzzled by some aspects of the monument. A turning-point in his own personal development was reached when, on an evening walk in the park, a friend:

> described it as a monstrous lie, a typical piece of European falsehood. He explained that the statues at the corners of the base represented areas in the former British empire – and that the African gazing at the European in the African corner was intended to represent the civilising influence of Britain on us 'Africans'. He pointed out the chain on the African's feet . . . and mentioned slavery.

Notions of racial identity in the Roman world seem not to correspond very closely to those of more recent times. In particular, Roman writers seem little concerned to explore the physical specifics of racial difference.[78] Yet it is hard to imagine that someone whose family came from Carthage would remain wholly ignorant of or indifferent to the significance of Carthage in narratives of Rome's rise.[79] And it is tempting to suppose that they might at times have felt some kind of kinship with Hannibal.

BARBARIAN MARBLES

As the Greek East came more securely under Roman control, the opportunities for acquiring desirable artworks as spoils largely disappeared (though

---

[75] On Augustan uses of Cleopatra, see Wyke (1992).

[76] On the presence of foreigners in Rome see Noy (2000) esp. 245–51 on Egyptians and 251–5 on North Africans.

[77] Dennis (1999) 319. I am very grateful to Will Stenhouse for drawing this to my attention.

[78] On this see Thompson (1989).

[79] Noy (2000) explores evidence, such as epitaphs, for self-identification among foreigners at Rome. While some soon came to identify themselves as Romans, it seems clear that many continued to identify themselves with their own or even their family's place of origin. Batty offers a suggestive exploration of a Carthaginian orientation in Pomponius Mela's *De Chorographia*, which he links with Mela's Spanish/Punic origins (2000).

Nero's depredations, extensively documented by Pausanias, form a significant exception). The Romans do not seem to have developed a taste for the
religious images of their barbarian subjects. Nevertheless statues continued
to offer a vivid means of representing the geographical extent of Roman
power, Rome's victory and dominion over even the most recalcitrant of barbarian peoples. A category of statues which became increasingly numerous
in Rome under the emperors is that of personifications – images which are
perhaps closer in function to the representations of the continents on the
Albert Memorial. In the Graeco-Roman world human forms were used to
represent virtues, for instance, but also – very importantly – geographical
areas.[80] An animated pageant of conquered nations might find its place in
a triumph; Cicero mentions the *simulacra oppidorum* carried in a general's
triumphal *pompa* (*In Pis.* 60), which may well have been personifications.[81]
Ovid, in the *Ars amatoria*, imagines as part of the triumph of Augustus'
grandson Gaius allegorical figures of countries including *Danaeia Persis*,
'Persia born of Danae' (1.217–28).[82] Writing a few decades after Ovid, Silius
Italicus imagines Scipio's triumphal procession of 202 BCE, which includes
Carthage stretching out her conquered hands to heaven, as well as images
of Spanish cities (*Punica* 17.635–42). The emperor Pertinax's splendid funeral (in 193 CE) included twenty subject nations, represented by bronze
images each in national garb, and followed by portraits of distinguished
Romans, which were paraded through Rome to the Campus Martius (Dio
74.4.5). Such images might also be found in the context of the iconographic
programmes for particular monuments.

The last years of the republic saw a shift towards ever grander structures
celebrating the achievements of individual Roman generals, outstanding
among them Pompey's theatre complex in the Campus Martius (which
in significant respects echoed Hellenistic royal monuments).[83] Standing in
the grounds of the theatre (or perhaps on the attic storey) were images of
fourteen nations, along with a statue of Pompey himself. The ensemble
had a clear political message; the fourteen statues represented the fourteen
nations Pompey had conquered, occasioning his triumph of 61 BCE.[84] This
appears to be the earliest instance of such personifications in Rome. Indeed,
this particular use of personifications seems to be distinctively Roman.[85]

---

[80] On this see Toynbee (1934) 7ff.   [81] As Toynbee suggests (1934) 11.
[82] See Beard's discussion of the passage in this volume, pp. 35–7.   [83] See Hanson (1959) 54.
[84] According to Varro, cited by Pliny, *NH* 36.41, the statues were made by one Coponius. Pliny's praise
of Pompey, *NH* 7.95–9, emphasizes the number of nations in Pompey's triumph of 61 BCE. See
Coarelli (1971–2), Nicolet (1991) 38.
[85] Smith notes that in the Hellenistic world, although political and geographic personifications are
not uncommon, they were not used for the visual enumeration of victories (1988, 70). Cf. Toynbee
(1934). 8. For the representation on coins of provinces as female figures, see Hannestad (1986) 23.

Augustus appears to have followed Pompey's example in setting up statues
in the city. According to Servius, 'Augustus made a portico in which he
assembled images representing the different peoples, on which account it is
called the Portico of the Nations' (Servius *ad Aen.* 7.721).[86] This structure
has not survived but some idea of how its iconographic programme worked
may be gleaned from that of the Sebasteion at Aphrodisias in Asia Minor
(constructed under the Julio-Claudians). For the latter was almost certainly
based on a particular model in Rome, most likely the figures of the *gentes*
in the Portico of the Nations.[87] The Sebasteion offers reliefs of female
figures representing a range of peoples and places within or bordering the
empire in the time of Augustus, which can, as Joyce Reynolds has argued, be
explained as parts of a series illustrating Augustus' victories.[88] The figures in
the Portico of the Nations, like the ones at Aphrodisias, would presumably
have represented those conquered peoples of greatest significance to the
regime[89] – perhaps reflecting the peoples listed in Augustus' *Res gestae*,
which was to be inscribed, a few years later, alongside his Mausoleum, a
short distance away.[90]

In his coinage, Augustus also drew on an earlier Roman tradition
of depicting symbolic representatives of conquered countries; a kneeling
Armenian and a kneeling Parthian symbolize Rome's successes in the East.[91]
Similar to the coin portraits of these kneeling barbarians are some huge
marble figures of male barbarians both kneeling and standing, found in the
heart of the city and almost certainly of Augustan date.[92] One group of three
colossal kneeling barbarians in Phrygian marble may have formed the supports of a tripod (Phrygian marble was no doubt deemed especially suitable

---

[86] *Porticum enim Augustus fecerat in qua simulacra omnium gentium conlocaverat: quae porticus appella-
batur Ad Nationes.* Velleius (2.39.2) writes of inscriptions (*tituli*) of nations (*gentes*) conquered by
Augustus adorning 'his forum', although no images of conquered provinces have been found near
the Forum of Augustus.

[87] As Smith argues (1988) 50–77. The Aphrodisias figures are in high relief rather than free-standing
statues. Smith suggests, however, that their bases were designed to look like statue bases, suggesting
that they were inspired by a line of statues in a colonnade (1988) 53.

[88] Reynolds (1981) 326–7 and (1986) 115.

[89] As Smith emphasizes, the full list would have been very lengthy, the Alpine *gentes* alone (as listed in
the monument at La Turbie) numbering 46, Smith (1988) 74.

[90] Nicolet emphasizes the close parallel between the lists of conquered peoples in *RG* and those
represented at Aphrodisias. He suggests that the model for the Aphrodisias Sebasteion may rather
have been the Forum of Augustus itself, proposing that elements in the decorative scheme may have
represented provinces or *gentes* (1991) 43.

[91] Toynbee (1934) 10, Zanker (1988) 187. For earlier examples, see Hannestad (1986) 23 on Faustus Sulla
and Julius Caesar. More generally on this topic see Levi (1952).

[92] Discussed by Schneider (1986) and Zanker (1970). There are some parallels, too, with reliefs depicting
conquered barbarians found on victory arches in the south of France. These are usefully collected
by Walter (1993), though the quality of the illustrations is poor.

for celebrating Rome's conquest of the East).[93] Another group of twenty-two standing barbarians formed part of the portico added to the front of the Basilica Aemilia under Augustus, the Porticus Gai et Luci of 14 BCE (these are of Phrygian marble apart from two in Giallo Antico).[94] These may have decorated the attic[95] (and thus perhaps served as the prototype for Trajan's Forum).[96] Both groups most likely commemorated Augustus' Parthian settlement of 20 BCE.[97] One could apply to these great figures Toynbee's observation, that they 'might be regarded as studies of... unfortunate captives as they walked in chains, or were dragged in waggons, in the train of their conqueror, or were herded in sullen groups through the streets of Rome'.[98] These powerful alien bodies were frozen in perpetual submission as a permanent reminder of Roman superiority.

Coinage from the reign of Trajan also shows a particular concern with personifications of provinces (apparently Arabia, Armenia, Dacia, Dardania, Germania, Italia, Parthia). Most of these are idealized female figures, exceptions being the representations of Dacia and Parthia as conquered males. Trajan's conquest of Dacia and its incorporation into the empire (after campaigns in 101–2 and 105–6) were celebrated in a number of monuments in Rome, most particularly Trajan's Column and Forum, constructed with the spoils of victory.[99] Statues of Dacians seem to have stood in the attics of the Forum's porticos. Two types of Dacians survive from the Forum, smaller ones of white marble, larger ones of Phrygian marble, with sockets for white marble heads and hands; the larger figures may have stood on the attic of the basilica, the smaller ones on the attics of flanking colonnades, where they appeared to support, like Caryatids, the cornice above (without it seems having a real supporting function).[100]

---

[93] Schneider (1986) 21. The statues were found in the Horti Farnesiani on Palatine. Other scholars have dated them to the second century CE on stylistic grounds (though this involves problematic comparisons with other works whose dates are also uncertain.). Two are now in Naples, fragments of a third in Copenhagen.

[94] Schneider proposes an important emendation of Pliny, *NH* 36.102 (concerning the Basilica Aemilia) to read *columnis e<t> phrygibus mirabilem* (1986) 120–1.

[95] Bauer suggests that they stood on the second floor of the interior of the basilica (1988) 210.

[96] As Coarelli suggests (1985) 296.

[97] Statues of barbarian in Numidian marble (Giallo Antico) similarly alluded to victory on frontiers of empire (Schneider (1986) 115–17).

[98] Toynbee (1934) 8.

[99] Trajan's victories were also commemorated by the trophy constructed at Adamklissi, in Dacia itself. The iconographic programme of this monument is discussed and compared with those of Trajanic monuments in Rome by MacKendrick (1975) 95–105 and Ferris (2000) 61–76.

[100] Packer (1997) 437 and Waelkens (1985) 650. The Dacians attached in the fourth century to the Arch of Constantine are often believed by scholars to have been taken from Trajan's Forum. There is no evidence, though (as Packer notes), that any part of Trajan's forum had been dismantled by the early fourth century. Most probably they were taken from another Trajanic monument.

Dressed in thick cloaks and barbarian trousers against the Dacian cold, these vast, bearded figures stand slightly downcast, their expressions hard to decipher. Some cross their arms below the waist, symbolizing their captivity, others hold their right arms across the chest in a gesture of mourning (fig. 3 – though this is from Arch of Constantine).[101]

Trajan's achievement in bringing the rugged Dacians under Roman control was strikingly commemorated. His forum complex continued to impress for centuries (it was the part of Rome which in 357 CE filled the newly arrived emperor Constantius II with greatest wonder, according to Ammianus 16.10.15). But were these statues unproblematic demonstrations of the perpetual subjection of the Dacians? Zanker, appropriating a phrase Vitruvius uses of Caryatids, calls the Dacians *exempla aeternae servitutis* (Vitr. 1.1.5).[102] What did these statues suggest to Roman viewers? Can we attempt to imagine their impact on Rome's Dacian subjects, if any happened to be in Rome?[103] The resonance of all these images is intriguingly suggested by a nightmare which Suetonius tells us troubled the emperor Nero, as he began to lose control of his empire. 'He dreamed that he was surrounded and prevented from moving by the statues of nations which had been dedicated at Pompey's theatre' (Suet. *Nero* 46).[104] The lifelike qualities given to statues by Rome's talented sculptors (most of them Greeks, of course) could give them a sinister potency. If Pygmalion's desire could bring a statue to life, then so too perhaps could a Roman emperor's fear.

CONCLUSION

The power of the Romans to capture the conquered in stone – whether by taking their statues or representing them as statues – is inextricably linked to the process of conquest itself and to its consequences. Some of the statues we have looked at were carried in triumphal processions, seductive spoils from the Greek East. Other statues were fashioned to resemble the human captives in such processions. Both categories served as perpetual reminders of this most glorious – but fleeting – celebration of Roman domination.

We have traced some significant slippages between statues *as* captives, captivating statues and statues *of* captives. Polybius – and Livy's Cato – worried that the statues taken from the Greek East might seduce their

---

[101] Waelkens (1985) 644–5.   [102] Zanker (1970) 512.

[103] The Adamklissi monument, referred to in n. 99 above, would of course have been familiar to many Dacians.

[104] *terrebatur ad hoc evidentibus portentis somniorum . . . vidit per quietem . . . se . . . modo a simulacris gentium ad Pompei theatrum dedicatarum circumiri arcerique progressu.*

Figure 3. Dacian from the Arch of Constantine (of the same type as those displayed in Trajan's Forum).

captors – a metaphorical reversal of Roman conquest. Later anxieties took a somewhat different form. Nero losing his hold on the empire allegedly dreamed of statues in a more openly aggressive mode. We may well suppose that when news came in the third century that Rome's hold on Dacia was slipping, some Romans in the city may have cast anxious glances at those brooding statues in Trajan's Forum. Desire, fear, grief, wonder and rage – the responses to the statues experienced by Roman and foreign viewers, as described in ancient texts (or imagined by the modern historian), reflected and crystallized the tensions and ambiguities evoked by empire itself on the part of both the rulers and the ruled.

A story told in the twelfth century reflects a continuing sense of the link between Rome's statues and Rome's empire. Magister Gregorius, an English visitor to Rome, tells of an ancient legend according to which a multitude of statues on the Capitol each represented a race or region of the Roman empire (*Mirabilia* 8). If any people rebelled against the Roman government, a silver bell would ring on the relevant statue, thus warning the Romans to defend their imperial power.[105] The almost magical potency of Rome's statuary could still be felt centuries after the empire itself had fallen.

---

[105] This may perhaps relate to the Portico of the Nations mentioned by Servius and discussed earlier. Different versions of this story appear in a number of medieval sources. Discussed by Graf (1915) 148–61.

CHAPTER 4

Inventing Christian Rome: the role of early Christian art

Jaś Elsner

INTRODUCTION

There is a certain irony in the way that Christianity, originally a non-iconic cult,[1] should have become in the fourth century a master-manipulator of material culture. By the end of the century, there were no material remains or remembrances of the saints which failed to be pressed to the greater glorification of Christ's Church – from relics, sites of burial and death, inscriptions and invocations, pictures in all media, amulets and the like, to grand basilicas and martyria. The use of such objects – the tangible and the visible – is one of Christianity's fundamental borrowings from the religions of the Graeco-Roman environment; and its exploitation of material culture in Rome to upstage that of traditional paganism is one of Christianity's most brilliant acts of outplaying its polytheistic rivals at the very game which they had themselves pioneered and mastered.

In seeking to illuminate some aspects of this process in the city of Rome, this essay is informed by the following propositions. First, to become established – as was suddenly the mission of Christianity after the conversion and victories of Constantine – required a religion which had defied localism in favour of salvific universalism rapidly to acquire a rootedness of place.[2] The very word used in Latin by Christians to define their most potent religious enemy – 'pagan' – speaks of their envy of, and desire for, the most resilient and persistent quality of ancient polytheism:[3] its rooting in local

[1] Despite the recent defence of early Christian iconism, by Murray (1981) 13–37, followed by Miles (1985) 43–8, Finney (1994) *passim*, but with summary at 290–3, and Jensen (2000) 13–20, we should not underestimate the residual resistance to art in a series of influential Church Fathers; see e.g. Barasch (1992) 95–157. For a recent discussion of the establishment of images in a didactic role in Christian late antiquity, see Brown (1999) 15–34, with Wood (1999) 35–46.
[2] For discussion of Christian universalism by contrast with other forms of universalism (such as those of the polytheistic Roman empire), see Fowden (1993) 49–50, 59–60, 90.
[3] Of course, there were monotheistic rivals to Christianity, both in Judaism and in pagan monotheism (on which see now Athanassiadi and Frede (1999) but neither was a serious opponent in the city of Rome itself.

identities and its encapsulation of such identities in parochial gods and rites.[4] Second, the search for a Christian localism grounded in more than a persecuted sect's (probably contradictory) oral traditions about a particular martyr cult, necessitated the rediscovery – even the 'invention' – of local saints, plenty of them, and simultaneously the manufacture of a plethora of material means by which to advertise their presence: hence images, relics, martyria, the whole gamut of devotional aids.[5] These saints and their visual or tangible evocations were to become the focus of cult.

All of this, in the specific context of the city of Rome, with which we shall be concerned here, was effectively to create an alternative sacred topography to the traditional one which had been in place for centuries. The fact that so much of the means for its creation was ruthlessly plagiarised from the opposition is less significant than certain fundamental differences between pagan and Christian practice. In polytheism, Rome's rituals, divine statues and temples stood for themselves: their correct cultivation was sufficient for the religious structure of the state to continue in what has been called a 'theodicy of good fortune'.[6] But in Christianity, the saints – including their pictures – stood not for themselves but for a complex superstructure of mediation and salvation reaching back to God himself. Every saint offered both a bridge into the eternal life proclaimed by Jesus Christ and a guarantee, through Christian theology and exegesis, of the salvation made possible by this bridge. St Peter, for instance, stood not just for himself as an important local martyr in Rome with at least two sites of cult by the third century. He also represented the apostolic tradition, the scriptures in which he had himself appeared, the scriptures which Christ had enjoined upon him to teach, the journey of the Faith from Palestine to Rome, and the rock upon which the Church was founded. On the model of Peter, every saint looked back to the founder of the Faith in the same way and offered sacred mediation for the worshipper with God himself through Christ. It is this hierarchical structure to the divine world which provided a cognitive reliability and effectively a form of insurance about the Faith – an ability to leave nothing whatsoever outside the remit of a Christian explanation – which pagan polytheism simply could not rival.

My aim in the following pages is to hit two targets. First, I want to advance a suggestion about the development of early Christian art in Rome

---

[4] See, e.g., Rives (1999) 135–54, esp. 135, 144–5, 154. An excellent account of localism in Egyptian religion of the Roman period is Frankfurter (1998) 65–144. Briefly on Greece and the East, see Elsner (1997) 178–99, esp. 191–6. On the importance of place to the (pagan) religion of Rome itself, see Beard, North and Price (1998) vol. 1, 167–210, 249–60.

[5] On the localism of the cult of the saints, see Brown (1981) 86–93.

[6] See Gordon (1990) 235–40.

from a self-assertion of initiate sectarian identity (against other Christian groups no less than against other religions) to the promulgation of a cohesive narrative of inclusive identity, designed to incorporate everyone. The fact that the fourth-century Roman Church was no less riven with schisms than the pre-Constantinian Church in Rome or the contemporary Church in the East, was perhaps itself a cause of the claims to unified and collective authority on the part of different Christian factions such as those variously represented by such figures as Callistus and Hippolytus in the third century, or Liberius and Felix as well as Damasus and Ursinus in the fourth.[7] Second, I want to argue for the significance of art, as visual hagiography, in the process of Christianizing Rome. Images became a highly devotional form of localism which aimed, by the end of the fourth century, to supplant paganism by the very means (that is the visual manipulation of art) at which the pagans had been the most skilled and established.[8] Yet we must not forget that the assertion of Christian localism – much as it might appear to be aimed at disrupting the pagan past – may also have been no less directed at firming up divergent positions within inter-Christian factionalism. One might argue that images played a smaller role in the process of fourth-century Christianization than say architecture, liturgy or even epigraphy; none the less, the sacred sites defined and propagated by architecture, liturgy and epigraphy in the period are inconceivable without a strong visual input which served a considerably wider set of purposes than simple decoration.

THE ORIGINS OF CHRISTIAN ART

I would like to begin with one of the fundamental problems of the rise of Christian art. It has been argued – following the evidence of numerous cults at Dura Europus with cult buildings literally side by side and all propagating themselves through images – that Christian art emerged around 200 CE as a competitive response to the impact of other religions and their iconographic 'propaganda'.[9] This position has not been significantly challenged, and indeed it has become the controlling positive thesis for the most recent (and controversial) account of the nature and development of early Christian art.[10] However, the evidence from the city of Rome (as reassessed

---

[7] On these oppositions see Brent (1995) 398–540 on the third century and Curran (2000) 129–42 on the fourth century.

[8] Here I shall follow the argument of Delehaye (1934) 117–46, that early Christian art is not merely a visual system but also a hagiographical method.

[9] See Grabar (1969) 20–30.

[10] See Mathews (1993) esp. 3–10. For critical reviews, though not attacking this aspect of his thesis, see Kinney (1994b) and Brown (1995).

in a couple of major recent discussions)[11] can help us nuance this picture somewhat. First, it is clear that images seem to have been used by different – competing – communities of Roman Christians in the third century to help define their own sectarian identities. Among the earliest examples of Christian art to survive (from roughly the first three decades of the third century)[12] are the frescos painted by members of the Callistus group to decorate cubicula in their catacomb on the Via Appia and the statue with inscriptions set up by the Hippolytus group, which was in direct opposition to them,[13] probably in the Hippolytan cult centre at the Ager Veranus near the Castro Pretorio.[14] We may surmise that it is at least as likely that the pro- duction of early Christian art was an aspect of sectarian self-assertion in the context of inter-Christian segmentary opposition, as that it was motivated by competition with outside cults.

The later evidence, I shall argue, shows the use of Christian imagery as an agent of Christianization, both in the affirmation of that once sectar- ian cult identity which was rapidly becoming universal during the fourth century and in the more specific assertion of localism. The function of the earliest Christian images to crystallize rival group identities within Rome's Christian communities – with visual palladia for the Hippolytus and Callistus factions – did not include a need to assert localism through representation. But then at this time localism was obvious: all the Christian groups which put images around their places of worship or burial were local communities, founded upon that particular site or set of sites, whether in Rome, or Dura or elsewhere. Moreover the ideological, though not necessarily the liturgical, trend of these Christianities tended away from parochial issues towards universal, salvific, even apocalyptic claims. But the move to localism in images during the fourth century in response to the new Constantinian dispensation and to the competition with Rome's traditional establishment (as evidenced by the Codex-Calendar of 354, for instance, which I shall discuss below) was hardly a radical break from earlier precedent in the use of art. The assertion of Roman local identities through

---

[11] I am thinking of Finney (1994) and Brent (1995).

[12] For the nightmare that is attempting to date early catacomb painting, see Février (1989) 102–34.

[13] On the opposition of the Hippolytus and Callistus 'house-schools' and the general context, see Brent (1995) 398–457.

[14] On the Callistus catacomb, see Finney (1994) 146–230 with bibliography; on the Hippolytus statue, see Brent (1995) 3–114 with bibliography, and 115–367 on the inscriptions and their significance for reconstructing Hippolytus and his corpus. Note that, unlike other very early examples of Christian art, such as the Shepherd lamp now in Berlin or the Piazzuola fragments beneath San Sebastiano (on which see Finney (1994) 116–35 and 231–46 respectively) or the gems, in these two cases 'material culture . . . probably represents a communitarian and collective decision', to quote Finney (1994) 150.

images of the Roman saints was a shrewd development of the affirmation of sectarian cult identity in the previous century. The use of post-scriptural (and specifically Roman hagiographic) imagery to fulfil and complete in 'real time' the scriptural message of Biblical images set in 'mythic time' was a natural adaptation of the typological use of New Testament themes to fulfil Old Testament prototypes which had been the foundation of Christian art in the pre-Constantinian era.

In effect, I shall be proposing that the history of Christianization in Rome was simultaneously a story of Christians versus pagans, both sides slugging it out for control of the empire's most prestigious city, *and* of different Christian factions – conceivably even somewhat different Christianities – competitively asserting their sectarian positions. Most fundamentally, the localism of fourth-century Rome was a sectarian statement of self-affirmation within Christendom generally, directed against the imperially backed aspiration to primacy of the Church in Constantinople. The affirmation of localism, which I propose was a strategy borrowed and adapted from the pagans, may have resulted in a topographical and liturgical rearrangement of the city, apparently in competition with its ancient polytheistic traditions. But it was, at the same time, no less the consequence of various appropriations of the authority of holy sites in order to valorize particular sectarian factions and even contested individual claims within a Church hierarchy riven by competition and dispute throughout the third and fourth centuries. Early Christian Rome was a crucible in which the argument of a united Church overcoming a resilient pagan establishment (something brilliantly achieved within the city's topography by Damasus' incorporation of the holy sites within a Papal programme) was itself the cover for a prolonged and internal Christian dispute about episcopacy and control.

FOURTH-CENTURY ROME

Rome in the fourth century was a schizophrenic city. The uniqueness of its position cannot be adequately explained by the usual culprits trotted out in diagnosis: cultural continuity or change, economic decline or innovation, the end of paganism and the triumph of incremental Christianization, or the revival of paganism and its suppression by law.[15] From the fall of Maxentius

---

[15] For an up-to-date survey of the historical questions, see Harris (1999b). Note his apology for the absence of a visual dimension to this book, p. 11. The fundamental starting-point on late antique Rome will now be Curran (2000), which is an admirably full and judicious account of a vast and disparate literature, both historical and archaeological.

in 312 until the fall of the city to Alaric in 410, Rome's civic life was poised between pagan polytheism and institutional Christianity.[16] The city's visual environment was caught between the demise of traditional forms of decoration (like statues or temples) and the rise of new kinds of adornment, such as Christian pictures and churches;[17] its patronage between the time-hallowed dedications of secular aristocrats and the new dominance of the Church.[18] Clearly, all cities in transition are interesting. But the transformation of what had (until November 324)[19] been the indisputable hub of empire into the symbolic centre of the universal Church was a remarkable process by any standards.

The fourth century presents us with a Rome poised between worlds, where 'pagan' and 'Christian' served not as a mutually exclusive antithesis (except in the vitriolic fulminations of certain prelates) nor as the clear temporal polarity which too much hindsight might suggest, but rather as a rich complex of options through which the identities of Rome's inhabitants could be expressed. The evidence of material culture shows us pagan and Christian images juxtaposed with flagrant panache in the domestic setting of the boudoir: in the casket from the Esquiline treasure for instance (surely commissioned and made at Rome), where Venus sits naked in a retinue of erotes and tritons above an inscription exhorting its owner to live in Christ.[20] Likewise, in the more sacrally charged sphere of the dead, we find a syncretism of overtly pagan and Christian subjects – for example in the frescos of the Via Latina Catacomb,[21] in those of room 79 of the Catacomb of Marcellinus and Peter (with its arcosolium of Orpheus juxtaposed against images of Daniel in the lions' den and the raising of Lazarus),[22] and the flamboyant assimilation of pagan iconographies to Christian themes.[23] On the level of high intellectual debate, the significance of a traditional polytheistic sacred monument for the competing histories and identities professed within the city is beautifully caught in the controlled rhetorical politesse of

---

[16] A general picture of the urban environment may be found in Krautheimer (1983) 7–40, 93–122 and (1980) 3–58; Curran (2000) 116–57. For a discussion of some aspects of the Christianization of the populace of Rome, see Brown (1982) 123–45.

[17] For a short account, see Elsner (1998) 736–61, esp. 736–9.

[18] See Ward-Perkins (1984) 14–21, 38–66.

[19] This was the date of the *consecratio* of Constantinople. See Krautheimer (1983) 42, with extensive bibliography at 134, n. 5.

[20] See Shelton (1981) 72–5. A recent discussion, with bibliography, is Elsner (forthcoming).

[21] A recent account is Elsner (1995) 271–80, with bibliography.

[22] See Deckers et al. (1987) 348–50.

[23] The standard discussion remains Huskinson (1974) 68–97. This deals only with specifically pagan themes rather than the more general assimilation of iconographical types like Endymion to Christian subjects like Jonah. On these, see Lawrence (1961) vol. 1, 323–34.

the different contributions by Symmachus, Ambrose and Prudentius to the question of the Altar of Victory in the Senate House.[24] Finally, there is the remarkable case of the Codex-Calendar of 354 – a de-luxe commission for a Roman aristocrat named Valentinus – whose repertoire of resolutely traditional images and pagan calendar of urban rituals is complemented with lists of bishops and martyrs which effectively create an alternative Christian festival calendar to supplement – but not yet to replace – the traditional cult of the city.[25]

The mixture of visual (and other) discourses speaks of a culture of Christian and pagan assimilation and easy interchange. At the same time, the Christian party – at least in the form of its elite proponents in the second half of the fourth century – was actively tracing and bolstering its own heritage, inevitably at the expense of its rivals.[26] At stake was the very identity of Rome itself and its inhabitants, poised between the great tradition and the new religion. In the case of pagans – with whom I shall not be especially concerned here – the past was easy, for it was theirs. It constituted in the fourth century a vast quarry of monuments, inscriptions and texts,[27] as well as the living traditions of ancient urban rituals so beautifully presented and illustrated in the Codex-Calendar.[28] The Arch of Constantine, to take an example from early in the century, mounted the argument of its entire visual programme on a complex interrelation of present and past vividly and materially juxtaposed through the bricolage of modern sculpture with ancient spolia.[29] In the canonical, time-hallowed past, traditionalist polytheists could root current identity and on it they could base modern artistic and religious practice. While the religious reforms of Julian or the 'pagan' imagery of the late Roman ivories (such as the Symmachus leaf with its libation,[30] or the Apotheosis ivory in the British Museum)[31] constituted

---

[24] The texts are Symmachus, *Relatio* 3; Ambrose, *Epistulae* 17–18; Prudentius, *Contra Orationem Symmachi libri*, all conveniently collected in M. Lavarenne's Budé of Prudentius vol. III, 1963, 85–196, and (for Symmachus and Ambrose) Klein (1972). See Matthews (1975) 203–11 and McLynn (1994) 166–8, 263–75.

[25] Most recently on the Calendar of 354, see Salzman (1990) esp. 25–55 for contents, 199–202 for Valentinus (possibly a Christian member of the family of Symmachus). Also, Salzman (1999) 123–34, esp. 124–7, and Curran (2000) 221–80.

[26] A good case against over-emphasizing the polarity of opposing Christian and pagan factions in this context is made by Cameron (1999) 109–21.

[27] On architectural and sculptural spolia in late antiquity, there is a large recent literature: see esp. Kinney (1997) 117–48 and Poeschke (1996), with bibliographies. On some aspects of literary 'spoliation', see Miller (1998) esp. 123–30 and Elsner (2000a) 149–84, esp. 163–77.

[28] See Salzman (1990) 32–4.   [29] See for instance Elsner (2000a), with bibliography.

[30] See most recently Simon (1992) 56–65; Kiilerich (1993) 144–9 and Kinney (1994a).

[31] See Eastmond (1994) 57–8 following Cameron (1986) 41–72; and Wright (1998) 354–69 for a different interpretation and date.

as much of an 'invented tradition' as the establishment of Christianity in the same period,[32] none the less the materials out of which fourth-century paganism fashioned its response to Christian ascendancy were absolutely grounded in the antique aura of authenticity. Despite the mystique of ancient rituals, the problem for pagans was the outdatedness of it all. In the face of imperial support and institutional establishment for Christianity, the pagans of Rome faced shrinkage into a small-group antiquarianism dependent on an outmoded canon of past glories.[33] It is, ironically, rather like the problems of the Church of England in trying to justify Establishment when only a small minority of the population holds to any of its rituals or beliefs.

Roman Christians, however, had the opposite problem. Their city, seat of a bishop who already claimed pre-eminence in Christendom, had a wonderfully distinguished but painfully pagan history:[34] its best Christian claims lay in the bones of those whose passage to sainthood had been aided by the city's executioners. The empire's east was full of sites with genuinely biblical associations – as recognized by Constantine's own patronage of churches in Palestine and Antioch, and as articulated in his own lifetime by our earliest surviving pilgrimage account.[35] At the same time, the capital had moved to a new metropolis whose patriarch vied with Rome's for seniority and whose churches competed with Rome's in their modern grandeur. Other cities in the empire – the Milan of Ambrose, for instance, or Constantinople – had still greater problems than Rome in discovering a Christian past; the task for them would involve the 'invention' of martyrs' relics on a grand scale throughout northern Italy and the import of saints' bodies into Constantinople in the later fourth and early fifth centuries.[36] Nevertheless, the task of constructing a Christian Rome which was not simply bolted on top of the ancient city, but rather had a deep-rooted heritage, was by no means an easy one. It involved rewriting the past as a Christian heritage and inscribing that new but hallowed Christian antiquity into the fabric and urban ritual of the city.[37] My subject in the next section is to

---

[32] On the invention of tradition, see Hobsbawn and Ranger (1983).

[33] Most recently on the fate of ancient cults and the multi-religious environment of fourth-century Rome (with bibliography), see Curran (2000) 161–259.

[34] For a recent discussion of how fourth-century Christians dealt with pagan sculpture, see Hannestad (1999) 173–203.

[35] On the Bordeaux Pilgrim of 333 CE, see Hunt (1982) 55–8, 83–5; Douglass (1996) 313–33; Bowman (1999) 163–87; Weingarten (1999) 291–7; Elsner (2000b) 180–94.

[36] Fundamental for the cult of the saints and relics are Delehaye (1912), (1927) and (1930). See also Brown (1981) and Mango (1990) 51–62.

[37] For some aspects of this project (spatial, temporal and gestural, all focused on the Roman liturgy) see Pietri (1983) 65–77 and Saxer (1989) 917–1033, esp. 919–36. For an urban topography of Christianization, see Reekmans (1989) 861–915, esp. 861–74.

look at some of the methods adopted by the city's Christian elite by which to establish Rome as the pre-eminent Christian city.

MATERIAL RHETORICS OF CHRISTIANIZATION

Here I shall examine two monuments from the sixth decade of the fourth century to unravel some strategies for the Christian appropriation of Rome. These monuments – the Codex-Calendar of 354 and the Sarcophagus of Junius Bassus (who died in 359) – are not only two of the most supremely lavish and accomplished high-quality products of the mid fourth century; they are also commissions by high aristocrats. They represent what might be called the elite pagan convert's educated and antiquarian response to the problem of Christianizing Rome, seen from a position that broadly affirmed a unified Christianity rather than any specifically sectarian faction within the Church. In the following section, I shall turn to the development of visual arguments for Christianization produced for display within what were surely rival sites of cult in Rome (at least until Pope Damasus, 366–84, brought them together under Papal authority). These objects (sarcophagi and catacomb paintings) were presumably created under the influence of the clergy, who controlled the sites which they adorned, rather than that of the lay aristocracy. I shall especially focus on the wake of the full-blown rise of the cult of the saints in the episcopate of Damasus.

After the beautifully illustrated pages of the official civil calendar of Rome in the Codex of 354 (section VI),[38] the compiler – perhaps the famous calligrapher Furius Dionysius Filocalus,[39] who signed the title page and was the text's probable scribe and perhaps illuminator – included lists of the dates of death of Christian bishops and martyrs (sections XI and XII).[40] These, like the pagan calendar, are presented as an annual cycle of festivals (beginning at Christmas, in the case of the Christians), but – since the popes and the martyrdoms can be dated – they are also capable of interpretation as a chronological sequence reaching back to St Peter. Beside these pagan and Christian cyclical calendars, offering liturgies of annual festivals, the manuscript contains chronological lists – of consuls going back to the foundation of Rome (section VIII), of urban prefects opening in 254 CE (section X) and of Popes reaching back to Peter's reign when Tiberius was emperor (section XIII).[41] That is, for both pagan and Christian Rome the

---

[38] On which see Salzman (1990) 116–89.   [39] On Filocalus, see Ferrua (1939) 34–47, and (1942) 21–35.
[40] The text of these lists is given by Mommsen (1882) 70–2 and Duchesne (1955) 10–12. See esp. Pietri (1976) 365–87, 603–24, and Salzman (1990) 42–50.
[41] See Salzman (1990) 35–9, 41–2, 47–50 with guidance to a huge bibliography.

Codex-Calendar provides two kinds of temporal patterning – a cyclical liturgy of festivals, tied in the case of the Christians to specific places on specific days,[42] and a myth-historical chronology rooting these current practices in the deep past of Rome's heritage. It happens that the *depositio episcoporum* (effectively a festival calendar of local sainted bishops) begins in 255 and thus nearly coincides with the list of urban prefects which goes back exactly 100 years from the Codex's making to 254. The depositions of bishops and martyrs both begin their annual cycle with the birth of Christ on 25 December and constitute a Christian liturgical calendar for every month except April, which was adequately catered for by Easter.[43] Section IX of the Codex supplies the missing month's celebrations by making a calculation of the dates of Easter from 312 to 411.[44]

While the strategy of temporal embedding of the past in the present (through liturgical commemoration) is common to both the pagan and the Christian elements of the manuscript (which may be competitive or complementary depending on one's view), clearly the Christian adoption of this method was innovative.[45] The Codex is careful to allude to both distant time – Christ's birth, the celebration of Peter and Paul (interestingly dated not only to Apostolic times in the evocation of these saints but also to the year 258 'when Tuscus and Bassus were consuls')[46] – and to the very recent past, so that the last bishop in the list of depositions is Julius, who died in 352. The Codex's cyclical calendar – its Christian rivalry with Rome's most fundamental traditions of state urban ritual – is thus rooted in a long chronology whose recent accuracy vouchsafes and validates its more mythical references to the dimly remembered deep past of persecution. Likewise, the pastness of Rome's apostles and martyrs – the city's major claim to a Christian identity – is rendered present and relevant through liturgical commemoration at the sites of their burial or special remembrance.

We have to be circumspect in using the evidence of any liturgical calendar in that it may represent – especially in the factional context of third- and fourth-century Roman ecclesiastical politics[47] – one side's position

---

[42] See Baldovin (1987) 119.

[43] Pietri (1976) 365; Salzman (1990) 34. For the way some of these festivals appropriated the dates of pre-existing pagan festivals in Rome, see Salzman (1999) 124–7.

[44] See Salzman (1990) 39–41.

[45] On the development of an urban liturgy in early Christian Rome, see Chavasse (1993) 13–26, 47–9.

[46] A major crux, on which see Salzman (1990) 46–7 with bibliography.

[47] On the factionalism of the Roman Church in the third quarter of the fourth century, see Curran (2000) 129–42, Pietri (1986) 31–58, esp. 31–45, and Pietri (1976) 407–31. On the complex of Damasus' late fourth-century readings of third-century 'schisms', see Brent (1995) 368–97, and on third-century factionalism *ibid*. 398–540.

(as articulated through its chosen rituals) rather than a general state of affairs.[48] Indeed, just as the Calendar's Christian sections can be read as letting some saints into the Roman canon, it presumably wrote others out too. Certainly, its willingness to give space to the controversial third-century presbyter Hippolytus appears to anticipate the later Damasan attempt to rewrite recent history as a story of happy concord,[49] and in their juxta-position (or perhaps opposition) of pagan and Christian, the text's lists certainly finesse any possible narrative of competing Christianities. The Codex-Calendar is a particularly difficult document. Not only does its physical survival belong to a set of recensions worthy of an Umberto Eco novel,[50] but it is unique. Its antiquarian lists are exceptionally accurate (the catalogue of consuls is the most reliable of all that have survived)[51] and its combination of pagan and Christian elements indicates an elite scholarly patron and author whose work may represent a highly idiosyncratic 'take' on the Rome of 354. However, what is clear is that by the reign of Constantius (whose resplendent imperial portrait as one of the two consuls of the year 354 occupies folio 13 of our principal manuscript copy)[52] a Christian identity had been constructed for the city which could be realistically set beside its great polytheistic heritage. Where Constantine had effectively bolted a series of spectacular churches onto the major Christian cemeteries of Rome in a great circle around the urban periphery,[53] by 354 these – as well as other funerary sites – had become integrated in a liturgical pattern of spatial *memoria* and temporal commemoration.[54] Not only were the martyrdoms and demises of sainted bishops located in the past, but the topography of their current places of burial (many of them cited in the Codex-Calendar's lists) offered tombs, material remains, possibly even

---

[48] As Brent (1995) 69–70 argues was the case with the Paschal calendar inscribed by the third-century Hippolytus community on the famous statue now in the Vatican Library.

[49] See Brent (1995) 379–81.

[50] The manuscripts we possess now – including the most important, the 'Romanus', which was executed under the supervision of the antiquarian Nicholas-Claude Fabri de Peiresc (1580–1637) – are sixteenth- and seventeenth-century copies of a lost Carolingian copy presumably made from the lost original Codex of 354.

[51] Salzman (1990) 36.   [52] Salzman (1990) 34 and fig. 13.

[53] Krautheimer (1983) 12–31; Ward-Perkins (1984) 236–7; Baldovin (1987) 108–12; Schumacher (1987) 132–86; Curran (2000) 90–115.

[54] In fact, while the Constantinian foundations of Sant'Agnese and San Lorenzo are mentioned in the Calendar, St Peter's on the Vatican is notably absent (a cause of long debate: see Pietri (1976) 366–80 and Salzman (1990) 46–7). The Calendar concentrates on the main catacomb sites including the catacombs of Callistus, Sebastian and Priscilla. If San Sebastiano, the Basilica Apostolorum, in fact antedates Constantine's conquest of Rome in 312 (see Krautheimer, Corbet and Frankl (1970) 144–5, 147 and Curran (2000) 99), then it may be that in this Christian outer ring, as in so much else, the new conqueror was taking up, transforming and completing a project already under way in his predecessor's reign.

Figure 4. Sarcophagus of Junius Bassus, marble, 359 CE. Front of the main coffin, a
five-niche double-register sarcophagus, with lid fragments (a further fragment has been
joined since this photograph was taken).

relics to Christian devotees keen to assuage their feelings of piety, and perhaps also to polytheists anxious to keep in with all of Rome's numerous
gods and sanctified heroes, including the Christian ones.

The Calendar's keenness in embedding the Christian present in a
Christian past reaching back for centuries within the city of Rome is not
unique. In the visual arts it finds an interesting parallel in a monument
close to it both in time and in its elite level of patronage. The sarcophagus
of Junius Bassus was carved for the Urban Prefect of 359, who died in office
on 25 August and was baptised on his deathbed, as we are informed by the
inscription on the coffin's upper rim (fig. 4).[55] Like Valentinus, the aristocratic patron of the Codex-Calendar of 354, Bassus came from the highest
rank of Roman society, his father having served as Praetorian Prefect from

---

[55] Generally on the sarcophagus, see Malbon (1990) with earlier bibliography. The best collection of
black and white photographs remains Gerke (1936). On Bassus himself, see Malbon (1990) 3–5 and
Jones, Martindale and Morris (1971) 155 (Bassus 15).

318 to 331 and as Consul in 331.[56] Like the Calendar, the Bassus sarcophagus is an exceptional monument – certainly the best-carved and most complex Christian sarcophagus of the fourth century; and, like the Calendar, both its content and its execution (in matters of style) show a certain antiquarianism of conception. While the Calendar uses a sophisticated patterning of liturgy and chronology to embed the present in the past, the sarcophagus makes a similar argument in visual and inscriptional means.

The inscription on the coffin's upper edge places its date firmly in the present, being careful to cite the time in terms of Bassus' life-span, in relation to his place on the *cursus honorum* as Urban Prefect and according to the traditional annalistic method of dating by Consuls:

IVN BASSVS V. C. QVI VIXIT ANNIS XLII MEN. II IN IPSA PRAE-FECTVRA VRBI NEOFITVS IIT AD DEVM VIII KAL. SEPT. EVSEBIO ET YPATIO COSS. Junius Bassus, a man of Senatorial rank, who lived 42 years and 2 months, went to God newly baptized, while he was Prefect of the City, on the 8th day from the kalends of September, when Eusebius and Hypatius were Consuls (25 August 359).

On the lid (now in a very fragmentary state) were traditional Roman 'biographical' scenes including a funerary meal, masks on the ends (probably Sol and Luna) and an inscribed epigraph in 8 elegiac couplets describing how the whole city – even the houses and the roof tops – fell to weeping as it mourned the deceased Prefect.[57] On the ends of the main box of the coffin are images of grape- and wheat-harvesting by winged putti as well as personifications of the Seasons – again highly traditional funerary imagery stretching well back into pagan times.[58] This traditional imagery of life and death, elegiac mourning and cyclical time, serves to generalize the very specific temporal placing of Bassus' death in a broader picture.

By contrast with these scenes – all entirely normal in pagan funerary art – the main front of the sarcophagus is adorned with ten Christian scenes placed between the intercolumniations of a double-register columnar sarcophagus. Reading from left to right, these images represent – on top – the sacrifice of Isaac, the arrest of St Peter, Christ enthroned over Caelus between Peter and Paul (fig. 5), the arrest of Christ and the judgement of Pilate. Below, in the lower register, are the distress of Job, Adam and Eve, Christ entering Jerusalem in triumph (fig. 6), Daniel in the lions' den and the arrest of St Paul.[59] Additionally, in the spandrels of the arches

---

[56] See Jones et al. (1971) 154–5 (Bassus 14).   [57] On the lid, see Malbon (1990) 104–19, 134.
[58] On the ends, see Malbon (1990) 91–103. Generally on the traditions of seasonal imagery, see Hanfmann (1951) and Casal (1990) 510–38.
[59] See Malbon (1990) 39–71.

Figure 5. Sarcophagus of Junius Bassus. Upper tier, central scene. Christ enthroned
between Peter and Paul, to whom he is handing the Law, above a personification of
Caelus. The columns on either side are carved with vinescrolls and vintaging erotes.

that spring from the columns of the lower register, there are six curious
scenes where lambs replace people. These represent the three Hebrews in
the fiery furnace, Moses or Peter (or both) striking the rock, the miracle of
the multiplication of loaves (fig. 6), the baptism of Christ (fig. 6), Moses
or Peter (or both) receiving the Law, and the raising of Lazarus.[60] These 16
Christian scenes – with the six spandrel images effectively making a middle
tier between the upper and lower registers – constitute a highly complex
typological group. Like the Christian elements of the Codex-Calendar, they

[60] See Malbon (1990) 72–90.

Figure 6. Sarcophagus of Junius Bassus. Lower tier, central scene. Christ enters Jerusalem riding on a donkey. To the side, columns with vinescrolls and vintaging erotes; above, an eagle-headed conch in the arch. In the two spandrel scenes above the capitals to either side are the multiplication of loaves and the baptism of Christ, with all the figures represented as lambs.

are separated from the 'pagan' parts of the sarcophagus,[61] though here they adorn its most important face beneath the main inscription – whereas the Calendar's use of illustrations marks out the pagan (or traditional) portions of the manuscript as the more significant (or at least more embellished).

What is interesting for our purposes is the range of 'times' evoked in these images. The Old Testament events of the Fall, the sacrifice of Isaac, the distress of Job, the ordeal of Daniel and the sufferings of the Hebrews

[61] Malbon (1990) 118.

in the furnace foreshadow the New Testament narrative of Incarnation and Passion, and are fulfilled by it. The two central scenes in the upper and lower registers show Christ in triumph (figs. 5 and 6) – both in his life when he entered Jerusalem to public acclamation, and after his Resurrection when he sits between his apostles enthroned over the world (upper register). But this dispensation of Old and New Testaments in scriptural time and place (that is, in events located in Palestine), is then carried towards the present by the allusion to the Roman martyr narratives of the arrests of Peter and Paul, echoing and mirroring the arrest of Christ. The key image of Christ enthroned handing the Law to the two Roman apostles (fig. 5) is the guarantee of the presentness of Biblical time and salvation in the apostolic Church established in the city by the very saints to whom Christ entrusted his salvific massage. This scene is framed by columns showing putti harvesting grapes, the spandrel images of the multiplication of loaves and the baptism and the inscription's VRBI NEOFITVS IIT AD DEVM. That is, this scene is surrounded by images alluding to the eucharist and baptism – exactly the sacraments handed down by Christ through the apostles to the contemporary worshipper in Rome (VRBI), including the newly baptized Junius Bassus. The spandrel scenes – which effectively efface the distinctions between Old and New Testament and apostolic subjects by representing all the actors as sheep – further emphasize the eternal presence of the sacred past.

Effectively, Bassus' sarcophagus – probably originally placed where it was first excavated in the last years of the sixteenth century,[62] near the tomb of St Peter on the Vatican – reflects the sacro-temporal rhetoric of the Codex-Calendar. Its Christian narratives encase the body of the dead Prefect in a symbolic structure rooting his baptism in both scripture and the specifically Roman inheritance of scripture. The allusions to Roman martyrdoms – including that of the saint associated with the site of Bassus' own burial – and the ways those saintly passions are made to parallel that of Christ (in the three images of arrest) give a strongly Rome-centred emphasis to the Christian heritage of initiation and death, of which Bassus is (in the rhetoric of the sarcophagus) the most recent heir. As in the Calendar, the present – especially the evocation of Roman *sites* (of burial and worship) in the reference to Roman saints – valorizes the scriptural imagery by making it relevant to the here and now. At the same time, the Biblical narrative rendered in typological images represents the conceptual underpinning for the implied message of Bassus' salvation.

---

[62] In 1595 or 1597 depending on conflicting archaeological reports. See Bovini and Brandenburg (1967) no. 680, pp. 279–83, esp. 279.

The resonances evoked by the images on the sarcophagus and the listed names and sites in the Calendar are interesting. They include specific times (from the incarnation to the present), specific places (where actions depicted took place or were commemorated), particular narratives (not just scriptural and martyrological texts, but also the entire 'oral history' of Roman Christianity as it must have existed in the 350s) and finally liturgical action – which is to say a cyclical dispensation of time and place in which the personal memories and experiences of Christian worshippers in Rome were inevitably evoked. All this related to Palestine, since that was where the scriptural story took place – not just in the sarcophagus' pictures but also in the opening liturgical feast of Christ's birth in the Codex-Calendar. But the Palestinian story of Christ and his Old Testament prototypes was capped and in its turn fulfilled by the Roman story of Roman saints and converts (in the Bassus sarcophagus) and Roman saints and bishops (in the Codex) in the here and now. This chronological dimension extending to Rome in the present day (let us call it a vertical axis) was then replayed in an annual cycle of feasts (a horizontal axis), which did not necessarily fall in chronological order, but all of which were celebrated at Rome.

It might be said that the spatio-temporal argument mounted by these objects – complex though it is – was to be developed further in subsequent centuries. The sixth-century mosaics of SS Cosma e Damiano or of San Lorenzo fuori le mura take the logic of the visual rhetoric one stage further. Christ in the centre, flanked by Peter and Paul, in turn flanked by more 'local' saints are all in their turn flanked by the reigning pope or church builder.[63] This powerful iconography, overtly exploited by the sixth century for propagandist political ends, had not yet evolved in the fourth century. But its foundations as a dynamic temporal line leading from Christ to the present were effectively already laid in objects like the Bassus sarcophagus.

The methods for establishing Christianity in Rome evidenced by the sarcophagus of Junius Bassus and the Codex-Calendar in the 350s are subtle. First, to make the city Christian is a matter of material intervention and interpretation: the argument about reinterpreting Rome as *Roma Christiana* is a materially based one, through sites, through the images and objects adorning those sites and through the representation of those sites figured as their patron saints in the visual arts. Second, there is an apologetic air about both objects. Their Christianity is affirmed side by side with the old traditions (the much damaged cult meal and burial scenes on the lid of the Bassus sarcophagus, as well as the seasonal scenes on its ends, the lists of

---

[63] On these mosaics, see Ihm (1960) 137–40.

consuls, prefects, emperors and traditional festivals in the calendar). This is a Christianity which asks to be included and then supplants by the persuasive rhetoric of faith. Third, every scene on the sarcophagus and every name and place in the Codex's lists evokes a series of interconnected connotations. That is, the great strength of the Christian reformulation of Rome is its 'multi-strand' force, whereby each symbol implies a range of interrelated referents that together create an overwhelming orchestration of integrated meaning.[64] This is a strength of Christian symbolism in general, but in the particular context of the Roman world in late antiquity it provided a 'deep play' of interpretative exegesis whereby any item could always be explained in terms of an intellectually satisfying set of meanings deriving ultimately from the Christian conception of God. One did not have to trace back every image to its Christian conceptual underpinnings – one merely had to trust (like Thomas) that they were there.

The power of this system was that any vision, image, place associated with a saint (for example) opened a potential gateway into the salvific dispensation with which Christianity was so rapidly and effectively displacing polytheism. There was an immediate and direct link (on a very simple and uneducated level) between material memoria and salvation, where salvation did not need explaining (but always could be explained by the educated hierarchy of the Church). Within a decade of the death of Junius Bassus, this strategy – already highly effective as we have seen – would be immeasurably boosted in the remarkable project inaugurated by Pope Damasus (366–84) to establish the cult of the saints, and especially of relics, through what was to be a hugely influential programme of finding relics, building or embellishing churches and inscribing Christian epigrams in the holy places.[65] By the later fourth century even Jerusalem could be mapped onto Rome – for instance in the apsidal mosaic of Sta Pudenziana with its representation of Christ and his apostles within the Holy Sepulchre.[66] By the fifth century, the events of the Passion were being celebrated in a stational liturgy around the main churches of Rome, in which Rome's key basilicas stood in for – one

[64] On 'multi-strand' activities, a formulation which I owe to Keith Hopkins, see Gellner (1988) 43–53.
[65] On the Damasan project, see Ferrua (1942); Pietri (1976) 514–51, 595–624; the various papers in *Saecularia Damasiana Atti del convegno internazionale per il XVI centenario della morte di Papa Damaso I, Roma.* 1986 and Curran (2000) 142–57. On the parallel and contemporary activities of Ambrose in Milan and Bologna, see Dassmann (1975) 49–68 and McLynn (1994) 209–17, 226–36, 347–50.
[66] Since this church, built into a pre-existing Roman baths, is eccentrically orientated (with the altar at the west end), the Jerusalem image might be a visual means of reaffirming the direction of the building towards an imaginary East. On the mosaic, see Ihm (1960) 12–15, 130–2; Hellemo (1989) 45–55; Schlatter (1992) 276–95; Mathews (1993) 98–114.

might say temporarily and liturgically *became* – the actual sites of those events in Jerusalem.[67]

But it is most important to note that these developments belong to the orbit of largely ecclesiastic patronage rather than the aristocratic culture of Bassus and Valentinus, which seems a Christian equivalent to the elite antiquarianism of Symmachus. Christian sectarianism is not at issue in the Bassus sarcophagus and the Codex-Calendar (which deal rather with universal Christian triumphalism in the case of the former and Christian equivalence with paganism at least in some respects in the latter). But with the objects collected by local Church hierarchies to adorn local martyr shrines within the city, there was always the potential for segmentary opposition even in the kinds of narratives encouraged by Damasus which suppressed the histories of conflict and opposition.

PETER, PAUL AND THE ROMAN SAINTS

Glancing back to the sarcophagus of Junius Bassus, let us press the allusions to Peter and Paul. They are quite specific. In the central scene of the upper tier – the one Christological image which shows the resurrected Christ – the Lord is depicted handing over his jurisdiction to his Roman apostles (fig. 5). This is a scene outside the normal confines of time and place – a mystical epiphany with Christ enthroned above the world as well as a key charter myth for the Roman Church, where variations of this iconography would be much repeated in the next half century.[68] But both the upper and the lower tiers of the coffin also depict distinctly Roman scenes in the arrests of Peter and Paul, themes which allude (as does the arrest of Christ) beyond themselves – to the martyrdoms of the saints, their tombs in Rome and their cults. This implicit imaging of place in the sarcophagus alludes generally to Rome but also much more specifically to the sites where Peter and Paul were venerated. In the fourth century, these were not just the basilica and tomb complexes recently constructed over ancient memoria on the Vatican (for St Peter, where the Bassus sarcophagus was found) and in the Via Ostiense (for St Paul), but also the famous joint monument of Peter and Paul 'ad catacumbas' in what is now the Church of San Sebastiano on the Via Appia, whose excavated remains have yielded a wealth of graffito invocations to the saints.[69]

---

[67] See Baldovin (1987) 147–57.
[68] See Huskinson (1982) esp. 3–63 for a survey of the visual material.
[69] The vastness of the literature on this complex issue is truly daunting. For summaries including discussion of the post-War excavations and bibliography, see O'Connor (1969) 116–206 and

The allusion via images of the Roman saints to sites of cult and (implicitly) to times of festivals – effectively a visual refiguring of Rome through its martyrs – became prolific in the second half of the century. We have a range of numerous relatively cheap tokens in bronze and especially in gold-glass, in which the main Roman saints (Peter, Paul, Agnes, Lawrence) are popular.[70] Likewise, at the more expensive end of the scale, we have images of the saints in wall-paintings, mosaics and sculpture. Sarcophagi with the two apostles appear to have been particularly associated with their sites of cult – at St Peter's, St Paul's outside the Walls and the joint monument at San Sebastiano.[71] Lateran 164, for example, a sarcophagus of the second half of the fourth century, found in the hypogaeum at the Confessio of St Paul's, shows the *crux invicta* – a symbolic image of the Crucifixion and Resurrection – with the arrest of Peter to the left and the martyrdom of Paul on the right (fig. 7). Sandwiching these Christological and martyrological images are Old Testament scenes showing the sacrifice of Cain and Abel on the far left and the distress of Job on the far right.[72] Here, even more than in the Bassus sarcophagus, the triple martyrdoms of Peter, Paul and Christ are the focus for and the fulfilment of Old Testament images of suffering and sacrifice misplaced. The end figures (God and Job) are seated and face inward looking beyond the characters in their own scenes to the apostolic martyrdoms represented further in to the coffin's centre. Christ himself does not appear here, except symbolically, which throws the weight of the sarcophagus' theological argument through images onto the Roman deaths of the two Roman apostles as guarantors of salvation for the owner and viewers of the coffin. An unfinished sarcophagus at San Sebastiano surrounds the figure of Christ as teacher (between two figures of whom that on the right looks like St Paul) with the scenes of the triple martyrdoms (fig. 8). Here the two intercolumniations on the left show the death of Paul, with the executioner in the act of drawing his sword, and the journey of Peter to his place of execution, while the two on the right show Christ before Pilate.[73]

Snyder (1985) 98–114, 141–7. For our purposes it is worth noting that Damasus celebrated all three sites in his inscribed verses: see Ferrua (1942) no. 1, pp. 81–7; no. 4, pp. 93–6; no. 20, pp. 139–44.

[70] See Huskinson (1982) 51–9. On the gold-glass medallions, see Morey (1959) with the examples listed by saint at p. 82.

[71] See Huskinson (1982) 20.   [72] See Bovini and Brandenburg (1967) no. 61, pp. 57–8.

[73] See Bovini and Brandenburg (1967) no. 189, pp. 119–20. Other sarcophagi with the two apostles from San Sebastiano are no. 212, pp. 128–9; no. 215, pp. 129–30; no. 220, p. 132 and no. 241, pp. 139–41.

Figure 7. Lateran Sarcophagus 164, marble, second half of the fourth century: front. This is a five-niche single-register tree sarcophagus (with trees replacing columns and arches). From left to right: Cain and Abel offering sacrifice to God, the arrest of Peter, the Crux Invicta with doves between sleeping Roman soldiers (symbolizing the Resurrection), the arrest or execution of Paul, the distress of Job.

Figure 8. Unfinished sarcophagus from San Sebastiano, marble, third quarter of the fourth century: front. This is a five-niche single-register columnar sarcophagus. From left to right: the execution of Paul, the arrest or journey to execution of Peter, Christ the teacher, the arrest of Christ and the judgement of Pilate. In the spandrels putti carrying martyrs' (?) wreaths.

Figure 9. Lateran Sarcophagus 174, marble, third quarter of the fourth century: front.
This is a seven-niche single-register columnar sarcophagus. From left to right: the sacrifice
of Isaac, Peter, Paul turning to Christ in the centre, Christ enthroned over Caelus and
between two figures (apostles? angels?), Peter receiving the Law from Christ, Christ
arrested, the judgement of Pilate.

Apart from the Bassus sarcophagus, a number of other coffins – roughly
contemporary with it and also found in St Peter's – emphasize the two
Roman apostles. Lateran 174, for instance, shows a *traditio legis* in the
centre with Christ enthroned over Caelus handing the Law to Peter and
Paul (fig. 9). On the right is the scene of Christ before Pilate and to the
left the sacrifice of Isaac and the arrest of Peter or possibly an unidentified
scene with Peter and an attendant – virtually a repetition of the upper tier
of the Bassus sarcophagus, although with seven niches instead of five and
all the columns carved with grapevines. On the ends of this sarcophagus
the Petrine imagery is extended with the denial of Christ and the cock
crowing on the left and a scene of parallel miracles by Peter and Christ
on the right (fig. 10).[74] In this scene, Peter and Christ, in broadly similar
dress and united by a continuous cityscape behind them, both turn to
the left to provide miracles to kneeling worshippers who stretch out their
hands. Christ heals a woman with the touch of his hand (probably the
woman with the issue of blood, though the subject has been contested),

[74] See Bovini and Brandenburg (1967) no. 677, pp. 274–7; Huskinson (1982) 25.

Figure 10. Lateran Sarcophagus 174: right end. As with most sarcophagi, the ends of this one are carved in shallower relief than the front. The image shows Peter's miracle of striking water from the rock and a miracle of Christ (probably the healing of the woman with the issue of blood).

while Peter strikes water from a rock with a wand. In this object, the emphasis is more directly focused on Peter (despite the iconographical closeness of the main face to the Bassus sarcophagus) as is appropriate in what was regarded by the second half of the fourth century as the major shrine of the saint. These kinds of images clearly bolster the shrine in which they were displayed – stressing the martyrological nature of the site and advertising the miracles of its saint. They also stand as visual invocations of the local saint for the particular person buried at his place of special worship. Interestingly, there is a general emphasis on the concordia of Peter and Paul and their joint apostolic mission which somewhat resists the New Testament's intimations of their discord.[75] This smoothing-over of a troubled past is firmly in line with the Damasan project of rewriting ecclesiastical history as a conflict-free harmony of progression. Since we know from the graffiti at San Sebastiano that much cult activity (including *refrigerium*, or the cult meal) took place, at least at that site, this kind of

[75] See Sullivan (1994) 59–80.

Figure 11. Catacomb of Commodilla, Cubiculum Leonis, frescos painted in the last
quarter of the fourth century. This view shows the interior of the cubiculum with the bust
of Christ between A and Ѡ on the vault, the image of Christ carrying a book between
Saints Felix and Adauctus in the rear arcosolium and the painting of Peter striking water
from the rock in the left-hand arcosolium.

imagery serves to adorn and make sacred the space already marked out as
holy by the memoria of the saints.

When such imagery extends outside sites specifically given over to the cult
of Peter and Paul, to other places of worship or funerary commemoration,
the referential effect is different.[76] In the Cubiculum Leonis, for example,
a late fourth-century hypogaeum in the Commodilla catacomb, the special
saints of the cemetery – Felix and Adauctus – are depicted twice. They stand
one on each side of the archway forming the entrance to the cubiculum,
and appear again together on either side of Christ in the niche of the
arcosolium at the end wall (fig. 11).[77] The viewer proceeds from the visual
announcement of their martyrdom to their heavenly presence beside Christ
himself as mediators gesturing to him and as imitators of Peter and Paul
in the traditional *traditio legis* scene. On the left and right walls of this

[76] Generally on the catacombs in the era of Damasus, see Nicolai et al. (1998) 48–57, 174–6 and Pergola
(1999) 95–101.
[77] See Deckers et al. (1994) 89–104, with bibliography.

Figure 12. Catacomb of Commodilla, Cubiculum Leonis. Detail of the right-hand arcosolium with the fresco of Peter (to the left) denying Christ beside a column crowned by a crowing cock, and Christ with a companion to the right.

arcosolium are various images (many unidentified) including Agnes, Daniel and images in which Christ appears as a lamb. In the two arcosolia, on the left and right of the room, are scenes of Peter striking water from the rock (fig. 11) and denying Christ while the cock crows (fig. 12). Here the specific local worship of Felix and Adauctus is bolstered by the inclusion of other Roman saints – in this case, Peter and Agnes – effectively a reference to other (perhaps more prestigious) sites in the city and to other (perhaps more famous) cults. This strategy of evoking a saint from elsewhere in Rome is found not only in paintings but in gold-glass medallions. In both the Pamfilus and Novegianus catacombs, gold-glass images of Agnes remain embedded in the plaster closing graves.[78] One presumes that most of the surviving objects of this type – now in museum collections and mostly unprovenanced – originally fulfilled a similar function.

In similar vein, in the famous ceiling fresco of room 3 of the Catacomb of Marcellinus and Peter (the 'Cripta dei Santi'), probably executed at the end of the fourth century, Christ appears nimbed and bearded between

[78] See Morey (1959) no. 221, p. 39; no. 226, p. 40.

the two Roman apostles (fig. 13).[79] Below this trio is a lamb with a halo, which contains the Christogram between A and ꙍ. The lamb stands over a rock from which four streams of water flow and is inscribed IORDAS (abbreviated from 'Iordanes' for the Jordan river). On either side of the lamb are two martyrs specific to the cemetery *inter duos lauros* where the catacomb, the later Constantinian basilica and its attached mausoleum were located. These are, from left to right, Gorgonius, Peter (not the Apostle), Marcellinus and Tiburtus, all with their right arms raised pointing to the lamb, but also mediating for the viewer with the lamb.[80] Here mediation with the local martyrs is again supported by the more general reference to Peter and Paul, respectively on Christ's left- and right-hand sides as is usual in the period,[81] who stand together in much larger scale as a superior trio, which the four martyrs and the lamb appear to support. Anticipating the way the cult of the saints would surround the major relics of a significant local saint with minor relics of other saints,[82] these images construct a topography which places the local martyrs of the Commodilla and Marcellinus and Peter catacombs within a broader Roman dispensation alluding to other major Roman martyrs and ultimately to Christ. These images function as if they were relics – though without the magical tangibility of the fragment of a sacred body which the cult of relics was soon to provide.[83] Like relics, they may be said to occupy space in two registers, denoting themselves as particular material representations of a saint and also a whole other world of increasing closeness to the saint himself – his tomb, his festival day, his actual remains, his presence in heaven, his bridging function between heaven and earth.[84] They create a complex cross-referencing of Roman Christianity in which the different saints are interconnected, just as the great basilicas around Rome's periphery and on its major arteries were interconnected by a web of liturgical celebrations and urban processions.[85] They work, therefore, like the 'chain of eternity' which – in the words of Victricius of Rouen, writing of relics in the last years of the fourth century – binds the disparate martyrs together.[86]

---

[79] See Deckers et al. (1987) 199–201, with bibliography.

[80] On these martyrs, the cemetery and their Damasan celebration, see Seeliger (1987) 67–70.

[81] Huskinson (1982) 114; Sullivan (1994) 69–75.

[82] For instance in the case of Bishop Gregory's use of relics to surround St Martin at Tours, see Van Dam (1993) 33–4, and for his use of collections of relics in the dedication of churches, see *ibid.* 65–7.

[83] On the 'tactile piety' of the cult of relics ('worship with the lips and the finger-tips'), see Wilken (1992) 116–17.

[84] For relics as occupying 'space in two registers', see Miller (1998) 113–38, esp. 125.

[85] On spatial interconnectedness through a network of holy places, see Markus (1990) 142–50.

[86] Victricius of Rouen, *De laude sanctorum* 11.50 (CCL 64.88), with Miller (1998) 126 and Clark (1999) 365–400, esp. 365–76 for context.

Figure 13. Catacomb of Saints Marcellinus and Peter, room 3 'Cripta dei Santi', vault fresco painted in the late fourth century. Upper tier: Christ between Peter and Paul. Lower tier: lamb standing over the Jordan flanked by the martyrs Gorgonius, Peter, Marcellinus and Tiburtinus.

CONCLUSION

Here, at the very dawn of the cult of relics, we find many of the features which would determine its operation and appeal already developed in the early Christian images of Rome. A remarkable piece of papyrus, which accompanied a collection of 26 glass ampullae containing oil from the martyrs' tombs in Rome that was given by Pope Gregory the Great to the Lombard queen Theodolinda at the end of the sixth century, gives a glimpse of the way this material rhetoric of a sacred topography would evolve.[87] The *notula*, which accompanied this gift, is a papyrus catalogue listing the saints whose oil the ampullae contained.[88] It gives the saints, beginning with Peter and Paul, in a geographical dispensation – presenting them according to where their tombs were sited in Rome. The list opens on the Vatican, moves to the via Ostiense and then circles the city with groups of martyrs at the Via Aurelia, Via Salaria Nova, Via Tiburtina, Clivus Scauri (the only site inside the walls), Via Nomentana, Via Appia, Via Salaria Vetus, Via Salaria Nova (twice), Via Salaria Vetus, Via Appia and finally Via Ardeatina. The sites are listed by saints, not by their locations on the map or their street names, as I have given them here: the geography of Rome as re-invented by the *notula* is an entirely martyr-specific one, ignoring all secular indications. It is rather as if one gave all one's directions to a town like Cambridge by the location of colleges rather than by street names. In terms of location, this is a strange set of groupings which – after the primacy of Peter and Paul – appears to follow some kind of liturgical pattern rather than any logical or ordered topography of the city's cemeteries. While there are 64 saints listed, the *notula* has 15 sites. The ampullae themselves were provided with small strips of papyrus (*pittacia*) on which the names of the saints whose oil was contained in a particular ampulla were written – effectively as labels.[89] By reference to the *notula*, any of Theodolinda's ampullae could be tied to the sacred topography of Rome. Effectively, this collection of relics – along with its labels and catalogue – not only commemorated Rome (now envisaged entirely as a martyrium)

---

[87] Sepulcri (1903) 241–62 remains fundamental. On the ampullae see *ibid.* 242–5; Lipinsky (1960) 146–73, esp. 163–6; Frazer (1989) 15–54, esp. 34–5.

[88] On the *notula*, see Sepulcri (1903) 248–57; Lipinsky (1960) 166–7; Merati (1963) 26–7. The text is published by Sepulcri (1903) 258–9 and Cabrol and Leclerq (1934) s.v. 'Monza', cols. 2753–6. For photographs, see Sepulcri (1903) facing p. 262 and Vitali (1966) pl. 41. On palaeographic grounds, the *notula* has been dated to the seventh century, suggesting that it is probably a copy of an original catalogue sent when the ampullae were despatched. See Sepulcri (1903) 254–7.

[89] On the *pittacia*, see Sepulcri (1903) 247 and 260–2 for the texts, also Cabrol and Leclerq (1934) cols. 2756–8.

but also refigured the city through the material means of its reliquary objects.

My point here is that the material and topographical dispensation for sanctity in Rome – so vividly brought to life in Theodolinda's reliquary ampullae and their catalogue – was already established in the Christian arts of Rome before the pontificate of Damasus. Its potent force as an agent of Christianization, through re-imagining the city as a sort of martyr-filled mother-earth, an eternal plenitude of devotional and disinterable sanctity, was created by the Christians' battle, against each other and against the pagans, to invent for themselves a past in the city of Rome. That they found such a past which would become in its own way as powerful as the pagans' traditional city is obvious. But this new Christian past – established as a territorial patterning of sacred sites whose meanings were defined, determined and differentiated from each other by the texts inscribed in them and the images which adorned them – was appropriated with radical and not entirely foreseeable effects by the Damasan project of emphasizing relics and integrating them in a cohesive topography of worship controlled by the papacy. Damasus was effectively inventing a united anti-schismatic history for Rome, targeted above all at establishing the city's primacy *vis-à-vis* Constantinople. But his focus on the Christian past as a population of sainted bodies appropriated the earlier visual rhetoric of images we have been examining for what was becoming the cult of relics. Its effects were soon exported to the exploding cult of relics in northern Italy and Gaul.[90]

---

[90] My abiding memory of being supervised by Keith Hopkins was the vision of him standing against the great semicircle of the window that dominated his wonderful rooms over the arch of the Gibbs Building in King's, kicking the frame and lamenting: 'Why have you not seduced me? I want to be seduced by your prose, not bored by it!' I don't suppose he will be much satisfied by this attempt at seduction, but it was written in his honour and with fond memories. Versions have been delivered to seminars in Oxford, Sussex and Munich, where I have had the chance to review and reformulate much of my thinking. My warm thanks are especially due to Allen Brent, Mary Charles Murray, Peter Stewart and Bryan Ward-Perkins for their acute critiques of an earlier draft, as well as to the Editors for their excellent suggestions.

CHAPTER 5

Slavery and the growth of Rome. The transformation of Italy in the second and first centuries BCE[*]

Willem Jongman

A WORLD OF CITIES

The city of Rome was and remained unique in European pre-industrial history. With its estimated one million inhabitants in the first century CE, it was by far the biggest city in the world, and remained so until the growth of the big Chinese cities of the Sung dynasty in the eleventh to thirteenth century CE.[1] In Europe, it was not until around 1800, in the early stages of the Industrial Revolution, that Rome was surpassed by London.[2] As Pliny the Elder put it: '...no city has existed in the whole world that could be compared with Rome for size'.[3] The ancients were particularly struck by the monumentality of the architecture. The huge walls measured 13.2 miles in circumference, certainly a daunting figure for any first-time visitor travelling from far-away lands.[4] Strabo, after a lengthy description of the monuments of the Campus Martius, continues 'on passing to the Old Forum, one should see forum after forum ranged alongside it, and basilicas, and temples, and should also see the Capitol and the works of art there and those on the Palatine and in Livia's Promenade; one would easily forget the things outside. Such is Rome.'[5] Aqueducts and sewers were particularly remarkable: 'The sewers, vaulted with close-fitting stones, have in some places left room enough for wagons loaded with hay to pass through them.'[6]

[*] Part of the research for this chapter was made possible by a grant from NWO. Parts of the argument were published earlier in Dutch: Jongman (1990); Jongman (2000a). It has been improved by comments from many friends and colleagues. In particular, I am grateful to Walter Scheidel for an invitation to present a shorter version in his Second Moses and Mary Finley Colloquium on the Comparative History of Slavery, at Darwin College, Cambridge. Jim Oeppen, Richard Smith and Sir Tony Wrigley of the Cambridge Group for the History of Population and Social Structure kindly shared their knowledge with me. Keith Hopkins was a gracious sparring partner. None of them may be held responsible for the conclusions.
[1] Hopkins (1978a) 96ff.; Elvin (1973) 175ff.; Elvin (1978). The similarities with Roman urbanization are remarkable, as are the differences with medieval Europe.
[2] Wrigley (1978); de Vries (1984) 96–101, 119, 152, 270.   [3] Pliny, *HN* 3.5.67.
[4] Pliny, *HN* 3.5.66.   [5] Strab. 5.3.8.   [6] Strab. 5.3.8.

However, other cities, too, in the Roman Empire reached an enormous size. Dio Chrysostom praises Alexandria as the second city in the world: 'Your city is vastly superior in point of size and situation, and it is admittedly ranked second among all cities beneath the sun.'[7] Alexandria, Carthage, and Antioch had a joint population of perhaps a million,[8] and there were yet other large cities.[9] Thus, the four largest cities of the Roman Empire had a joint population of perhaps 2 million people, or almost 4 per cent of the entire population of the Empire.[10] That is remarkable, because in pre-industrial societies it has never been easy to maintain such large cities: they were difficult to feed because transport costs were high, and they were difficult to populate because urban mortality was gruesome.[11] And yet, by comparison there were more large cities in the Roman world than in early modern Europe: around 1500 the four largest cities in Europe had a joint population of only 450,000 people.[12] Even in 1700, there were only eleven cities with more than 100,000 people.[13] It was not until well into the Industrial Revolution that Europe exceeded the levels of urbanization which had obtained under the Roman Empire.

Roman urbanization, moreover, was not restricted to a few big cities: there were many small cities all over the Empire. Thus, the ancient world really was an urban civilization. Its high culture was largely urban, and its most impressive material culture was also in the towns. With their passion for marble as a building material, the Romans probably quarried more marble than in all centuries after.[14] Political units often consisted of cities with their hinterlands, and even in the larger political system of the Roman Empire, cities remained centres of administration and local government. Economically, towns were also important. As in all pre-industrial economies, agriculture was by far the largest sector, and it provided the elite with the bulk of its income. However, the Roman elite mostly resided in the cities: Roman cities were important because, unlike medieval cities, their

---

[7] Dio Chrys. *Or.* 32.36.   [8] Hopkins (1983a) 88–9.

[9] We do not know which they are. Direct evidence is not available. However, the size distribution of cities is likely to have been subject to geometrical progression. There were more small cities than large cities. Good theoretical discussion in de Vries (1984) 85–120.

[10] The population of the Empire has been estimated at 54 million during the reign of Augustus. It may have grown even larger during the first century CE. Beloch (1886) is the classic statement.

[11] Jongman and Dekker (1988), Jongman (2000b) and Jongman (2001) esp. 1081–3 for discussions of urban food supply. Scheidel, this volume pp. 161–3 for high urban mortality.

[12] De Vries (1984) 34–5.

[13] De Vries (1984) 34–5 and catalogue on 270ff.; together those had now 2.4 million inhabitants. Even around 1800, only 3.3 per cent of Europe's population lived in cities with more than 100,000 inhabitants: de Vries (1984) 34–7; Wrigley (1978), 215–16.

[14] Good recent surveys in Dodge (1991), Fant (1993) and Jongste (1995).

elites controlled the largest sector of the economy (providing a steady urban demand for goods and services). In the Roman Empire, a larger proportion of the population lived in towns than in almost any pre-industrial society before or after. The Italian heartland of the empire was exceptionally urbanized: there were many cities, and some of them were very large.[15] Perhaps almost a third of the Italian population lived in cities.[16] Elsewhere in the empire, the level of urbanization was generally lower, but even there, it was often higher than it would be for centuries, if not millennia. Proportionally, many Romans lived in cities.

From a comparative historical perspective, Roman urbanism was, therefore, exceptional; what is the meaning of that?[17] Urbanization is often seen as an index of economic development. Eighteenth-century political economists such as Adam Smith even viewed cities as the engines of economic development: towns stimulated farmers to produce a surplus for the market. In return, urban manufactured goods became available for rural consumers. The increased division of labour between town and country expanded the market sector and stimulated economic development. Others have argued that the emerging towns protected a different culture, more amenable to economic innovation. The feudal world had been traditional, and hostile to economic change. In contrast the urban bourgeoisie embodied a new rational and secular mentality aimed at profit and improvement. To quote Postan: '[The towns] were non-feudal islands in the feudal seas; ... places which enjoyed or were capable of developing systems of local government and principles of law and status exempting them from the sway of the feudal regime.'[18] Did the urbanization of Roman Italy create some of the conditions for a similar economic development?

The ancient city has indeed been at the core of the debate on the nature of the ancient economy. It was Moses Finley who (following in the footsteps of earlier scholars such as Max Weber and Werner Sombart) argued that not all urbanization was the same.[19] In contrast to medieval and early modern so-called 'producer cities', ancient cities were 'consumer cities'. Their elites were not involved in trade and manufacturing for distant markets, but derived most of their incomes from agricultural property. What trade and manufacturing there was, was largely to satisfy local elite demand for consumer products, and was controlled by people of relatively small means and low status. Urbanization, therefore, did not generate a new economic

---

[15] Beloch (1886); Duncan-Jones (1982) 337ff.
[16] Hopkins (1978a) 69h. That rural/urban split, however, is based on occupation rather than location.
[17] Jongman (1988) 15–62; 91–5; Jongman (forthcoming a).
[18] Postan (1975), 239; Jongman (1988), 50.   [19] Finley (1984); Jongman (2000b).

mentality, the economic integration of distant markets, or the advantages of a geographic division of labour. Trade and manufacturing remained relatively small, and the economy did not grow.

Finley's model of the ancient economy and the role of cities has met with passionate criticism from scholars who tried to show that, really, there was far more trade in antiquity, and that the elite were involved, although sometimes at arm's length.[20] Others have argued that whereas Finley's model is broadly right, there were particular times and places where increased commercialization did occur after all. Keith Hopkins in particular has come up with two fascinating and interconnected models.[21] The first is his 'taxes and trade' model, which argues that Roman provincial taxation stimulated exports from provincial cities, to pay for the taxes. The second is his model for the impact of the growth of the city of Rome. He argued that the growth of the city of Rome increased urban demand for agricultural products. This, and the migration of poor peasants to the city of Rome, led to a commercialization of Italian agriculture, a shift to more profitable crops, and higher labour productivity.[22] That is the rosy and optimistic view. What, however, if the level of urbanization expresses the rate of fleecing of peasantry and provinces? What, if urbanization is not always the same?

GROWING PAINS

The growth of the Italian urban population in particular had indeed been remarkable. During the last two centuries BCE it had grown from perhaps 600,000–700,000 to something like 1,900,000.[23] Italy had been quite an urbanized society early on, but during these two centuries the level of urbanization in Roman Italy grew from some 10–15 per cent to about 30 per cent. The growth of the city of Rome, from perhaps 250,000 in 225 BCE to almost a million inhabitants in 28 BCE (when Augustus held his first census – though not of the urban population specifically), was particularly

---

[20] Three important surveys of the debate are Andreau (1995), Morris (1994) and Morris (1999). Jongman (1998), Jongman (2000b), Jongman (2000c) and Jongman (forthcoming a) for some of my own recent thoughts.

[21] Hopkins (1978b); Hopkins (1980); Hopkins (1995/6).

[22] Hopkins (1978a), 48–74. Cf. Morley (1996).

[23] These figures are based on the estimates in Hopkins (1978a) 68–9 and 96–8. See also Jongman (2001), esp 1077–9. Hopkins estimates that the free population of the city of Rome quadrupled from 150,000 in 225 BCE to 600,000 in 28 BCE, and that joint free population of the other Italian cities doubled from 250,000 to 500,000. So, over a period of two centuries, the free urban population of Italy, in Rome and in the other cities, increased from 400,000 to 1.1 million, an increase of 700,000. Add an increase of the urban slave population of at least half a million over these two centuries, and the total urban increase is a staggering 1.2 million, or more.

spectacular. With the growth of its political and military power, the size of the city had increased. Rome alone accounted for perhaps two-thirds of the urban increase. By comparative historical standards, urbanism in Roman Italy was exceptional.

The chronology of Italian urban growth closely followed the growth of Roman imperial power: the growth of cities was not the only change that had taken place in Late Republican Italy. During the same period, captured slaves arrived in Italy in large numbers. Estimates differ somewhat, and must remain tentative. As William Harris has said, however, already in the first Punic War 'the slave market was clearly able to dispose of [captured] slaves by the tens of thousands'.[24] Roman imperialism generated a major supply of slaves, most of whom ended up in Roman Italy. As a result, the slave population of Roman Italy grew significantly. Hopkins has estimated that it quadrupled from about 500,000 in 225 BCE to about 2 million in 28 BCE.[25] The slave proportion of the population increased from some 10 per cent to about a third, a level comparable to that in other and more recent slave societies.[26]

Finally, Roman social inequality increased stupendously. The Roman elite had never been the one of modest means and simple tastes so admiringly portrayed by later Roman writers. During the last two centuries of the Republic, with the conquest of a world empire, the Roman elite grew vastly wealthier, and adopted the lifestyle of a cosmopolitan ruling class of a world empire.[27]

The first Scipio [Africanus] opened the way for the world power of the Romans; the second opened the way for luxury. For when Rome was freed of the fear of Carthage, and her rival in empire was out of the way, the path of virtue was abandoned for that of corruption, not gradually, but in headlong course.

Elite residences became larger and larger, their walls decorated with quite exotic paintings of Hellenistic inspiration – elegant backdrops for sumptuous dinners. Greek statues provided symbols of cultural achievement, underscored by libraries full of often Greek manuscripts. Such houses were so large that many domestic servants were needed. Their number, however, often increased well beyond what was practically necessary, even to cope with large banquets. Thus, the elite also became more differentiated and stratified internally. Some senators acquired resources on an almost regal scale, and began to act the part politically. That in turn did not generally make them any poorer. At the other end of the social spectrum, there are increasing tales of impoverished peasants, urban poor, and revolting slaves.

[24] Harris (1979) 81.   [25] Hopkins (1978a) 68.   [26] Hopkins (1978a) 101.   [27] Vell. Pat. 2.1.1.

The growth and transformation of Rome during the last two centuries of the Republic is a dramatic and bewildering tale. In ancient accounts, the story is dominated by the struggle between a senatorial elite bent on retaining cohesion as a group, and individual leading senators who came to dominate political life more and more, until Augustus finally established monarchy. Sympathies in our sources differ. Many Republican accounts deplore the abuses of the new leaders with their armies more and more loyal to them rather than to the state, or the infringements on senatorial power and wealth. Cicero wrote of the Gracchan agrarian law that 'the people acclaimed it, for it seemed to restore the fortunes of the impoverished; but the *optimates* vigorously opposed it because they saw it breeding disorders and felt that to dispossess the wealthy from holdings of long standing was to strip the state of its first line of defence'.[28] By contrast, some imperial accounts denounce the new rapacity of the Senate as a group, and admire popular leaders for their concern with traditional rights of ordinary Roman citizens. Plutarch, writing early in the second century CE, praises Tiberius Gracchus:[29]

Tiberius, fighting for an honourable and just cause with an eloquence that would have dignified even a meaner cause . . . spoke on behalf of the poor. 'The wild beasts that roam over Italy,' he said, 'have their dens, each has a place of repose and refuge. But the men who fight and die for Italy have nothing but the air and light . . . they fight and die to protect the wealth and luxury of others; they are styled masters of the world, and have not a clod of earth they can call their own.'

Clearly, writing history was a highly ideological activity; quoting such histories as unproblematic sources of social fact rather than as sources of contemporary sentiment is naive; above all they reflect the culture and values of the period in which they were written.

Modern histories, however, often stay surprisingly close to these sources. In particular, they seem to share the aristocratic sense of doom and crisis. The modern story goes something like this. When larger and larger Roman armies began to fight longer and longer wars in more and more distant lands, military service became increasingly burdensome to ordinary peasant citizens, the traditional backbone of the legions. As a result, many lost their land to the ever more powerful rich, and left to increase the number of the urban poor. The rich, grown richer from the spoils of conquering the world, acquired large estates through the purchase and occupation – legal or otherwise – of public or private land. To work the land they used the ever increasing number of slaves captured in Rome's wars of expansion.

---

[28] Cic. *Sest*. 44.96–46.100, 48.   [29] Plut. *Vit. Ti. Gracch*. 9.

The most lucid and elegant exposition of this story is in the first chapter of Hopkins' *Conquerors and slaves*, a chapter read and reread by every teacher and almost every undergraduate in the world for the last two decades. To put the argument in his own words: 'Roman peasant soldiers were fighting for their own displacement.'[30] It is a powerful model, because it integrates all major developments: imperialism, slavery, urbanization and social conflict.

Methodologically, the model is conventional, however. For its explanation of events in the Late Republic it relies heavily on ancient – but by no means contemporary – literary sources. It also writes economic history at the pace of political history. The great political transformations of the period demand an explanation, and rapid economic changes are invoked. The similarity to now heavily criticized 'economic' explanations of the French Revolution is striking.[31] For these explanations to work, the economy must change at the same rapid pace as politics. However, pre-industrial economies rarely do that.

What I want to do in this chapter is to undermine the modern orthodoxy. In particular, I want to argue first that the urban growth of Roman Italy owed more to 'pull' factors than to the misery on the land, and that the largest need for immigrants was permanent and due to high urban excess mortality. Second, I want to argue that the transformation of the agrarian economy was far less complete than the modern orthodoxy presupposes. Large slave estates growing cash crops emerged indeed, but many small peasants survived to grow cereals for themselves and for the market. In my view, Roman urbanism and Roman slavery were far more directly related: cities grew and stayed large primarily because slavery came to occupy such a large place in urban society.

WARM BODIES

Italy's urban population roughly tripled in the last two centuries of the Republic. This urbanization was so rapid and substantial that, I want to argue, it required massive and continued migration, not only from the Italian countryside, but also from elsewhere in the Empire.[32] Every year, on average, some 6,000 more people lived in the cities than in the year before. This urban growth was entirely due to immigration, because urban mortality was so high that even in the best of times there were more urban

---

[30] Hopkins (1978a) 30.   [31] From a vast bibliography: Furet (1978) and Hunt (1984).
[32] Jongman (1990).

deaths than births. Moreover, as Wrigley has argued in his famous article on the growth of London, this need for immigrants translates into more than twice as large a demand on rural births: people migrate as young adults, but before they can do so, quite a few of their coevals have died.[33] An immigration of 6,000 adults (at age 20) required 13,800 rural births (life expectancy at birth = 25).

In fact, as Wrigley has demonstrated so elegantly for London, gigantic numbers of immigrants were needed even to maintain the population of especially the larger pre-industrial cities, and compensate for excess deaths. Pre-industrial cities were horribly dirty and unhealthy. In the city of Rome, some 50,000 (or more) corpses had to be disposed of every year, to be thrown in pits (*puticuli*), together with dead animals and household refuse.[34] Clearly, that offends our sensibilities, even if it helped the decomposition of the corpses. A tomb on the Via Appia was not for all. Sometimes corpses were not even collected. When Vespasian was dining, a dog came in from the street, to drop a human hand.[35] Corpses, moreover, were not the only filth. Stench was everywhere, from waste lying in the streets, from urine and faeces, or from drains which returned their content when the Tiber was high.[36] Romans paid a heavy price for their passion for – unchlorinated – baths, and for their belief that digestive and skin diseases above all others required a visit to the baths. Urban mortality exceeded natality by quite a wide margin; there were many empty places to fill. We can, therefore, transplant Wrigley's argument to Roman Italy, and estimate the rough order of magnitude of the issue. Let us try to calculate the number of immigrants necessary to maintain the urban population of Roman Italy at the level it reached by the late Republic and early Empire. For London, Wrigley has estimated an excess of deaths over births of 10 per 1,000, and for other pre-industrial European cities de Vries thinks 5 per 1,000 was typical.[37] Let us make a perhaps not so bold assumption, and pretend Rome was like London, and the other cities of Roman Italy were like average cities of pre-industrial Europe. If that is so (in this volume Walter Scheidel plausibly argues that Rome was probably even more unhealthy), to maintain the urban population of Roman Italy at late-Republican and early-Imperial levels required an annual flow of about 14,000–15,000

---

[33] Wrigley (1978), esp. 218. Landers (1993) and Galley (1998) for urban mortality.
[34] Hopkins (1983b) ch. IV for evocative analysis.   [35] Suet. *Vesp* 5.4.
[36] Scobie (1986) for an evocation of this other antiquity.
[37] Wrigley (1978) 217; de Vries (1984) 179–98, 202. Compare de Vries (1984) 201 for the required natural rural population increase (7 per 1,000) to supply migrants to maintain the cities of central Holland.

immigrants, corresponding to 32,000–35,000 rural births.[38] The city of
Rome was responsible for two-thirds of this (the explanation must be the
pull from the city, since the push from poverty cannot explain why they
ended up in Rome). Significantly, therefore, after the first urban growth
the bulk of immigration served simply to maintain the urban population,
and that of the city of Rome in particular. The need for that remained for
as long as Italy remained highly urbanized, i.e. well into the late Empire.[39]
That is important, because it contradicts the common view that urban
migration in Roman Italy was concentrated in specific periods (the second
and first centuries BCE), and related to particular series of events (the im-
poverishment of Italy's rural population and the growth of large estates).
Thus, a simple demographic simulation shows that what appeared to our
sources as a unique event, was really the beginning of a long-lasting and
highly structural feature of Roman society.

The growing urban death trap was not, however, the only demographic
drain on the rural population of Italy. Traditionally, historians have emphasized the migration of citizens to the provinces.[40] Some of these colonists
came from the cities, and from Rome in particular, but most of them were
veterans who on discharge from the army were rewarded with provincial
land. Italian peasants who served in the army to retire as colonists in the
provinces depleted the numbers of Italy's rural free population. However,
with the exception of the last few decades of the Republic, the drain from
emigration was quite small compared to the permanent devastation from
urban mortality.[41]

---

[38] This is based on the estimates for the size and composition of the population in Hopkins (1978a)
      68–9: the free population of the city of Rome grew from 150,000 in 225 BCE to 600,000 in 28 BCE
      During that same period, the free population of the other cities in Italy increased from 250,000
      to 500,000. The urban slave population grew by about half a million to something like 800,000,
      of whom perhaps 300,000–350,000 lived in the city of Rome; Scheidel (this volume) 175. Of a
      cohort of rural men, only 40–45 per cent survived until they were twenty years old (43.5 per cent in
      Coale and Demeny (1983) model south, level 3, life expectancy at birth = 24.6). We cannot estimate
      immigration into the cities of Roman Italy by just adding my two estimates, the first one to make
      the cities grow, and the second for what was required to keep them from shrinking. Italy's cities did
      not continue to grow for ever, whereas in an earlier period they had required far fewer immigrants to
      retain their smaller sizes. Even so, Late Republican immigration to the cities of Italy may perhaps be
      estimated as something like 15,000–20,000 adults per year, requiring about 30,000–45,000 births.
[39] Mazzarino (1951) 230–8 and Hodges and Whitehouse (1983) 51.
[40] Brunt (1971) 159–265; Hopkins (1978a) 67.
[41] Until the middle of the first century BCE, there were about 1,000 adult male emigrants annually in
      Brunt and Hopkins's estimates (Hopkins (1978a) 68, table 1.2, c; Brunt (1971) 262–4). Emigration
      became a major demographic drain only in the Late Republic: Brunt and Hopkins estimate 265,000
      adult male emigrants in the forty years from 49 BCE to 8 BCE, or an annual average of about
      6,500 adult males; Brunt (1971) 262–4; Hopkins (1978a) 68–9. Scheidel (1996a) 93–5 rightly cautions
      against underestimating the impact of military recruitment.

The cities of Roman Italy needed large numbers of warm bodies to grow and then maintain their populations. How many such migrants could the Italian countryside supply? Again I want to mirror Wrigley's research. He argued that London had a dramatic impact on British demography and culture: 'the survivors to adult years of almost one sixth of all births taking place in the country would be living in London twenty years or so after the arrival of the birth cohort...'[42] For Roman Italy, the figures are perhaps even more remarkable. As I want to show, rural Italy could, in fact, not supply enough warm bodies for migration to Rome. Let us do some of the sums first, and then worry about the implications.

Wrigley estimated that in the relatively favourable conditions of eighteenth-century England the rural birth surplus was unlikely to have been more than 5 per 1,000.[43] If that high figure applied to Roman Italy, it translates into a rural birth surplus of at most 20,000 births.[44] That may have been just enough around 225 BCE (10,000 births were needed to compensate for the natural urban decrease of 4,500, leaving 10,000 births for urban growth), but not thereafter. We may conclude, therefore, that the urban demand for warm bodies exceeded rural supply in Roman Italy by a significant margin. For a long period, rural Italy can have supplied only about half the necessary immigrants.

The two ways to cope with urban demand for immigrants were either, indeed, rural depopulation, or mass immigration from outside Italy. Traditionally, and in the wake of ancient authors, rural depopulation and the replacement of citizen peasants by slaves have been given a great deal of attention. The problem with it, however, is that it can only serve as a one-off supply of urban immigrants. If I am right that the demand for urban immigrants continued to exist, owing to high urban excess mortality, then rural depopulation can only have served for a short period. After that, some other source would have had to be found with even greater urgency, or the cities would have declined again. In my view, the alternative to rural depopulation, mass immigration into Italy, deserves more attention. Indeed, as Juvenal wrote: 'Long since Syrian Orontes has flowed into the Tiber, and has brought with it its language and manners.'[45] The mainly long-term and structural demand for urban immigrants needed a steady and long-term supply.

---

[42] Wrigley (1978) 221.   [43] Wrigley (1978) 218.
[44] During the last two centuries of the Republic, Italy had a rural population of 4–4.5 million people: Hopkins (1978a) 68.
[45] Juv. 3.62.

SOLITUDO ITALIAE

The classic accounts of the rural history of Roman Italy under the Republic all stress the profound changes which took place under the impact of Roman imperialism. Roman magnates acquired larger and larger tracts of land, either from impoverished peasants, or through the legal or not so legal occupation of public land. On these new properties, they practised a new kind of agriculture, characterized by large production units, a stress on market crops, and wine and olive oil in particular, and the presence of a sometimes quite luxurious residence for the landowner: the villa. As a workforce, instead of the former peasants, they used the newly captured slaves. Thus, Hopkins argued, they could use labour more intensively, and move to crops with higher added values.[46]

This image of an Italy given over to large slave estates working for the urban market is derived almost directly from some ancient literary sources. Not surprisingly Marx, Engels, and their later admirers were highly impressed.[47] Classic is Plutarch's graphic description of Tiberius Gracchus' journey through Etruria:[48]

when Tiberius on his way to Numantia passed through Etruria and found the country almost depopulated and its husbandmen and shepherds imported barbarian slaves, he first conceived the policy which was to be the source of countless ills to himself and to his brother.

Appian is not so dramatic, and gives the account that found its way directly into the textbooks:[49]

for the rich, taking possession of the greater part of the undistributed lands and being emboldened by the lapse of time to believe that they would never be dispossessed, absorbing any adjacent strips and their poor neighbours' allotments partly by purchase under persuasion and partly by force, came to cultivate vast tracts instead of single estates, using purchased slaves as agricultural labourers and herdsmen, since free labourers could be drawn from agriculture into the army. At the same time the ownership of slaves brought them great gain from the multitude of their progeny, who increased free from danger because they were exempt from military service. Thus certain powerful men became extremely rich and the class of slaves multiplied throughout the country, while the Italian people dwindled in numbers and strength, oppressed by penury, taxes, and military service. If they had

---

[46] Hopkins (1978a) 2–3.
[47] Schtaerman (1969); Kolendo (1980); Gabba and Pasquinucci (1979), reviewed in Barker (1982); Carandini (1988), reviewed in Rathbone (1990); Giardina and Schiavone (1981) reviewed masterfully in Rathbone (1983).
[48] Plut. *Vit. Ti. Gracch.* 8.   [49] App. *BCiv.* 1.7.

any respite from these evils, they passed their time in idleness, because the land was held by the rich, who employed slaves instead of free men as cultivators.

These are powerful images. Moreover, they can be complemented archaeologically. Numerous villas have been found and excavated, originally mostly for their luxury finds, but later also to validate the existence of a slave mode of production. Whoever had any doubts could visit a real villa, with cells for slaves, and iron chains for the night.

My argument against this paradigm consists of two parts. First, I want to discuss ancient evidence. I want to remind you that our literary evidence is in fact limited and mostly late. I also want to remind you of the growing archaeological evidence for the continuity of small-scale farming and of cereal farming. Second, I want to show you that a major shift from cereal agriculture to wines and olives is implausible because that would not produce what people needed. It would have left Italy both fatally hungry, and dangerously drunk.

ANCIENT EVIDENCE

I am not the first to caution that the literary evidence for the modern orthodoxy is in fact quite limited.[50] There are a few key passages quoted over and over again, and that is about it. Moreover, the two main sources, Plutarch and Appian, were in fact written more than two centuries after the events. What I have quoted is enough to show that they did not share Republican senators' distaste for the Gracchan efforts at reform. Ideologically, we are in different worlds. Their accounts are too obviously coloured by imperial concerns to be unproblematic sources of simple truth. In fact, the moralizing about agriculture and the need for peasant soldiers are recurrent imperial themes. Domitian's concern that viticulture threatened cereal agriculture, or Pliny's praise for the imperial *alimenta* are leaves from the same book as the imperial accounts of the Gracchi.

Let us now return to Plutarch's graphic description of Tiberius Gracchus' journey through Etruria. John Ward-Perkins' decision to mount what would become the first large modern field survey in Etruria rather than anywhere else is one of those decisive moments in the history of scholarship.[51] Year by year a new and far more varied picture emerged from what could

---

[50] The scholar who imagines he has something new to say about the Roman Republic often has to discover that Ernst Badian has been there before. Badian (1972) is fundamental for the debate, and a fascinating example of how despite different methodologies and intellectual tastes somewhat similar conclusions may still be reached. From a vast bibliography, see also Earl (1963) and Boren (1969).

[51] Potter (1979).

actually be seen and found on the ground. Villas there were indeed, but
also many traces of smaller sites. Others are much better equipped than I
am to discuss the results and implications of the many field-surveys that
followed the South Etruria survey. Two observations should be made, however. The first is that what once was a unified picture, has now become a
picture of great regional variation. Some of that may be due to the ideological preferences of the scholars working in particular regions, but some of
it seems real. The second observation is that within particular regions we
often find a continuation of smaller farms besides the newer bigger farms
and villas. Much of the earlier imagery of villa agriculture as the dominant
mode of agricultural exploitation had been inspired by the highly visible
remains of Pompeian villas and viticulture.[52] They had impressed the young
Rostovtzeff, and thus became part of the standard fare of ancient historical
teaching.[53]

As so often in ancient historical argument the problem of interpretation
is in the jump we have to make from data that rarely prove more than
the existence of phenomena to an argument about their prominence. How
many villas do we need before we can confidently say villas not only existed,
but were also prominent, or even dominant? For Pompeii, I have argued
that the highly visible remains of the villas obscure the continuation of
small-scale cereal agriculture in much of that city's territory.[54] When you
want to prove the prominence of the slave mode of production, and decide
to excavate a villa, of course, what you find is a villa.[55] We now know that in
many parts of Italy, below the highly visible surface of new villas, a *longue
durée* of many small farms remained.

AGGREGATES

We cannot reconstruct Italian agriculture from the remaining literary and
archaeological data. Here, we must try to estimate aggregate production
and consumption of food in Roman Italy. We should not be under the
illusion that we can attain aggregate level by adding up known instances.
Even true stories can make untrue history. More than anyone, it has been
Keith Hopkins who has cautioned us against the perils of such inductive
reasoning. He also pioneered the parametric methods to simulate the past.[56]

---

[52] Jongman (1988) 112–23.   [53] Jongman (forthcoming a) for a discussion.
[54] Jongman (1988) 97–154.
[55] Carandini and Settis (1979); Carandini (1985). See also the bibliography cited in my n. 47.
[56] His innovations in historical demography have been most important, and paved the way for
     what has become the biggest innovation in ancient history of the last few decades. For a

Such estimates are not a frivolous game of numbers, as is sometimes suggested. On the contrary, it is a game with tight rules. These rules can be so tight because in pre-industrial societies the limits of the possible were narrow, and mostly dictated by nature. Most people were living near subsistence, and were not much more than hungry mammals. They consumed little more than basic food, and of that often only just enough to avoid starvation. The age-specific incidence of their deaths was within a narrow band, mostly determined by human physiology and by the epidemiology of infectious diseases. Compared to the insecurity of our written sources, such estimates are a big improvement.

The rules of this game are also tight because the variables in our models are interconnected. What we believe about one variable dramatically reduces what we can realistically believe about another. Mortality, for example, may be high or low, but if it is high, either the birth rate or immigration must be high as well to avoid population decline.[57] A failure to appreciate the interconnection between variables is probably at the root of some of the wildly problematic estimates for population, consumption, or production in the older scholarly literature.

Before we go into a detailed discussion of production and consumption estimates, it may be useful to show why the traditional view that a significant part of Italian agriculture was transformed into viticulture is implausible. If only a quarter of Italy's cultivable land was indeed used for viticulture, this could have produced enough wine for the entire population of the Roman Empire.[58] Moreover, shipping all that wine from Italy to other areas across the Mediterranean was a twenty-five times bigger job than supplying the city of Rome with grain.[59] If vineyards were as prominent as tradition suggests, Italy was drowning in wine.

We can also reconstruct the relative importance of viticulture from the other side: roughly how large was urban demand for wine, and how much land was needed to produce that wine?[60] One hectolitre is a realistic rough

---

survey: Jongman (2000b), 267–71. For an excellent recent discussion of Roman demography: Scheidel (2001a).

[57] Scheidel (1997) is a good example of the logic.

[58] Italy had probably about 100,000 sq. km of cultivable land. One hectare could yield perhaps 2,000 litres of wine. Total wine production, therefore, would be 2.5 million × 20 hectolitres = 50 million hectolitres. For details, below, p. 114.

[59] Even with large ships of 400 tonnes, this freight represents some 12,500 shiploads. Hopkins (1983a) 97–102 for the size of ships. If the city of Rome had a population of 1 million, and if people ate grain at a rate of only 200 kg per head, total grain consumption was about 200,000 tonnes. For these and other estimates: Jongman (2000b), and Jongman (2001).

[60] My model is simple: it ignores the possibility of net imports of wine and oil. If we assume that there were such net imports, urban demand for Italian wine and oil must have been even less important.

estimate for annual *per capita* wine consumption.[61] Given the prominence
of (young) children in the age distribution, it boils down to something like
the proverbial bottle of wine a day for an adult. As a population average, that
is quite high, but comparable to early modern consumption figures from
France and Spain. The productivity of vineyards may vary enormously, but
quantity goes at the expense of quality. Perhaps 2,000 litres per hectare is a
realistic annual average.[62] Therefore, to produce enough wine for an urban
population of 1.9 million (1.9 million hectolitres) took no more than 95,000
hectares, or about 1 per cent of the cultivable land of Roman Italy.[63] To
produce all good wine for elite demand took even less land: for that, an area
of just over 11 × 11 kilometres was more than enough.[64] The production of
quality wines undoubtedly made some people rich and others happy, but it
is no more than a footnote in Italy's agricultural history. It is unlikely that
Italy was covered in vineyards.

A similar calculation for olive oil is more problematic. Both consumption
per head and production per hectare are far more insecure. However, let
us see whether that affects the argument. I shall use Mattingly's estimates,
because he tries to argue that olive oil production and consumption were
enormous. His estimates are unlikely to be too low. His consumption figure
is 20 litres per head per year. On this basis, total Italian urban demand
amounts to 380,000 hectolitres. He estimates an average production of
400 kg = 440 litres[65] of oil per hectare. In short, the production of all
olive oil for the cities of Roman Italy needed about 85,000 hectares, or
850 sq. km. That is almost the same as was required to produce the wine
for Italy's cities.

---

[61] Hopkins (1978a) 3 calculates a figure of 100 litres for mid eighteenth-century Madrid. Ringrose (1983) 119–21 gives lower figures for the eighteenth century, but higher figures for the seventeenth century. Braudel (1979) 1 202 quotes 100–120 litres for mid-sixteenth-century Valladolid, and 120 litres for Paris on the eve of the Revolution. When higher figures are quoted, they are almost invariably for adult males. Children drink less.

[62] Duncan-Jones (1982) 40, 45; Rathbone (1981) 12–13; Jongman (1988), 132.

[63] I follow my earlier estimate for agricultural land in Roman Italy in Jongman (1988) 67: 100,000 sq. km.

[64] The entire Italian elite of senators, equestrians and decurions, and their families, perhaps amounted to something like 125,000 people (I follow my estimates in Jongman (1988) 193: I assume that there were 600 senators, 5,000 knights and 20,000 decurions in Italy). At a consumption per head of 100 litres per year – I do not think that the rich drank appreciably more than this average for the population at large – total elite consumption of quality wines may thus be estimated at about 125,000 hectolitres per annum. Let us assume that productivity of quality wine is well below average, at 1,000 litres per hectare. Even with a fairly high consumption estimate, and my low productivity estimate, only 12,500 hectares were required to produce all wine for the elite. That is a square of eleven kilometres, or only just over 0.1 per cent of all Italian agricultural land.

[65] The specific gravity of olive oil is about 0.9.

A vast urban demand for wine and olive oil did not require much land.[66] An implication of this is that we should not be surprised that relatively small areas could become major centres of specialized production. We may think of Spanish or North African oil or of some of the famed viticultural districts. It was easy to become a major producer of a relatively minor crop. The real contribution of olives and olive oil was that they were high-quality nutrition making up the deficiencies of a cereal-based diet, and that, as with wine, they allowed a significantly higher production of calories per unit area.[67]

Compared with the small area needed to produce oil and wine for urban consumers, far more land was needed to satisfy their hunger for cereals. The estimate of the consumption of grain per head is relatively secure. We know that cereals provided most calories in the diet, and the total caloric requirement is tightly set by human biology. Let us assume that on average 200 kg of wheat were required per head per year.[68] On that assumption, total Italian urban demand for wheat would be 380,000 metric tonnes per annum. How much land was required to produce all that? Let us assume a two-field system with a net yield of 400 kg per cultivated hectare. If that is realistic, then feeding Italy's cities with cereals required 1.9 million hectares / 19,000 sq. km of arable land. That is ten times more than the joint requirement of wine and oil production, and about 20 per cent of Italy's agricultural land.

The argument would not be affected by slightly different figures. In the end, my argument rests on the simple fact that under prevailing conditions, a hectare of agricultural land could feed about one person with cereals, but produce enough wine for about twenty people. Therefore, cereal agriculture must have remained the mainstay of agriculture.[69]

Italy's agriculture may not have changed as dramatically as some scholars have claimed. Cereal agriculture continued to dominate rural life. More than before, however, this grain went to the cities. The needs of the city of Rome even exceeded the production potential of Italian agriculture, and

---

[66] I appreciate that land use is only one way of measuring the importance of a crop. Cereals require much land. Olive oil and wine also require a fair amount of capital. Viticulture, moreover, is labour-intensive. The ancient agronomists agree that wine was the most profitable crop. As a result, the production of olive oil and wine are more important than would appear from just their land use. However, I do not believe that my argument is greatly affected.

[67] Here, I refer to work in progress by my student Bouke van Laethem.

[68] Wheat was not the only cereal consumed. It was, however, the preferred choice. In Rome the distributions were of wheat. Romans also consumed other food, such as vegetables, dairy products, some meat, and wine and oil. To avoid spurious complication I ignore these for now. See Jongman (2001) 1081–3 for a more nuanced analysis of the diet, and its implications.

[69] Spurr (1986) is fundamental.

required the taxation of provincials.[70] To a varying degree, cereal farmers in Italy and the provinces became integrated into a wider world. Whether that improved their lives, or not, is a different matter, which we cannot go into now.[71] But perhaps we should remind ourselves of the refeudalization of the lands east of the Elbe in the eighteenth century: that occurred as a response to their integration into the West European grain market. Exploiting peasants had become more profitable when a market for their products emerged. Roman peasants of the Late Republic may have experienced similar difficulties.

SLAVES

In the last part of this chapter I want to discuss what my views imply for the location of slaves in Italian society. In particular, I want to argue that, perhaps because of the powerful images of plantation slavery in the Americas, we have been too ready to assume that Roman slavery's place was primarily in agriculture, and in villa agriculture above all. We must not forget that the overwhelming majority of individually known slaves from antiquity lived in the cities. In fact, the vast majority of all known inhabitants of the city of Rome were slaves or freedmen.[72]

The city of Rome harboured the power elite of the entire empire, and their attendants. A few thousand senators and knights, each with at least a few dozen domestic slaves, imply at least a hundred thousand (and probably many more) slaves who lived in Rome. Even without many people like the urban prefect Pedanius Secundus, whose four hundred slaves were put to death as punishment for the murder of their master, the slaves owned by the imperial elite were many.[73] Add to this perhaps twice as many rich people who would have been town councillors if they had lived in other cities, each with a dozen slaves, and we have at least another hundred thousand slaves. Add to that the slaves of the imperial household and bureaucracy, and all those slaves in domestic service or crafts owned by those who were

---

[70] Jongman (2000b) 279 for the argument that the demand of the city of Rome exceeded the potential of the Italian countryside: 'in practice every area with some means of relatively easy sea or river transport (i.e. Sicily and the western coastal areas) would have had to feed Rome. There would not have been food for other urban life in these parts.' Moreover, Italy was exempt from taxation, so supplies would have had to be bought in the market.

[71] De Neeve (1984); Johne, Köhn and Weber (1983).   [72] Cf. Huttunen (1974).

[73] Tac. *Ann.* 14.42–5 for this tale of Roman harshness. As to numbers of domestic slaves, we must appreciate that my tentative numbers include children. So actual working slaves would be far fewer, given the large proportion of children in an urban population. However, the age distribution may be very uneven: below, pp. 117–18.

neither rich nor particularly poor, and it is clear that, whatever the precise numbers, slaves were a large proportion of the urban population. Beloch estimated that between them, resident aliens, soldiers and slaves numbered about 300,000.[74] That is probably too conservative.

Slaves are indeed very visible in our record, even if scholars have tried to play down the significance of that record. In my view, however, the overwhelming presence of slaves and, particularly, freedmen in the urban epigraphy has been argued away too light-heartedly. Traditionally, that epigraphic prominence has been explained by an epigraphic mentality. Overjoyed by their newly won freedom, freed slaves were keen to commemorate their lives and relationships to the outside world. I can well imagine that they were, but the emphasis in many of the somewhat more informative memorials is on familial relationships, career in life, or the special circumstances and tragedy of death. I really see no reason why those should be concerns of freed slaves only. In fact, much of the same was commemorated in the funeral epigraphy of the Roman elite. Of course we should not take the proportion of freedmen in the urban epigraphy as proxy for the proportion of freedmen in urban life. The valid argument that they may be epigraphically over-represented, however, may be pushed too far if we treat the evidence as no more than a cultural phenomenon.

Sometimes, moreover, we have sets of data where a potential epigraphic habit is irrelevant. We may note, for example, the large numbers of freedmen in professional associations.[75] Clearly, freeborn and freed mixed in these *collegia*, and clearly the freeborn did not hide their presence. There simply were many freedmen in these associations. Another set of data is the set of witnesses in the documents of the Pompeian auctioneer L. Caecilius Iucundus.[76] If, as I argued, they represent some cross-section of the more well-to-do Pompeians, then the overwhelming presence of freedmen is truly remarkable.[77]

The evidence for large numbers of urban freedmen is not confined to any particular period of late Republican or Imperial history. Clearly, for many generations, freedmen were a large part of the free urban population. In fact, they are so prominent that that in itself creates a problem. In principle, their status was a transient one. Children born after the manumission of their mothers were freeborn. The conventional assumption that urban manumissions were frequent and early was a stock theme of ancient moralists' complaints, but it is incompatible with a high proportion of freedmen

---

[74] Hopkins (1978a) 96–8.   [75] Royden (1988).   [76] Andreau (1974); Jongman (1988) ch. VI.

[77] Jongman (1988) 264–73; Jongman (forthcoming a), for some recent thoughts on the subject of Pompeian demography and social reproduction.

in the urban population. It would have increased the freeborn population by too much. Therefore, manumissions were perhaps less frequent and also later, leaving in slavery the offspring born before manumission. Particularly if manumission was late, slaves and freedmen were not so much members of different social groups, but members of different age cohorts.

The urban slave population may have lost fewer reproductive members through manumission than previously thought. It did lose some, however. Scheidel has recently developed some scenarios for this: 5.7 per 1,000 in his intermediate schedule.[78] If slave owners wanted to continue to manumit, then they needed to acquire new slaves to replace those manumitted and not replaced by their own offspring born in captivity. The slave population also lost many to nature, however. Just as Scheidel argued that natural reproduction was by far the most important source of new slaves, I want to argue that urban excess mortality was probably the most important drain on an urban slave population. I have argued earlier that excess mortality for the urban population as a whole was probably in the order of 5–10 per 1,000. This figure would be the same or, if anything, higher for slaves. Between them, manumission and the Big Reaper accounted for an annual decrease of the urban slave population of 10–15 per 1,000, if not more. Those are substantial numbers.

These hypothetical figures also show how manumission of slaves could and probably would have made up for a large part of the natural decrease of the free urban population. In short, I think Scheidel is perfectly right that slave reproduction is likely to have been the most important source of slaves from one generation to the next. However, owing to very high urban mortality there was a shortfall in the cities that had to be made up with recent slave immigrants if the slave population was to maintain its size. Since through manumission the slave population probably also provided a large part of the warm bodies needed to maintain the free population, all the more fresh slaves were necessary. Demographically it was slavery that underwrote an unprecedented urbanism under horribly unhealthy conditions. It was manumission which in due time transformed slave immigrants into free citizens. Manumission, after all, was mostly an urban thing.

Finally, I want to return with you to the transformation of the Roman elite in the Late Republic. They were, after all, the main buyers (or captors) of this new bulk of immigrants. They apparently exercised most of the demand for urban labour. Why did they want more and more slaves? My answer would be that that is part of the transformation of the life-style of the

---

[78] Scheidel (1997).

Roman elite, and of those aspiring to be part of it. Clearly, from all accounts during the last two centuries BCE they began to live in larger and larger houses, surrounding themselves with more and more domestic servants, and with more and more luxurious goods. Within those households more and more separate functions were distinguished. The Roman elite had become significantly richer, and could well afford the expense. In any pre-industrial society, living in a large house with numerous domestic staff is one of the defining elements of wealth and status. It made life more convenient, but, clearly, beyond some level that was not the point. Domestics underscore one's prestige in a society where public prestige was important, and where competition for status was getting fiercer all the time. What was more fitting for the cosmopolitan elite of a World Empire than to live in almost royal style, and to be surrounded by slaves from conquered lands and beyond?[79]

EPILOGUE

The urban population of Roman Italy grew enormously during the last two centuries of the Republic. Of Italian cities, it was Rome itself which grew most of all. That is uncontroversial. Disagreement emerges when we imagine how this could happen, and what else happened. Traditionally, the growth of Rome is attributed to the flight of destitute peasants to the city, and their replacement by newly imported slaves. In that view, the migration was a one-off process. Once the city of Rome reached its new and much larger size, and once the country was largely depleted of free peasants, there was little need or possibility for continued migration. Thus, for a few centuries agriculture was thought to have been dominated by a slave mode of production.

Instead, I have argued that it cannot have been like this for two groups of reasons. The first is that urban mortality, particularly in the city of Rome itself, was likely to have been so high that the need for immigrants was not only large, but that migration was also continuous and structural, if a decline of the urban population was to be avoided. More immigrants were needed each year than even a prospering rural Italy could have provided, let alone a countryside depopulated of its peasants. The second group of objections is that the traditional model conflicts with more recent archaeological research, and exaggerates the changes in the rural economy beyond the plausible. So, I have argued that the archaeological picture is now more

---

[79] Solin (1971) rightly argues that Greek cognomina need not necessarily denote Greek ethnicity, but may indicate former slave status. Therefore, it was fashionable to give slaves Greek names, even if they were not Greeks. It emphasized the foreignness of slaves.

diverse, with more evidence for the continuity of small farms alongside
the new villas. Finally, I have argued that production of wine and oil per
unit area was so high, that at no period were really large areas required
in order to produce sufficient quantities of both products. The traditional
reconstruction with an Italy overgrown with vineyards and olive groves, if
true, implies a large import of cereals, and, particularly, a massive export of
wine and oil, to the extent that the entire Empire would have been drunk
on Italian wine.

My argument also illustrates the difficulties of writing ancient history.
Late and tendentious literary sources proved a treacherous guide. Moreover,
archaeology was hardly better as a source of unmediated 'facts'. Beyond the
usual problems with the interpretation of what survives, the bigger problem
was and is to interpret what did not survive, and to reconstruct behaviour
that did not even leave any traces at the beginning. How about the small
farms that, until quite recently, nobody really wanted to see?[80]

Induction from patchy data is difficult. We cannot reach aggregate level
by adding up known instances. However, as Keith Hopkins has shown ancient historians, the range of the possible is often quite narrow. Moreover,
he has argued that what we assume about one variable often closely cir-
cumscribes what we may assume legitimately about another. It is what he
has called a compatibility theory of truth. We know little, but if we assume
that the urban death rate was higher than the urban birth rate, cities either
needed a continuous flow of immigrants, or else they declined. Without
explicit models to interrelate the variables, isolated facts cannot become
evidence.

My analysis also illustrates the difficulties of writing about historical
change. The ancient world was a pre-industrial society, living within the
limitations of a technology that hardly changed, with a high mortality rate,
and without significant economic growth of the kind that we know in our
world. It was the pessimistic world of the *longue durée*. Thus, for the last
few decades, ancient historians, including myself, have written mostly static
accounts of the structure of 'the' ancient economy, with little reference to
any change. The exception to this has been the recent interest in risk and
uncertainty: antiquity was also a world of the unpredictable. Agricultural
yields were not only low, they also varied enormously from one year to the

---

[80] I have argued something quite similar in Jongman (1988) 97–154. The Pompeian evidence has often
been used to validate the traditional picture. Archaeology has other problems too: how about the
status of those peasants? Were they freeholders, tenants or, even, slaves living and working on their
own?

next.[81] Mortality was high, and also variable and unpredictable.[82] Thus, ancient historians have begun to address the implications of such volatility for social relations.[83] Keith Hopkins, for example, has shown that the Senate was anything but the stable social group it pretended to be: the Roman Senate owed its stability to the effective socialization of new entrants rather than to genetic continuity.[84] We think of traditional society as a world where nothing ever changes, but the opposite is true: it is a world of fundamental uncertainty, mortal risks and extreme volatility. However, that volatility existed within an envelope of long-term continuity, and of ceilings that could not be breached. It was a world of changeless change.[85]

Thus, we have a paradigm that relates the two extremes of historical time: the very long run, and the very short run. Traditionally, however, historians have mostly written about changes and events in an intermediate time-frame: changes in the lives of people that took one, or perhaps a few generations to take effect, and that, by and large, were not reversed almost immediately. Centuries and the reigns of monarchs are historians' stock tools to organize time, and political history has dominated. Writing economic and social history at this intermediate level is more difficult, but the challenge remains: Rome in the Augustan age was undeniably different from Rome in the second century BCE. Traditional accounts of the economic history of the period follow the drama and speed of political events, and mirror aristocratic gloom over the decline of the Republic – if only pre-industrial economies change as fast as that. Roman economic history from the literary sources is a succession of crises and decline.[86] However, the scale of the Roman economy actually increased quite significantly, and at least the rich had become far wealthier (it is more doubtful if there was real economic growth[87]). Intellectually, we are only just beginning to develop models and concepts for such change. My contribution here has been quite modest. I have not done more than what may be called comparative statics: a static structure is brought into disequilibrium by an intervening variable (the growth of Empire and the concomitant growth in the demand for people in Rome), until such time as a new (political and demographic) equilibrium emerges in the Augustan age. However, that was dramatic enough – even if the real drama escaped contemporaries.

---

[81] Gallant (1988); Halstead (1987); Halstead and O'Shea (1988),   [82] Above, pp. 106–9, 113.
[83] Saller (1994); Jongman (forthcoming b).   [84] Hopkins (1983b) chs. 2 and 3.
[85] Jongman (1988) chs. 6 and 7; Jongman (forthcoming a).
[86] Cf. the revealing analysis in Edwards (1993).
[87] Real economic growth presupposes a sustained growth of aggregate national income, and of per capita incomes as well. I will soon return to this elsewhere.

The city of Rome was indeed unique in European history. Renaissance men, living in its ruins, were right to be amazed: it must have felt like living in New York, a century after the explosion of a neutron bomb. Their admiration for ancient Rome has since been questioned by the Romantic insistence that the Middle Ages were not a Dark Age. Moreover, after the dramatic social changes of the Industrial Revolution, it has become much harder to be impressed. We live in a radically different world. Thus, ancient historians have forgotten what their predecessors knew: Rome was the marvel of European history. They have allowed the debate on the ancient economy to become stuck in a discussion of relations between town and country, and forgotten that the Roman Empire was first of all a huge Empire; economically it was more than the sum of many Pompeiis. They have allowed themselves to believe that, really, Rome was a less developed ancestor of the medieval and early modern world. More seriously, they have allowed antiquity to disappear from the research agenda on economic growth and development. Nowadays, and almost without exception, the history of European urbanization or economic development (or any European history) is taken to begin somewhere around the year 1000. That only makes sense to the extent that the decline after antiquity was indeed horrendous. Of course, it is uncomfortable that the modernization of Europe was more complex than a simple and unilinear story, but so be it. Ancient history matters.

Ancient Rome was not only unique in its achievements, but also in its horrors. My reconstruction of the demography of Roman urban growth (especially when taken together with Scheidel's contribution in this volume) and its voracious appetite for fresh bodies demonstrates that Rome was also quite unique in its miseries and hardship. Poor peasants and, particularly, slaves from all over the known world had to be moved forcibly to Rome, to replace those who had died in the disease-infected city. Nothing drives home better the gap between the Romans and us than the high and unpredictable mortality that prevailed, particularly in the cities. When Martial recounts the story of the beggar dying in the streets of Rome, surrounded by dogs and vultures, the point of the story is whether the beggar will be eaten dead or alive.[88]

---

[88] Mart. 10.5.11–12.

CHAPTER 6

Rivalling Rome: Carthage

Richard Miles

INTRODUCTION: MAPPING THE WORLD

In the late fourth century CE, Decimus Magnus Ausonius, a wealthy and successful member of the Gallo-Roman elite, wrote a poem in celebration of those cities within the empire which he considered to be the most remarkable. The poem, *Ordo nobilium urbium*, lists twenty cities in descending order of importance: Rome, Constantinople, Carthage, Antioch, Alexandria, Treves, Milan, Capua, Aquileia, Arles, Seville, Cordova, Tarragona and Braga, Athens, Catana, Syracuse, Toulouse, Narbonne and Bordeaux. Even taking into account its author's understandable bias towards the Latin West where most of his career had taken place, it would be hard to read this poem as a representation of the geo-political reality of the Roman empire in the 380s CE. There is a noticeable paucity of cities from the eastern empire, and the importance of some of the loci listed such as Syracuse and Capua could be consigned to the distant past.

Ordo nobilium urbium is in many ways a mapping-out of Ausonius himself. The cities are physical co-ordinates charting a glittering career; Toulouse was where he had studied; Milan and Aquileia, seats of government from which his former pupil the emperor Gratian had appointed Ausonius and members of his family to high office; Treves, Capua, Arles, Narbonne, Carthage, Catana and Syracuse, cities which had all come under his joint jurisdiction when appointed *praefectus Galliarum* in 378 CE; and, most importantly, the two cities, whose positions at the beginning and end of the *ordo* mark the starting-point and summation of his life achievements: Bordeaux, his city of birth and the location for a well-appointed marriage and a successful academic career, and Rome, where he had been elevated to the consulship in 379 CE.[1]

---

[1] See Matthews (1975) ch. 3 for the public careers of Ausonius and his family. For Ausonius' life and career in Bordeaux see Sivan (1993) 31–93.

Perhaps more importantly, *Ordo nobilium urbium* also functions as a guide to the cultural landscape which Ausonius claims to inhabit. A recent study of literary representations of Rome has argued convincingly that the city was, and still is, constructed with texts as well as stone, bricks and mortar.[2] To know a city was not just a matter of being informed about its buildings but also about having knowledge of its past, a past which was constructed by, and represented through, texts. Ausonius furnishes his reader with a series of anecdotes about each city which stand as a mighty testament to the *paideia* of the author. These anecdotes do not stand in isolation from one other but link the different cities with one another and in doing so forge a coherent and precise vision of Ausonius' world.[3]

Ordo nobilium urbium celebrates the supremacy of the city of Rome. Her pre-eminence is emphasized by the linear structure of the poem. Rome features first in a descending order of importance. It is also striking that Rome requires just one line stating rather than arguing for her special position in sharp contrast to the wordy justifications in which the claims for other cities are made.[4] Rome's supremacy is also highlighted by its exemption from the poem's strict linear progression. By constant reference to and juxtaposition with the other cities, Rome emerges as the central reference-point in Ausonius' vision of the world. The reader is told that the great buildings of Milan are not overshadowed by having Rome so close by; Arles is 'the little Rome of Gaul'; Capua had once had pretensions to be 'a second Rome' and his love of Bordeaux has to be tempered by his allegiance to the city of Rome.[5]

With its emphasis on the importance of the city of Rome in the construction of Roman identity, *Ordo nobilium urbium* does not present a radical departure from previous works written by those who had come to the capital city and done well. The final lines of the poem with their insistence that every Roman had two *patriae*, his place of birth and Rome itself, echo the words of Cicero in his exploration of his respective relationships with the city and his home-town of Arpinum.[6] What it emphasizes is the pervasiveness of this discourse even in a period when the city of Rome had lost

---

[2] Edwards (1996). This book has greatly influenced my thinking on Carthage as a 'textual' city.
[3] For the importance of the written word in the representation of imperial space see Nicolet (1991) 1–14.
[4] Auson. *Ordo nob. urb.* 1, *Prima urbes inter, divum domus, aurea Roma*.
[5] Milan = Auson. *Ordo nob. urb.* 7.11, *nec iuncta premit vicinia Romae*; Capua = *ibid*. 8.16, *Roma altera quondam*; Arles = *ibid*. 10.2, *Gallula Roma*; Bordeaux = *ibid*. 20.40, *diligo Burdigalum, Romam colo*.
[6] Edwards (1996) 18.

its position as the administrative and governmental centre of the western empire.[7]

Through her omnipresence in a series of texts purportedly sketching the geographical setting and historical past of a number of cities within the Roman empire, the place of the city of Rome at the centre of empire is continually reasserted. In this way *Ordo nobilium urbium* is a prime example of how imperialism is as much about the production and control of the texts through which communities are imagined as it is economic, political or military subjugation. As one recent commentator has argued: 'The ineluctable necessities of conquest and government are to understand (or to believe that one understands) the physical space that one occupies or that one hopes to dominate.'[8]

In the case of the Roman empire, or indeed any imperial conglomerate, no one city is constructed around its own exclusive set of texts: each is created by the same group of contested texts. As an imperial centre, Rome was made up of many different cities and was herself present in every city that made up the Roman empire. It is in this sense, perhaps more than any others, that the city of Rome can be regarded a true Cosmopolis.

Nowhere is this made clearer than in the treatment of the city of Carthage in *Ordo nobilium urbium*. Carthage is portrayed as being in keen competition with Constantinople for second place behind Rome. Ausonius sets this up as a battle between past and present.

One has the advantage in her ancient wealth, the other in her newborn prosperity: the one has seen her day, the other is now rising and by the magnitude of new achievements outshines past renown.[9] (Auson. *Ordo nob. urb.* 4–6)

The dispute is taken to celestial arbitration. Both cities are reminded that it was through heaven's will that their destinies had been altered. The reader is reminded that they had once been Byzantina Lygos and Punica Byrsa. This can be read as a tacit recognition that the agent of these divinely sanctioned changes had been Rome. It was subjugation by Rome that had brought about these metamorphoses. However, this map makes few concessions to temporality. The past and present are fused. Yet it is the author who controls the text by controlling access to the past.

Ausonius is only willing to allow Constantinople its rebirth as a Roman foundation. The new foundation of Carthage as a Roman colony by Gaius Gracchus, Julius Caesar and then Augustus himself is not alluded to.

---

[7] For Rome in late antiquity see Curran (2000).   [8] Nicolet (1991) 2.

[9] *vetus hanc opulentia praefert, | hanc fortuna recens; fuit haec, subit ista novisque | excellens meritis veterem praestringit honorem.*

Carthage is represented by Elissa, the legendary founder of the Punic city. In contrast, the eastern imperial capital is allowed a far more contemporary advocate, the emperor Constantine. Roman Carthage remains locked into looking back at a glorious Punic past whereas Constantinople has been re-born and can look forward to a bright future. Carthage's elevated position in *Ordo nobilium urbium* not only reflects its relative political and economic importance in the fourth century CE, but also the central role played by its Punic forebear in the textual construction of the city of Rome.

This essay is a study of literary accounts of Roman Carthage from its foundation until the mid-fifth century CE. However, in essence it is a study of the city of Rome. As Catharine Edwards argues, there is 'a sense in which the particular resonance of Rome is negotiated against that of other cities'.[10] Carthage, perhaps more than any other urban conglomerate in the empire, helped to define what the city of Rome was in the eyes of contemporary commentators.

The first section of this essay will explore the significance of Punic Carthage in textual representations of the city of Rome throughout the imperial epoch. It will argue that this central role ensured that the re-founding of Carthage consisted of not only of the construction of a new Roman city but also the rebuilding of Punic Carthage. This is not to sug-gest a dichotomization between a 'physical' Roman and a 'textual' Punic city: inscriptions are just one medium which should warn against such an approach. Nor should this be perceived as an assertion of a uniform imperial vision of Roman Carthage: as has been argued above, the city is a culturally contested locus which allows many different visions and ver-sions of it to exist simultaneously. Nor is this a question of separating the 'reality' of Roman Carthage from the self-aggrandizing pseudo-historical fantasies of an educated Roman elite: this was a created body of theory and practice, in which, for many generations, there had been a consider-able material investment.[11] Roman Carthage prospered in the late second and third centuries CE, and as a port became a place on which the city of Rome became increasingly reliant for its grain supply, whilst also providing a launch pad for those challenging for imperial power. The ancient rivalry between Punic Carthage and Rome offered a compelling narrative into which these developments could be placed and justified.

The second section of this essay takes as its subject one particular revolt, that of Gordianus, governor of Africa Proconsularis, in 238 CE. What makes

---

[10] Edwards (1996) 19.
[11] See Ceausescu (1976) for such an approach in relation to reported imperial plans to move the capital of the empire to Alexandria.

this episode so interesting for our purposes is that we have accounts from two very different cultural viewpoints: Herodian, whose intended audience was made up of the senatorial elite of the Greek East in the mid third century CE and the Scriptor Historiae Augustae writing for their Latin counterparts in early fourth-century Rome. It will be argued that these two accounts represent conflicting narratives; one concerning Carthage as a replica of, and possible substitute for Rome, the other as the Punic city, the enemy which had played such a central role in the construction of Rome's past.

From their divergent rhetorical standpoints, one as 'ruler' and the other as 'ruled', both the Scriptor Historiae Augustae and Herodian illustrate the complex relationship between physical place, text and the past in the construction of a Roman imperial discourse. It will be contended that Roman Carthage provided a lens through which the position of the city of Rome as the fulcrum of the empire could be explored and even re-evaluated. What will become clear is that the city of Carthage afforded contemporary commentators the opportunity to make sense of their own relationships with the cosmopolis that was Rome.

KNOWING CARTHAGE, KNOWING ROME

Now it is a colony of the Roman people, but it was once their [the Romans'] determined rival for imperial power. In fact Carthage is now wealthy again, but it remains more famous for the destruction of its ancestor's claims than for the wealth of its present inhabitants.[12]

For contemporary observers the fact that Roman Carthage inhabited the physical space where the Punic city had once stood was of the utmost significance.[13] Just as in literary representations of Rome, places were important as repositories of memories, so too in accounts of Roman Carthage, the Punic city was always present.[14]

An awareness of the perceived threat that the site of Carthage posed must lie behind the tales of Scipio, the conqueror and destroyer of Punic Carthage, variously consecrating the site or placing a curse on anyone who

---

[12] Pompon. Mel. *De chor*. 33. In a recent article Batty (2000) has argued that Mela's is a Phoenician or Punic vision of the world. Mela's extensive reference to Carthage is seen to be indicative of that. However, as will be argued below, the quotation above is very much part of a Roman literary discourse about Punic Carthage.

[13] See Pliny, *HN* 5.24, Livy, *Epit*. 60, who both emphasize that Roman Carthage was built on the site of the Punic city.

[14] Edwards (1996).

attempted to colonize it.[15] The Punic past had left an indelible stain on
the physical landscape of Carthage. Plutarch recounts how during the civil
wars, Pompey's army was swept with rumours that the Carthaginians had
hidden their riches on the site of Carthage during a time of crisis. The
general was powerless to stop his troops picking up tools, and engaging
in an impromptu treasure hunt.[16] Buildings could be pulled down and
whole populations removed but the memories could not be expunged. The
actual physical site where Punic Carthage had once stood was pregnant
with meaning for the educated Roman. Velleius Paterculus in his history
of Rome depicts Marius, the famous Roman, forced into exile by his rival,
Sulla, living a life of poverty in a hut amongst the ruins of Carthage; 'there
Marius, as he looked upon Carthage, and Carthage as she gazed upon
Marius, might well have offered consolation to one another'.[17] An explicit
link is forged between the Punic past and the plans for a new Roman
colony on the site of the city. Appian relates a story about Julius Caesar,
when encamped with his army near the site of the destroyed city, having
a dream in which he saw a whole army weeping. He immediately made a
memorandum stating that Carthage should be colonized.[18]

Caesar's initiative would not have been well received in some quarters.
For many of his peers, a new foundation at Carthage would not provide
a clean break with the past but would rather germinate the seeds for fresh
discord.[19] These concerns are evident in the stories associated with the
various attempts to found a Roman colony on the site in which the reader
is confronted with a series of reminders of the threat that a renascent
Carthage could present to the city of Rome. Appian recounts the following
about the first attempt to found a colony on the site of Carthage by Gaius
Gracchus in 123 BCE:

The officials who were still in Africa laying out the city wrote home that wolves had
pulled up the boundary marks made by Gracchus and Fulvius, and the soothsayers
considered this an ill omen for the colony. So the Senate summoned the *comitia*,
in which it was proposed to repeal the law concerning this colony. When Gracchus
and Fulvius saw their failure in this matter they were furious and declared that the
Senate had lied about the wolves.[20]

---

[15] For the consecration of the site see Cic. *Leg. agr.* 1.5, 2.51. For the cursing of the site see App. *BCiv.*
1.24, *Pun.* 1.35.
[16] Plut. *Vit. Pomp.* 11.3–4.
[17] Vell. Pat. 2.19.4, *cum Marius aspiciens Carthaginem, illa intuens Marium, alter alteri possent esse solacio.*
A similar story is recounted in Plut. *Mar.* 40.9.
[18] App. *Pun.* 8.136.   [19] For such a view see Cic. *Leg. agr.* 2.33.
[20] App. *B Civ.* 1.3.24. The same story is recounted by several other sources: Plut. *Vit. C. Gracch.* 11 also
states that the leading standard was broken into pieces and the sacrificial victims lying on the altars
were scattered by a violent storm. The account of the fifth-century Christian writer, Orosius (5.12),
is the same as that of Appian.

Appian's account is interesting because it suggests that both the Gracchan faction and their enemies were aware that the choice of the wolf as the agent of this ominous warning, an animal which was so central to the foundation stories of the city of Rome, would create alarming associations in the minds of the citizenship. The unease engendered by Punic Carthage might also lie behind Appian's false assertion later in his history that Augustus built the Roman city near by but not on the original site.[21]

Punic Carthage was an important co-ordinate on the cultural landscape of the western Roman empire. The three Punic wars waged between Rome and Carthage in the third and second centuries BCE were perceived to be a turning-point in the development of the city of Rome. Commentators rarely describe the wars as a clash between two empires but rather as that between two cities fighting for the headship of the world.[22] The importance of Punic Carthage to the city of Rome is perhaps best highlighted by the fact that one of the most important historiographical questions asked from the late Republic through to late antiquity was did Rome need Carthage? For those with an agenda of showing that they were themselves living in a period of decline the answer was a resounding yes. For Sallust, trying to make sense of the political malaise of the Late Republic, and Augustine of Hippo and Orosius, anxious to show that it was not with the advent of the Christian emperors that empire had reached its nadir, Rome's descent could be traced to one particular event, the destruction of 'that great whetstone of their brilliance and sharpness, Carthage'.[23]

Carthage is therefore inexorably linked with the city of Rome. The importance of Punic Carthage in the development of the city of Rome was not lost on the Augustan writers.[24] The work of Virgil, Horace, Livy and Ovid amongst others, ensured that Carthage was second only to Troy in its association with the foundation and growth of the city of Rome. In creating a past for the city of Rome, Augustan writers and those who had preceded them also created a past for Punic Carthage.[25]

For the educated elite of Rome to be Roman was to know the city itself. To know the city of Rome required knowledge of Punic Carthage. This

---

[21] App. *Pun.* 8.136.

[22] Sil. *Pun.* 1.7–9 'for a long time it remained unclear, on which of the two citadels Fortune would establish the capital of the world'.

[23] Oros. 4.23. Cf. *ibid*. 5.8, August. *De Civ. D.* 2.18, Sall. *Hist*. 1.9 Vell. Pat. 2.1.

[24] See in particular Feeney (1991); 125–7 for how Virgil and Horace used a literary tradition probably stretching back to Ennius and Naevius in their association of the goddess Juno with Carthage.

[25] The continued importance of Virgil in the literary canon of the late antique western empire (see for instance the commentary of the *Aeneid* by Servius and the *Saturnalia* by Macrobius) was of course a major reason why Punic Carthage retained its relevance. In regard to this see Stahl (1952) 17–23; Collins (1909) 7–10. It is also worth noting that Book 4 of Orosius' *Historiae* commences with a quotation from *Aeneid* 1.203.

was a discourse which was still strikingly relevant to Roman authors writing many generations after the re-foundation of Carthage as a Roman city. The *Punica* of Silius Italicus, a retelling of the Punic wars in epic form, written in the second century CE, was not as one commentator has put it a work 'in which the historical past can only be evoked with the dignity of a museum piece, having become too distant to be used in interpreting the present'.[26] The events and the sentiments expressed in the *Punica* were still as strong a cultural marker for Silius Italicus and his audience as they had been a century or so before.

The same point can be made in regard to the *evocatio*, the formula of prayers supposedly uttered by Scipio to entreat the deities of the besieged city of Carthage to desert their charges. This tradition persists in Latin literature up until at least the fifth century CE, once again highlighting the importance of physical place as a repository of memories in the Roman psyche.[27] The *evocatio* with its promises of new temples and shrines in Rome for the deities of the besieged city as a reward for their desertion is on one level an attempt to tangibly appropriate the past. One late antique source explicitly states that the statue of Caelestis, the patroness deity of Carthage, was indeed brought to Rome by Scipio after the destruction of the city.[28]

The spectre of Punic Carthage imposed itself in other ways on the topography of Rome and Italy. The fact that Hannibal and his army had almost reached the walls of the city, that Carthage nearly had come to Rome, allowed its later inhabitants to indulge in the 'what if?' scenarios of 'virtual history'. The building of a road by the emperor Domitian in 95 CE was occasion for the poet Statius to celebrate the fact that 'no Libyan hordes' under the command of 'their foreign chief' were passing through the Campanian countryside 'in treacherous warfare'.[29] Even treasured objects could be fantasized as having Hannibal himself as a previous owner.[30] The

---

[26] Santini (1991) 8.

[27] Macrob. *Sat*. 9.6–13. It is also worth mentioning Macrobius' exegesis of Scipio's (the conqueror of Carthage) Dream, which had made up the last section of the sixth book of Cicero's *De republica*.

[28] Serv. *Praef*. 12.841. This statement has been accepted by certain scholars. See Picard (1954) 101; Harlesberghe (1984) 2208; Zecchini (1983) 152–3. These have all argued that the cult statue was returned with the foundation of the Gracchan colony. See also Paz Garcia-Bellido (1989) who argues that some of the iconography on a series of late Republican coinage represents Caelestis, thereby proving that her cult had first arrived in Rome with Scipio. Others have remained sceptical. Rives (1995) 67–8 contends convincingly that there is simply not enough evidence to argue for or against such an event. For a discussion of the evidence of the later transferral of the statue to Rome by the emperor Elagabulus and the extent of the cult of *Dea Caelestis* in Rome see below.

[29] Stat. *Silv*. 4.3.4–6.

[30] Stat. *Silv*. 4.6.75–84, a poem about the Hercules statuette of Novius Vindex.

final scene in the *Punica* is of Hanno, Hannibal and Carthage herself walk-
ing in the streets of Rome not in triumph but as part of the triumph of
Scipio.[31] Punic Carthage itself even had a physical presence within the city:
Pliny the Elder recounts that three statues of Hannibal still stood in the
city of Rome 'within the walls of which he alone of its enemies had thrown
a spear'.[32]

Punic Carthage's influence on the physical topography of Rome is also
portrayed in more subtle ways.

Vellius Paterculus, writing during the reign of Tiberius, takes the familiar theme of the onset of moral decline after the final destruction
of Carthage and weaves it into the actual physical fabric of the city of
Rome.

> The state passed from vigilance to slumber, from the pursuit of arms to the pursuit
> of pleasure, from activity to idleness. It was at this time that there were built,
> on the Capitol, the porticoes of Scipio Nasica, the porticoes of Metellus already
> mentioned, and, in the Circus, the portico of Gnaeus Octavius, the most splendid
> of them all; and private luxury soon followed public extravagance.[33]

As a Cosmopolis, Rome was made up of many different cities whose pasts
were intertwined within its own. Throughout its history, to know Rome
meant knowing Carthage. Punic Carthage was therefore a hugely important cultural signifier for those claiming to belong to, or disassociating
themselves from the city of Rome. As we shall see in the next section the
spectre of Punic Carthage is also much in evidence in the foundation and
development of Roman Carthage.

'COLONIA CONCORDIA'?

The foundation of a Roman colony on the site of Punic Carthage was a
long-drawn-out affair. Although originally planned and partly executed
under the direction of the tribune, Gaius Gracchus, in 122 BCE, it was then
refounded by Julius Caesar in 44 BCE and a major building programme
seems to have been undertaken by his adoptive son, the emperor Augustus,
around 29 BCE.[34] The city was built on the classic Roman grid system. The
centre of the city was located on the capitol of the Punic city, the Byrsa. The

---

[31] Sil. *Pun.* 17.625–54.   [32] Pliny, *HN* 34.32, *cuius intra muros solus hostium emisit hastam.*

[33] Vell. Pat. 2.1–2, *in somnum vigilis, ab armis ad voluptates, a negotiis in otium conversa civitas. tum
Scipio Nasica in Capitolio porticus, tum, quas praediximus, Metellus, tum in circo Cn. Octavius multo
amoenissimam moliti sunt, publicamque magnificentiam secuta privata luxuria est.*

[34] For a discussion of the dating of the foundation of Roman Carthage see Le Glay (1985) and Rives
(1995) 21, n. 10.

entire summit of the hill was levelled and 100,000 cubic metres of earth was pushed down the slopes, which were then supported by a series of terracing walls. On the flattened summit, an enormous rectangular platform was constructed on which a series of monumental buildings such as a basilica, temples and forum were built.[35]

This was a consciously undertaken eradication of the physical topography of Punic Carthage, which, even by the exacting standards of the Augustan building programme, was an enormous and ambitious undertaking. Pierre Gros, in an influential article bringing together new information gleaned from the recent excavations on the Byrsa hill with more problematic material uncovered earlier in the twentieth century, has argued that in many ways the Augustan building plan mirrors the Virgilian thesis of the refounding of Carthage as 'un acte de réconciliation à la fois politique et ethnique'.[36] The dramatic reshaping of the physical landscape and the construction of a new religious and administrative topography for the citadel of Carthage not only proclaimed the supremacy of Rome but was also a testament of the peace and concord offered by the new regime after the long years of civil war.[37]

The fact that the foundation of *Colonia Concordia Iulia Karthago* could act as such a powerful symbol of reconciliation stands as a startling admission of the importance of Punic Carthage in the construction of Rome's past.[38] The Augustan foundation in many ways stands as a paradox. On the one hand, this was the self-conscious physical obliteration of the Punic past, whilst, on the other, its status as symbol of imperial *concordia* required that the *discordia* between Carthage and the city of Rome that had precipitated the destruction of the Punic city should not be forgotten. It is this paradox which lies behind many of the accounts of the Roman city of Carthage. For the educated Roman, Carthage, unlike other cites such as Alexandria could never be an *altera Roma*.[39] Unlike Troy, which could never be rebuilt because 'Rome, as Troy's successor, displaces Troy, subsuming its gods, and its glory', Carthage *had to be* rebuilt because the city of Rome was, in part, constructed on the rivalry between the two.[40] In the next section we will see

---

[35] For the clearest summary of the Augustan foundation of Carthage see Rakob (2000).
[36] Gros (1990) 557.   [37] Gros (1990).
[38] Dio Cassius uses the foundation of a Roman colony at Carthage by Julius Caesar as an indication of his *clementia*.
[39] The collection of sources marshalled together by Ceausescu (1976) shows that the idea of Alexandria as a possible subsititute for Rome still provoked considerable discussion right up until late antiquity. However, a note of caution should be sounded over Ceausescu's assertion that these literary vignettes really reflected contemporary imperial policy.
[40] Quote from Edwards (1996) 64. For the Augustan vision of the relationship between Troy and Rome see Edwards (1996) 63–7.

how the pervasive influence of this discourse underpinned the important role that imperial patronage played in the further development of Roman Carthage.

REBUILDING PUNIC CARTHAGE

Despite its being provincial capital of Africa Proconsularis by 38 BCE, the development of Roman Carthage as a major imperial capital was a gradual affair.[41] It was not until the mid-second century CE that Carthage became one of the largest and wealthiest cities in the empire, mainly because of its strategic position as the principal port for the North African corn trade.[42]

Its growing importance attracted imperial patronage: after a disastrous fire, the emperors Antoninus Pius and Marcus Aurelius had instigated a major enlargement of the monumental centre of the city on the Byrsa hill.[43] Another major building phase was undertaken in the reigns of Septimius Severus and Caracalla, including a tax rebate for the funding of a new aqueduct.[44] In the fourth century Carthage again benefited from extensive imperial munificence, beginning with Constantine after its sack on the orders of his imperial rival, Maxentius.[45] Several emperors were given the title of *Conditor* (founder of the city), an honour which had been accorded to the emperor Augustus himself.[46]

The granting of the title *Conditor* highlights not only the pervasive importance of the Augustan principate in the legitimization of later emperors but also that the city of Carthage was still a potent symbol of the *concordia* that underpinned Roman imperial ideology.

Thus, the Punic past played a central role in the development of Roman Carthage: not least for the inhabitants of the city themselves. There has been much recent scholarly interest in the question of 'Punic survivals' in Roman Carthage. Particular attention has been paid to the survival of the Punic language and the religious continuity provided by *Dea Caelestis* and Saturn, who often seem to have been conflated with the great Punic deities Tanit and Baal.[47] However, these major breakthroughs in our

---

[41] Hurst (1985) shows that building on the *insulae* furthest from the administrative centre on the Byrsa hill did not begin until the late first or early second century CE. Even during that period the original street grid does not seem to have been filled in.

[42] Whittaker (2000) 534–6.   [43] Gros (1985); Audollent (1901) 58–9.

[44] Birley (1970); Pera (1979) 106–7.   [45] Lepelley (1981) 12–18.

[46] Although it had been his adoptive father, Julius Caesar, who had refounded the city. See n. 31.

[47] For the survival of Punic see Lancel (1995) 436–8. For *Dea Caelestis* see Harlesberghe (1984) 2208; Zecchini (1983); Audollent (1901) 369–94. Hurst (1999) has put forward a convincing hypothesis that the temple of Caelestis at Carthage was located on the very site of the Punic sanctuary of Tanit, the Tophet. For Saturn see Le Glay (1966).

understanding of the complex cultural identity of the city should not obscure the fact that Carthage was a *Roman* city.

The proud claim made by one of its most celebrated inhabitants, 'Carthage, venerable teacher of our province. Carthage celestial muse of Africa; Carthage, Camena of the toga-clad people', informs rather than contradicts the 'Punicity' of the city.[48] For the elite of Roman Carthage, as for other elites all over the empire, the attainment of *paideia* was an essential prerequisite to their standing within society. Their knowledge of the Punic past was as likely to have been attained through Virgil and the epic poets as it was through worshipping at the shrine of *Dea Caelestis* or the language spoken by their tenant farmers on their estates.[49]

A recent study has shown has how the elite of Carthage actively promoted Romano-African deities such as *Dea Caelestis* in order to forge a strong civic identity. Such cults fulfilled an important mediatory function in the relationship between the Antonine and Severan emperors and the Carthaginian elite. Through a set of coinage issues and dedicatory inscriptions, both parties were able to articulate their relative roles and responsibilities towards one another. By including the emperor as an important figure in the cult, the Romano-African elite showed their obedience to Rome whilst the emperor, by publicly emphasizing the significance of the cult of Caelestis, recognized the importance of Carthage within Africa and the empire as a whole.[50]

The coins with their depictions of *Dea Caelestis*, as the patroness of the city, and superscriptions proclaiming the *Indulgentia Augustorum in Carthaginem*, point more towards a common cultural viewpoint of the past rather than an active programme of cultural assimilation.[51] This was a symbolic re-enactment of the *concordia* between Carthage and Rome.

---

[48] Apul. *Flor.* 20.10 *Carthago prouinciae nostrae magistra venerabilis, Carthago Africae Musa caelestis, Carthago Camena togatorum.*

[49] See for example the references to Punic Carthage in the surviving works of M. Cornelius Fronto, born at the Roman colony of Cirta in Numidia around 95 CE. Writing to console Antoninus Pius after a Parthian victory in Armenia, Fronto recalls a whole series of wars in which Roman defeats preceded ultimate victory. Among his examples he cited the second Punic war. 'After the disaster at Cannae, the Punic general sent to Carthage three bushels of golden rings heaped up, which the Punic soldiers had drawn from the fingers of Roman knights slain in the battle. But not many years later, Carthage was taken, and those who had drawn off the rings were themselves put in chains' (*De bello Parthico* 8, Naber p. 217). Fronto's identification with the Roman side is clear.

[50] Rives (1995) 132–53.

[51] *RIC* 4.1.116–19, nos. 25, 266, 194, 759; *RIC* 4.1.231, nos. 415, 280 and 418. For discussion of the coinage and imperial patronage in Roman Carthage see Rives (1995) 70; Pera (1979) 107; Lepelley (1981) 11.

Paradoxically the aim of this ritual act of reconciliation was to bolster an imperialist discourse which required that the rivalry between Rome and Carthage should never be forgotten.[52]

If Roman Carthage was a 'city of memories', these were not just the distant echoes of the pulverized Punic city buried under tons of African soil. Punic Carthage was part of a body of knowledge and practice which not only justified the existence of the Roman emperor but also placed the city of Rome at the centre of the empire. If the re-foundation and subsequent imperial patronage of the new city of Roman Carthage was in part dictated by the Punic past, it was one which had been extensively reworked in the pages of the Latin literary canon. As will be shown below, the ancient rivalry between the cities of Rome and Carthage was not a static entity consigned to the distant past. In the third and fourth centuries CE, Rome's increasing reliance on the corn of North Africa, and a series of revolts, provided contemporary Latin commentators with an opportunity to add a new episode to the Punic wars.

THE REVOLT OF THE GORDIANS

The economic prosperity and strategic importance of Carthage in the imperial epoch can to a great extent be attributed to the corn trade. North Africa, along with Egypt, had become the principal supplier of the *annona* to the city of Rome. Carthage as the principal port of Africa Proconsularis boomed. The reliance of the city of Rome on the African corn fleet and hence Carthage itself was further increased in the fourth century when the Alexandrian fleet was diverted in order to supply the new urban metropolis of Constantinople.[53]

It was this strategic importance in relation to the city of Rome that ensured that Carthage and the province of Africa Proconsularis became a favoured base for those who sought imperial power. The revolt of Papirius Dionysius in 190, although in Rome, seems to have been provoked by the deliberate withholding of corn supplies from Carthage. The Gordians in 238, Domitius Alexander in 308, Gildo and Boniface in the late fourth / early fifth centuries all attempted to use control of Carthage in order to control the corn supply of Rome.[54]

---

[52] One might wish to think here of the repeated collective 'forgetting' of the American Civil War discussed in Anderson (1991) 200–1.
[53] Jones (1964) 698, 828.
[54] For the revolt of Papirius see Whittaker (1964); Picard (1959) 59–60. For the Gordians see Loriot and Nony (1997) 688–724. For Gildo see Cameron (1970) 93–123.

These events threw the relationship between the cities of Carthage and Rome into sharp relief for those who looked on. The revolt of 238 CE, led by M. Antonius Gordianus Sempronianus, governor of Africa Proconsularis, against the emperor Maximinus is particularly interesting because it is the subject of accounts from the Latin West and the Greek East. The writers concerned are Herodian, writing in the 240s CE, and the Scriptor Historiae Augustae, writing in the late fourth / early fifth century CE.[55] Although it has not been conclusively proved whether the SHA had read Herodian or both authors utilized the same sources; it is striking that despite broadly agreeing on the chronological events that took place, the tenor of their accounts differs widely.[56]

I make no apology for breaking with chronological convention in dealing with the *Historia Augusta* first. It will be argued that the SHA's treatment of the city of Carthage is part of a longstanding tradition which sought to continually reassert the hegemony of Rome over other cities in the empire. In turn, Herodian's account of the revolt of the Gordians should be viewed partly as a confirmation and partly as a reaction against such a vision of the Roman world.

LOOKING SOUTH: THE SHA

The SHA is broadly in favour of Gordian and his son and hostile to the Maximini, the ruling imperial dynasty whom the Gordians are trying to usurp. Gordian's noble lineage from the house of the Gracchi and the emperor Trajan, his *paideia* and even his physical appearance (a close resemblance to Augustus) mark him out as a suitable candidate for imperial office in contrast to the barbarous, ill-educated Maximinus (even as a youth he had barely mastered the Latin tongue).[57] Perhaps more important for the SHA are their respective relations with the city of Rome. Despite often portraying the citizens of Rome in very scathing terms as being cowardly,

---

[55] For the date of Herodian see Whittaker (1969) ix–xix. For a late fourth-century / early fifth-century date for the *Historia Augusta* see Honoré (1987), Barnes (1978) 85.

[56] Sidebottom (1998) 2781–3 and Whittaker (1969) lxv–lxviii argue that Herodian was aware of, and probably used, the work of Dio Cassius (although the SHA recommends Herodian to his readership (*Clod. Alb.* 12). Barnes (1978) 85–9 agrees with this but sees no clear evidence for the SHA using Dio Cassius or Herodian. Whittaker (1969) lxix–lxxi gives a qualified assent to Herodian using Marius Maximus, a major source of the SHA (Barnes (1978) 98–107). Birley (1970) 86 argues that Herodian is the major source for the SHA's account of the revolt of the Gordians. For the convincing arguments for single authorship of the *Historia Augusta* see Honoré (1987), Barnes (1978), Birley (1970), Syme (1971).

[57] Gordian's education and learnedness, SHA *Gord.* 3; appearance, SHA *Gord.* 21. 5. Maximinus' lack of education, SHA *Max.* 6.

fickle and self-serving the SHA mentions approvingly the fact that Gordian had been born in Rome (his family owned the house of Pompey) into a senatorial family that could boast a long line of consuls and that his political career had included many acts of munificence to the city and its citizens. Gordian's origins are made to stand favourably against Maximinus' lowly birth to barbarian parents in Thrace, his rise to power through a military career, and his hatred of the city of Rome born of his insecurity over his own barbarian and humble origins.[58]

For the author of the *Historia Augusta*, the city of Rome is an important cultural signifier. But it was less important to have been born in Rome than to have a profound knowledge of the city.[59] It is this idea that binds the SHA to a small group of writers, born in the Latin West, who had all held high political or bureaucratic office in the mid to late fourth century.[60] It is not just to Ausonius and his *Ordo nobilium urbium* that one could turn to discover similar sentiments.[61] The imperial biographies of Aurelius Victor underline the importance of the city as a repository of the communal memories that were so important in the construction of Roman identity.[62] Aurelius Victor's work is underpinned by a strong sense of relationship between the topography of the city of Rome and the past. Physical space is used as a way of exploring the relationship between past and present. His disapproval of the abandonment of Rome as an imperial capital by the fourth-century emperors, symbolized above all by the decision to bury the emperor Constantine at Constantinople, is articulated through his praise of the building programmes carried out by a long list of previous emperors from Augustus to Constantine.[63] Rome resounds with memories, and an intimate knowledge of those memories was central to Aurelius' vision of Romanness. Victor is particularly scathing of the failure of the imperial authorities to commemorate the 1,100th anniversary of the founding of Rome, in contrast to the celebrations that had marked its 800th, 900th and 1,000th birthdays.[64]

---

[58] Gordian's family background, SHA *Gord*. 2; senatorial career, SHA *Gord*. 3; munificence, SHA *Gord*. 3, 4 For Maximinus' parentage, SHA *Max*. 1; military career, SHA *Max*. 2–7; hatred of Rome, SHA *Max*. 9.

[59] It is interesting to note that scholarship has been united in viewing the birthplace of SHA as not having been Rome but one of the western provinces. Honoré (1987) 170–3 argues for Gaul, Birley (1970) 80 for Africa.

[60] See Honoré (1987) 170–3.

[61] Honoré (1987) 170–3 argues for the SHA being a protégé of Ausonius.

[62] See Bird (1984) 5–6 for the possible African origins and career in imperial service of Aurelius Victor.

[63] Bird (1984) 60–3 for discussion of Aurelius Victor's attitude towards the city of Rome.

[64] Aur. Vict. *Caes*. 4.14, 15.4, 28.1, 28.2–6. See also Eutropius, *Epit*. 28.3.

For this educated provincial elite, who had prospered under imperial patronage, the city of Rome, as both a physical and textual entity, provided the central locus of a coherent geographical, political and cultural thought world. In the SHA's account of the revolt of the Gordians, it is the position of Rome as the legitimate capital of the empire which informs and underpins the narrative. Quite simply, Gordian, although his upbringing and manifold qualities suggest that he is more than worthy to be emperor, fails in his plans because it is Carthage rather than Rome that is the stage for his acclamation.

The initial acclamation of Gordian and presentation *cum pompa regali et fascibus laureatis* in Carthage and consequent affirmation by the Senate in Rome is portrayed by the SHA as a subversion of the natural order by which such decisions should be made.[65] In the life of Tacitus, the reader is confronted with the textbook example of how the SHA considers that Roman emperors should be acclaimed: by the Senate in Rome.[66] Only later should be the provinces should be informed by letter. To emphasize his point the SHA even includes a 'copy' of the letter sent by the Senate to the people of Carthage.[67] The author's disapproval comes to the fore in his description of the Roman Senate being informed of the revolt. The consul declaimed:

Conscript Fathers, the two Gordians, father and son, both ex-consuls, the one your proconsul, the other now your legate, have been declared emperors by a great assembly in Africa. Let us give thanks then to the young men of Thysdrus, and thanks also to the ever-loyal people of Carthage; they have freed us from that savage monster, from that wild beast (Maximinus). Why do you hear me with quaking, why do you look around? Why do you delay? This is what you have always hoped for.[68]

The author's later comments about the perfidy of the Carthaginian people coupled with the hesitant reaction of the senators signal the grim irony of *gratias Carthaginiensi populo semper devoto*. In the pages of the SHA, the reader is taken back to Punic Carthage, whose relationship with Rome is deeply ambivalent and indeed hostile. This is achieved by the author by direct allusion to the proverbial bad faith of the ancient Carthaginians that one finds in the pages of Livy, *perfidia plus quam Punica*.[69]

Gordian's manifold qualities are tragically undermined through his trust in the Carthaginians. The SHA puts into the mouth of Maximinus two speeches which strongly make this point. On hearing of the revolt whilst on campaign Maximinus addresses his assembled troops thus:

---

[65] Gordian in Carthage, SHA *Gord*. 9.6; *Max*. 14.4.   [66] SHA *Tac*. 3.7.   [67] SHA *Tac*. 18.1–5.
[68] SHA *Gord*. 11.4–7.   [69] Livy 21.4.9. on Hannibal.

The Africans have kept Punic faith. (*Afri fidem Punicam praestiterunt*). They have acclaimed the two Gordians emperors; one of whom is so broken with old age that he cannot rise, the other so wasted with debauchery that exhaustion serves him for old age. And lest this not be enough, that glorious Senate of ours has approved what the Africans have done.[70]

In the end Gordian commits suicide after the people of Carthage desert him (*ad quem omnis fide Punica Carthaginiensium populus inclinavit*)[71], 'well knowing that there was much strength in Maximinus and in the Africans none, nay rather only a great faculty for betraying' (*et in Afris nihil virium, multum quin immo perfidiae*).[72]

It would be a mistake to dismiss this as merely another example of a member of the western late Roman *literati* displaying his *paideia*. For as with all imperial discourses, the latent threat that Carthage posed to the city of Rome was one in which there had been, and still was, considerable material investment. Perhaps the most striking example is an inscription dated to the third century found in the eastern area of the *Forum Romanum* in the city of Rome. It reads INVICTA ROMA FELIX CARTAGO.[73] Its high-profile location within the city points to the power of this discourse in defining the identity of both Rome and Carthage. The same motto is also found on a series of coins minted in Carthage on behalf of L. Domitius Alexander, the *Vicarius* of Africa, who led a revolt against the tetrarch Maxentius from 308 to 310 CE.[74] On the reverse of the coins is the superscription: IN [VICTA RO]MA FELIX KARTHAGO. The image on the reverse side of the coin is of *Dea Caelestis*, the patron goddess of Carthage, with a diadem on her head and sheaves of corn in her left hand.[75] This coinage emphasizes both the strength and weakness of having Carthage as a base for a bid for imperial power. Control of Carthage meant control of the corn supply for the city of Rome. But it also put any claimant for imperial power in a potentially dangerous position, susceptible to accusations from their rivals that this was in fact an attack by age-old enemies on the sovereign power of Rome. Taken within this context the coinage of Alexander should be seen as an attempt to seize the ideological initiative from a rival who was at that time in control of the city of Rome.[76]

---

[70] SHA *Gord.* 14.1. See also SHA *Max.* 18.1–2, 'Fellow soldiers, we are revealing something you already know. The Africans have broken faith. When did they ever keep it?' (*Afri fidem fregerunt. nam quando tenuerunt?*)

[71] SHA *Gord.* 15.1–2.   [72] SHA *Max.* 19.2–3. See also SHA *Gord.* 16.3 *et fides Punica perurgueret*.

[73] *CIL* VI 29850a.   [74] *PLRE* I.43.   [75] Clover (1986) 2.

[76] This was a strategy also utilized by later *Comites* of Africa who were seeking imperial power. See Clover (1986) 13–15, for a discussion of a set of silver coins minted in Carthage sometime during the late fourth and early fifth centuries CE. These coins bear the image of the emperor Honorius

This image of the city of Carthage wielding a malign and subversive influence on Roman *imperium* is juxtaposed with the legitimacy that the city of Rome confers on those who seek imperial power. The SHA justifies this stance by setting his account of the revolt of the Gordians within the context of the Punic wars. Roman Carthage becomes the heir of Punic Carthage, a place which is in direct opposition to the city of Rome.

LOOKING WEST: HERODIAN

Herodian's period of imperial service in Rome might in part explain his interest in that city.[77] In his 'history of monarchy', which revolves around the characters of the individual emperors, there is a firm emphasis on the city of Rome itself as a legitimizing qualification for those who held or wished to attain imperial power.[78] This perhaps suggests a common cultural assumption as to the importance of physical place in constructions of cultural identity and power for members of the Greek as well as the Latin elite of the Roman empire.

That is not to say that Herodian holds a consistent position on this matter. The emperor Commodus is advised by his brother-in-law not to rush back to Rome on the death of his father, Marcus Aurelius, for 'Rome is where the emperor is.'[79] The young emperor ignores this advice and the temptations of the city eventually corrupt him and lead to his downfall.[80] However the attainment of Rome is presented as being central to the success of Septimius Severus' bid for power. Severus has a dream set on the Sacred Way and the Forum of Rome in which his predecessor Pertinax is thrown from a horse, which then allows Severus himself to mount it.[81] On his acclamation, Severus proclaims

Let us be the first to take Rome, the very seat of empire. Starting from there we shall easily control the rest of the world.[82]

on their obverse side whilst the reverse bears a seated Roma and the legend VRBS ROMA. Clover convincingly argues that these coins were minted by either one of two dissident *Comites*, Gildo (397–8) or Boniface (422–9). Clover thinks that it is more likely that they should be ascribed to the latter rebel. By proclaiming their allegiance to the city of Rome either Boniface or Gildo were attempting to head off any accusations hurled at them by their rivals (who controlled Rome) that their claims were nothing but an attempted African *coup d'état*. These concerns are of course borne out by the use made by Claudian of the spectre of the Punic wars to consolidate support for his patron Stilicho against Gildo. (See Cameron (1970) 93–123.)

77 Whittaker (1969) xix–xxiv in a detailed discussion on the background and career of Herodian suggests that it is most likely that he was a *scriba* in the imperial service.
78 Quotation from Sidebottom (1998) 2803.   79 Herod. 1.6.4–6.   80 Herod. 1.8–17.
81 Herod. 2.9.5–6.   82 Herod. 2.10.9.

Herodian juxtaposes this successful strategy against that of Septimius' rival Pescennius Niger who contents himself with dallying in Antioch.[83] Herodian gives an account of Niger's proclamation as emperor by the citizens of Antioch. He is invested with the purple and 'all the other tokens of imperial dignity' but we are then told that these were 'made out of makeshift materials'.[84] His own private house is turned into an imperial court. The citizens of Antioch are portrayed as constantly celebrating festivals and completely ill-suited to the rigours of war.[85] The whole episode carries with it an air of insubstantiality and indeed illegitimacy. This description functions as a pointer to the eventual failure of Niger's claims.

Much of Herodian's history is concerned with each emperor's attainment and commitment to Greek culture.[86] The city of Carthage presented Greek authors writing about the Roman empire of which they were subjects with an opportunity to play the part of the objective observer. Carthage was not a Greek city but could also be constructed as not being Roman. Herodian's account of the (re?)introduction of *Dea Caelestis* (he uses her Greek name Urania), the patroness of Carthage, into the city of Rome by the emperor Elagabulus is good example of this.[87] Elagabulus sent for the statue of Caelestis so that she could be married to his own god, Sol Invictus. The gold from her temple and other collected monies were to serve as her dowry. Herodian is at pains to point out the Phoenician roots of both the goddess and the city that she protected. She is a foreign and, most importantly, an oriental deity.[88] For both Herodian and Cassius Dio, who also recounts the story, the introduction of *Dea Caelestis* is yet another indication of how far Elagabulus deviates from his role as Roman emperor. The introduction of a 'barbarian' goddess into the pantheon of Rome sits well with Elagabulus' oriental dress, bizarre food restrictions and penchant for circumcision and human sacrifice.[89] The fact that Elagabulus' orientalizing behaviour transgresses both Greek and Roman cultural *mores* allows both

---

[83] Herod. 2.7.7–2.8.9.   [84] Herod. 2.8.6.   [85] Herod. 2.7.9–10; 3.1.3.

[86] Sidebottom (1998) 2803–12.

[87] There has been much debate over exactly when the cult of *Dea Caelestis* was introduced and established in Rome. See above (n. 36) for a discussion on the introduction of the cult after the third Punic war. Scholars are in agreement that Von Domaszewski's (1895) 62–79 thesis of *Dea Caelestis* playing an important role in Septimius Severus' and Julia Domna's 'orientalization' of Roman religion (see Mundle (1961) for a convincing refutation of this) and that there was resurgence of interest in the cult during the reign of Elagabalus. However the longevity and importance of the cult in Rome is disputed. Zecchini (1983) 160–3 and Harlsberghe (1984) 2213–21 argue that the cult of *Dea Caelestis* played a significant role in the religious life of the city of Rome during the reign of Elagabalus. Rives (1995) argues that in fact the surviving evidence points to the cult playing a limited and very minor role in Rome.

[88] Herod. 5.6.3.   [89] Dio. 80.11–13; Herod. 5.5.3–5.6.3.

Herodian and Dio Cassius to identify with Rome as an imperial capital, whilst at the same time remaining true to their concerns with imperial attainment of Greek *paideia*.

The role of the city of Carthage in Herodian's account of the revolt of the Gordians mirrors that of Antioch in the acclamation of Niger:

Then he [Gordian] left Thysdrus and marched to Carthage, the largest and most heavily populated city (as Gordian knew), so he could act exactly as if he were in Rome. The city is the next after Rome in wealth and population and size, though there is rivalry for second place between it and Alexandria in Egypt. With him went the whole imperial escort, the soldiers stationed there, and the tallest young men in the city acting like the bodyguard in Rome. The fasces were garlanded with laurel (a sign that distinguishes an emperor from an ordinary man) and fire was carried before him in procession, so that for a short time the city of Carthage was a kind of replica of Rome itself in its prosperous appearance.[90]

Once again Herodian places a provincial city in comparison with the city of Rome and yet again it is found wanting. The Carthaginians' pretensions are mocked by the emperor Maximinus in his speech to his troops. These were not worthy and dangerous rivals like the Germans or the Persians

but the Carthaginians, who have gone mad. They have persuaded or forced a feeble old man, who has taken leave of his senses in the extremity of old age, to be emperor as though it were a game in a procession. But what sort of army are they relying on, when lictors are enough for them as attendants on their governor? What sort of weapons will they use, when they have nothing but the lances used by gladiators in single combat against wild animals? Their only combat training is in choruses or witty speeches and rhythmic dances.[91]

These observations are backed up by subsequent events. When confronted by a well-trained army, the Carthaginians, 'brought up in absolutely peaceful conditions, forever whiling away their time in festivals and easy living, completely divorced from weapons and instruments of war', were easily defeated.[92] Gordian the elder commits suicide and his son is killed in battle.

Herodian's final judgement of the episode is: 'So Gordian, to whom life had been fortunate in its early stages, met his end masquerading as an emperor.'[93] Carthage is a pretend capital for a pretend emperor. The message is that only Rome can be head of the Roman empire.

Here, as with Niger's Antioch, the emphasis is on a subject city whose ill-founded aspirations to actually be Rome are disastrously at odds with the reality of the situation. The hegemony of Rome has absolved the citizens of Carthage of any sense of responsibility for their city apart from the

[90] Herod. 7.6.   [91] Herod. 7.8.   [92] Herod. 7.5–9.   [93] Herod. 7.10.

provision of leisure activities. This is a tyranny of peace. For Herodian and his readership taken from the Greek elite of eastern empire, Rome had to be the capital of the empire, because how else could Rome's position as an occupying power be explained? If other cities could become the imperial centre of the Roman empire, then the suggestion would have to be that the empire was in some way a politically and culturally co-operative rather than coercive affair.[94] By constructing the city of Rome as a unique entity which could not be successfully emulated, the Greek writers of the Roman empire attempted to create a space between themselves and the empire which they belonged to and operated within.

To this end, Herodian also employs the standard Greek rhetorical position of the disinterested and ignorant observer when commenting on the city of Rome.[95] In Herodian's account of the revolt of the Gordians, the lack of any mention of the past rivalry between Carthage and Rome is striking. It is most unlikely that either Herodian or his readership were unaware of the Punic wars. Dio Cassius, a member of the Greek elite who had risen to the Roman consulship and whose readership would have been very similar to that of Herodian, refers to them in his history.[96] Herodian's brief reference to the foundation myth of Carthage, which has Dido cutting up an ox's hide in order to claim enough land on which to build her new city, also suggests that the author knew something about Punic Carthage.[97]

Even Theodoret, bishop of Cyrrhus, writing in far-off Syria in the fifth century CE, used the story of the capture of Carthage by Scipio in order to evoke sympathy for members of the Carthaginian elite driven out by the Vandals. Theodoret obviously assumes that his correspondents, several senior imperial officials in Constantinople, will know the story.[98] By professing no knowledge of Rome's traditional enemy, Carthage, Herodian is claiming to have no understanding of the capital city's past. In this way, Herodian makes a powerful statement of his and his readership's detachment from the city of Rome. Yet again, we find the city of Carthage playing an important role in defining Rome itself.

CONCLUSIONS: *ALTERA ROMA* OR *CARTHAGO POENA*?

These two accounts of the failed revolt of a well connected Roman aristocrat in Africa Proconsularis have a far wider significance than simply as an insight

---

[94] *Contra* Swain (1996) 401–8 (writing about Dio Cassius), I see no clear differentiation between Roman political loyalty and Greek cultural loyalty in the writing of the Second Sophistic.
[95] Sidebottom (1998) 2822–6.
[96] Dio. 43.50, Zon. 9.30. He also paraphrases accurately three lines of the *Aeneid* (75.10.2).
[97] Herod. 5.6.3.   [98] Theodoret, *Epp.* 28, 29.

into the political uncertainties of the third century CE. They were part of, or a reaction to, a much wider discourse of power which sought to explain and to justify the position of Rome at the head of the empire. Both Herodian and the SHA, with their very different agendas, stress the uniqueness of the city as the seat of imperial power. One of the most important ways that both authors highlight that uniqueness is through comparison with other cities within the empire. There is a paradox at work here: by arguing that Rome is unlike any other city in the empire both Herodian and the SHA show the extent to which she was a true Cosmopolis, a city made up of many different cities.

The fact that many of the traditions on which Rome had been constructed both as a textual and physical city, were intricately woven around her ancient rivalry with Carthage, ensured that the latter held a unique position in the cultural *imaginaire* of the educated elite of the Latin West. The city of Roman Carthage's strategic importance to Rome was not limited to its present position as provincial capital and chief port for Africa Proconsularis: she stood as a testament to the *concordia* guaranteed by the imperial regime. The munificence endowed on the city by successive emperors was part of the process whereby this *concordia* between Rome and Carthage was re-enacted.

As with all constructions of the past, the rivalry between Rome and Punic Carthage was in a constant state of flux and development. As Rome came increasingly to rely on African corn for its *annona*, Roman Carthage took on a new strategic importance for those vying for imperial power. Carthage once again could be constructed as representing a real threat to the city of Rome. For those looking on, it was the past which could be relied upon to provide a justification for the present situation.

For the SHA, writing in a period when the position of the city of Rome as imperial capital was under threat from the new Tetrarchic settlement, the story of the failed revolt of the Gordians allowed the author to assert his own commitment to the city of Rome. Under the pen of the SHA, the complexities of imperial politics become simplified into the threat posed to the suzerainty of the city of Rome by Punic Carthage. This is no longer a co-operative empire made up of equals but the story of an imperial city-state that has to be continually vigilant against the plotting and machinations of its subject peoples.

For the SHA, so self-consciously part of the literary traditions of the Latin West, Carthage could never be an *altera Roma*. Carthage was a dangerous rival in her own right, a city that was greedy for her own empire. Her Punic past explained her present treachery. Gordian, although his imperial credentials were impeccable, is portrayed as having made a fatal error in putting his trust in a city which had an inbuilt disposition for attempting to undermine and destroy the *imperium* of Rome.

Herodian's account of the revolt of the Gordians is also concerned with highlighting the position of the city of Rome as the centre of the Roman empire. Carthage is one of a number of cities which are juxtaposed with Rome through their attempts to become the capital city. In the case of Carthage, Herodian explicitly makes the observation that at Gordian's acclamation, Carthage comes to look like Rome. By exploring the possibility of Carthage being like Rome, an idea that goes against the role of Punic Carthage in Roman imperialist discourse, Herodian self-consciously highlights his and his elite Greek audience's disengagement from Rome's past and by association its present.

The fact that Carthage's pretensions to be an imperial capital are found pathetically wanting allows Herodian to present the empire as being dominated by one city, Rome. The years of living under the hegemony of Rome had turned its citizens away from statecraft and military affairs towards a love of games and festivals. For Herodian and his audience, Carthage can perhaps be taken as a metaphor for their own cities in the Greek East. In Herodian's narrative the Roman empire is simply split between the ruler, the city of Rome and the ruled, the other cities of the empire.

Unlike Herodian, the cities of Rome and Carthage seem to have held little interest for the elite of the Greek East in the fourth century CE. Their attention had turned to the new eastern imperial capital at Constantinople. Ironically it was a Greek from the city of Alexandria who kept the Latin discourse of Punic Carthage very much alive. Claudian, court poet of the imperial regent Stilicho, was quick to deploy such imagery in his work celebrating his Rome-based master's victory over the *Comes* of Africa, Gildo.[99]

In the Latin West, even in the mid fifth century CE, long after the city of Rome had ceased to have any empire to rule over and Carthage had fallen to the Vandals, an anonymous Gallic chronicler wrote about the latter in terms which the SHA would have sympathized with. Carthage is portrayed not so much as a Roman city that had fallen into barbarian hands but as a place once controlled by Rome and now a threat to her power. In his account for the year 425 CE, it is noted that

Carthage was surrounded by a wall. This city had been forbidden by the sanction of the Romans to be fortified since the old city was destroyed, lest it afford a refuge for rebellion.[100]

---

[99] This is an area explored in Cameron (1970) ch. v.   [100] *Chron.* 98 (425).

Another entry, for the year 444 CE, states that

Carthage, having been captured by the Vandals, with disaster and deplorable loss to all of Africa, threw off the power of the Roman empire.[101]

As one recent study has commented: 'It is almost as if the reader is being shown Hannibal's Carthage resurrected: first the city is given back its walls and then, less than twenty years later, *Carthage* throws off Roman rule.'[102]

At the same time, in another part of Gaul, a Christian monk had also turned his attention southwards to the city of Carthage. For Salvian of Marseilles, it was the Punic wars which provide the introduction for his discourse on Carthage.

The chief of all cities of that land, and in a way mother of them all, the eternal rival of Rome's citadel, of old in arms and courage, afterwards in splendour and dignity. It is Carthage of which I speak, the greatest rival of the city of Rome, and a sort of Rome in the African world; she alone suffices as an example and witness of my words, since she has contained within herself all the resources and governance of statecraft in the world.[103]

Salvian attempts to distance himself and his Christian audience from the pagan past which, in his eyes, was represented by the city of Rome. For Salvian, unlike earlier Latin writers, Carthage *could* be considered to be like the city of Rome. The uniqueness of the city of Rome as the capital of empire is condensed down to the presence of government and judicial offices, educational establishments and a military camp. In other words, Rome can be judged on the same terms as other cities. However, Salvian, as with all the Christian intelligentsia of the late antique West, betrays his commitment to the same cultural assumptions as we find in Ausonius and the SHA. His account of Carthage was still framed within the context of the Punic wars. Even for Salvian, the city of Rome was still a benchmark against which other cities were to be judged albeit for its licentiousness and worldliness.

[101] *Chron.* 129 (444)   [102] Muhlberger (1990) 178.   [103] Salvian, *De Gub.* 7.16.

CHAPTER 7

Migration and the Metropolis

Neville Morley

*The Mediterranean: early morning, fine weather. View from the forward deck
of a ship, the prow cutting through the waves. Sound: water, wind, occasional
shouts from elsewhere on deck.*

Voice 1 (an old man, reminiscing): Why, oh Lord, did I leave my home
in Africa to travel to Italy? It was not because I could earn higher fees
and greater honours as a teacher of literature that I wanted to go to Rome,
though these were the rewards promised me by my friends, who urged me to
go. Naturally these considerations influenced me, but the most important
reason, and almost the only one, was that I had heard that the behaviour of
young students at Rome was quieter. Discipline was stricter and they were
not permitted to rush insolently and just as they pleased into the lecture-
rooms of teachers who were not their own masters. In fact they were not
admitted at all without the master's permission. At Carthage, on the other
hand, the students are beyond control and their behaviour is disgraceful.
As a student I had refused to take part in this behaviour, but as a teacher
I was obliged to endure it in others. My life at Carthage was a real misery
and I loathed it; but the happiness I hoped to find at Rome was not real
happiness . . .

My mother wept bitterly to see me go and followed me to the water's
edge, clinging to me with all her strength in the hope that I would either
come home or take her with me. I deceived her; for I pretended that I had
a friend whom I could not leave until the wind rose and his ship could sail.
It was a lie, told to my own mother – and to such a mother, too! But she
would not go home without me and it was all I could do to persuade her
to stay that night in a shrine dedicated to Saint Cyprian, not far from the
ship. During the night, secretly, I sailed away, leaving her alone to her tears
and her prayers.[1]

---

[1] Augustine, *Confessions* 5.8.

The ship reaches harbour. Cut to a series of images of people disembarking and flowing into a crowd moving towards and past the viewer. Sound: a jumble of voices, accents, languages, some sufficiently distinct to be understood.

Voice 2 (a woman in her 30s): I came from Thrace with my sister, whose husband is *beneficarius* of the tenth cohort of the Praetorian Guard in the city.[2]

Voice 3 (a man in his 50s): While still a youth I left Nicaea in Bithynia and came to Rome to teach accounts and measures.[3]

Voice 4 (a man in his 20s): I left Egypt and became an imperial freedman at Rome so as to gain citizenship and gain access to an official appointment in the civil service.[4]

Voice 5 (a man in his 40s): As a sculptor whose skills are always in demand, I passed through many cities, accompanied by my wife and son, before settling here.[5]

Voice 6 (a woman in her 60s): My husband is a dealer in *garum* from Malaga and an officer of the Corporation of Traders there, but he stays here to oversee the business.[6]

A confusion of voices: I came from Phrygia as a slave. I came from Smyrna as a slave. I came from Carthage as a slave. I came from Thebes as a slave.[7]

Voice 7 (a man in his 50s, with an exaggeratedly harsh manner): I cannot put up with a city of Greeks. [*a sudden hush*] And yet how much of this dregs is truly Achaean? The Syrian Orontes has long been discharging into the Tiber, carrying with it its language and morals and outlandish harps, complete with piper, not to speak of its native timbrels and the girls who are told by their owners to ply their trade at the race track…[8]

This voice is gradually drowned by the noise of the crowd, pressing onwards towards Rome. Dissolve to a view of their destination, at a distance.

Narrator: Rome was the greatest city of the ancient world: the largest and the richest, grown fat on the spoils of empire. It seems scarcely surprising that it should attract large numbers of migrants; but perhaps we should not take this so easily for granted. We, after all, come from a world of ceaseless movement and instability, driven by the demands of the capitalist economy.[9] The ancient world lacked both the technology and the motivation for such mobility. The Roman Empire brought about an unprecedented degree of movement of peoples through the Mediterranean:

[2] *CIL* vi 2734.   [3] *IGUR* 1176.   [4] *P.Oxy.* xliv 3312, discussed by Noy (2000) 25–6.
[5] *IGUR* 1222.   [6] *CIL* vi 9677.   [7] *AE* (1972) 14.   [8] Juvenal, *Sat.* 3.60–5.
[9] Works on migration in the modern world include Cohen (1987), Chambers (1994), Pooley and Turnball (1998), Rappaport and Dawson (1998), Van Hear (1998).

armies, captives, administrators, ambassadors, traders.[10] Even so, the vast majority of its inhabitants lived and died in the same locality, and even those who were sent abroad by the empire doubtless hoped to return home. The fact that significant numbers of people left their homes and settled in the city of Rome does require explanation, and the consequences both for the migrants and for the city as a whole need to be explored.[11]

Approaching Rome, the view is dominated by the lines of tombs on either side of the road. Dissolve to a series of images of tombs, columbaria, the catacombs.[12]

Narrator: Death pervaded ancient Rome. As was the case in other pre-industrial cities, mortality rates were significantly higher there than in the countryside.[13] Urban living conditions, and the sheer density of people, provided ideal conditions for the rapid spread of disease.[14] Moreover, certain pathogens, such as measles and smallpox, were endemic in the city.[15] Whereas other regions of the empire suffered only occasional epidemics, devastating in the short term but easily compensated for with an increase in the birth rate, Rome's population was constantly at risk from diseases which most often affected the young, before they had a chance to reproduce.

Images: scenes of plague, bodies lying in the streets, the burial pits on the Esquiline.

Voice 1: At Rome I was at once struck down by illness, which all but carried me off to hell loaded with all the evil that I had committed against you, Lord, against myself and against other men. My fever rose. I came close to dying, close to losing my soul.[16]

Cut to a book-lined study in which we find the Historian. She is clearly a little uneasy about the conflicting demands of entertainment and scholarship, but determined to make the best of things.

Historian: Of course, we don't actually have much evidence for any of this; we're scarcely better off than the emperor Elagabalus, who tried to estimate the population of Rome from the weight of cobwebs that had been collected in the city.[17] On the other hand, we don't have any good reason

---

[10] See e.g. Stanley (1990).
[11] Cf. Horden and Purcell (2000) 377–400, who see mobility as characteristic of the Mediterranean world throughout its history, although they do acknowledge the possibility of a 'cultural predilection' for continuity and stability (384).
[12] Hopkins (1983b) ch. 4; Purcell (1987); Patterson (1992).
[13] 'Urban natural decrease': Wrigley (1978) 216–17; Finlay (1981); de Vries (1984) 179–97. Cf. Scheidel in this volume.
[14] Scobie (1986); Manchester (1992b); Morley (1996) 39–42.
[15] Grmek (1989) 89, 177–97, 277–82; Sallares (1991) 243, 244–62; Morley (1996) 42–3.
[16] August. *Confessions* 5.9.
[17] Hume (1875) 414, citing SHA *Heliogab.* 26. Generally on the problems of studying Roman demography, Hopkins (1974) and Parkin (1992).

for believing that the demographic structures of Rome were significantly different from those of other pre-industrial cities which we *do* know something about, and there's no denying the existence of 'urban natural decrease' there. The importance of ancient evidence can often be overestimated.

Cut to more scenes of people travelling towards Rome.

Narrator: The urban population was unable to reproduce itself; simply to maintain a steady level, the million or so estimated for the time of Augustus, Rome needed thousands of migrants, perhaps ten thousand or more, every year.[18] In the period of its rapid expansion in the last two centuries BCE, the numbers must have been even greater. Some migrants came willingly, in search of fame or fortune; some came for want of a better alternative, fleeing war, famine or economic crisis; many were brought against their will, to serve the needs of the conquerors of the world. A lucky few were able to return home if they wished; most died in an alien city. Rome consumed bodies as insatiably as it consumed food, wine and other goods.[19]

Back to the study.

Historian: It gives a misleading impression to talk of Rome 'needing' migrants.[20] We have to deduce the importance of migration from the size of the city, but we mustn't forget that it was actually the other way round: the size of Rome was a consequence of the level of migration. Given what we know of problems with the city's food supply, it seems perfectly possible that Rome would have worked better with a lower population; but, as modern experience shows, even if the authorities perceive a problem with the level of immigration there are strict limits on their ability to deal with it.[21]

Images of the streets of Rome, crowded and bustling.

Voice 8 (a man in his 40s): Behold this concourse of men, for whom the houses of immense Rome scarcely suffice: most of this throng are now deprived of their country. From their towns and colonies, from the whole world, in fact, they have flocked hither. Some have been brought by ambition, some by the obligation of a public office, some by an envoy's duty having been laid upon them, some seeking a convenient and rich field for *luxuria*, some by a desire for study, some by the public spectacles; some have been drawn by friendship, some, seeing the ample opportunity for displaying energy by the chance to work; some have presented their beauty for sale, some their eloquence – every class of person has swarmed into

---

[18] Morley (1996) 43–6.
[19] Extensive discussion of the evidence for migrants, their backgrounds and motivation, in Noy (2000).
[20] *Contra* Morley (1996) 44, and Noy (2000) 31.
[21] Food supply: Garnsey (1988), 167–243; Rickman (1991) on the Tiber bottleneck; Noy (2000) 37–41, on expulsion of foreigners in times of food crisis.

the city that offers high prizes for both virtues and vice. Give orders that each be called by name and asked 'Where do you come from?' You shall see that the greater part have left behind the place where they were born and come to this city, the greatest, the most beautiful city, perhaps, but not their own.[22]

Images: a series of faces, emphasizing variety of age and physiognomy; few women. Captions underneath each one.

Doctor; Lawyer; Teacher; Philosopher; Goldsmith; Dancer; Sculptor; Stonemason; Wine Merchant; Carpenter; Actor; Gladiator; Poet; Prostitute; Tallest Man in the World.[23]

Narrator: These migrants have two things in common. First, they all made a living by servicing the needs and desires of the wealthy Roman elite, which funded its luxurious lifestyle from the proceeds of empire. Second, they were sufficiently successful in their professions to be able to afford tombstones, in many cases having first managed to obtain their freedom, or they were sufficiently prominent in city life to attract the attention of elite writers. Other migrant workers, equally vital to the life of the city, failed to leave a trace in the epigraphic evidence: building workers, porters, dockhands and the like, men who were either unskilled or simply unable to find an opening in their chosen profession.[24]

Images: construction sites, the docks, the streets of Rome.

Voice 9 (male, scholarly): The Emperor Vespasian was once offered a machine which would haul some huge columns up to the Capitol. He rewarded the inventor but declined the invention: 'I must always ensure', he said, 'that the poor plebs can earn enough money to buy food.'[25]

Historian: Vespasian as a Keynesian *avant la lettre*? It seems unlikely. Nevertheless, the fact that this story was told of the emperor is significant in itself. We must never underestimate the importance of hope – one of those irrational emotions which historians find it so difficult to discuss. It was hope that brought people to Rome – few if any, besides the slaves, can have arrived in full certainty that they would be able to find proper employment. It was hope, including the hope founded on the knowledge that the emperor cared for his subjects, that kept the peace in the face of dramatic economic and social inequalities. Or so one might speculate.

Images: groups of men, sullen and bedraggled, standing or sitting idly; some playing with dice, some staring with resentment at the camera. A striking contrast with the ceaseless movement that has dominated the screen until now.

---

[22] Seneca, *Ad Helviam* 6.2–3.   [23] References in Noy (2000) 90–123. Cf. Treggiari (1980).
[24] Brunt (1980), *contra* Casson (1978).   [25] Suetonius, *Vesp.* 18.

Narrator: Free wage labour was always marginal in antiquity. What little work was available depended on the season, and workers were hired on a daily basis; the labourer's position was highly precarious.[26] In Rome, in contrast, wage labour played a far more significant role, perhaps second only to slavery. Work was available all year round; on the other hand, there were always far more available workers than jobs. The urban elite benefited from the effects of competition on wages, but they also had to deal with the presence of a large group of people, predominantly younger men, who were intermittently unemployed and largely alienated from the traditional social structure.

Voice 10 (male, tones of moral outrage): All who were especially conspicuous for their shamelessness and impudence, those too who had squandered their patrimony in riotous living; finally all whom disgrace or crime had forced to leave home, had all flowed into Rome as into a cesspool. Many, too, who recalled Sulla's victory, when they saw common soldiers risen to the rank of senator and others become so rich that they feasted and lived like kings, hoped each for himself for like fruits of victory, if he took the field. Besides this, the young men who had maintained a wretched existence by manual labour in the country, tempted by public and private doles had come to prefer idleness in the city to their hateful toil: these, like all the others, battened on the public ills.[27]

Voice 11 (male, official): Emperors Gratian, Valentinian and Theodosius Augusti to Severus, Prefect of the City. If there should be any persons who adopt the profession of mendicancy and who are inclined to seek their livelihood at public expense, each of them shall be examined. The soundness of body and the vigour of years of each of them shall be investigated. In the case of those who are lazy and not to be pitied on account of any physical disability, the necessity shall be placed upon them that the zealous and diligent informer shall obtain the ownership of those beggars who are held bound by their servile status, and such informer shall be supported by the right to the perpetual conscription of labour of those beggars who are attended by only the liberty of their birth rights, provided that the informer should betray and prove such sloth.[28]

The Forum: bustling, crowded, a confused mass, as senators mingle with beggars.

Narrator: The Roman elite mistook some of the symptoms of the peculiar nature of the urban economy for the disease itself; the same may be

---

[26] Garnsey (1980). Cf. Matthew 20.1–16.   [27] Sallust, *Cat*. 37. Cf. Whittaker (1993) 1–3.
[28] *Codex Theodosianus* 14.18 (382 CE).

said of their often-repeated complaints about the dominance of money in urban social relations.[29] They responded in a similar manner to any signs of change in the existing social structure. High levels of mortality in the city created the conditions for social mobility, even into the senatorial order, as 'new men' were recruited to fill the depleted ranks.[30] Some at least of those rising in society – even at the very highest level, as the Senate began to draw members from outside Italy – were migrants, including ex-slaves. But this process was perceived by some members of the elite not as replacement but displacement, not as a renewal of Roman society but as a dilution of its central values.

The camera focuses on the red face, bulging eyes and violent gestures of Umbricius, who turns out to be Voice 7 from the beginning of the programme.

Umbricius: Why should our friend here sign before me as a witness and recline above me at dinner – one who was blown to Rome by the wind, with figs and damsons?

Interviewer (off camera): If he is a citizen, and a man of integrity, why not?

Umbricius: Does it count for nothing at all that I, from earliest childhood, breathed the Aventine air and was fed on the Sabine berry?

Interviewer: Tradition says that Romulus built up his city by welcoming all comers, including criminals and escaped slaves, and making them citizens.[31] Surely that offers a different idea about what it is to be 'Roman', not just a matter of birth?

Umbricius: There's no room here for any Roman; the city is ruled by some Protogenes or other, some Diphilus or Hermarchus.

Interviewer: You haven't answered the question.

Umbricius: They are making for the Esquiline and the Viminal, intent on becoming the vital organs and eventual masters of our leading houses. I must get away from them and their purple clothes.

Interviewer: You talk as if this was a recent phenomenon. Foreigners have been coming to Rome for centuries. There can be few people in this city who don't have a bit of foreign blood in them.

Umbricius: And look at them! Wearing their *trechedipna*, with their *niceteria* around their *ceromatic* necks! Oh, Romulus, if you could see your people now ...

The camera pulls back to view the studio audience, laughing and applauding. The Interviewer tries unsuccessfully to keep a straight face, but 'Umbricius' remains in character, striking dramatic poses of outrage.

---

[29] E.g. Juv. *Sat*. 3.140–4.   [30] Hopkins (1983b) ch. 2.
[31] Livy 1.8.4–6; Plutarch, *Rom*. 9.

Narrator: 'Umbricius' is by no means the first or last comic creation whose words have been taken at face value even or especially by those whose values and rhetoric his creator had set out to satirize.[32] He speaks for those who had everything to lose from any change in the existing social order. Although much of his diatribe is directed against those whom he perceived as competing with him for a limited fund of status and resources, his anxieties encompass city life as a whole. Underlying his litany of complaint is a deep-seated fear of the dissolution of social boundaries and the loss of identity, of being bruised and crushed by the workings of the urban economy, of being swallowed up by the crowd and ceasing to exist as an individual.

Moving through the crowd, the camera is jostled and buffeted by passers-by.

Voice of Umbricius: Hurrying through the streets of Rome we are blocked by a wave in front; behind, a massive multitude crushes my pelvis; *he* digs in with an elbow, *he* with a hard-wood pole; then *he* hits my head with a beam, and *he* with a wine-jar. A giant fir-tree on a swaying cart comes bearing down; another wagon carries a pine; they nod overhead and threaten the people. For if the axle transporting Ligurian marble collapses, tipping its mountainous load down on the hordes beneath, what is left of their bodies? Who can identify their limbs or bones? Each casualty's corpse is crushed out of existence, just like his soul.

Narrator: Such fears were surely common to migrants as well as natives. The latter feared the loss of their social position, their status and identity; the former had already lost them, in the act of moving to the city. This might present itself as an opportunity, for those who, freed from old social ties, had the resources and the good fortune to enable them to construct a new identity for themselves. It might equally be perceived as a threat to their survival.

Tombs: beginning with the conventional, moving on to the lavish and ostentatious monuments of Sestus and Eurysaces, culminating in a series of epitaphs in Greek and Hebrew.

Narrator: Some migrants were able to reinvent themselves completely as Romans, parading their acquisition of citizenship in their new language. Others sought to preserve links with their former life, continuing to identify themselves with their homeland through language or religion.[33] Many, natives as well as migrants, sought new forms of community, in *collegia, stationes,* neighbourhood cults or taverns.[34] All, even the elite, had to

---

[32] On Umbricius, Winkler (1983) 220–3, Braund (1996) 230–6.   [33] Noy (2000) 157–60, 164–97.
[34] MacMullen (1974) 68–86; Stambaugh (1988) 208–12; Whittaker (1993) 23; Noy (2000) 160–4 on *stationes*; Hermansen (1981) 185–205 on taverns.

struggle to establish some kind of stability in the face of the chaos and constant flux of urban life.[35]

Voice 12 (male, pensive): In our own city we were like foreigners wandering and drifting, until your books, Varro, led us, so to speak, right home, and enabled us at last to realize who and what we were.[36]

Voice 10 (still outraged): The plebeians are now much mixed with foreign blood, freedmen have equal rights of citizenship with them and slaves are dressed in the same fashion as their masters.[37]

A rapid, confused montage of buildings, juxtaposing squat, rustic temples with marble-clad Hellenizing edifices, elegant domus *with dingy* insulae, *the Rostra with the temple of the Deified Julius, and a whole array of 'foreign' architecture – obelisks, pyramid tombs, theatres.*

Voice 13: What a city is to its boundaries and its territories, so this city is to the whole inhabited world. Just as the earth's ground supports all men, so it receives men from every land, just as the sea receives the rivers.[38]

Narrator: Rome itself was too large and too fragmented to serve as a focus for the identity of its inhabitants, even if it continued to fulfil that role for the people of the empire. Death and money combined to create a world of constant fluidity and uncertainty. Migration overturned boundaries and undermined stable notions of separation and distance.[39] Other cultures were no longer encountered only at the periphery, or paraded as the spoils of conquest, but paraded themselves in the centre of daily life and in the heart of *Romanitas*. There was no longer one single model of how to live in the city, or even – if this is not actually the same thing – of what it meant to be Roman.

We move from the architectural confusion of Republican Rome – the temples of the Largo Argentina, the Forum, the narrow streets – to the elegance and unity of the imperial Fora, the complex around the Ara Pacis, and Nero's new streets.

Voice 14 (male, academic): Signals, styles, systems of rapid, highly conventionalized communication, are the life-blood of the big city. It is when these systems break down – when we lose our grasp on the grammar of urban life – that violence takes over. The city is soft, amenable to the dazzling and libidinous variety of lives, dreams, interpretations. But the very plastic qualities which make the great city the liberator of human identity also cause it to be especially vulnerable to psychosis and totalitarian nightmare.[40]

---

[35] Cf. Whittaker (1993) 16–17 on anxieties about status and social mobility.   [36] Cicero, *Acad.* 1.9.
[37] Sallust, *BC* 2.120.   [38] Aelius Aristides, *Or.* 26.61–2.   [39] Chambers (1994) 2.
[40] Raban (1974) 10.

Back to the study.

Historian: This is all very thought-provoking, though for a start one might be a little wary of invoking Juvenal to explain the crisis of the late Republic. Of course it is impossible to avoid interpreting the ancient sources through our own prejudices and experiences, but surely there's a risk of over-doing it? The fact that we lack understanding of the grammar of urban life in Rome does not mean that its inhabitants had the same problem. A time traveller would doubtless experience the city as fragmented, incomprehensible and alienating, and would be quite incapable of producing a coherent account of it, but that doesn't mean we should elevate such a reaction to a principle of urban life.

View of Rome from the perspective of a pigeon flying just above the rooftops, sudden swerves to avoid taller buildings included.

Voice 15: It is this city who first proved that oratory cannot reach every goal. It is impossible not only to speak about her properly, but even to see her adequately.[41]

Even from a greater height, Rome still fills the screen.

Voice 15: For beholding so many hills occupied by buildings, or on plains so many meadows completely urbanised, or so much land brought under the name of one city, who could survey her accurately, and from what point of observation?

The vast urban sprawl continues to dominate the view as the credits roll.[42]

* * * * *

From the cutting-room floor: back in the study.

Historian: Which proves nothing. Aristides is a foreign visitor, he's in more or less the same boat as us, *and* he's looking to flatter his audience, not offer a serious study of urban alienation. The obvious problem with this style of presentation is that the sources lack all context; which is, I suppose, deliberate, as any editorial commentary on their reliability would simply reinstate the quasi-objective voice of the historian as the sole source of authority.[43]

Voice 14 (off camera): The city as we imagine it, the soft city of illusion, myth, aspiration, nightmare, is as real, maybe more real, than the hard city one can locate in maps and statistics, in monographs on urban sociology and demography and architecture.[44]

---

[41] Aelius Aristides, *Or.* 26.6

[42] Particular thanks to David Noy and Andrew Skingsley, for their work in collecting and analysing evidence relating to migrants and beggars respectively, and to my family.

[43] Cf. Berkhofer (1995) 170–201.   [44] Raban (1974) 9.

Historian: Agreed, the task of the historian is to offer both perspectives, the critical analysis and the imaginative reconstruction, and agreed, this is a matter of presentation as much as substance.[45] The gods'-eye view of urban life is all too familiar, as is historians' reliance on the literary techniques of nineteenth-century realist fiction.[46] What alternatives are there? We can offer a perspective that is explicitly individual and situated, though we soon run up against the limits of the evidence and the problem of how much we are entitled to make use of imaginative hypotheses – that is, making things up. Besides, it must be admitted that the professional writers of fiction are more often than not rather better than your average historian at such things as characterization and dialogue. Our reconstructions can only pale in comparison, even if ultimately their versions succeed by assimilating Rome to something more familiar – the conventions of *film noir* with added togas.[47] I suppose that the documentary form works as well as anything else in evoking fragmentation and confusion, which, even if they were not endemic to life in ancient Rome, certainly characterize our knowledge of it. Are we done now?

[45] Hopkins (1999) 2.   [46] White (1978) 42–6.   [47] E.g. Davis (1989), (1990).

CHAPTER 8

Germs for Rome

Walter Scheidel

Rome was a doctor's dream. As Galen drily pointed out, physicians practising in the capital had no need to consult Hippocratic accounts or other written sources for descriptions of semitertian fever, because its symptoms could nowhere better be observed on any given day than in the city of Rome.[1] This comment highlights a conspicuous if neglected facet of Rome's exalted status: its undisputed supremacy as the capital of infection and disease. An abundance of human hosts notwithstanding, microbial competition was fierce: the parasites behind Galen's malarial fevers vied for prey with a wide range of worms, amoebas, bacteria and viruses. But it would not do merely to list diseases. Infective agents operate, thrive and fail within a complex ecological framework, mutually interacting with other species of micro-organisms as well as environmental factors from climate and human population density to hygiene, nutritional status, and housing. We cannot hope to understand the ground-rules of life and death in Rome without a comprehensive model of the metropolitan disease environment, of microbial fitness and competition – in short, of causes and consequences. In the absence of Roman statistics of morbidity and mortality, we need to place and interpret scattered observations within a comparative framework derived from the more recent past.

My reading of the evidence suggests that life in Rome was probably nastier and certainly shorter than many historians are likely to appreciate, and that as a consequence, the urban plebs was a highly unstable body. If correct, these findings are of considerable relevance to appraisals of family formation, social structure, political activity and the preservation of civic memory in the capital.[2] Ideally, in devising a broad and tentatively

---

[1] Gal. 7.135.

[2] Purcell (1994) offers a perceptive survey, stressing 'the mobility of the individual, the fluidity and mutability of social groups and the transience of family and household structures' (654). It may be worth pointing out that the survival of the four urban *tribus* depended on the continuing influx of manumitted slaves: without them, the entire metropolitan citizen population would eventually have come to consist of members of the thirty-one rural tribes.

quantitative model from a blend of non-quantitative ancient source material and statistical data of more recent origin, we may gain more profound insight into the demography of an ancient city than its own inhabitants could ever hope for. This objective, no less immodest than exciting, would hardly seem feasible without Keith Hopkins' repeated demonstration that through parametric modelling and judicious analogy we are sometimes able to explain and even quantify processes that are crucial to our understanding of Roman history – from the link between taxation and trade to the spread of Christianity – but were never analysed or even adequately documented in contemporaneous sources.

READING FILTH

What was it like to live in Rome? From bits and pieces of literary sources and archaeological remains, we gain the impression that for all its outward splendour, Rome may not have been a particularly pleasant place to live in. In a seminal survey, by then long overdue, Alex Scobie drew attention to the serious shortcomings of Roman sanitation and housing and their probable, or indeed inevitable, impact on health and survival.[3] Marshalling an impressive array of data, Scobie portrayed a city of filth and squalor, faeces and carcasses. This picture, however sobering, is unlikely to raise eyebrows among historians familiar with early modern capital cities. But not every classicist wants to be a historian, and given the current rush to deconstruct literary images, it was perhaps only a matter of time that Scobie's project should come under fire for its goal, now unfashionable at best, 'to establish an objective framework for viewing life in ancient Rome', and so to shed light on something as irrevocably lost as past *reality*. In particular, the critic takes issue with Scobie for his failure to compare 'like with like':

He takes a modern Western standard and compares this with Rome's pre-industrial cities. Often the Roman conditions are elucidated with reference to situations in developing countries and are seen to be similar ... Scobie's discussion of water-supply and overcrowding is reminiscent of the nineteenth-century treatises on the problems of the city ... [H]e takes a standard that had never existed and looks for abuses of that standard ... These standards need not have occurred to the inhabitants of Rome, whose environmental perception was not constructed in the same way.[4]

Yet are modern standards of hygiene irrelevant simply because they are unknown? Does contamination not threaten people's health as long as

---

[3] Scobie (1986).   [4] Laurence (1997) 2, 12, 14.

some pre-modern 'construction' of their 'environmental perception' keeps them from appreciating that filth is bad for them? We might call this the Blissful Dinosaur Fallacy: the assumption that the dinosaurs could not be harmed by an asteroid impact because they did not know the first thing about astronomy.[5] Rather, it is exactly *because* the Romans were unaware of modern notions of hygiene that we must apply our own deliberately anachronistic standards in ascertaining the probable consequences of their absence. What is more, for every sardonic aside in Juvenal or every other dubious anecdote 'that creates a negative impression of sanitary conditions in Rome',[6] we have access to independent data from archaeological surveys to legal provisions and medical observations that are fully consistent with the bleak picture painted by Scobie. Straight-faced advice to those troubled by their bowels to bathe their anuses in the hot pools of the public baths or a warning not to expose infected wounds to the filthy contents of such pools – not necessarily two entirely unrelated observations – might invite scepticism if uttered by a satirist: proffered as they were by the physician Celsus, these comments were hardly made in jest. There is no lack of Roman authorities with no obvious axes to grind, no good reason to throw out the baby with Celsus' soiled bathwater.[7]

All the same, the pessimistic model of life in Rome does not stand or fall with Scobie's sample of miscellaneous evidence. Even if all of his references were to be excised from our accounts, the satires together with the laws and stones and indeed every single ingredient of his masterly survey, we would draw the same conclusions from precise observations in the medical literature, from casual talk about the weather, and from thousands of epitaphs salvaged from the suburban catacombs, all of them interpreted within a comparative framework.

---

[5] For an idea of how the environmental perception of dinosaurs may have been constructed, see Bakker (1995); for contrast, compare Verschuur (1996).

[6] Laurence (1997) 12.

[7] Celsus, *Med*. 4.25.3, 5.26.28c. Other, methodologically less trendy attempts to clear Rome's reputation cannot impinge on Scobie's work. Residual infatuation with 'the grandeur that was [the imperial city of] Rome' can encourage special pleading: in a 783-page tome on life in the metropolis, Kolb (1995) mysteriously refers to unspecified public prevention measures against epidemics and other diseases (577) and knows of a hospital complete with isolation station (!) on the Tiber island (578), but suppresses mention of epidemics in the city after the early Republic (now listed by Duncan-Jones (1996) 111) and fails to refer to – or show any awareness of the implications of – Scobie's work. In a different vein, Lo Cascio's more upbeat reappraisal originates in an independent more wide-ranging and revisionist model that requires its adherents to minimise urban mortality and thus migration to Rome in support of inflated estimates of the size of the population of Roman Italy (Lo Cascio (forthcoming)).

COUNTING DEATH

Funerary inscriptions provide a preliminary starting-point. Epigraphic evidence of mortality can be used as proxy data for the underlying disease environment. On previous occasions, I have discussed the seasonal distribution of deaths recorded in late antique epitaphs in the city of Rome and other parts of the Roman empire.[8] The metropolitan sample reveals an unusually high amount of seasonal mortality variation among teenagers and adults that merits closer scrutiny. After all, these age groups are ordinarily fairly resistant to endemic seasonal infections. Moreover, the scale of seasonal mortality amplitudes is often correlated with mortality rates as such: both tend to rise and fall in tandem.[9] Thus, pronounced seasonal mortality variation in disease-resistant age groups is indicative of extremely high mortality overall.

Unfortunately, these texts only show that a large proportion of all annual deaths were concentrated in a particular season, without giving us a clue as to their actual number. In a recent study, Paine and Storey attempt to squeeze additional information from these documents by combining the attested seasonality pattern with recorded ages at death. In referring to epigraphic age data for the purpose of demographic analysis, they revive a line of enquiry forcefully discredited by Hopkins half a lifetime ago.[10] This is all the more astonishing since thanks to his efforts, 'it should by now be clear that ages of death recorded on tombstones are wholly worthless as demographic evidence; the surviving evidence is hopelessly skewed by underlying differences in who was commemorated and who was not'.[11] This conclusion is not in need of revision. In order to deflect such scepticism, Paine and Storey limit their analysis to epitaphs containing precise and potentially accurate information of ages at death, namely inscriptions that record the ages of the deceased in years, months and days, and sometimes even hours. From this sample, which consists of 2,237 cases and shows little digit preference, they derive an age-distribution of mortality which compared to standard model life tables implies an extremely high incidence of death from ages five to twenty-five relative to lower and higher ages. This pattern, though judged 'extreme', is taken to 'fit a real biological phenomenon, catastrophic mortality, which may be consistent with public health conditions in Rome and other preindustrial cities'. However, Paine

---

[8] Scheidel (1994), (1996a) ch. 4.
[9] This point is well illustrated by Sakamoto-Momiyama (1977) 67 fig. 4.8.
[10] Paine and Storey (1997); Hopkins (1966), (1987).   [11] Crawford (1996)

and Storey do not even attempt to show that the attested frequencies are not caused by higher rates of formal commemoration of older children and young adults – a phenomenon well documented throughout the empire – and completely fail to address Hopkins' critique of comparable reasoning in earlier scholarship. Because of their irrelevant and misleading focus on age-awareness and the accuracy of recorded ages, they blithely sidestep the pivotal question of biased commemoration practices. Their reference to the epidemics of the second century CE, when many of these texts were set up, as a possible cause of 'catastrophic mortality' is similarly unhelpful: severe plagues must have depressed formal epigraphic commemoration. All in all, their study fails to make a case for straightforward demographic interpretation of Roman age-at-death data.

But all is not lost. Seasonal mortality variation is caused by fluctuations in the incidence of the principal determinants of death. 'Since many diseases follow distinct seasonal patterns, seasonality can often be used to identify the causes of epidemics and the major components of mortality.'[12] Recent surveys of the epigraphic evidence have revealed considerable differences between seasonality profiles from various parts of the ancient Mediterranean,[13] differences which need to be explained in terms of local and regional disease patterns. In late antique Rome, about 38 per cent of close to 4,000 attested deaths occurred in August, September and October.[14] The mean death rate in this quarter was 1.8 times as high as during the remainder of the year. On previous occasions, I have associated this conspicuous seasonal concentration of deaths with a high prevalence of malignant forms of malaria, or more precisely with the synergistic interaction of malaria with other infections that are typical of the hot season, such as gastro-intestinal disorders.[15] This interpretation is consistent with the timing of the annual outbreak of falciparian malaria in nineteenth-century Rome, which used to commence rather suddenly in July and peak between August and October. The overall death rate rose accordingly.[16] The late Roman epitaphs register a sharp upturn in burials during these very months.

Interpreted in this manner, the epigraphic data may be correlated with particular diseases which in turn imply certain levels and patterns of mortality unrecorded in ancient sources. It is true that faced with a multiplicity of possible meanings, the leap from attested seasonality to imputed cause is

[12] Alter and Carmichael (1996) 47.
[13] Scheidel (1996a) ch. 4; Shaw (1996); Scheidel (2001a) ch. 1.   [14] Shaw (1996) 115 fig. 5.
[15] Scheidel (1994) 157–65, (1996a) 149–53.   [16] E.g. Aitken (1873); Rey and Sormani (1881).

fraught with uncertainty.[17] In this case, however, explicit and detailed testimony of experienced contemporaneous observers provides independent corroboration. Medical accounts describe the symptoms of every single type of malaria present in the Mediterranean: malignant tertian fever (caused by *Plasmodium falciparum*), benign tertian fever (*P. vivax*), and quartan fever (*P. malariae*). In addition, pernicious quotidian or subcontinuous fevers (i.e. primary attacks of *P. falciparum*), 'semitertian' fever, and mixed infections were likewise reported in the capital (see below).

GODDESS FEVER

In what began as part of our collaborative study of the impact of infectious endemic disease on the demography of the Roman world and has now become a separate monograph, Robert Sallares presents a sophisticated comparative and interdisciplinary analysis of malaria in central Italy. The following pages owe much to his efforts. For full documentation and further discussion, readers are referred to his recent volume.[18]

According to Asclepiades of Bithynia, a doctor practising in Rome in the first half of the first century BCE, quotidian fevers – which are now known to be typical of the initial and most dangerous stages of *P. falciparum* infection – were common in the capital and frequently accompanied by cerebral complications described as 'catalepsy' or 'lethargy', which could often be fatal. These conditions reportedly prompted repeated discussion by this physician.[19] More than two centuries later, Galen's researches in Rome led him to very similar conclusions. His reference to the ubiquity of malaria, quoted at the beginning of this paper, is backed up by several more detailed observations. In his view, semitertian fevers, which he expressly described as extremely dangerous, were more widespread in Rome than anywhere else: 'just as other diseases thrive in other places, this one abounds in that city'.[20]

His comments on the age-specific incidence of particular types of malaria are of particular significance for our reconstruction of the metropolitan

---

[17] Landers and Mouzas (1988) 62–3. For instance, comparably high peaks of the death rate in the spring documented by epitaphs from Roman and early Islamic Egypt appear to be unrelated to malaria: Scheidel (2001a) ch. 1.

[18] Sallares (2002). For an earlier preview, see Sallares (1999). Sallares' extraction of *P. falciparum* DNA from a late Roman child skeleton from Umbria – the first genetic evidence of malaria in classical antiquity – has attracted considerable media attention (e.g. *The New York Times*, 20 February 2001).

[19] Cited by Caelius Aurelianus 2.63–4 ed. Drabkin. For parallel observations in nineteenth-century Rome, see Marchiafava and Bignami (1894) ch. 7.

[20] Gal. 7.465, 17A.121–2.

disease environment. Quotidian fevers, the most dangerous of all, primarily (*malista*) struck small children (*paides mikroteroi*), while semitertian
fevers were common among men in the prime of life (*andres akmazontes*).[21]
Through these casual remarks, Galen unwittingly hands us a key to an
improved understanding of the demography of the largest conurbation of
the classical world. The ancient physician, unaware of underlying causes,
was reduced to reporting observable phenomena. It is only with the help of
modern epidemiological knowledge that we may fully appreciate both the
internal consistency and the demographic implications of his statements.

Quotidian fever, a daily febrile paroxysm, is characteristic of the early,
pernicious stages of *P. falciparum* infection.[22] Outside the tropics, for this
condition to be concentrated in early childhood, transmission rates and
thus the overall incidence of infection must be very high, a scenario known
as hyperendemicity. Parasites are transmitted seasonally and morbidity is
concentrated under age five. Under conditions of hyperendemicity, 50 to
75 per cent of the population carry malaria parasites; spleen enlargement
is found in over 50 per cent of children under the age of ten and in over
25 per cent of adults. Survivors of primary attacks in infancy and early
childhood gradually develop acquired immunity to locally active strains of
P. falciparum in response to repeated infections. As a consequence, episodes
of acute illness become less frequent with increasing age.

Children living in a highly endemic malarious area without chemopro-
phylaxis or any protection against mosquito bites and continuously exposed
to the infection are, until the age of about 5 years, at a particularly critical
stage of their host–parasite relationship. Many of them die with cerebral
malaria, severe malarial anaemia or with repeated generalized convulsions
and prostration.[23]

This is the situation implied by Asclepiades and Galen. At significantly
lower levels of infection (as under mesoendemicity), by contrast, primary
falciparian infections would be more evenly spread across the life cycle.

Severe cases of semitertian fever among fully grown adults would probably be rare in a population inured to unceasing exposure from birth.
However, imperial Rome continuously received large numbers of adult immigrants. Comparative evidence shows that it was above all the health-
iest – that is, elevated and consequently malaria-free – parts of Italy
that produced significant demographic surpluses and therefore emigrants.
Immigrants who had not acquired immunity during their first years of

[21] Gal. 11.23 (children), 7.468 (adults).
[22] Standard handbooks on malaria include Pampana (1963) and Gilles and Warrell (1993).
[23] Gilles and Warren (1993) 47.

life must regularly have been struck by various infections either at once or within a short period of time upon their arrival. Numerous accounts from early modern Rome invariably stress the vulnerability to malaria of recent adult immigrants, whereas indigenous survivors of childhood infection exhibited higher levels of resistance later in life. Incidentally, the same was true of immigrants to the malarial marshlands of south-east England.

In terms of severity, the Hippocratics considered semitertian fever second only to quotidian fever, associated with primary attacks of *P. falciparum*. Since the late nineteenth century, the condition which in antiquity was described as 'semitertian fever' has been known to be yet another, related manifestation of falciparian infection. In antiquity, by contrast, its symptoms had generated widespread but inconclusive debate. Galen and others interpreted semitertian fever as a combination of quotidian and tertian fevers.[24] On the face of it, given the attested prevalence of both species in Rome, mixed infections of this kind may well have been common among non-immune adult immigrants. At the same time, the often irregular patterns of *falciparum* fever obscured the cyclical nature of attacks and so prevented pre-modern observers from identifying semitertian fever as an exacerbated form of malignant tertian fever. Moreover, differences in the symptoms of primary falciparian infection between small children and adults may have prompted observers to draw terminological distinctions between age-specific manifestations of the same phenomenon. Galen describes an environment in which primary attacks of falciparian malaria were common among small children *and* among adult men: under these conditions, a large majority of small children contracted malaria, as did many adult immigrants who lacked acquired immunity.

As a consequence, it was in the malaria season, *insaluberrimum tempus*, that newcomers to the city succumbed to its *infamis aer* (an early precursor of *mal'aria*).[25] Although Tacitus does not specify whether the soldiers of Vitellius' Rhine army who, encamped between the Vatican and the Tiber, died in droves during the summer of 69 CE fell a victim to intermittent fevers, a wealth of comparative evidence from the Middle Ages and the modern period suggests that this may well have been the case.[26] Detailed assessments of the malarial geography of early modern Rome have revealed a patchwork of dangerous low-lying and less exposed elevated sections. Thus, Cicero and Livy appear to have been uncannily precise in praising

---

[24] Hippoc. *Epid*. 1.11. Debate: Gal. 17A.120. Combination: Gal. 7.363, 369.
[25] Plin. *Ep*. 4.2.6 (*tempus*); Frontin. *Aqu*. 88.3 (*aer*).   [26] Tac. *Hist*. 2.93. See Sallares (2002).

the salubrious *hills* of Rome, islands as it were in a sea of pestilence.[27]
However, in the imperial age, with a metropolitan population about ten
times as large as around 1600,[28] the malarial plains close to the river and
between the hills were inevitably much more densely populated than at
any other time before the twentieth century. Run-off water from the hills,
the constant overflow from public water-basins and the stagnant residue
of the notorious Tiber floods left no shortage of breeding grounds for the
anopheline carriers of malaria. And unwittingly helping to level the playing-
field, open *impluvia* in the courtyards of altitudinous *domus* extended a
warm welcome to mosquitoes and their parasites. Comparative evidence
from Mumbai reveals the hazards of this custom.[29]

    As a consequence, 'high living' did not afford sufficient protection. Just
like their medieval and early modern successors, affluent Romans and their
entourage made sure they steered clear of their capital city at the peak of the
malaria season. Under the Principate, the Senate adjourned for the months
of September and October to allow its members to decamp to their more
salubrious country estates. During this annual recess, only a quorum of
senators chosen by lot was left behind, although important events could
force a temporary recall. Although it remains unclear whether or to what
extent a similar custom was observed in the Republic, it would be surprising
if it had been unknown.[30] These were the months when the Younger Pliny
would visit Tifernum Tiberinum,[31] a healthy locale, as he assured a friend,
up in the mountains that was far removed from the malarious plains. The
clients of the powerful followed their example if they could, as did Horace,
when he denounced the fever season of Rome from the safety of a country
retreat. The urban masses stayed behind: with little hope to be spared, they
could be said by Juvenal, cynically but not implausibly, to wish for a quartan
fever, clearly the lesser evil on offer.[32] At that time of the year, the grace

---

[27] Cic. *Rep.* 2.11; Livy 5.53.4.   [28] Schiavoni and Sonnino (1982) 98–9.
[29] Scheidel (1994) 158 n. 37.
[30] Principate: Talbert (1984) 211–12. Republic: Stein (1930) 110–11 argued for some kind of recess from
    mid-April to mid-May in the mid-first century BCE; an idea dismissed by Bonnefond-Coudry
    (1989) 259–60. A recess at that time would not make sense either in terms of disease avoidance
    or estate management. Of ninety-two sessions of the Senate in the first century BCE discussed by
    Bonnefond-Coudry (1989) (as listed 807–9), only fourteen (or 15.2 per cent) fell into the months
    of August, September and October. Needless to say, these somehow noteworthy sessions do not
    constitute a random sample and the implied slump may be accidental; even so, the trend is suggestive
    of avoidance behaviour during the malaria season. The fact that in the mid-first century BCE,
    the official calendar deviated from the astronomical year by a margin from one week to more
    than two months (Brind'Amour (1983) 320–30) further complicates interpretation of the available
    records.
[31] *Ep.* 5.6, 8.1–2, 9.16, 9.20, 9.36, 10.8. In 1.7.4 he envisages returning to Rome in mid-October.
[32] Plin. *Ep.* 5.6.1–6; Hor. *Epist.* 1.7.1–9; Juv. 4.56–7.

of Dea Febris must have been in high demand,[33] yet she collegially shared the booty: a plethora of autumnal deaths duly brought 'bitter gain' to the sanctuary of the Goddess of Death, Libitina, recipient of a registration fee for those deceased whose relatives could afford to abide by this custom.[34]

But how many died, and how? While it remains impossible to *measure* Roman mortality rates, the hyperendemicity of malaria at Rome permits us to draw on comparative data to sketch out the most likely pattern of disease and death. In the nineteenth century, Grosseto, a regional centre of the Maremma in coastal Tuscany, was a notorious hotbed of falciparian malaria. In 1840/1, about 60 per cent of all recorded illnesses were intermittent fevers, while 19 per cent of all deaths were directly attributed to malaria.[35] Impressive though these numbers may be, malaria infection was likely to have even greater *indirect* effects on morbidity and mortality. The synergistic interaction of malaria with other diseases deserves much more detailed examination than is possible here.[36]

On its own, *P. falciparum* not only causes fever of up to 41 °C but may induce anaemias (by invading up to 60 per cent of the host's erythrocytes) and malarial haemoglobinuria or 'blackwater fever' (the excretion of haemoglobin in the urine), as well as splenomegaly, jaundice, renal dysfunction and pulmonary oedema. Maternal malaria infection is known to reduce the birthweight of infants, thereby exacerbating infant mortality through enhanced vulnerability to diarrhoeal diseases even if malaria is not actually present in those children.[37] Moreover, malaria readily coexists with gastro-intestinal infections, such as typhoid, paratyphoid and amoebic dysentery. It tends to suppress immune responses to typhoid, and dual infection is common. In general, under conditions of malarial hyperendemicity, gastro-intestinal infections are more dangerous than in the absence of malaria.

Malaria also raises the fatality rates of respiratory diseases, both acute (tuberculosis, pneumonia) and chronic (asthma, bronchitis). In the late nineteenth century, when malaria in Rome had widely abated, chronic malaria was still found to cause complications that resulted in higher mortality from respiratory diseases than in many other major European cities.[38] Although malarial fevers can make it difficult for *Mycobacterium tuberculosis*

---

[33] Three temples of Dea Febris are attested in Rome (Val. Max. 2.5.6). Her cult later continued under the guise of Christianity, at Santa Maria delle Febri in the Vatican area. In the Roman period, divine quartan fever received a dedication in Nîmes (*CIL* 12.3129); cf. Burke (1996) 2269–71 for further texts. The existence of a dedication to Dea Tertiana, a personification of *P. vivax*, on Hadrian's Wall is doubtful (*RIB* 1.1209 *contra CIL* VII 999).

[34] Hor. *Sat*. 2.6.19.   [35] Del Panta (1989) 48 n. 23.   [36] See Sallares (2002).

[37] Desowitz (1992) 118.   [38] Rey and Sormani (1881).

to infect a body, the introduction of malaria to a human body already suffering from tuberculosis greatly exacerbates the latter. Of course, the incidence of tuberculosis in the ancient city of Rome is unknowable. Only if
Roman epitaphs accurately reflected age-specific mortality could we hope
to trace the distortions widespread tuberculosis is known to cause in the
mortality profile of adolescents and young adults. However, owing to the
commemorative biases inherent in these sources (see above), this path remains blocked.[39] Even so, evidence of lethal cases even within the orbit
of the Roman elite is strongly suggestive of considerable dissemination of
tuberculosis in the cramped living quarters of the poor.[40] There can be no
doubt that pulmonary tuberculosis was present in Rome and must therefore
have interacted with malaria.

Malaria overlapping with diarrhoeas accounts for exceptionally high levels of child mortality. However, to judge by the extant early Christian
epitaphs from the catacombs of late antique Rome, the upsurge in deaths
in the late summer and early autumn was as pronounced among young
and middle-aged adults as among small children.[41] Although *P. falciparum*
was undoubtedly capable of killing recent non-immune adult immigrants –
in fact, Galen specifically referred to adult men as the main victims of autumnal semitertian fever, when new infections were most dangerous – this
can only be part of the answer. In this connection, it is important to realize
that a number of diseases that could be aggravated by malaria, in the first
instance typhoid, paratyphoid, relapsing fever and tuberculosis, used to be
more typical of adolescence and more mature ages than of infancy and early
childhood.[42]

As a consequence, high mortality at mature ages is a characteristic feature of populations in the grip of hyperendemic malaria. In Grosseto in the
middle of the nineteenth century, mortality from ages twenty to fifty stood
at 60 per cent, a proportion far in excess of the predictions of the most pessimistic standard model life tables. Much the same was true for the heavily
malarial Crotonese in Calabria. Many of these deaths were caused by diseases that had been rendered lethal only by concomitant malaria infection.
Comparable, albeit less severe, distortions of the adult mortality pattern
were observed in the English marsh parishes well into the nineteenth century: in that setting, *P. vivax* exerted a predictably less deadly influence than
P. falciparum did in Italy.[43] When Del Panta compared nineteenth-century
Grosseto with Treppio, an Apennine community unaffected by malaria,

---

[39] *Pace* Russell (1985) 93–110.   [40] Grmek (1989) 193–4.   [41] Shaw (1996) 118 fig. 9, 120 fig. 11.
[42] Gal. 7.468. Diseases of adolescence and adulthood: Sallares (2002); Scheidel (2001a) ch. 2.3.
[43] Grosseto: Del Panta (1989) 22; Crotonese: Arlacchi (1983) 182; England: Dobson (1997) 169–70.

he established mean life expectancies at birth of twenty years in malarial Grosseto and thirty-seven years in Treppio. Dobson found corresponding rates of thirty-four and fifty-eight years in malarial and healthy parts of early nineteenth-century Kent.[44] The data from Grosseto in particular give us a good idea to what extent hyperendemic falciparian malaria must have shaped the demography of imperial Rome. I will return to the question of quantification by analogy at the end of this chapter.

RIVALS

By the beginning of the imperial period, malaria had long been firmly entrenched in the Tiber valley and the fertile lowlands of Latium. But Rome also kept importing afflictions from afar. Since the city was located at the crossroads of commerce and migration, every contagious disease known to its empire was bound to enter it sooner or later. Infective agents often depend on a critical mass of hosts to survive and prosper: Rome's uniquely high population density inevitably helped microbial newcomers gain a foothold. Contemporary observers could not fail to appreciate this undesirable state of affairs. At the beginning of the 26th book of his *Natural history*, the Elder Pliny discussed 'novel' diseases that had been introduced to Rome and Italy in the recent past, some of which persisted while others had soon disappeared. Provence, for instance, was said to have dispatched *carbunculus*.[45] But above all, it was Egypt that had earned a reputation as the leading source of new health hazards.[46] Following the political unification of the Mediterranean and ever closer trade ties between the city of Rome and Egypt, the inflow of grain was matched by an invasion of germs. Pliny singles out *lichen* or *mentagra*, and *elephantiasis*. The former, a pustulous lichen on the chin, transmitted by kissing, that was reportedly confined to the upper classes, cannot safely be identified with any modern condition.[47]

The 'elephant disease', by contrast, poses no difficulties of identification.[48] Caused by *Mycobacterium leprae*, lepromatous leprosy appears to have been common in Egypt (at least) from the Hellenistic period onwards. Its devastating effects are well known: injuries to peripheral nerves

---

[44] Del Panta (1989) 22; Dobson (1997) 172 table 4.5. Again, the difference between the two malarial mortality rates reflects the difference between *falciparum* and *vivax* infection. The demographic impact of malaria is discussed much more fully in Sallares (2002).

[45] *HN* 26.4: anthrax? Grmek (1991) 209.   [46] Marganne (1991) 158.

[47] Plin. *HN* 26.2–4, 7–8. Cf. Grmek (1989) 208.

[48] On leprosy in classical antiquity, see Grmek (1989) ch. 8; Manchester (1992a). R. Sallares is currently preparing a comprehensive study of this subject.

cause loss of sensation, while severe damage to the nose and upper jaw results in conspicuous malformations that often leave sufferers shunned by society. In the first century BCE, Lucretius was still able to maintain that *elephas morbus* was only found in the Nile valley and nowhere else. According to the Elder Pliny, it had not occurred in Italy before the time of Pompey, and had disappeared before his own lifetime; a bit earlier, Celsus had deemed it 'almost unknown in Italy'.[49] Leprosy spreads very slowly. As a result, its geographical distribution pattern showed substantial variation, with a gradient from the south-east, especially Egypt, to the north and north-west. Galen observed that leprosy was rife in Alexandria but rare in other parts of the Roman world, such as Mysia (which was presumably known to him from his days in Pergamum) and Germany, and almost unknown among the Scythians.[50] Although he omits any explicit reference to Rome, it seems reasonable to suspect that by that time, the capital had come to occupy an intermediate position between highly affected Alexandria and the largely untouched north. It took leprosy well beyond the end of the Roman empire to fulfil its potential. As Sallares argues in unpublished work, the low frequency of leprosy observed by Galen in Asia Minor and Germany appears to have been the leading edge of a single epidemic which was to spread across medieval Europe.

In nineteeth-century Egypt, leprosy was (still) concentrated in the most densely populated parts of the country including Alexandria. Under the Ptolemies, the disease could only have been introduced to the new city of Alexandria by massive immigration of infected Egyptians. Leprosy is strongly associated with poverty, overcrowding, malnutrition and poor hygiene. In principle, therefore, Rome's large intake of immigrants, its high population density and its poor living conditions ought to have facilitated a gradual expansion of leprosy. However, the specific disease community of the capital may actually have worked against this new bacterium. The precise nature of the interaction of malaria and leprosy is open to debate. In modern Italy, it was hard for tuberculosis to establish itself in malaria sufferers, perhaps because of elevated body temperatures associated with malaria, which also afford some protection against syphilis.[51] It is not inconceivable that leprosy, caused by a species of bacteria closely related to that responsible for tuberculosis, was subject to similar constraints. For this reason, a high incidence of malaria may have helped to curb the spread of leprosy in Rome and in Italy in general. In addition, *M. tuberculosis* is known to compete with *M. leprae*. While existing tuberculosis inhibits infection with

---

[49] Lucr. 6.1114–15; Plin. *HN* 26.5; Cels. *Med.* 3.25.1.   [50] Gal. 11.142.   [51] Collari (1932).

leprosy, leprosy patients easily contract tuberculosis.[52] Thus, the presence of both hyperendemic malaria and some amount of tuberculosis may have left little room for leprosy, which might otherwise have proved as successful in Rome as it had been in Alexandria.

While the competitive disease community of the metropolis tended to suppress infections with very low transmission rates, it failed to keep away those favoured by rapid proliferation. Ancient evidence, despite its sketchiness, leaves little doubt that Rome was regularly ravaged by deadly epidemics.[53] An autumnal epidemic said to have claimed 30,000 lives (a conventional figure) barely merited mention.[54] Although we cannot prove that the metropolitan population was hit harder than lesser cities or the countryside, it is generally true that large conurbations are more heavily affected by epidemic outbreaks. For one thing, urban crowding made it harder to avoid infection. Moreover, as Herodian claimed with reference to the 'Antonine plague', mortality was higher in Rome than elsewhere 'because of its very large population, and because it took in immigrants from all over'.[55] If this pandemic, which struck Rome in 166 CE, was indeed smallpox, it could conceivably have killed up to a third of the inhabitants of Rome, a proportion that translates to as many as 300,000 fatalities, or several thousand per day.[56] Even a death toll half as high could easily have trebled the annual death rate. For what it is worth, Dio Cassius speaks of 2,000 deaths a day in 189 CE, a figure which need not be wide of the mark.[57]

---

[52] Manchester (1986) 29.   [53] Duncan-Jones (1996) 109–11.   [54] Suet. *Ner.* 39.1.

[55] Herodian 1.12.1, also quoted by Hopkins (1995/6) 60. The case of malaria shows that this was true not merely of epidemics but of infectious diseases in general.

[56] SHA, *Marc.* 13.3–6; Littman and Littman (1973) 245–52. Compare the analogous tally surmised for the smallpox outbreak in Athens in 430 BCE: Hansen (1988) 14; Sallares (1991) 258–9. Bubonic plague is said to have produced daily death tolls of several thousand in cities of considerably smaller size than Rome, such as late medieval and early modern Cairo: see Raymond (1972) 205–9; Dols (1977) 178–9, 208–9, 212.

[57] Dio Cass. 72.14.3. The figure 2,000 is at best a rounded one (cf. in general Scheidel (1996b)), but one that is neither ostensibly impossible nor wildly improbable. If the population of Rome had by then dropped from (say) one million to 700,000, and the annual death rate had stood at (say) 60 per 1,000 (see below), and if the epidemic of 189 CE had doubled the regular annual death rate (cf., e.g., Perrenoud (1979) 457) and had lasted two months, the average daily number of excess deaths would have been 700, a figure that may be consistent with a peak value of 2,000. Alternatively, if we speculate that this outbreak primarily affected those born after the initial epidemic of 166 CE, it might have killed up to one-third of the juvenile and adolescent population, perhaps 90,000 alltogether or 1,500 per day. These speculative calculations may be of limited value in corroborating Dio's claim but imply plausible manpower losses that seem compatible with the reported figure. Dio's claim that this had been the worst epidemic he knew is a topos that goes back to Thucydides' appraisal of 'his' plague (1.23 and 2.47, with Woodman (1988) 31, 37. Duncan-Jones (1996) 115 lists plague-related parallels); it does not tell us about the actual force of the initial outbreak. Other figures are similarly generic but not impossible. According to Jerome (*Chron.* 188 ed. Helm),

At the first stage of the 'epidemiologic transition',[58] occasional epidemic waves were not at all unusual or necessarily confined to large cities. The real question is whether Rome would have been spared some of these outbreaks if it had it not been at the crossroads of the movement of goods and people across the Mediterranean, and whether such waves had any lasting effects. The first of these problems, although interesting, is difficult to address. If the early annalistic sources for the fifth and fourth centuries BCE are anything to go by, Rome had already been the target of epidemics when it had still been much smaller and more isolated than in later centuries. Although the spread of the 'Antonine plague' must have been facilitated by troop transfers, the history of later epidemics in a less unified world suggests that they may merely have sped up an unstoppable process. More to the point, there is no evidence that occasional epidemic waves resulted in the introduction to the capital of novel diseases that were successful in the long term. Even though Rome was sufficiently populous to support endemic smallpox, this disease cannot be shown to have established itself there for good in the 160s CE. The same is true of Alexandria and the densely populated Nile valley. In its endemic form, turned into a disease of early childhood, smallpox was first attested for the Near East around 900 by ar-Razi, and for Italy only as late as 1546 by Fracastoro.[59] Even so, the possibility that smallpox managed to become fully endemic in Antonine Rome cannot be dismissed out of hand.[60] In that case, child mortality in the capital would have risen higher still, an increase that could have persisted into the fifth or sixth centuries when population numbers finally dropped below the endemicity threshold. When bubonic plague hit Rome

in 77 CE (but probably under Titus), a plague in Rome killed 10,000 people per day for many days on end. SHA *Gall.* 5.5, on the unidentifiable epidemic of the mid-third century CE that allegedly claimed 5,000 lives a day, may also refer to Rome. Daily casualty figures of '5,000' and '10,000' are stock ingredients of later plague narratives (see esp. Procop. *Goth.* 2.22.2, and the previous footnote). As noted above, the 30,000 victims of an epidemic in 65 CE (Suet. *Ner.* 39.1) also represent a symbolic figure, despite the reference to some *ratio Libitinae* (death rolls?) of questionable reality.

[58] Omran (1971).

[59] Ar-Razi: Greenhill (1848) 28–30. Fracastoro: Hopkins (1983b) 30. Medical writers of the Roman period nowhere describe the symptoms of endemic smallpox: e.g. Bertier (1996); Hummel (1999). Although it is true that these authorities showed relatively little interest in childhood diseases, it would be surprising if they had failed to mention this extremely conspicuous and deadly phenomenon at all had it become common in the population centres of the imperial age. In Constantinople in the early 1050s, Michael Psellos lamented the death of his nine-year-old daughter; the symptoms described point to smallpox: Hummel (1999) 80–1, 267–8.

[60] In his forthcoming PhD thesis at Columbia University, Yan Zelener argues that during the Antonine plague, smallpox gained permanent footholds in Rome and Alexandria. I am grateful to Mr Zelener for sending me a first draft of the relevant chapter.

repeatedly in the sixth and seventh centuries, the city had already shrunk to a shadow of its former self.[61]

UNBECOMINGLY ROMAN

We may conclude that at least from the late Republic onwards, the disease community of Rome was dominated by hyperendemic malaria and other diseases developed accordingly. Thus, while slow infections like leprosy may have found it difficult to spread under these conditions, many others, above all gastro-intestinal disorders and probably also pulmonary diseases, were regularly exacerbated by malaria and rendered more lethal than they would otherwise have been. As a result, foetuses, small children, pregnant women and adult immigrants faced particularly grave risks.

There is no strong reason to assume that nutritional status could significantly affect the impact of malaria either way. It is generally true that well-nourished bodies are better prepared to combat infections. However, even with the grain dole, a diet sufficient in protein was beyond the means of the urban masses, while the wealthy preferred to avoid infection altogether by resorting to seasonal migration. On the other hand, it is doubtful whether extreme malnourishment, which lowers the reproduction rate of the malaria parasite once contracted, offers effective protection: one study associates acute hunger in India from 1868 to 1940 with concurrent malaria epidemics.[62] In any case, near-starvation increases susceptibility to other infections, thereby offsetting any health gains from diminished malarial fevers. The distribution of free grain may have saved poor Romans from acute hunger. At the same time, more moderate levels of chronic malnourishment or vitamin deficiency – which must have been endemic in the capital[63] – would not help contain malaria.

Privileged access to material resources may have enabled the few to engage in avoidance behaviour,[64] but could otherwise afford little protection against infectious disease. Surviving rosters of discharged soldiers point to considerably higher attrition rates among military elite units stationed in the capital compared with frontier garrisons.[65] Higher adult mortality in the capital seems to me the most plausible explanation.

By the time of Galen, and probably much earlier, malaria had established a stranglehold on the city. According to medieval and modern sources,

---

[61] Biraben (1975) 27–41 lists outbreaks in 543, 570, 590, 599/600, 608 and 654.
[62] Zurbrigg (1994).   [63] Garnsey (1998) ch. 14, (1999) ch. 4.
[64] But see Scheidel (1999) for low life expectancy in the Roman elite.   [65] Scheidel (1996a) 128–9.

this situation remained unchanged until the nineteenth century. Even so, imperial Rome stands out for two reasons: at that time, the city was larger than at any time before the twentieth century, and attracted immigration on a correspondingly huge scale. In later centuries, papal wealth exerted a steady pull. Between 1598 and 1797, the Roman population rose from 90,000 to 160,000 even though deaths exceeded births for most of this period.[66] Yet under the emperors, the court, aristocratic mansions, food distributions and cash handouts created more splendour and largesse than the papacy ever could,[67] enticing even larger crowds of newcomers. It was only after the *risorgimento* that the city once again approached its ancient size. By that time, however, malaria prevention measures had finally begun to succeed. In no other period was Rome ever as big *and* as unhealthy as in antiquity. For this reason, comparative evidence capable of conveying an adequate impression of the scale of mortality and morbidity in the ancient metropolis simply does not exist.

Nevertheless, information from the more recent past enables us to chart the limits of the plausible. As I have noted above, in nineteenth-century Grosseto, hyperendemic falciparian malaria cut mean life expectancy at birth to a mere twenty years. Even in the English marsh parishes, in the somewhat less deadly presence of *P. vivax* malaria, Crude Death Rates of 50 to 60 per 1,000 were not unusual, together with higher levels in particularly bad years. Mortality rates of the order of 60 per 1,000 are also found in the nineteenth-century Crotonese. In 1622, a strong year for malaria, 54.1 deaths per 1,000 were recorded in the city of Rome.[68] Needless to say, early counts regularly under-reported infant mortality, thereby underestimating the true extent of mortality: the actual rate must have been higher still. And imperial Rome was much larger and much more crowded, with hundreds of thousands of people packed into blocks of tenement buildings. Under these conditions, mortality may soar to levels that are unknown in larger (e.g. national), composite population samples. In Mumbai in 1920, to name just one example, *reported* mortality during the first year of life stood at 55.2 per cent. Among poor families that occupied only a single room (a situation hardly unknown in ancient Rome), the respective proportion was as high as 63.1 per cent.[69] Against this background, we may safely assume that Crude Death Rates at Rome regularly reached or even exceeded

---

[66] Schiavoni and Sonnino (1982) 98–100, 105.

[67] Whittaker (1988) 57–68; Hopkins (1995/6) 58–60.

[68] England: Dobson (1997) 133–59; Crotonese: Arlacchi (1983) 181; Rome: Schiavoni and Sonnino (1982) 107.

[69] Dyson (1997) 131 table 7.9.

60 per 1,000 and that mean life expectancy at birth fell below twenty years.[70] The resultant shortage of births relative to deaths must have been enormous. So was immigration.

RULES OF ATTRACTION

Of the 3,495 Christian inhabitants of Rome who revealed their provenance in the census of 1526/7, only 16 per cent had been born in the city while 64 per cent had moved there from other parts of Italy and 20 per cent from abroad.[71] Although I hesitate to follow Delumeau in considering it 'not implausible' that these statistics faithfully mirror the make-up of the urban population of some 55,000 as a whole, these percentages hint at very considerable levels of immigration overall. In fact, migration on a massive scale was an indispensable precondition of rapid population growth in the teeth of heavy malarial attrition: despite largely negative natural growth, the urban population rose to 90,000 in 1598 and 135,000 in 1699.[72] Since the late Republic, ancient Rome must have accommodated a comparable influx of newcomers. In much the same way as in the sixteenth century, the ancient city may well have grown by some 60 per cent within seventy years. If the metropolitan population had numbered 150,000 in 200 BCE and steadily grown at that rate, Rome would have been home to 600,000 people at the beginning of the Christian era and to a million by the time of the Flavians. (In reality, net growth may have been more rapid early on and slowed down later.) From this perspective, the guesstimates proposed by Morley seem comfortingly conservative, all the more so as Wrigley's blanket estimate of an average annual excess mortality of 10 per 1,000 in early modern London favoured by Morley is hardly applicable to an urban environment dominated by hyperendemic falciparian malaria.[73] Reckoning with annual rates of births and deaths of the order of 40+ and 60+ per 1,000, respectively, the average Roman shortfall could easily have been twice as large.[74] Hence, even if Morley's own computations should fail to stand

---

[70] For what it is worth, the age distribution derived from the metropolitan census returns of Roman Middle Egypt (mostly from Arsinoe, Oxyrhynchus and Hermopolis Magna) implies a mean life expectancy at age fifteen of twenty-two to twenty-three years, which is about one-quarter lower than the most pessimistic prediction proffered by standard model life tables (Model West Mortality Level 1 Males: Coale and Demeny (1983) 42): see Scheidel (2001a) ch. 2.3.

[71] Delumeau (1957) 1 198–9.   [72] Schiavoni and Sonnino (1982) 98–9.

[73] Morley (1996) 44–6; Wrigley (1978) 217.

[74] For the suggested death rate, see above. Although correspondingly higher birth rates are possible in theory, in this context they would seem improbable for a number of reasons including a high incidence of stillbirths owing to malaria infection, below-average nuptiality and fertility among first-generation immigrants (cf. Morley (1996) 44–5), and the possibility of male-biased sex ratios.

up to closer scrutiny,[75] a more realistic set of parametric variables that takes full account of the peculiar disease community of ancient Rome cogently predicts continuous immigration on a tremendous scale.

More metropolitan wealth meant more immigration; more immigration meant more residents; and more residents meant more deaths. The ultimate consumer city in history, Rome set new standards in wasting lives as much as in largesse and monumental splendour. A few years ago, Hopkins called the imperial capital 'a huge death-trap, which consumed both goods and people'.[76] This simple model of the metropolitan disease community and the demographic profile it generated will help us to appreciate the true scale of this vicious circle. In this respect, as in so many others, *Roma vorax hominum*, as the shrivelled city could still be called around 1060 by a bishop of Ostia in his tetrastichon on 'Roman fever',[77] was dwarfed by her previous incarnation, the *Roma vorax populorum*, as it were, of the imperial age. If population pressure was indeed a problem under the Principate, as now seems likely, the capital acted as a much-needed safety-valve.[78] Hopkins has argued that Rome stimulated the economy of her empire through exploitation.[79] But exploitation takes many forms. The Ottoman empire raised tribute in humans (*devshirme*); and although the Romans refrained from such measures, the mere presence of their capital imposed a demographic tax on their subjects: voluntary for some (from traders and officials to soldiers and preachers), involuntary for others (above all, slaves), and perhaps a mixture of both for most (that is, poor peasants and freedmen). Not unlike monetary taxes, this levy may ultimately have been of some benefit to the overwhelming majority – to those who stayed away. In the end, our models of taxes, trade and disease all raise the same paradoxical question. Was it through the conspicuous consumption of goods and bodies that the city of Rome contributed most to the well-being of her empire?

---

[75] As suggested by Lo Cascio (2001) 113–19.   [76] Hopkins (1995/6) 60; cf. Sallares (1991) 89.
[77] *MGH Ep.* IV 2, no. 72, p. 344.
[78] Frier (1999) 103–4, (2001). Smaller cities provided similar services on a correspondingly smaller scale: compare Scheidel (forthcoming) ch. 2.4, for a parametric model of population growth and urbanization in Roman Egypt.
[79] Hopkins (1980), (1995/6); Freyberg (1989).

CHAPTER 9

Embracing Egypt*

Caroline Vout

ROMAN WALLS AND PYRAMIDS, THE PARAMETERS OF THE DEBATE

Anyone approaching Rome from its main port at Ostia had to haul themselves and their merchandise northwards up the Via Ostiensis towards
antiquity's most celebrated city. Backs breaking under the weight of their
belongings, minds racing with stories of their destination, they would finally catch sight of the gleaming masonry, which would reassure them that
they had reached their goal. 'The capital of the Roman empire', they would
realise, as they paused for breath at the first major monument. It was by
no means the only man-made structure that they would pass en route: the
city's houses and tombs sprawled far beyond its boundaries. But, thirty-
seven metres in height, this edifice had a privileged position in the fork of
the Via Ostiensis, which ran left towards the Tiber, Forum Boarium and
harbour district, and right towards the Circus Maximus and Porta Capena;
this gave it an enviable visibility. Whichever way they went, this landmark
could be seen as a signifier of their arrival. So what was its identity? Not
an arena, forum, temple, such as we have come to expect from Rome's
image-makers, past and present. It was a pyramid. Nor was it built by an
ancient Al Fayed who had managed to gain his citizenship, but by the heirs
of a priest and praetor of one of the oldest families in Rome.[1]

The port of Ostia was soon to be superseded by Trajan's new harbour at
Portus, but the pyramid still stands its ground as one of the most enduring
and intact of ancient Roman sites, relatively unharmed by the waves of

---

* I thank Mary Beard, Catharine Edwards and Greg Woolf for their helpful comments on various versions of this manuscript, John Patterson for providing a clearer picture of ancient Roman topography,
and John Riddy for his wonderful photograph of Cestius' pyramid.
[1] The most comprehensive account of the pyramid's appearance and history is Ridley (1992). See also
Neuerburg (1969), and entries in Claridge (1998) 364–6, Richardson (1992) 353–4, and Roullet (1972)
6–7 and 42–3. For the inscription recording its erection in accordance with Cestius' will, *CIL* vi
1374 = *ILS* 917. And for the Via Ostiensis, see Steinby (1999) vol. 5, p. 143.

Figure 14. The pyramid of Gaius Cestius as it stands today.

restoration and demolition which have so shaped (indeed are) the city's history.[2] It was constructed in around 12 BCE as the final resting-place of the man whose name is inscribed on the side of it, Gaius Cestius, *septemvir*, praetor and tribune of the people, and was one of the largest and last of the tombs to private individuals, which lined the roads beyond the city limits.[3] But as the urban landscape grew, and later the threat of invasion, increased pressures demanded that a huge circuit of walls be built to provide Rome with a stronger sense of protection and identity. By the end of the third century CE, the emperor Aurelian was incorporating the pyramid into the very fabric of these new defences (as though the brick-faced concrete of his wall were slicing through the triangular structure), thereby bringing it and its symbolism inside the parameters of the town (fig. 14).[4]

---

[2] Patterson (1999) 143 argues that the fact that the third-century CE *Porta Ostiensis* has a double gateway suggests that the road past the pyramid remained an important route.

[3] An additional inscription, *CIL* VI 1375, lists one of Cestius' heirs as Marcus Agrippa, whose death in 12 BCE gives a *terminus ante quem* for the construction of the pyramid.

[4] For the latest on the margins of the city, see Patterson (2000a).

His actions, arbitrary or otherwise, were to have a far-reaching effect on how the pyramid was treated. Some of the earliest extant maps of Rome show that there were two other pyramids of sorts, one where the Church of Santa Maria dei Miracoli stands today on the southern side of Piazza del Popolo and the other on the *Ager Vaticanus*. The last of these seems to have been the largest of the three and became known in the Middle Ages as the 'Tomb of Romulus'.[5] This association presumably stemmed from its location close to that area of Rome from which Romulus so suddenly disappeared.[6] Coincidental to this and integral to our purpose is that Cestius' pyramid became the 'Tomb of Remus'.[7] This accolade may have been due in part to its proximity to the Aventine, the hill that Remus was said to have occupied.[8] But – bearing in mind that Remus is supposed to have died for daring to cross his brother's defences – its title most likely depends upon its straddling of the wall. Centuries later, from the eighteenth century onwards, the region around Cestius' tomb became the Protestant cemetery. Their faith (or lack of it) prevented many of Rome's most ardent admirers from being buried within Catholic boundaries. The result is that Keats and Shelley strangely rest in the shades of a pyramid, a pyramid tied to the foundation myths of Rome.[9]

The colosseum, the forum, a pyramid – identifying points in the city of Rome's magnificence. Those in the eighteenth and nineteenth centuries thought little of the inclusion of an Egyptian-looking monument in their canon of Roman Classicism.[10] Nor should they. They took tea in the Caffè degli Inglesi, opposite the Spanish Steps, luxuriant with Piranesi's Egyptianizing decor, and were accustomed to seeing Egyptian and Classical antiquities side by side in the Vatican and British Museums.[11] But

[5] Middleton (1892) vol. 2, p. 287, Eisner (1986) 223–4 and Ridley (1992) 13–14. For the discovery of the foundations of the Popolo 'pyramid', also see Visconti and Vespignani (1877) 186–90. And for the Vatican 'pyramid', which stood until the sixteenth century at the intersection of the Via Cornelia and Via Triumphalis, Peebles (1936) 21–63, Platner and Ashby (1929) 340, and Richardson (1992) 252–3.

[6] For Romulus' disappearance, enveloped in mist on the Campus Martius, see Livy 1.16.1–2. And for further hypotheses, see Ridley (1992) 19.

[7] See e.g. Urlichs (1871) and Poggio Bracciolini (1723) 9.

[8] For Remus' occupation of the Aventine, see Dion. Hal. 1.85.6, Plut. *Rom.* 9.4, and Fest. 345 L.

[9] For Shelley's eulogy of the cemetery, *Letters* (1964 edition) vol. 2, pp. 59–60.

[10] For example, Cestius' pyramid is one of the sites in Edward Gibbon's famous reportage of Bracciolini's overview or essence of Rome and one of the four key sites, together with the Pantheon, Trajan's column and the Temple of Vesta, visited by Gregorovius on his second day in Rome (1907) 3. It was also a popular subject for eighteenth-century poets and painters – see e.g. Musée de la civilisation gallo-romaine (1998) cat. nos. 73, 74 and 94, Bignamini and Wilton (1996) cat. nos. 75 and 82, pp. 118 and 124–5, and entries in Edwards and Liversidge (1996) cat. 1, nos. 38 and 39, pp. 119–22.

[11] For an introduction to the Caffè degli Inglesi and its interior design, see Bignamini and Wilton (1996) cat. nos. 73 and 74, pp. 116–17, and Scott (1975) 224–6. Cestius' pyramid was also among the first nineteen plates of Piranesi (*c.* 1748), *Vedute di Roma*. See Scott (1975) 312–13.

for Classical scholars today, the notion that a pyramid could function as a flagship of *Romanitas* does not come so naturally. Pyramids are Egyptian icons, and fascinating for their foreign nature. Ancient authors corroborate this reaction: they suggest that animal worship, the Nile, and the pyramids were amongst the most common stereotypes with which the Romans epitomized Egypt and Egyptian history. I shall be examining the specifics of this distillation and of Rome's relationship with Egypt in a moment. But the validity of the pyramid–Egypt equation even in antiquity already urges us to question a Roman's motivation in wanting to be buried in such a structure. It begs us to find an explanation as to how something so patently Egyptian could fit a Roman frame.

LOCATING THE EGYPTIAN

The most common and, in some ways, obvious conclusion to reach is that Cestius' tomb, and the Egyptian connotations it carries with it, do not fit, and never did fit, comfortably with the rest of Rome's culture. Art-historians have described its design as an 'anomaly',[12] 'vagary of personal taste',[13] 'striking aberration',[14] more outside than inside the edification of the Roman wall. There is a good chance that their views concur with those of the majority of Romans (and for that matter, Egyptians) who hurried past the pyramid daily. Not only was the structure, as Paul Zanker has pointed out, one of the last and least subtle of the memorials to dare to challenge Augustan autocracy, but it was shaped like one of the chief emblems of Egypt, the adversary, which Rome had recently defeated at Actium in 31 BCE. Certainly, the outcome of Actium, and the anti-Egyptian politics of its aftermath, seems to have made everything Egyptian more charged than it had been before, or would ever be again, in Rome's history. The ancient literature for this is well known. Horace and Virgil paint a picture of an alien world of excess, artfulness, and unintelligible religion, spearheaded by Cleopatra, a licentious, monstrous queen.[15] Their hostility is perhaps best epitomized in Virgil's:

> omnigenumque deum monstra et latrator Anubis
> contra Neptunum et Venerem contraque Minervam
> tela tenent.[16]

---

[12] Zanker (1988) 293.   [13] Boëthius and Ward-Perkins (1970) 299.   [14] Ridley (1992) 28.
[15] See e.g. Virgil, *Aen.* 8.671–714.
[16] Virgil, *Aen.* 8.698–700: 'Monsters all, these gods of every shape and yapping Anubis, brandish weapons against Neptune and Venus and against Minerva.'

The uncompromising opposition that these words present between the circus of Egyptian deities and the stalwarts of Rome (and by extension, everything Egyptian and Roman) conspires to make Cestius' choice particularly surprising. The most extreme conclusion to reach is that only anarchists or sympathizers of Cleopatra's consort, Antony, would want to tie themselves to Egypt, hardly the safest course of action under the new Augustan regime.

But this is just one interpretation of Cestius' pyramid, and the pyramid is only part of the story of Egyptian influence and reception in Rome. One could equally argue the other way, namely that *because* Egypt was such a 'hot topic' in the Augustan period, Cestius' selection is more understandable, predictable even. The excess and licentiousness bemoaned by Horace and Virgil are, as they were well aware, as beguiling as they are sinful. What makes us think that their curiosity about Egyptian culture was not matched by patrons and viewers of the visual arts? Perhaps some passers-by considered it amusing or even admirable that Cestius' heirs had commemorated him with a pyramidal structure, and echoed, on a tiny scale, what Octavian had done (and was still doing in the form of obelisks and corn-supply) in adding Egypt to Rome. Whether or not their aspirations were really this grand, pyramids were commonly associated with royal power and enduring fame in authors such as Pliny and Horace, who compares his literary production to them explicitly and favourably in these terms:

> Exegi monumentum aere perennius
> regalique situ pyramidum altius,
> quod non imber edax, non Aquilo impotens
> possit diruere aut innumerabilis
> annorum series et fuga temporum.[17]

I concede that there is still an element of opposition here, Egyptian achievement versus (and vanquished by) Roman, but it is healthy competition. Any residual doubts as to the positive potential of a pyramid are alleviated by the fact that already in the second century BCE, those at Giza had entered the Classical canon as one of the seven wonders of the ancient world.[18]

Unfortunately, there are no extant ancient written responses to the tomb of Cestius to help clarify the issue, nor to any of the other representations

---

[17] Hor. *Carm.* 3.30: 'I have completed a work of art more lasting than bronze and loftier than the stately scale of the pyramids, a work which stinging rain cannot destroy nor a raging north wind, nor the countless chain of years and the speedy passage of time.'

[18] See the *Laterculi Alexandrini* (PBerol. 13044ᵛ, cols. 8–9) and Antip. Sid. *Anth. Pal.* 9.58.

of pyramids in and around Rome, or in two dimensions on the Nilotic
Mosaic at Praeneste. But a more careful reading of the ancient literature
confirms the double-edged nature of Rome's response to Egypt – as, on
the one hand, the evil enemy and, on the other, a culture to be copied –
both in the aftermath of Actium and throughout the Roman period. Obviously, individuals would have varied in their admiration or animosity, with
Tacitus, for example, appearing almost entirely negative in his writing,
Apuleius more susceptible to its pleasures (most notably the cult of Isis),
and Germanicus and Julia Balbilla mad keen on visiting its antiquities (the
latter going as far as to scratch poetry, the ancient equivalent of 'Jules woz
here', on the Colossus of Memnon!).[19] But almost everyone, these included,
was probably more difficult to pin down to a consistent stance than most
historians have credited.[20] Juvenal's fifteenth satire, for example, is often
evoked as evidence of anti-Egyptian feeling, when its primary dichotomy
is one of past achievement versus present depravity, over and above Egypt
versus Rome.[21] This is not to say that the Egyptians, and the cannibalism
they practise, are not functioning as the Other for Juvenal, but that, as with
almost all representations of the Other, they embody, potentially at least,
something of all of us. Their civilisation too was once great. It is only now
that ancient Thebes lies in ruins.[22] The overriding message is that their
current behaviour is emblematic of all behaviour, and a benchmark against
which the human race everywhere is judged.

It can also be argued that Virgil and the context in which he was writing
were more equivocal than they appear on the surface. The invective that he,
Cicero and, ultimately, Octavian directed against Antony, and the ammu-
nition that Antony's allegiance with Cleopatra afforded them, conspire to
create a wholly contemptuous picture of Egypt. Yet this description clashes
with the reality that far from turning his back on its monstrous deities,
Octavian annexed the province to his empire. Not only that, but he is
even represented wearing a pharaonic headdress in a portrait displayed on
Egyptian soil.[23] If we go back to book 8 of the *Aeneid*, we can find, alongside the uncompromising trashing of Antony, the first seeds of this relationship. The last image of those described on the shield, that of the River
Araxes, alludes to the bridge which Augustus had built there to replace that

[19] See e.g. Tac. *Hist.* 1.11.1 and 4.81.2 and Apul. *Met. passim.* For Germanicus' visit to Egypt see, Tac.
Ann. 2.59–61 and Weingärtner (1969), and for Balbilla's graffiti, Bernand and Bernand (1960) nos.
28–31.
[20] See e.g. the summaries of Leclant (1958) and Smelik and Hemelrijk (1984).
[21] For a more balanced view, see Fredericks (1976).   [22] Juv. *Sat.* 15.4–6.
[23] E.g. the relief of Augustus from the temple at Dendur, now in the Metropolitan Museum, New
York. See Kiss (1984) cat. nos. 24–6 and 36–9, pp. 126, 129–30 and 31–7.

built by Alexander.[24] Earlier in the book, we find Hercules written into the foundation myth of Rome, a figure strongly associated with the Ptolemaic dynasty (of which Cleopatra was part) and, again, Alexander the Great.[25] Virgil is not alone in linking Augustus and the Ptolemies. Horace repeatedly evokes Hercules as a model for Octavian, imagining, for example, Rome's *princeps* sipping nectar with Pollux and Hercules in a similar motif to Theocritus' Ptolemy Philadelphus sitting with Hercules and Alexander in heaven.[26] These images work against the anti-Egyptian line of argument to stress emulation as opposed to rejection. Post-Actium Rome is now the new Alexandria, taking its inspiration from Egypt and the East. Seen from this acute angle, it is easier to accept Cestius' pyramid. If Octavian could dress up as pharaoh, Virgil hail him as a Hellenistic-style dynast, and Cicero criticize Egypt in public, but write to Atticus in a letter that he would like to pay it a visit,[27] then it would be almost more surprising if someone somewhere in Rome had not erected such a structure. How many Romans berated Egypt and all it stood for, but yearned for its textiles and coloured granites in their homes?

If we follow this line of argument to its logical end, we realize that influences as *au courant* and exotic as those of Egypt must have pervaded all areas of Roman culture, artistic as well as literary. The visual remains of the city of Rome confirm this conclusion. Taking the pyramid of Cestius as our entry point into understanding 'Egyptianizing' imagery in Rome, we shall focus on a further three monuments in the capital as stepping-stones or stimuli for discussion: the 'Tomb of the Egyptians' or Tomb Z beneath St Peter's (a necropolis dated to between 125 CE and 200 CE), the 'Aula Isiaca' on the Palatine, and the 'Basilica' of Junius Bassus, which was built on the Esquiline in 331 CE. In some ways, these sites constitute a random selection covering a daunting and distinct three centuries. They are but a tiny fraction of the material available, from antefixes and table legs in the shape of *uraei* and sphinxes to statues of baboons and crocodiles, not to mention the architectural fantasias of Hadrian's Villa at Tivoli and the gardens at Pompeii.[28] But each of them presents problems, which play an important part in how we place Egyptian influences (and foreign influences

---

[24] Virgil, *Aen.* 8.728.

[25] For Hercules and Cacus, see Virgil, *Aen.* 8.193–305, although from 1.10, *insignem pietate virum, tot adire labores*, it can be argued that Aeneas and Hercules are linked. I thank Richard Hunter for first alerting me to the importance of Hercules and his Ptolemaic connections in the *Aeneid*.

[26] Hor. *Carm.* 3.3.9–12 and Theoc. *Id.* 17.13–33. Also Hor. *Carm.* 3.14.1–4; 4.4.61–4 and 4.5.33–6.

[27] Compare e.g. Cic. *Rab. Post.* 12.35 and *Nat. D.* 1.16.43 with *Att.* 2.5.1.

[28] See e.g. de Vos (1980), Zanker (1988) 269–74, Roullet (1972), Blake (1936), Whitehouse (1977), MacDonald and Pinto (1995) 109–11, 150–1 and 195–6, and Grenier (1989) and (2000).

more broadly) in a multicultural city. The primary question is: What might it have meant to a Roman audience to see and use Egyptian shapes and motifs? We shall end in an analysis of a particular application, the suitability of Egyptian iconography for Roman memorials and tombs. In the process, however, of examining the apportioning of meaning, other issues will come to the surface. The cult of Isis, for example, because of its origins in Egypt, has become a common explanation of Egyptianizing elements. Are there potential problems in this equation? Are there other explanations? Can the search for a meaning sometimes deceive?

As if this were not enough evidence to contend with, hundreds upon thousands of Rome's columns and statues were made from green granite, basalt or porphyry, materials mined exclusively in Egypt. Were these objects and their contexts ever deemed Egyptian? Was an emperor suddenly seen as Egyptianizing, if his image were cast in purple stone? The question of what constitutes 'Egyptian' in ancient Rome is obviously crucial to anyone attempting to understand the place of Egyptian influence in the city. Jean-Marcel Humbert, for example, has argued that a Hellenized depiction of a sphinx with softer contours than its Egyptian relative can still be Egyptianizing, whilst even the most faithful version of a sphinx cannot be called Egyptianizing unless it wears a *nemes*.[29] His contentions are, in part, convincing. As far as the Romans were concerned, sphinxes were as much at home in Greek mythology as they were in Egyptian (although technically speaking, the Classical species had the head and breasts of a woman rather than the head and body of a hawk, ram or man). But his formulation of the problem chooses not to take account of the context of each example. It is presumably a different matter for a Roman when the sphinx in question, with or without a headdress, is represented in the same frame as an Egyptian deity, Apis bull or Nilotic scene.

Most art-historians expect Roman versions of Egyptian figures to be naïve in their representation. There was a 'deep misunderstanding of Egyptian representations by the Romans', writes Anne Roullet in what is still the most comprehensive catalogue of Egyptian and Egyptianizing monuments in imperial Rome.[30] 'To judge from the inaccuracies and misunderstandings shown in certain details of the figure of Horus (?), the paintings are probably the work of a Roman artist', conclude Jocelyn Toynbee and Ward-Perkins in their analysis of the frescoes of Tomb Z beneath the Vatican,[31] whilst Helen Whitehouse berates the western world's general 'superficial imitation of Egyptian art'.[32] But by setting the objects of their censure

[29] Humbert (1994) 21.   [30] Roullet (1972) 21–2.   [31] Toynbee and Ward Perkins (1956) 55.
[32] In Baines and Málek (1980) 222.

within the same frame of reference as Rome's use of Greek artistic motifs, we can start to bring them, and their meaning, under the aegis of Roman Classicism. Art-historians have recently debunked the terminology, which refers to Roman renderings of Greek art as 'copies'. They now largely look positively upon variation, and concentrate upon collections of images, and the dynamics of their new Roman display.[33] A brief consideration of how the Romans treated the Erechtheum's caryatids supports the case for reassessment. Extant examples include the self-supporting statues of Hadrian's Canopus, the versions in the eaves of Augustus' Forum, and the two-dimensional, dainty caryatids of wall-paintings at Pompeii.[34] All are original and witty takes on a corner-stone of Athenian culture. A set of casts and moulds, discovered at Baiae on the Bay of Naples, proves that the Romans could make exact copies, when this was their objective.[35] But more often than not, they chose to exert their freedom. Rarely were they satisfied with the slavish imitation of Greek art.

Similar claims can be made for the Roman image of Horus on the north wall of tomb Z beneath St Peter's, and by extension, images of Egypt-inspired figures from mosaics and paintings throughout Rome and its environs (fig. 15).[36] Regardless of the image's poor state of preservation and the 'distorted' rendering of its details (with its torso more twisted, in line with its legs than is normal in frontal Egyptian decoration), the combination of its polychromy, kilt and sideways stance conjures up immediate intimations of Egypt. For a moment, its alien expression (with what appears to be a large eye in the side of its head, *anck* in its left hand and sceptre in its right, hence its identification as the hawk-headed Horus), and the presence of a second ideographic figure, an Apis bull with its characteristic crescent-moon insignia, and sphinx elsewhere in the chamber, transport the viewer from a necropolis of Rome to an Other-world on the Nile. Authenticity need not come into this equation. It is a mistake to assume that the patrons of the tomb (whether Eygptian or otherwise) necessarily intended their god to match the mother ship at Edfu. If this had been their aim, then scholars would be right to treat his image as an interloper in an alien landscape. But, as he stands, modulated by the hand of an artist accustomed to painting more fluid drapery, and sharing his standard brick-faced chamber with the common classical cipher of a gorgon (a symbol which seems to have come

---

[33] Compare the approaches of e.g. Bieber (1977) with those of Marvin (1993) and (1997).

[34] For those in Augustus' Forum, see Kleiner (1992) 100–1, fig. 83, those at Hadrian's villa, Kleiner (1992) 247, figs. 214–15, and those in Pompeian painting, Ling (1991) 34, 37, figs. 31, 35 and plate IIIA.

[35] See publication of the site by Landwehr (1985).

[36] See Toynbee and Ward Perkins (1956), 51–5, and Mielsch and von Hesberg (1995) 225–33.

Figure 15. Tomb Z with later sarcophagi in the foreground. The now faded figure of
Horus is high in the centre of the back wall.

into the Greek visual vocabulary from Mesopotamia) as well as a bull and
sphinx, he is as comfortable as the bodies of Leda and the Swan on the wall
of tomb Phi, the next-door chamber.[37] He does not embody Egypt proper,
but an Egypt of the Roman mind.

DESTABILIZING THE EGYPTIAN

But there is a danger in the way in which this discussion is moving,
a methodological lesson in how to interpret external influences in a
'multicultural' city or society, especially influences with as much political

[37] For tomb Phi, see Mielsch and von Hesberg (1995) 235–55, fig. 288.

baggage as Egyptian art had for Rome. So keen was I to kick against
the reductionist approaches of those scholars who were unable to find a
place for Cestius' pyramid within Roman culture, or those, like Roullet,
who did find a place for it, but were unable to make it work for them as
Roman, that I was sorely tempted to overlook the opprobrium of Virgil
and Tacitus, and embrace all Egyptianizing objects, whatever their style
and function, unproblematically as Rome. 'Roman culture was, by definition, a cosmopolitan fusion of influences from diverse origins rather than
purely the native culture of Rome itself', wrote Otto Brendel in his famous
essay of 1979.[38] One does not have to tackle Brendel's 'What is Roman
about Roman art?' question head on to sympathize with its standpoint.
His synopsis is as valid for Rome as it is for any metropolis, New York and
London included. Augustus' mausoleum, for example, is widely recognized
to have been inspired both by the aristocratic tombs of the Republican period (those of the Scipios, Caecilia Metella and Cestius), and the Carian
tomb of Mausolus, a monument that was already a synthesis of architecture from Athens, Persia and Egypt.[39] His portraiture combined Polycleitan
and Lysippan imagery, whilst what was to become the icon of Mussolini's
Romanità, the Ara Pacis, echoes the iconography of the Parthenon, the
standard-bearer of democratic Greece. Historians have come up with all
kinds of arguments to downplay the Greekness of these objects (so the
mausoleum becomes a product of Octavian's early, untempered ambition,
and the Classicism of his portraiture is mitigated, on the Ara Pacis at least,
by the veil of Roman religious piety), but the bottom line is that all use
Greek vocabulary to mark Augustus out from Rome's veristic rabble. This
vocabulary, no matter how seamlessly or obviously integrated into Rome's
visual culture, is still resonant with manifold meanings, some positive,
others less so. The validity of Brendel's statement should not obfuscate
the fact that influences from foreign cultures, no matter how Romanizing
in their packaging, carry with them intimations and stereotypes of their
source.

A comparable set of issues surfaces in relation to the study of the empire at
large and the so-called 'Second Sophistic', the blanket-term used to describe
the literary and, most recently, artistic, production of the ancient world
from 60 to 230 CE. The label was coined by the second-century CE writer
Philostratus, who used it to legitimate his own intellectual pursuits and

---

[38] Brendel's thesis as epitomized by Millett (1990) 1.
[39] For the the Scipios and Caecilia Metella, see Boëthius and Ward Perkins (1970) 175–6 and
302, and for Mausolus' tomb, Ashmole (1972) 147–193, Waywell (1978) and Hornblower (1982)
223–74.

those of his fellow sophists by comparing them to the 'first sophists' of fifth-century Athens.[40] But the breadth of its application grows daily as modern scholars find in it new legitimation. Almost everything in the second-century Roman world is now culturally unified as 'Second Sophistic', and said to characterize (and be characterized by) a distinctive, self-conscious relationship with Classical Greece. The shortcomings of this periodization are several. For example, how strong is the justification for claiming that Lucian's prose is more Hellenizing than Catullus' poetry, or all authors in the second century as interested in Atticizing Greek? In addition, images produced at this time, such as those of Hadrian's male lover, Antinous, and the responses to these in outlying areas of the empire, are wrapped up neatly as 'manifestations of Hadrian's Hellenism'.[41] They are entered on the check-list of acceptable behaviour under 'acculturation', together with the emperor's *pallium* and beard.

The principal problem with these kinds of formulations is that they allow no room for conflict. 'Der Gegensatz zwischen griechischer und römischer Tradition verflüchtigte sich weitgehend', writes Zanker in relation to the second century specifically. He continues, 'die klassische Kultur wurde zur gemeinsamen Kultur des Imperium Romanum'.[42] That Roman identity changed dramatically is almost impossible to refute (could Augustus have 'got away with' sporting a philosopher's beard or Nero monumentalized his male lover, Sporus?). But just as it is optimistic to assume that all subjects would have accepted Augustan iconography without comment, so too it is improbable that there was ever a common language which could completely efface local accents. No matter how smoothly Greek and Roman iconographic traits were fused in the sensuous contours of Antinous' statues, it is almost impossible to imagine that such an unprecedented display of passion can have been received without comment or contention. How much more humiliating or absurd could Roman conquest get for some provincials than an invitation to venerate the emperor's boyfriend? Had Antinous' statues been just another example of the fashion for philhellenism, how do we explain their power, their capacity to capture the imagination, the fact that poems were still being written about him at the end of the third century CE?[43]

[40] Philostr. *VS* 1.481.
[41] Birley (1996) 663. For Antinous' image, see Meyer (1991) and Charles-Gaffiot and Lavagne (1999).
[42] Zanker (1995) 193: 'the opposition between Greek and Roman tradition largely disappeared as Classical culture became the common culture of the Roman empire'.
[43] See e.g. the most recent papyrus find from Oxyrhynchus, which preserves part of a poem in praise of Antinous, written at the accession of Diocletian in 284 CE, *P. Oxy.* 63.4352. Also *P. Oxy.* 4.705, which records how games were established in Antinous' honour in 202 CE.

Similar conclusions can be drawn about Cestius' pyramid. It may well be less anomalous than most scholars have assumed, an unsurprising manifestation of a multicultural city's interaction with, and absorption of, a richly decorated country, but it is still an arrogant structure at one of Rome's busiest intersections. It derives meaning from, and gives new meaning to, its Egyptian format (a meaning dependent on its size, position and function as a funerary monument), as much as it is an expression of a prevailing trend in Egyptomania. Scholars have argued for decades over whether Egyptianizing art in Rome was redolent with meaning (religious, political, personal) or was simply an ancient equivalent of eighteenth- and nineteenth-century Chinoiserie.[44] Obviously, any argument must take into account each object's individual context. But the notion that this could then be fitted safely into one or other of these categories, even in antiquity, is deceptive (deliberation goes into even background music or wallpaper). The tendency to see the material in 'either/or' terms has meant that those in opposition to the Chinoiserie camp have overcompensated in their interpretation of the evidence. Assumptions have been made about extant visual examples, which further mislead.

At least we have a date and a function for the structures of Cestius and the Vatican necropolis. Although even here, assumptions have been made about the Egyptian nationality of the owners of the Vatican tomb, a conclusion which becomes less easy to believe the more Egyptianizing iconography we see. But the problem with most of this material is that it rarely comes with a precise archaeological context, making its meaning and date impossible to substantiate. Any effort to date Egyptianizing statues or wall-paintings stylistically is complicated by the fact that we are dealing with figures whose ideographic quality is one of their chief characteristics. Most have been dated after Actium or in the reign of the, rhetorically speaking, most multicultural emperor, Hadrian, but we have already seen how Rome's interest in Egypt was not confined to the second century or 31 BCE. Desperate to define Egyptianizing art and accord it more scholarly weight than the term 'fashion' allows, those who have given any time at all to contextualizing the material within Roman culture have turned to the cult of Isis to give their work meaning. Devotion to Isis becomes the 'rabbit out of a hat', or reasoning behind the bulk of Egyptianizing decor. Studies of the subject, from Roullet's catalogue of ancient material to Humbert,

---

[44] Whitehouse touches on this issue in the last paragraph of her discussion of Egyptianizing elements in Pompeian wall-paintings (1977) 65. Her conclusion is typically polarizing in its formulation: 'it is perhaps best to compromise and say that in some cases the choice of landscape may have been determined by more than the fashions of the day, and the Julia Felix triclinium may be one of these'.

Pantazzi and Ziegler's publication of the Louvre exhibition of Egyptomania throughout western culture, begin and end with Isis.[45] As is so often the case, religion provides a dispensation from more detailed scrutiny.

'In Pompeii, followers of Isis painted scenes from the Nile on their walls', states Christine Ziegler in the introductory essay in the Louvre catalogue.[46] Another monograph on the same subject, this time by Stevens Curl, catalogues two marble Egyptianizing antefixes, one from Ostia and the second from Rome, but which lack precise find-spots, as 'probably from the temple of Demeter-Isis at Ostia' and 'probably from the Iseum Campense'.[47] The only basis for these attributions is the Egyptianizing nature of the subject-matter, and it is a methodology which is not confined to these examples. Several pharaonic-looking statues, including a couple which are traditionally identified as Domitian, and some Sarapis, Isis and Harpocrates heads were found in Beneventum and Rome's *regio* III, respectively.[48] All have been absorbed into supposedly neighbouring Isea. The implications of such strategies are of huge importance both for Egyptianizing art and the cult of Isis. First, as Beard, North and Price clearly summarize, the cult may not have been as Egyptianizing as we now think. After all, most western statues of Isis are Hellenistic rather than Egyptian in their representation. The degree to which the cult is paraded as Roman or Egyptian depends on which ancient authors one reads.[49] But more than this, they raise the question of how far the visibility of the cult in Rome is due to the wider (and wrongly assigned) significance of Egyptianizing material. How many of these neighbouring sites were not what we now categorize neatly as Isea?

Wild's work on known sanctuaries of Isis and Sarapis in the Roman period, for example, excludes Beneventum.[50] He concludes that he can find no definite location for the sanctuary or sanctuaries attested to in surviving inscriptions, whilst I can see no obvious iconographic reason to link the pharaonic heads with Domitian. Although Wild does include the *regio* III example, the foundations for this entry were, at the point of publication, no more stable.[51] As with Beneventum, there had certainly been a sanctuary to Isis somewhere in the area: not only was the region known as Isis Sarapis in the late imperial period but its inhabitants were called 'Isiaci' after its name.[52]

---

[45] Roullet (1972) 1; Ziegler (1994) 15; Stevens Curl (1994) 9. Even Meyboom's monograph on the Palestrina mosaic (1995) 99 suggests that it was inspired by images from the Serapeum at Puteoli.

[46] Ziegler (1994) 17.

[47] Stevens Curl (1994) fig. 8, p. 18. Both are now in the Museo Greg. Egizio, nos. 94 and 96.

[48] For Beneventum, see e.g. Müller (1969) *passim* and Daltrop, Hausmann and Wegner (1966) 39–40, 97–8 and plate 23d. For the heads from *regio* III, see Visconti (1887) 133–6.

[49] Beard, North and Price (1998) 281–2.   [50] Wild (1984) 1744, n. 21.

[51] Wild (1984) cat. no. 33, pp. 1813–14.   [52] *SIRIS* 372–3 and *CIL* VI 3189b.

But the precise situation of the temple depended upon a report by Bellori, published in 1664, which claimed that, 'The chapel of the goddess Isis was discovered in 1653 in a garden below the Caelian Hill close to the church of SS Peter and Marcellinus.'[53] Although there is no real reason to suppose that he was lying about the discovery of the building, the problem again comes in the justification of its function. Bellori writes, 'In it were discovered very beautiful paintings of Egyptian figures.' Even if the account is reliable and accurate in its attention to detail, the sole basis for the classification of the site is the Egyptian nature of its decor. There is no mention of a potential candidate for a cult statue of Isis, nor even a positive identification of Isis amongst the painted figures. 'Among them were idols and winged animals, ibises and sphinxes, priests standing and other priests kneeling in front of crowned and winged monsters, (priests?) with baskets of grain and of flowers.' There is little doubt that together, these elements conjure up an image of Egypt and, more specifically still, the Roman stereotypical view of Egypt's religious mystery. But Isis? Even if Isis were evoked in some viewers' minds, the prevalence of Egyptian imagery in Cestius' pyramid, tomb Z, and elsewhere in Rome, underlines the obvious objection that the building need not have been specifically for Isis nor for any kind of religious activity.

Since Wild's publication, however, two seventeenth-century drawings of the scenes described by Bellori have come to light in the collection of the Royal Library at Windsor.[54] Their discovery goes some way to alleviating the scepticism displayed above: one of them clearly shows the figure of Isis beneath an ornamental canopy with her robe characteristically knotted at the front. Ongoing archaeology in the Via Labicana area has even gone so far as to identify the vaulted structure in which the paintings were originally sited (a little further north than the association with the church implies) and suggested that it may have been part of a larger portico and pool complex, discovered between the modern Vie Buonarroti and Bonghi, and identified as the main Iseum.[55] Whether this hypothesis is right or wrong (and there are conflicting opinions about the function of the latter complex, as well as incongruities in the style of the paintings and the Republican date

---

[53] Appended to the Rome edition of Lunadoro (1664) 62. See also Bartoli in Fea (1790) vol. 1, ccxxii: 'an Egyptian temple has been discovered near the church of SS Pietro e Marcellino, the figures of which were designed by order of Cassiano dal Pozzo'.

[54] Royal Library Windsor Castle inv. 11398–9.

[55] This Iseum is now known as the 'Iseum Metellinum' after a reference in SHA *Tyr. Trig.* 25 and the Metelli identified as Metellus Pius and Metellus Numidicus (*RE* 111 Caecilius 98 and 97). For recent location attempts, see de Vos (1996) 110–12 and for the ongoing work of the GIS[A] FORTVNA project in this area, see e.g. with additional bibliography, Häuber and Schültz (1999).

of both the extant architecture and the Iseum's supposed patrons), recent
research is still unwilling to concede that not all of the Isiac or even broadly
Egyptianizing material in the area (Bellori's structure included) need have
belonged to a sanctuary or had a strictly cultic context. The very existence
of an eponymous sanctuary to Isis, and the likelihood that there were ritual
objects and miniatures for sale, would only have made it more likely that
Isiac decoration became popular in settings which did not belong to staunch
devotees. The heads of Isis and Sarapis mentioned above, and assigned to
the Iseum, were found over a wide area, built into later structures. They
too may have been part of this general popularity. They, and the paintings,
need not have belonged to the important Iseum.

More serious doubts surface in relation to the so-called 'Aula Isiaca', the
vaulted hall under the northern corner of Domitian's palace on the Palatine,
which was accessed (and drawings made of its wall-paintings) as early as
1724, but which was excavated fully in 1912.[56] This time, the drawings,
and sections of the paintings themselves, survive, found in their original
archaeological context (fig. 16). These too encompass Egyptian elements
within a complex illusionistic backdrop: there is, for example, an Egyptian-
style statue on a plinth represented in the rarefied architecture. But more
than this, a decorative border of symbols used in Isiac ritual (*situlae, uraei,
vasi rotondi*) winds its way prettily along the top of each wall and across
larger rectangular panels on the ceiling. A priestess of Isis has been identified
in one of the small panels on the wall in the shape of a veiled, female figure
clad in white. The conveyor-belt of cult objects stakes a claim to religious
specificity, and potentially even the belief system of the building's owner,
but it, and the figure of the priestess it qualifies, are far from the full story. In
fact, these details form but a fraction of a decorative schema which includes
a panel of a fleshy, Hellenistic cupid balanced on the curling tail of a sea-
monster, as in the Munich relief of the Altar of Domitius Ahenobarbus, and
of the same dimensions as the panel with the supposed priestess, and (more
importantly, to judge from its larger size) a scene which survives only in the
eighteenth-century drawings of the chamber and shows a male helmeted
hero in the style of the 'Borghese Ares' helping a female figure down from
a boat.[57] There is nothing explicitly Egyptian in the style or content of
these panels, nor anything ritualistic, such as attributes or clothing, to tie

---

[56] See monographs by Rizzo (1936) and Iacopi (1997), as well as entries in Claridge (1998) 135 and
Richardson (1992) 46. The wall-paintings are now displayed in the second court of the palace
complex.

[57] For the Altar of Domitius Ahenobarbus, see e.g. Kuttner (1993) and on the 'Borghese Ares' type
and its import in Rome, Kleiner (1981).

Figure 16. Water-colour by G. Piccini (1724) showing a section of the decoration of the 'Aula Isiaca', including the frieze of cult objects and panels of a sea monster with cupid and Paris and Helen.

them to the worship of Isis. But so pressed have scholars been to try to explain, or give a deeper significance to, the few Egyptianizing elements of the building, that these elements have taken over to give it its name and identity. Even the image of man, woman and boat, generally agreed to be a representation of Paris and Helen disembarking from Sparta, is now interpreted in a specifically Isiac light.[58]

This over-determination of the frescoes' Egyptianizing elements has had a dramatic effect on the dating and broader historical discussion of the building, so much so, in fact, that Carlo Boni's original publication of the site in 1913 as a 'Republican house', the remains of which belonged to the stage of building before the imperial palaces claimed the space, has been practically forgotten, replaced instead with the more attention-grabbing falsehood that it was built by Caligula in around 40 CE.[59] 'On the Palatine, this sovereign built himself a palace of Isis', wrote Witt, one of the most influential scholars to have worked on Isis and her evidence.[60] By the time we reach Stevens Curl in 1994, 'Caligula encouraged the cult of Isis, imported a large obelisk to beautify Rome, erected the Aula Isiaca on the Palatine Hill, and emphasized the Egyptian-Isiac character of the cult of Emperor-worship by marrying his own sister.'[61] His sentiments do for Caligula what scholars have done for Hadrian in packaging Antinous with the emperor's *pallium* and beard. Only this time, there is more to exonerate. The charges of incest aside, the connection between the 'Aula Isiaca' and Caligula comes exclusively from the emphasis on their alleged Egyptianizing natures and, more critically still, contradicts the archaeology which pushes the structure back fifty years or more into the Republican period. The Italian art-historian, Rizzo, was the first to circumvent the context of the structure and identify its decoration with Caligula. For him, the decoration spelled Isis, and Isis Caligula, the emperor who is reported to have been the most enthusiastic about her worship.[62] The fact that few scholars have questioned his conclusions, or paused to compare the building to other known Isiac sites in Rome, underscores how the urgency to situate Egyptian iconography and give meaning to its exoticism has reached an alarming degree.

Amanda Claridge is a shining exception, and reinstates the 'Aula Isiaca' to its rightful position as Republican. Ostensibly, at least, she leaves the meaning of its Isiac motifs to others. We should all be similarly loath to link decoration with function, after witnessing the recent research on

---

[58] Iacopi (1997) 39 following Rizzo (1936) 36–7.   [59] Boni (1913) 247.   [60] Witt (1971) 223–4.
[61] Stevens Curl (1994) 18.   [62] Rizzo (1936) 38–9.

wall-paintings at Pompeii.[63] But what she does say is that the building is 'painted in the Egyptianizing style of about 30 BCE'.[64] Despite declining to comment on the iconography, the few Egyptianizing elements still trap her. It cannot be a coincidence (can it?) that the date she assigns to the decoration is one year after Actium. It is a date which is supported by the second style of the paintings and by the stone-work of the structure, but one which relies ultimately on the emphasis of its Egyptianizing and Isiac elements (elements which are not necessarily one and the same) and seeing these as a localized response to Rome's most publicized encounter with Egypt. The appearance of the wall-paintings and the overly precise limitations of the four styles as a dating tool mean that they could potentially have been executed at almost any point between 50 BCE and 50 CE. Let us not forget that the literature shows a fascination with things Egyptian throughout the Roman empire. As with most extant Egyptianizing artifacts, without a secure context, and sometimes even with a secure context, there is nothing innate to help with dating, nor in justifying their iconography.

WRAPPING IT UP?

So where do these workings leave us and Cestius' pyramid? It is a rather wishy-washy conclusion to say that no matter how well integrated into Rome's multi-cultural society Egyptianizing aesthetic elements, and external artistic influences more broadly, were, they were not without a certain degree of native (or rather the Roman take on their native) meaning. If we then argue that this meaning was not necessarily religious, nor tied specifically to Isiac sanctity, what *was* the motivation behind the evocation of an Egyptian landscape, animal-headed god or pyramid? Or to put it another way, what was this building in *regio* III, if not a functioning Iseum? The boring reality, of course, is that it too may have been a private house like the 'Aula Isiaca'. But why the choice of décor? The sweeping statements of 'Second Sophistic' discourse – 'cultural conquest', 'unification' or 'stylistic synthesis' – go only some way to answering this question. None of them clarify the specifics of a site's significance, nor a particular patron's reasoning, to a tight enough historical degree. My only hope of refining my conclusions is to end with a building for which we do have a context: we know its date, a date which is nowhere near the exculpatory chronologies

---

[63] See e.g. Clarke (1998) esp. 195–6, who tackles the misconception that the presence of a sexually explicit painting at Pompeii dictates that the building or room was a brothel. On this ill-conceived basis, Pompeii had 35 brothels (!) *Pompei: l'informatica al servizio di una città antica* (1988) 71.

[64] Claridge (1998) 135.

of the Battle of Actium or Hadrianic eclecticism, the identity of its patron, and despite controversy over its precise function, that it was definitely not an Iseum. Perhaps here, in the so-called 'Basilica' of Junius Bassus, built on the Esquiline in the first half of the fourth century, there lies a more precise picture of why at least one wealthy Roman saw fit to use Egyptian-izing symbols as part of his commemorative language.[65] By comparing the context of this language with that of Cestius' pyramid and tomb Z beneath the Vatican, monuments for which we also, and unusually for Egyptianiz-ing sites, know both date and function, there is a possibility that (despite the fact that each patron will have had his own reasons for emulating his part of Egypt's visual landscape) we can come to some broad conclusions about the connotations of Egyptian culture in at least a subset of Rome's imagery.

The subset in question is funerary or, more loosely defined, commemo-rative imagery. Whether the 'Basilica' of Junius Bassus was actually meant as a mausoleum, as has been argued by Schumacher, a cenotaph or building in honour of someone buried, in accordance with Roman law, beyond the city limits, or a basilica, as is now generally accepted by way of a convenient or obfuscatory short-hand, the apsidal hall on the hill surely functioned as a memorial to the man whose name is displayed on the inscription, the *consul ordinarius*, Junius Bassus, and stood as a concrete marker of his presence and status in this world and for centuries to come.[66] In this sense, and in so far as it was a building for a powerful Roman individual, with a large investment in the city's political system, the structure is not dissimilar in its purpose from the pyramid of the praetor, Gaius Cestius, with its osten-sibly funereal function. I am not about to surmise whether the 'basilica' ever housed, or was constructed to house, Junius Bassus' body. Unfortu-nately, the structure was demolished in the 1930s, leaving only Ashby and Lugli's excavation reports, the marble wall panels, which will be discussed below (figs. 17 and 18), and drawings made by Giuliano da Sangallo late in the fifteenth century, and none of these sources offer any firm evidence on this matter.[67] But despite their different chronologies and their differ-ent ways of doing things, both Bassus and Cestius (or at least the heirs of Cestius) saw an Egyptian-suggestive visual vocabulary as a ready means of celebrating and magnifying their lives and achievements in the Roman world.

---

[65] *CIL* VI 1737.

[66] Schumacher (1958) 117, n. 90, and as a cenotaph, *RE* XI 1 s.v. *Kenotaphion*, c. 171.

[67] Ashby and Lugli (1932) 221–55. For easy access to Sangallo's drawings, Hülsen (1910) 45–7 and (1927) 53–67, and for the Windsor 'copies' of the drawings, Waetzoldt (1964) 29.

Figure 17. Intarsio panel showing Hylas and the nymphs with its Egyptianizing border
from the 'Basilica' of Junius Bassus.

As far as we know, the Egyptianizing elements of the 'basilica' were
confined to narrow bands or friezes of ideographic figures, which framed
two of the intarsio panels, originally decorating the space. The best known
of these panels depict tigers capturing calves, and are now in the Capitoline
collection, but it is those of Hylas and the nymphs, and a male figure in
a chariot, which are emphasized by the Egyptian bands above. The chariot
scene is most typical of Roman art of the late antique period: it shows a
male figure, with a broad horizontal band across his toga, a flat, frontal
torso, and saucer-like stare. His outstretched arm could be said to echo that

Figure 18. Recut intarsio panel of consular figure in a chariot surrounded by riders from
four circus factions from the 'Basilica' of Junius Bassus.

of the Primaporta statue of Augustus and works together with the horses,
which lead the chariot and the viewer through the centre of the scene,
to expose his body to visual attack. One of the closest parallels to this
configuration comes from the base of the obelisk of Theodosius from the
hippodrome at Constantinople, where the emperor and his family stand
facing forwards and, framed by the royal box, gaze out at their real and
represented audience.[68] Such powerful associations, combined with the
observation that our protagonist wears an embroidered toga or *toga picta*
to denote either triumph or imperial or (as in the ivory diptychs of the
fifth and sixth centuries or the image of Constantius II from the copy of
a codex-calendar produced in Rome in 354 CE) consular office, command
our attention and afford him status.[69] It is a logical assumption to suggest
that he represents Junius Bassus, the patron, who the building's inscription
claims was consul in 331 CE.[70]

---

[68] On the obelisk of Theodosius, see Kiilerich (1993) 31–9.

[69] On the *toga picta* and triumph, see Tac. *Ann.* 4.26; Livy, 10.7.9 and 30.15.11 and Flor. 1.5.6; on its
imperial context, Flor. 1.5.6 and SHA *Gordiani Tres* 4.4; on its later use in consular iconography,
Weitzmann (1979) cat. nos. 45–9, pp. 46–50, and on the codex-calendar in particular, Salzman
(1990).

[70] This is not without contention. See e.g. Becatti (1969) 197.

Sadly, or perhaps fortunately for art-historians intent on finding answers in the life-history of their subject, we know nothing about Bassus' biography (whether he was once praetor in Egypt, worshipper of Isis, that kind of thing). But there is a sense in which the standard nature of the iconography of the chariot scene makes it even more striking that it should be framed by Egyptianizing figures. Once it was removed from its original setting in the 'basilica', the panel was reduced in size, and recut into a rectangle, but drawings by Guliano da Sangallo show that it had a similar shape and Egyptian setting to the Hylas panel, now displayed intact in the Palazzo Massimo Museum. In both of these cases, beneath the central scene, a procession of small, stiff figures moves across a white background towards a series of enthroned Egyptian deities. These figures carry cult objects or weave their way past candelabra or vases. They spread beyond the dimensions of the central scene to decorate a further fringe, which hangs in swathes in the form of fabric to the floor. The fact that the Egyptian elements should have been part of a pastiche, which seems to have been designed to resemble drapery, might reinforce the notion that one of the main purposes of their presence was to enhance the opulence of the building by simulating silks from Egypt.[71] But we are missing something, I think, if we do not allow the juxtaposition or situation of the late antique Roman imagery, whether chariot scene or Hylas, with(in) its Egyptianizing context to signify something richer than the luxuriant status of the hall.

If we consider the companion piece to the chariot scene, that of Hylas and the nymphs, we notice that Hylas' hand is raised in acclamation to the viewer, signalling perhaps its similarity to the outstretched arm of the aristocrat described above.[72] If we want to pursue this link between the two panels, as potentially prompted to do by their similar Egyptianizing settings, then we see that nymphs have taken the place of the horsemen in the background. They snatch their subject from his life on earth down into the waters below. It takes little imagination to understand why this image from a myth about a man who died young and beautiful was a common motif on funerary monuments throughout the Roman period.[73] But there is evidence that chariot scenes too, stemming presumably from their association with (especially imperial) apotheosis, were also part of this specialist commemorative repertoire, as Romans were represented in

---

[71] In line with the *luxus* described by e.g. Plin. *NH* 34.34 and 36.16 and Ath. 196A.

[72] For close iconographic parallels to this scene, see e.g. the third-century CE floor mosaic of Hylas from the House of the Venus Mosaic in Volubilis, Morocco, *LIMC* v cat. no. 17, p. 575.

[73] For a bibliography on Hylas and his funerary context, see Cumont (1942) 97, n. 2 and 402, n. 3.

triumphant splendour racing to the afterlife.[74] In addition to these connections, similar shaped drapes or *vela* to those in the 'basilica' can be seen
on stelae and sarcophagi of the third and fourth centuries, and have been
interpreted as the material which envelops the soul of the deceased before
his or her entry to the celestial world above.[75]

The overriding image then would seem to be commemorative, if not
specifically funerary. Might this conclusion explain the appropriateness
of its Egyptian imagery? Again, using the Egyptianizing elements as his
starting-point, Becatti, whose publication of the 'basilica' is still the cor-
nerstone of our studies of the site, has argued that the Egyptianizing details
are an integral part of a programme which displays a specifically neo-
platonist attitude to dying.[76] The bare bones of his justification are that
neo-platonists were interested in the mysteries of Egypt (Plato having supposedly gained his wisdom in Egypt, Pythagoras spent much time there,
and Plotinus been involved with the cult of Isis) and that the Hylas and
chariot panels could be read as fitting their philosophical doctrine as alle-
gories of the soul.[77] This time, the 'rabbit out of a hat', Isiacism, has been
substituted for the equally obscure yet precise neo-platonism. Similar criticisms apply here as for Isis: one does not have to be a practising platonist
(whatever that might mean) if one has Hylas or a chariot on one's wall.

Instead, what the evidence does suggest, once set in a broader cultural
context next to Cestius' pyramid and tomb Z of the Vatican, is that the
Romans saw Egyptian iconography, or the idea of Egypt which was con-
veyed in their version of Egyptian iconography, as a useful mechanism for
referring to the afterlife. Whatever its connotations, positive or negative,
Egypt was the ultimate 'other world', an assimilated yet ethereal landscape,
whose history was ineffably linked with monumentality and the notion of
endurance after death. This essay has already highlighted how the Romans
shared our twenty-first-century enthusiasm for the antiquity of Egypt's
colossal statues and temples, with Horace, for example, offering the pyramids as the ultimate measure of mortality. There is also evidence to suggest
that they were fascinated by the Egyptian custom of embalming. Both
Diodorus Siculus and Cicero write positively about the process of mummi-
fication, whilst Dio Cassius indicts it as one of the clichéd charges, which
he has his Caesar throw against the forces of Antony.[78] The body of Nero's
second wife, Poppaea, is said by Tacitus to have been embalmed in spices

---

[74] Compare e.g. Cumont (1942) plate xLV and figs. 97–9, pp. 461–4.
[75] Compare e.g. De Ruyt (1936) 160–4 and Cumont (1942) 476–7.   [76] Becatti (1969) 204–11.
[77] For more on the neo-platonist connection to Egypt, see Smelik and Hemelrijk (1984) 1953–5.
[78] Diod. Sic. 2.1.2; Cic. *Tusc.* 1.108 and Dio Cass. 50.24.6.

in keeping with the Ptolemaic tendencies she is given (Cassius Dio describes her as bathing in asses' milk like Cleopatra) whilst alive.[79] Against this background, it is perhaps easier to appreciate how the Egyptianizing borders fit their context. Not simply decorative, nor specifically neo-platonist, rather they frame the panels within them. They lift them out of the sway of everyday drama into the hermeneutic sphere of a world beyond. As Carrott has argued in relation to nineteenth-century America and its use of Egyptian imagery, '[Egyptian] funerary affiliation, [is] perhaps the most persistent image ever projected by a culture'.[80] Together, the building dedicated to Junius Bassus, Cestius' pyramid, and tomb Z beneath the Vatican suggest that this was a sentiment that the Romans themselves might have shared.

This is not to say that all other unidentified Egyptianizing material in Rome was originally funerary. This essay has warned against such unification of meaning and argued instead for a more polymorphous Rome in which Egypt could assume a spectrum of shades and shapes. Recognition of this spectrum is crucial. In recent years, scholars of Classical culture have shifted focus from concentrating on Rome's relationship with, and representation of the Other, to her cultural conquest and synthesis with the empire. They have sought examples in which sub-cultures and their heritages have melded with Rome to create a dominant, unified race. Countless new lines of inquiry have emerged from this change of angle. Investigation into the once relatively neglected second century CE is now thriving, as is research on the cultural eclecticism of Rome's changing language of imperium and visual display. This essay has chosen to concentrate on the status of Egyptianizing influences in the multicultural capital. By extension, it has examined strategies for coming to terms with foreign influences more broadly in what is now casually called, 'a cultural melting-pot' or cosmopolitan space. In the current intellectual climate, it sounds absurd to call Cestius' pyramid an 'anomaly'. Instead, it has become a natural expression of Rome's contact and political unification with the south and the east. But the danger with this 'anything goes' environment is that everything goes, including the meaning. This process of cultural assimilation becomes an end in itself as opposed to a springboard for further discussion. The impact of Cestius' pyramid is reduced to an entry in Rome's catalogue of conquests. The specifics of the monument's appearance, function and position each give place.

The enduring problem, however, with so much of the surviving Egyptianizing art from Rome is that its date and context are unrecoverable. As

---

[79] Tac. *Ann.* 16.6 and Cass. Dio 62.28.   [80] Carrott (1978) 132.

with the so-called 'Aula Isiaca', assumptions are made about its meaning which cannot be supported by literary or archaeological data. Overly optimistic stabs at meaning are more insidious than saying that something is simply 'characteristic of Roman art'. So where do we go from here? Well, just as we must work with the duality that an object might be *both* wallpaper *and* the result of a long and hard decision-making process on the part of artist and/or patron, so too must we use the growing secondary literature on cultural syncretism alongside data on specific sites to give new life and meaning to Rome and her representation. One thing is for certain: yet more catalogues on Egyptianizing art in Rome are not the way forward. Once we take the notion of Rome as Cosmopolis as a given, or point of departure, we can carefully insert Egypt inside Rome's boundaries, and (if the objects allow) explore meaning in terms of genre or functional category: not Egyptianizing versus Hellenizing, but domestic, imperial, funerary. Only then can we make an inroad on the many expressions of Rome's multicultural face.

CHAPTER 10

The City of Letters

Greg Woolf

THE WORLD'S CITY

He calls Rome the people (*demos*) of all the earth. Indeed he says too that it would not be far off the mark to call the City of Rome an *epitome* of the civilized world, for within it every city may be seen to have planted a colony. Most cities he refers to by their famous epithets, Golden Alexandria, Fair Antioch, Nicomedia the Beautiful and 'that most radiant of all the cities ever made by Zeus'.... Athens, of course. But a whole day would not be enough for me to recount all the cities he numbers within the celestial City of the Romans. In fact, a year's worth of days would not be enough, so numerous are they. For entire nations have come to live there, such as the Cappadocians, the Scythians, the Pontians and many others. (Athenaeus, *Deipnosophists* 1.20b–c)

This passage takes us through familiar territory.[1] Rome is unlike all other cities in its scale and in its splendour. It is a city that stands for the world, a city that words cannot capture.[2] Then, again by a familiar trope, the world city shimmers out of focus. Vast barbarian populations, their names evocative of the great slaving-grounds of the Republic, colonize this complex of Hellenistic capitals.[3] In the paragraphs that follow we read how the 'gathered *demos* of all the world' idolized a dancer-philosopher and named him after 'the most ancient and royal of cities', Memphis, the ancient capital of Athenaeus' native Egypt. The despised tastes of the *plebs urbana* lead us back to another comparison with the past, a test which Rome now fails. All these moves were as familiar to ancient readers as they are to us. Rome had acquired an established place in the tropical universe, was equipped

---

[1] I am extremely grateful to Denis Feeney and Catharine Edwards for reading and commenting on this chapter.

[2] The conceit is a central image in Aristides' panegyric *To Rome*, and the notion of Rome as an *epitome* of the *oikoumene* was attributed to Polemo by Galen. On these and other examples of the trope see Swain (1996) 363–5.

[3] For cosmopolitan Rome rewritten as barbarized and de-Romanized, Juvenal, *Satires* 3 is the *locus classicus*, on which Edwards (1996) 125–9.

with routine comparisons and oppositions, was praised and reproached in all the same ways that every imperial capital has been.

Yet Rome was not the imperial capital. Or rather it was not, in Athenaeus' day, a centre of government in the same sense as Periclean Athens or Victorian London, or even Ciceronian Rome. The seat of government was located wherever the emperor himself happened to be sitting. That might be in Rome, but might equally be in Sirmium or Corinth, at Tivoli or on Capri. If Rome was still an imperial capital after the fall of the Republic, it was so more in the sense that New York was in the early part of the twentieth century. As the totemic vestibule to America and as symbol of its melting-pot ideology, the great metropolis of the Empire State put on display unrivalled magnificence and squalor. It was celebrated for this in art and novels, in song and on film. Rome of the emperors too epitomized an empire it did not rule. This chapter is about the transformation of the city of Rome from one kind of capital to another.

For moderns, as perhaps for the urban plebs, it is the accumulated physical grandeur of the city and the ceremonies that brought it to life that mark Rome out as a cultural capital. But monumental Rome was invisible from the provinces. Coins might depict individual buildings, and some metropolitan landmarks were imitated in provincial cities, but the cityscape of the Cosmopolis could not be grasped through those media alone.[4] The emperors invented new ceremonies, like the *adventus* and *osculatio*, that they could take with them on their journeys. No Woody Allen movies celebrated Rome in each provincial town. Visiting sophists filled provincial *odea* with the praises of their host cities, Corinth and Alexandria, Athens and Ephesus, rather than with eulogies of the metropolis. The physical magnificence of the City on the Tiber was perhaps a shock to many visitors, if we are to believe the trope of amazement on first *seeing* Rome.[5]

If you were to pass back through the ancient forum and were to behold one forum ranged after another and the royal stoas and temples, and were to see the Capitol and all the monuments on it and the Palatine and the porticus of Livia, you might easily forget everything outside the City. (Strabo, *Geography* 5.3.8)

Most of Strabo's readers would not, however, view the metropolis at first hand. Instead, they would read about it; and so this chapter is about texts,

---

[4] Besides, the provincial *Stadtbilder* of the Augustan age were in many cases not constrained or given meaning by existing structures and resonances in the way that monuments in Rome were, with the result that their 'Roman' centres looked quite unlike the centre of Rome. For examples, see the papers in Trillmich and Zanker (1990), Goudineau and Reborg (1991), Fentress (2000).

[5] One to which Lucian, *Nigrinus* 18 gives a twist in having the philosopher declare that he lives in Rome like a man sitting high in a vast theatre, observing the spectacle of vice it offers.

not monuments, and about the rewriting of the imperial city, not its re-building. The texts concerned are mostly in Latin, as I shall be examining a cultural game played more in the West than in the empire as a whole. As my initial text indicates, Rome's Greek subjects had other capitals. But there was no hermetic seal between the high cultures of empire. Greek littérateurs will intrude themselves back into the story, just as Juvenal claims they always did,[6] and sometimes they even told similar stories about the Cosmopolis.

But it is not enough to simply comb ancient testimony for images of the City in the hope of finding stereotypes for consumption by dumb provincials. Roman writers were not cameras, and their literature was not disinterested or realistic reportage. Evident as these propositions are, their implications are not always appreciated by those who have written the daily life of the City as a pastiche of anecdotes from Juvenal and Pliny, Martial and Statius. One aim of this chapter is to explore some ways in which precisely these texts can be used by historians in ways that do less violence to their literary agendas. But that will involve a necessary detour through the sociology of Latin literary activity, by which I mean consideration of the political and social location of writers and readers.[7]

It is probably helpful at this point if I summarize the argument. Rome, I have been suggesting, *was* represented as a cultural capital to the readers of Latin literature, and those readers *were* mostly provincials. But those writers were not engaged in a conscious shared project to represent Rome to the provinces, let alone one promoted by the imperial state or the Roman aristocracy. Roman literary modes of writing *were* well suited to marking out cultural distance, but in general their target was not the provinces but closer to home. Latin literature developed this discourse of differentiation in part as a consequence of the relationship established between the Latin intelligentsia and the Roman aristocracy. The independence this won Roman writers meant, however, that literature always had to compete with other potential markers and activities of the Roman leisure class. One tactic was the appropriation of the energy of alternative pursuits. Another response was a sustained cultural project to give the City of Rome a central place

---

[6] Much of what follows represents a meditation on the image of the cultural life of Rome conjured up in the first part of volume III of Friedlander (1928). Keith Hopkins introduced me not only to this marvellous work but also to many of the argumentative techniques with which I now propose a slightly different picture.

[7] That project has barely begun but I have gratefully drawn for this chapter on Fantham (1996), Bloomer (1997), Habinek (1998). Perhaps the linguistic turn in literary studies and a sociological one in ancient history left Roman historians and Latinists heading in different directions for a while. The contrast with Hellenic studies, where a sense of historical context has enriched readings of Greek texts for a decade, is striking.

in Latin literature by writing it up as a literary capital. Portraying Rome as a cultural centre, and its elite as absorbed in literary pursuits, emerged as much from the local political concerns of writers in the Cosmopolis as from any desire to export Rome to provincial audiences. All the same, provincials were drawn in, both as participants and because provincial locales had long been imagined as convenient vantage points from which to regard the City. Imperial society provided few barriers to movement or cultural participation. Unlike more recent colonial elites, then, the provincial littérateurs of the West produced neither distinctive literatures nor perspectives on the City. Rome's new-found status as the cultural capital of the West suited many interests, but its creation was otherwise fortuitous, an accidental product of other 'culture wars'. Written Rome, on the other hand, was profoundly shaped by its new significance within an imperial culture, just as the City found a new location for itself in the empire.

LATIN LITERATURE AND THE CONSTRUCTION OF CULTURAL DISTANCE

My starting-point is the capacity of Latin literature to induce a sense of cultural alienation, to induce in its readers a sense of a community divided by hierarchies of cultural competence. That capacity was a precondition for creating the gulf between provincialism and metropolitan sophistication, but arguably it predated those imperial agendas.

Ancient historians often complain about the unevenness of the written testimony at their disposal, and of the limited range of viewpoints represented by their authors. But these limits can be a strength if we wish to empathize with Rome's provincial readers. Like provincial or other subaltern readers,[8] we worry that we are too dependent on texts for our knowledge of Rome, and that perhaps we have not got enough texts, or not the right ones, and maybe do not know quite how to read them properly. Latin literature characteristically operated to induce a similar sense of inadequacy in its readers.[9] Complex allusive practices were directed towards two literatures and on a broad mythological and historical field; elaborate synonyms for

[8] Those readers, that is, who read about Rome without feeling fully part of it, or fully competent at reading. My guess is that this group comprised the vast majority of readers of Latin literature, whether resident in the provinces (eastern as well as western), Italy or indeed the City itself. The argument that follows might be summarized as a proposition that Latin literature was written in such a way as to make subalterns of its readers, to culturally disfranchise most of those whom literacy might be thought to have empowered.

[9] Henderson (1997) explores some of the ways Juvenalian satire manages this trick.

proper names were sought; conventions that were rarely made explicit characterized particular genres, or the treatment of particular themes. Literary Latinity often sought registers remote from everyday spoken or written Latin.

Consider, for example, the opening lines of Statius' *Thebaid*, composed at the end of the first century CE.

> Fraternas acies alternaque regna profanis
> decertata odiis sontesque evolvere Thebas,
> Pierius menti calor incidit. unde iubetis
> ire, deae? gentisne canam primordia dirae,
> Sidonios raptus et inexorabile pactum
> legis Agenoreae scrutantemque aequora Cadmum?
>
> (Statius, *Thebaid* 1.1–6)

Fraternal battle and alternating kingdoms opposed in impious hatred and guilty Thebes is the tale Pierian fire rouses me to unfold. But where do you bid me begin, goddesses? Shall I sing of the origins of that hateful race, the Sidonian rape, the inflexible terms of Agenor's law, and Cadmus searching over all the sea?

The epic plunges the listener or reader into an assault course of allusion. Our commentaries supply answers to questions a Roman reader might feel he or she was expected to have coped with unaided. Myth first. Who are the warring brothers? Which kingdoms does he mean? In what sense did they alternate? What was so terrible about Thebes, and where or what is Pieria? Who raped whom at Sidon? Who was Agenor, and what was so inexorable about his law? For what or whom was Cadmus searching? But there are questions about epic too, since the metre and lexis immediately identify the poem as such. 'Fraternal' evokes civil war, and the beginning of Lucan's *Pharsalia*, itself pointing back to the second half of the *Aeneid*. But isn't Latin epic, ever since Ennius, supposed to be about a *Roman* past? The suspicion that the *Thebaid* is, despite its overt subject, really about Rome will hover at the back of the reader's mind, to be stoked up by Statius all the way through the poem. There are questions of criticism too. The opening issue of whether any epic could have a clearly defined beginning or end, was by Statius' day well travelled terrain. A competent reader should recognize this in the long *apostrophe* to the muses that is also a *praeteritio*, a declaration that Statius will *not* tell of Sidon, Agenor and Cadmus, of the farmer who sowed battle, of Amphion's song and the mountains of Tyre, of Bacchus' anger against his ancestral walls... and so on, cryptic allusion after allusion leading to Oedipus. Until, just when the co-ordinates of the beginning of *Statius'* Theban epic seem set (line 17), with an abrupt change of direction a second *praeteritio* declares that Statius will also not sing of 'Italian standards and northern triumphs, of the Rhine twice yoked, of Transdanubia twice invaded by legions, of the defeat of the Dacians', and so on. That *recusatio*, the poet deferring an epic about his imperial Roman patron, is by now a trope of imperial verse, even if Statius has surprised the reader by inserting it into 'epics I shall not sing'. But can we take this claim seriously? Is the *Thebaid* about Domitian after all, the way the *Aeneid* is about Augustus, and if so which character or characters evoke the emperor and his family? Civil war might be a traditional theme of Roman epic by Statius' day, but the subject has a new, post-Lucanian resonance after 69 CE brought the Flavians to power. But is it safe to read the *Thebaid* according to the conventions of *Roman* epic, when it is sung by a Greek on a Greek theme, inspired by Greek muses, and played (line 33) on the *chelys?* And yet, the last time we were comfortably settled in Greek myth (at line 17) Domitianic warfare burst into the poem . . . and so on, and so on. This anti-introduction keeps even the skilled reader guessing about what will follow, and about how the epic is to be read.

The introit to the *Thebaid* shows that there was more to the allusiveness of Latin literature than a simple desire to exclude. Allusion enriched texts by appropriating the energy of literary predecessors, of scholarly researches, of cult, of belief and of social memory. The complexity of Latin literary treatments of important social rituals – dining for example – reflected the complex etiquette of aristocratic mores.[10] The invention of less ordinary styles of speech overtly competed with similar tactics in Greek rhetoric.[11] Yet the price for these effects – esotericism – was paid willingly, and sometimes relished. Reading Latin literary texts was clearly hard work, and meant to be. Even when an author deliberately adopted a more inclusive style, as the Younger Pliny did in his letters, that effect is achieved partly by ostentatious abstention from the devices of routine exclusion, in order to signal a (temporary and voluntary) departure from the norm. Any reader who felt gratitude must at the same have been made aware that concessions were being made, that the text condescended to being widely readable.

Latin literature thus constructed cultural distance between authors and readers. Scholars more usually stress the converse, that a common literary

---

[10] That is, of course, earlier texts claimed as predecessors, as classics, as rough prototypes now surpassed and so forth by various kinds of allusion. On all this see Hinds (1998). On the appropriation of cult and belief see Feeney (1998), on dining as a literary motif Gowers (1993). Other social rituals that might be given the same treatment include courtship and marriage and, as will emerge, 'literary life' itself.

[11] Bloomer (1997), also exploring the links between Latinity, Roman identity and social conflict in Rome.

culture had the potential to bind together as an elite group those who were confident readers of this esoteric discourse. For the rich of Rome, participation in literary activity might become part of the life of luxury, a marker of membership of the leisure class.[12] It offered itself as a form of conspicuous consumption, less costly than euergetism, which was in any case dangerous in the capital where even absentee emperors jealously guarded the patronage of the *plebs urbana*.[13]

All this is perhaps true, although we might wonder how many readers of the *Thebaid* were justifiably confident that they had passed the tests it set. And tests of that kind were often set by the aristocrats' social inferiors. The status dissonance between high-ranking but incompetent readers and lower-ranking expert writers was one pressure leading to the social promotion of many of the latter.[14] And then there was the danger of becoming *too* learned.[15] Perhaps this was a game it was safer not to play?

We should, perhaps, be cautious before concluding that literary activity played a central part in the self-definition of the Roman imperial aristocracy. Certainly those classes that no longer ruled the world – who were becoming an aristocracy of status rather than of office[16] – were offered the chance of attaining cultural supremacy through letters. But there was a price to pay. Accepting a cultural definition of elite status (as opposed to a moral or political one) involved submitting to the scrutiny of cultural experts, men whose social status was mostly significantly inferior to your own.[17] This offence against hierarchy was a serious matter in Roman society, especially for the senatorial elite who had been compensated by the emperors for a loss

[12] The term coined by Veblen (1926).
[13] Eck (1984) for a demonstration of this in relation to the Augustan principate, developed by Griffin (1991).
[14] The upward social mobility of those who could produce literature or teach it to the great was another consequence, as Hopkins (1961) long ago made clear.
[15] An anxiety brilliantly lampooned by Juvenal, cf. Henderson (1997).
[16] The characterization is that of Hopkins (1983b) 176–93. This movement was, naturally, interdependent with the transformation of Rome from political to cultural centre. At no period were the imperial elite normally dispersed throughout the empire as, for example, tenants-in-chief were in the kingdoms of the mediaeval West.
[17] Much has been written on the social status of poets under the empire. Poets might emerge from almost anywhere in the educated classes. Hence senatorial poets existed, for instance Lucan, Seneca the Younger and the Younger Pliny, and poetic composition was evidently a pastime for many aristocrats as for some emperors. The same was true of the equestrian order. But White (1978), (1982) and Saller (1983) agree that the norm was for Latin poets to be of lower status. Establishing the status of individual poets is made more difficult by the convention of adopting an authorial *persona* appropriate to the genre, and by the unreliability of the extant ancient biographies of poets. Fantham (1996) 191–200 provides a careful survey of the social world of those who made their living from literary acumen.

of political power with even clearer marks of their social pre-eminence.[18] And poets could not be relied on to praise – or rather could not effectively praise if they were not granted licence to abstain from eulogy, or even to blame. Poets might praise you as a patron of the arts and perhaps even as a poet yourself, but equally you might be damned for tastelessness and cultural incompetence.

Lucian's hilarious satire *On taking up salaried posts in a great house* portrays the Roman patron as an ill-educated boor, keeping a paid intellectual for show but having no real interest in the acquisition of *paideia*. His Greek employee competes for attention (and tidbits) with dancing-masters and *kinaedoi*, troupes of gymnasts and singing dwarves. Subordinated to slaves (10), he surrenders family, freedom and ancestors (23) for poor hospitality, casual insults, and a lousy salary. The duties include minding the mistress's lapdog (34) and praising the master's bad verse (35). Lucian's satire deliberately offers an outsider's view of the cultural life of the capital. The City is de-familiarized by the emphasis on the Hellenism of the paid scholar. Roman friends of the master are hostile and make innuendoes about Greeks (17). The hireling has to suffer the barbarism of the Roman language (24), and trailing round after his patron is made even worse by Rome's wretched hills. 'You know what that city is like.' It is a world that revolves around the leisure of grand houses – no political activity is mentioned, no senatorial ceremony or social or religious ritual, in fact no *officia* at all, since friendship and hospitality are so abused. The emperor is absent. This Rome is a prototype of the late antique City attacked for similar vices by Ammianus.[19]

That skit, and others like it,[20] cannot be plausibly read as faithful representations of the bond between the literati and the rich. But nor can Statius' *Silvae*, which celebrate the poet's 'friendship' (no mention of pay here) with rich aristocrats who are poets themselves, nor Martial's dedicatory epigrams.[21] It is not even the case that *Silvae* and satire together mark the limits within which the game might be played, as if some sober scholar could fix some middle point between flattery and abuse and deem

---

[18] Wallace-Hadrill (1983) 101–8, Hopkins (1983b) 174–84 for good treatments of Roman sensitivity to social status.

[19] Ammianus Marcellinus 28.4.18. For discussion see Matthews (1986). Another Greek, Galen, in *On prognosis* 1.1–5, asserts that doctors too are treated the same way, and at 1.13 attacks the lifestyles of the rich. But he generalizes his complaint to the rich of all the cities until 2.1, when he recounts his own experiences in Rome. For comparison of Galen's ideas with those of other Greek writers see Swain (1996) 363–79.

[20] Juvenal's third and fifth Satires are the usual comparanda, without of course the complaints about anti-Greek prejudice, the barbarity of Latin and the City's atrocious topography.

[21] For example *Silvae* 1.2 on Stella and 1.4 on Rutilius Gallicus (on which Henderson (1998)). On the individuals named in these poems, and in Martial's, see Hardie (1983) and White (1975).

it realism. Better to admit that both genres appropriate the social energy of aristocratic life, and recruit it to poetic ends.[22] Both too keep the cultural distance between aristocrat and poet firmly in the eye.

A final example of this kind of trope of differentiation is provided by Martial, *Epigrams* 10.19, written for Pliny, who quotes part of it in a letter on Martial's death.[23] The two texts present a rare opportunity to observe a relationship depicted by both sides. Pliny writes that he had given Martial a *viaticum*, the cost of his journey back to Spain when he left Rome. 'I gave this for friendship's sake and I gave it also for some little verses which he composed about me.'[24] Pliny goes on to set his gift to Martial in an ancient tradition of rewarding praise-singers, a tradition Pliny claims has nearly died out,[25] and then quotes the second half of the epigram, which represents Pliny in a manner close to Pliny's own self-fashioning through the *Letters*.[26]

But Martial has not merely reflected Pliny's chosen self back to him in verse. The epigram as a whole adopts the form of an address to the muse Thalia directing her to Pliny's Esquiline mansion. Each component of the poem contributes to a portrait of Pliny. The choice of a muse as messenger, the description of Martial's *libellus* as not learned enough or serious enough (for Pliny), but not rustic either offers a picture of Plinian taste. The mansion is represented as near to the forum (so the home of a politician) but high up (so in an exclusive district). Landmarks are appropriately chosen – a fountain depicting Orpheus for the poetic senator, and a statue of Ganymede riding the eagle of Zeus for the emperor's friend. Finally the home of an Augustan epigrammatist perhaps alludes to Martial? His muse is a festive one, warned not to knock on Pliny's door drunkenly when he is hard at work preparing speeches for the *centumviri* to hear, and also for posterity to read and judge Ciceronian. Instead the poems should call in the evening, when wine is flowing and even stern Cato would read them. Certainly the epigram is a tribute to Pliny, but for the reader of book 10 of

[22] For this approach to literary patronage at Rome, see Zetzel (1982). More often modern treatments of the relationship between poets and patrons at Rome depend on fairly literal readings of remarks addressed to or about patrons in Latin verse, and sometimes even of satirical writing on the subject. For a gentle demolition of this approach see Cloud (1989).

[23] Pliny, *Epistles* 3.21. The letter, concluding book 3 and perhaps the first published collection of letters, by quoting from Martial's *encomium* serves as a memorial for Pliny as well as for Martial himself, allowing Pliny to inoffensively sign off with self-praise.

[24] *dederam hoc amicitiae, dederam etiam versiculis quos de me composuit.*

[25] So much for the survival of literary patronage, if we believe him!

[26] The salient features include a comparison of Pliny's rhetoric with Cicero's, on which Riggsby (1995), the balance of *officium* with *otium* and the use of a banquet with literary entertainment as a symbol of the latter; cf. Pliny, *Epistles* 1.15 with Gowers (1993) 267–79.

the *Epigrams* it achieves its effect, like one of the *Silvae*, through a brilliant pen portrait of a public figure. The distance Martial establishes between himself and Pliny[27] – the drunken muse, the Ganymede statue reminding the reader of the homoerotic revels celebrated by other epigrams in the collection (and by Trajan?) – offers a collusion between author and reader, looking on Pliny from afar. Pliny has been turned into a poem, and not just for his own entertainment.

UNLITERARY ROME

Aristocrats did not have to put up with this treatment. Many modern scholars have assumed that a literary definition of Roman identity and elite status was widely accepted in the Capital. Perhaps there were some provincial readers who held similar views. But if so, perhaps it was because, like us, they were largely dependent on ideals of aristocracy created and promulgated by literary texts. The Martials and Statiuses had, naturally, a vested interest in promoting their preferred versions of Roman and elite identity. There are, however, clear signs that not all Roman aristocrats pursued this sometimes risky symbiosis with the poets. Others found alternative pursuits and fields of self-glorification. This section sketches this alternative Rome, and examines how the poets laid siege to it.

No poets promoted un-literary Rome, but it remains possible to sketch out its form,[28] and it is the form of a debate over the nature of aristocratic virtue. The fiercest debate often focuses on senators who preferred pantomime artists to philosophers, or equestrians who liked to fight in the arena. If some engaged in these activities to gratify a private and socially despised taste, others may have done so to seek an alternative kind of approval. Perhaps they were always in the minority. The issue is clearer, however, if we turn to pleasures that were neither vicious nor literary. Poets did not always celebrate alternative elitist pleasures, but their efforts to polemicize against them and appropriate their social energy to poetic ends makes it possible to observe the un-literary elite at play.

Consider for a moment Pliny's *Letters*. The text resists easy classification, partly because it exploits the fragmented nature of a collection of letters,

---

[27] Note the answering distancing in Pliny's letter marked by *partial* quotation and the equivocation that follows it, 'He did as much as he could for me, and would have done more had he been able . . . You object that what he wrote will not stand the test of time? Maybe not, but he wrote it intending that it should.' The critic, as ever, has the last word.

[28] The argument that follows owes much to Hopkins (1978c) which makes clear, *inter alia*, the dangers of according importance to aspects of ancient culture in proportion to the frequency with which they figure in literary sources.

purportedly composed on different occasions to different addressees, to achieve a *variatio* of tone and subject that mimics the varied lifestyle it promotes.[29] Nevertheless it is possible to read the *Letters* as modelling a vision of senatorial virtue, one comprising particular attitudes to social obligation, to leisure, to political ethics, to literary pursuits and so on. That vision of virtue is presented largely through idealizations of Pliny, of his correspondents and of certain exemplary figures described in the *Letters*. One feature of this idealization is participation in a literary life that includes reading drafts of compositions by one's friends, attending *recitationes* – readings of their works – and so on. It is not too strong to say that Pliny's aristocracy is united in part by common literary values.[30] Is Pliny's vision representative? Some have taken it to be, although his view of literature stands in obvious contrast to those of some contemporaries. I have already discussed his distance from Martial.

But there is a bigger issue here, that of genre. By making use of an epistolary format, Pliny, sets himself in a didactic tradition that in Latin includes Seneca as well as Horace. And any overtly didactic text advertises the existence of alternative positions. Pliny is not (only[31]) advocating virtue, he is arguing for a particular definition of it, implicitly against alternative versions. His general advocacy of the literary life, and his relative lack of engagement with critical issues of the kind that preoccupied Tacitus' *Dialogus* or the now fragmentary dialogue attributed to Florus entitled *Was Virgil an orator or a poet?* suggest that Pliny does not just have alternative literary canons in his sights.

So what alternative aristocratic virtues are there? Rather than opposed and starkly contrasting codes, perhaps we should envisage a variety of ethics that differed most in the relative importance they gave to different kinds of activity. The sixth letter of the first book of *Letters* offers a glimpse of one rival to literary *otium*, the hunt. Pliny, writing to Tacitus, describes himself attending a hunt, and even catching three boars. Anticipating a surprised reaction, Pliny then declares that he had spent the time sitting by the nets with writing materials, and expands on how inspiring this sort

---

[29] This is especially clear if Pliny's *Letters* are contrasted with those of Seneca, the sole addressee of which is barely characterized.

[30] This can be shown in more detail by the attitudes Pliny models towards different genres. Oratory and short poems – elegy, erotic verse – are central, drama less so, epic and satire hardly appear, philosophy is respected but participation in it is not encouraged; cf. Tac. *Agric.* 4. History is admired, but again from afar. On Pliny's poetics see further Hershkowitz (1995). Fantham (1996) 200–21 draws attention to other limitations of Plinian literary life.

[31] The *Letters* do also condemn vice, of course, and point to contemporary lapses from praiseworthy custom in the manner of other Roman moralists.

of activity is and how the silence and the woodland setting encouraged his thought. He even advises Tacitus to follow his example and discover that the mountains are inhabited by Minerva as much as Diana. The letter sets up hunting and literary activity as conventional opposites, and then, by familiar appropriation, makes the hunting expedition serve literary ends, both this letter and the acts of composition and reflection it describes.[32] The choice of Tacitus, portrayed here as a keener hunter than Pliny, as addressee also indicates an awareness that these tastes were often combined.

Hunting was in fact enormously popular in the early second century CE.[33] Enthusiasm for it was widespread. Hunting was associated with heroic lifestyles, and with the pleasures of Macedonian and Persian monarchs. Hunts were portrayed in every medium from sarcophagi and mosaics to silver plate and *terra sigillata*. Even the urban masses had their *venationes* in the amphitheatre, and the language of hunting provided metaphors for other spheres of aristocratic activity, such as legacy hunting. But actual participation in grand hunts with horses and hounds or else with nets and spears, often organized by trained slaves and held in private reserves, was the preserve of the rich alone.

Hunting may stand for a universe of alternative aristocratic vocations, ill represented in imperial literature. Through physical exercise and weaponry it connects easily with warfare, still an avenue open to some senators and *equites*.[34] The imperial elite was held together in part by bonds of common service in the *militia equestris*, and by patronage exercised in the camps as well as in the City. And there were less physical alternatives to literary pursuits: art collecting, for example, or an interest in building or in music.[35] Part of it was held together still by real or pretended hereditary status, that 'grand set' whose pretensions were attacked by Juvenal in Satire 8:[36] ancestry is noticeably absent from Pliny's *Letters*, both the biographies of his heroes and his own cumulative autobiography. Literary taste might substitute for or complement the hunt and warfare, cult and connoisseurship, genealogy

---

[32] Martial 12.14 performs a similar trick, offering a warning against the dangers of the hunt in an epigram that imitates the pace and excitement of the chase with a series of two-line periods, peppered with active verb forms and dactyls. Other examples include Pliny, *Epistles* 5.18 and Martial, *Epigrams* 12.1, both opposing hunting and literary pursuits. For serious pursuit of this theme, Henderson (2001b).

[33] Aymard (1951) remains the best account, supplemented by Green (1996). Pliny praises Trajan's virile hunts in *Pan.* 81 and Hadrian's enthusiasm for hunting is noted in SHA, *Hadrian* 2, 20 and 26. Arrian's *Cynegeticus* attests interest in the Greek world, while tomb reliefs and inscriptions from Gaul indicate it was popular in the western provinces too.

[34] Like hunting, this sort of virtue might also be appropriated for literary purposes, not always in ways that endorse that vocation. Tacitus' military heroes – even Agricola – often seem designed to demonstrate the limits of that style of aristocratic self-fashioning.

[35] Cf. Rawson (1985) 100–2 on the various likes and dislikes of Atticus.

[36] For the grand set see Hopkins (1983b) 171–3.

and business. But it was in the end only one of a number of means through which the rulers of the empire and the City found a common vocation and definition.

It is difficult to measure the scale of literary Rome against its un-literary *alter ego*. What sort of aristocrats would submit to the praise of poets, and offer themselves up to be transformed by their art? Not the grandees, perhaps, nor the military heroes with their triumphal *ornamenta* and offices proclaimed in great career inscriptions carved on their family tombs.[37] Literature, like hunting, suited only some tastes and capabilities. But perhaps it is not surprising that our great 'patrons' turn out to be lesser luminaries,[38] men like G. Plinius Secund(us/-rate) and L. Arruntius (not-quite) Stella(r). Perhaps we have overestimated, or rather been led to over-estimate, the significance of literature in the life of the Roman elite. If so, however, we may be comforted by the probability that many provincials were also duped. Visible only through texts, these un-literary pursuits will have been seen mostly through texts that appropriated them to their ends. If we doubt the success of littérateurs in this respect it is only necessary to consider the astonishing success of Latin education in the West, testified to in late antiquity by a very broad familiarity not just with curriculum classics like Virgil and Cicero but also with the works of later Latinists, not least Pliny.

THE CITY OF POETS

Literary appropriation was only one possible response to un-literary definitions of aristocratic virtue and Roman culture. A second tactic was the rewriting of the City as a literary hub, a sort of prototype of Johnson's London or Joyce's Paris. So Latin literature became a literature about the City and its wealthy rulers. There were plenty of precedents available. The frenetic creation of Latin literature in one generation of the third century BCE had taken the form of a collective cultural project, funded and directed by the Roman aristocracy, to naturalize a literary culture in Rome.[39] In the

---

[37] Like those of the Plautii at Ponte Lucano, *CIL* XIV 3606–8, with subtle discussion in Beard (1998) 98–114.

[38] Hardie (1983) 68–70 surveys the dedicatees of the *Silvae*, showing them to be predominantly western or Italian, mostly of newly eminent families. The only consular is Gallicus (1.4), himself a *novus homo* from Transpadana. Martial and Pliny, each with many more addressees, cover a wider social range, but Italians and equestrians are prominent. Imperial dedicatees, of course, are ubiquitous but here perhaps poets and emperors both had less choice. Rawson (1985) 97 suggests that in the Republic too the grandest families were rarely very much involved in intellectual activities.

[39] Among a number of recent accounts of this process see Habinek (1998) 34–68 and, more generally, Gruen (1992).

imperial period Latin verse elaborated a new vision of literary Rome, and allusive games might be played now not only on mythological, textual and historical fields but on a concrete urban topography.

So Pliny's friends rush through the City between *recitationes*. They gather in urban *domus*, suburban *villae* and Italian retreats equipped with fine private libraries. They constantly bump into friends with similar interests, and generally have the leisure to take these opportunities to engage in impromptu yet elevating discourse. Certainly Pliny and his peers built on Republican models, Pliny generalizing from the locations employed by Cicero in his philosophical dialogues,[40] Juvenal setting most of his satires in an urban landscape elaborated by Horace on a Lucilian model. But continuity too needs explanation. The contrast is striking between this literature of empire, so preoccupied with the (cultural) capital and that of the British Empire revelling in the exoticism of its periphery. Not all British writers were Kiplings and Conrads, to be sure, but as Edward Saïd has shown empire impinged closely even on narratives that unfolded against a metropolitan backdrop such as the novels of Austen and Dickens.[41] Rome's empire, however, is hardly visible from much of its literature.

Tacitus' *Dialogus* provides a nice example. The dramatic scene is a chance visit – the air of insouciance is ubiquitous in this kind of literature[42] – paid by two literary figures on a third to discuss his *recitatio* of the previous day, a *recitatio* that has allegedly set the city ablaze with anxious excitement. Naturally, they find him engaged not in farm business or negotiating a loan for overseas trade, but in revising the previous day's text for publication and in planning its sequel. Equally naturally their debate is interrupted not by an enquiry about a runaway slave, by news of frontier wars nor a man selling hunting dogs but by yet another chance visit from an equally literate grandee. The *recitatio* setting operates for Latin writers, in other words, rather as the *symposium* does for Greek ones.[43] But other occasions are exploited. Gellius has Favorinus declaiming against the background of the imperial palace on the Palatine, at the temple of Carmentis at the foot

---

[40] Themselves developing Platonic models, but their subsequent transformation from an appropriate locale for philosophical debate into a landscape of aristocratic life seems more elaborated in Pliny.

[41] Saïd (1993).

[42] At least in relation to *otium*. Pliny's tone describing forensic engagements or imperial business is appropriately different.

[43] It would hardly be necessary to insist on the highly stylized settings in these texts if they were not routinely used as realistic descriptions of the lifestyle of the Roman elite, including surprisingly in Dupont (1997). Like many of Cicero's dialogues the Tacitean one has a dramatic date of some time before its actual composition, a device used to play with the topos of declining oratorical standards with which the *Dialogus* is partly concerned.

of the Capitol, in the Baths of Titus and also in the Forum of Trajan.[44] Juvenal complains of lectures in public baths.[45] Chance encounters while rummaging in bookshops are also occasionally used as settings,[46] as well as the Platonic device of a conversation accompanying a gentle stroll in any urban setting.[47] Pliny describes his speeches in the Senate, in the centumviral court, at a dedicatory ceremony in Comum, read (inevitably) to a small group of friends at a *recitatio*, and he also alludes to funeral orations. Speeches to the troops or to provincial audiences do not, however, feature in his correspondence. The cultured world knows its limits.

Let me close this section with a final pair of examples. The thirteenth letter of Pliny's first book of *Letters* is the culmination of a sequence that advertises Rome as a centre of literary life.[48] Pliny describes the host of new poets, all giving readings, so many in fact that audiences are scarce throughout the month of April. Moving to an explicitly didactic mode he then sets about criticizing the manners of the audiences, sitting around gossiping in public, arriving late, leaving early, failing to come when invited . . . and yet the poets continue to recite. Pliny himself is an assiduous attender, if restrained in giving recitations himself. When his literary *officia* are done he finally retires from the City to write something himself. Here, in the guise of a critique of public morals, Pliny has smuggled in a City that is *entirely* literary, peopled by no-one but poets and audiences, a population with no other activities to provide alibis or legitimate alternative occupations. Admittedly business and politics were less busy in April, much of which was dominated by the Megalensian, the Cerialian and Floralian Games, but even these do not feature in Pliny's letter. Rome the cultural capital has squeezed out all the other Romes. My second example, the opening lines of Juvenal's first satire, plays with the same conceit. But now the ubiquity of literary performances stifles the speaker and arouses his anger. So many *recitationes*, such verbosity, the dreadful and artless repetition of tropes filling aristocratic mansions and schoolrooms with the same old themes. 'Restraint is stupidity. When one keeps bumping into so many inspired poets on every side, why spare the papyrus?'[49] Pliny's literary Utopia has

---

[44] Gellius 4.1.1, 20.1.2 (the Palatine), 18.7.1 (the temple of Carmentis), 3.1.1 (the Baths), 13.25.1 (Forum Traianum).

[45] Juvenal 1.17–18.

[46] Gellius 9.4.1 and also Galen in the opening of *On my own books*.

[47] As used, for example, by Minucius Felix in his *Octavius*, beginning with a walk to Ostia (Rome's Piraeus), cf. Gellius 18.1.2.

[48] Compare especially the beginning of 1.10 'If ever our city flowered with literary arts then now it flourishes more than ever.'

[49] *Satires* 1.17–18.

become Juvenal's illiterate purgatory. But the common message from Pliny and Juvenal to their provincial readers is clear. The City of Rome is packed with culture.

READING ROME IN THE PROVINCES

And suppose all you knew of Rome you learned from reading Latin literature? How would you imagine the City? Rome was, of course, known to everyone by rumour too and through travellers' tales and other tall stories. As the archetypal City in the West, many perhaps imagined it simply as a larger version of their own metropolis. But their elementary Latin classes had taught provincial readers that that was false.

The City men call Rome, I thought, Meliboeus, stupid as I then was, must be like our own home town to which we shepherds often used to drive the tender offspring of our sheep. As pups resemble dogs, as kids their mothers, in this way I compared small things with great. And yet this city raises her head as high above all other towns, as a cypress tree towers above twining osiers. (Virgil, *Eclogues* 1.19–25)

What else was Rome unlike? Rome was not like Massilia, 'where Greek charm and provincial moderation mix and form a happy compromise.'[50] Nor was it like peaceful, studious Tarraco,[51] where the speaker in *Was Virgil an orator or a poet?* finally found rest. After travelling the world too ashamed to return home to Africa after failure in the Capitoline Games, he took up an honourable career teaching the children of well-born provincial families. Nor was Rome like Bilbilis, from where Martial wrote of his 'provincial solitude.'[52]

Rome's status as cultural capital of the West was asserted in part by tropes of alienation. The difference of the City from the provinces could be expressed from either perspective. The cultural pretensions of the provinces might be disdained, as when Pliny affects surprise that his books may be bought in Lyon.[53] Alternatively, the provinces might be represented as free of Roman literary decadence, as in the passages of Tacitus and Florus cited above, or when Juvenal proclaims that if you want to make a living from forensic oratory you'd better emigrate to Gaul or Africa.[54] The machinery of differentiation that Latin literature had developed to map the cultural

---

[50] Tacitus, *Agricola* 4.
[51] Accepting the usual identification of the dramatic location of *Virgilius orator an poeta?*
[52] Martial, Preface to book 12.   [53] *Epistles* 9.11.2 with an explicit contrast to the City.
[54] *Satires* 7.147–9. Needless to say all these testimonia have been used in attempts to map the spread of Roman education and culture in the provinces.

geography of metropolitan society was easily employed to show and make use of the cultural distance of the provinces from Rome.

Martial's preface to book 12 of his *Epigrams* is one of the more complex comparisons of literary life in Rome and in the provinces. It begins with a mock formulaic apology for not having written more in three years. Martial has no excuse that would have been acceptable even if he were still burdened with those urban routines which so often make nuisances rather than dutiful clients of us. So far the text evokes countless other satires on the client's daily round. But then the polarity shifts. 'There is even less excuse in this provincial solitude, where, unless I throw myself into my work, I have no comfort in my retirement any more than any excuse. Let me explain. The biggest reason of all is that I miss that audience [literally "the ears"] of my fellow citizens to which I have become accustomed: I feel as if I were pleading in a foreign court.' Now Martial, the Spaniard returned home, expresses alienation from his fellow Spaniards and nostalgia for Rome. 'If I had written anything at all worthwhile in my books, the audience would pick it out. The sophistication of their criticism, the mass of material on which to write, the libraries, the theatres, the meeting-places where labour is insensibly transformed to pleasure. In short all those things that my delicate sensibility led me to abandon, I now long for as if I had been deprived of them.' Martial has made an exile of himself.[55] But even in exile the Rome he laments is literary Rome. He goes on to complain of the small-town rivalries of Bilbilis that have discouraged him from work. Then again the tone changes. Priscus' imminent arrival from the City has inspired Martial to take up his pen again and to produce something worthy of such a audience. The preface ends with conventional protestations that the work had been dashed off in a hurry, and then the request to Priscus not to let Martial send it to Rome if the book turns out to be Spanish rather than Romano-Spanish.[56] Priscus' arrival is a metropolitan stimulus that will counter provincial torpor. Martial's friend and countryman will bring Roman ears to Spain, and use them to make sure no book of provincialisms will reach the audience that really matters, in the City. The compliment is elegant, just as the deft reversal of direction and deployment of tropes demonstrates that Martial is far from barbarized.[57]

Many of Martial's readers ought to have appreciated the joke. There is little doubt that Latin literature of this period had far more readers than

[55] On the tropes of exile, and their use to characterize Rome, Edwards (1996) 110–33.
[56] *non mittamus Hispaniensem librum sed Hispanum.*
[57] A more bullish assertion of the literary potential of Spain is provided by *Epigrams* 1.61, in which Spanish Latin writers are explicitly set on a par with the Roman canon.

it had hearers, and that most of them lived outside the City of Rome.
The evidence is feeble, but it is impossible to explain the emergence of
Latin writers from all over the West without presupposing wide access to
education for the children of local elites. Virgilian graffiti, mosaic images
depicting poets and painted scenes from literary works all make this conclusion certain.[58] This dispersed if educated readership may well have smiled
with recognition at Martial's play on provincialism and metropolitanism.

The cultural gradient Martial described was, after all, a relatively easy
one to traverse, as Martial's career, like that of many other Latin writers in
the first century CE made clear. The point is made, again, by a contrast with
more recent empires. Benedict Anderson memorably linked the emergence
of national sensibilities and national literatures in the modern world to the
plight of creole elites.[59] Culturally rooted in Europe but politically debarred
from moving easily between their metropoles and the various provincial
worlds they inhabited, these elites developed their own literatures. Often
modelled on western genres, even written in European or colonial languages, these texts were none the less highly distinctive. They tended to
be suffused with rich local allusion – argot, place-names, an emphasis on
local geography and climate and, of course, a sense of their authors' and
intended readers' colonial situations. As such they contributed (along with
local newspapers, local film and the like) to a new esoteric discourse that
was one vehicle for the development of shared identities from which new
nationalisms, sometimes precariously, emerged. The literate Latin elites of
Roman Spain and Africa were, on the other hand, free to visit Rome, and –
given enough wealth and the right connections – to penetrate the highest
echelons of the literary and or aristocratic elites.

Many provincials did visit Rome, on all sorts of business or none at
all. And some important groups moved backwards and forwards between
provinces and metropole: senators of provincial origins and traders, touring
sophists and competitors in Domitian's games, imperial slaves and provincial equestrians on the make all come into this category. Many of these
were educated and some presumably had some interest in literature. Did
Rome satisfy or disappoint their expectations? It is difficult to recover Latin
reactions to the City, as opposed to those Greek ones discussed already. We
might imagine that, just as a first-time visitor to Paris whose reading has

---

[58] For some thoughts on Roman education at the beginning of the principate see Woolf (2000) 119–21.
Hoogma (1959) lists epigraphic citations from Virgil: many more recent finds remain to be added
to this corpus.
[59] Anderson (1991). The importance of these factors was not apparent to Anderson in the first (1983)
edition of his book.

prepared him for the Boulevard St Michel and the Quartier Latin may see only that, so too some provincial visitors would have found the Rome of Pliny and Juvenal, and imagined that the world of the *Silvae* lurked behind each aristocratic portal guarded by its stern *ianuarius*. Perhaps, like some modern visitors to New York, a sense of wonder mingled with a sense of familiarity. Maybe a literary knowledge of the City gave educated visitors a sense of ownership to balance the provincial alienation induced by the same texts. The City of Letters was not, after all, a falsification of Rome, simply an exaggeration, or a selective representation, and all representations are selective.

But we are dealing in speculation, however plausible. Certainly the creation of Rome as a cultural capital made it susceptible to being understood in those terms, rather than, say, as the place from which emperors were often absent, or as the *former* political capital. Moving Rome into the same category as Athens or Alexandria could work to the advantage of the empire's rulers. For the leisure class, Rome's supposed cultural hegemony was an acceptable face to show the tax-paying[60] world, and a compensation for their loss of power. For the emperors, a western cultural capital provided some rivalry to eastern centres.[61] Besides, the emperors were not always absent, and Rome was a stage on which they occasionally needed to play. But it would be a mistake to explain literary Rome entirely in such functional terms. The City of Letters had been built for other reasons. Written for an imperial people, Latin literature had become temporarily tangled around a single place, and subsequent generations had, if only metaphorically, to live there. Latin literature at least provided them with the tropes with which to love it or loathe it.

---

[60] Or 'tax-exporting'? Cf. Hopkins (1980) for the patterns of economic inequality that underpinned these literary differentials.

[61] Among conscious attempts by the emperors to develop Rome as a cultural capital, Domitian's Capitoline Games stand out, on which see Caldelli (1993).

Bibliography

Abrams, P. and E. A. Wrigley (eds.) (1978) *Towns in societies. Essays in economic history and historical sociology.* Cambridge

Aitken, L. (1873) 'The sanitary state of Rome', *British Medical Journal* 1: 311–12

Alcock, S. E. (1993) *Graecia capta.* Cambridge

Alter, G. and A. Carmichael (1996) 'Studying causes of death in the past: problems and methods', *Historical Methods* 29: 44–8

Anderson, B. (1991) *Imagined communities. Reflections on the origin and spread of nationalism.* Revised edition, London

Anderson, J. C. (1984) *Historical topography of the Imperial Fora.* Brussels

Andreau, J. (1974) *Les affaires de monsieur Iucundus.* Rome

(1995) 'Vingt ans après *L'économie antique* de Moses I. Finley', *Annales. Histoire, Sciences Sociales* 50/5: 947–60

Arlacchi, P. (1983) *Mafia, peasants and great estates: society in traditional Calabria.* Cambridge

Ashby, T. and G. Lugli (1932) 'La basilica di Giunio Basso sull'Esquilino', *Rivista di Archeologia Cristiana* 9: 221–55

Ashmole, B. (1972) *Architect and sculptor in classical Greece.* New York

Athanassiadi, P. and M. Frede (eds.) (1999) *Pagan monotheism in late antiquity.* Oxford

Audollent, A. (1901) *Carthage romaine.* Paris

Austin, R. G. (1971) *P. Vergili Maronis Aeneidos. Liber primus.* Oxford

Aymard, J. (1951) *Essai sur les chasses romaines des origines à la fin du siècle des Antonins.* Paris

Badian, E. (1972) 'Tiberius Gracchus and the beginning of the Roman revolution', in *ANRW* 1 1: 668–731

Baines, J. and J. Málek (1980) *Atlas of ancient Egypt.* Oxford and New York

Bakker, R. T. (1995) *Raptor red.* London

Baldovin, J. (1987) *The urban character of Christian worship.* Rome

Barasch, M. (1992) *Icon.* New York

Barkan, L. (1999) *Unearthing the past: archaeology and aesthetics in the making of renaissance culture.* New Haven

Barker, G. (1982) review of Gabba and Pasquinucci (1979), *JRS* 72: 192–4

Barnes, T. D. (1970) 'The Goddess Caelestis in the Historia Augusta', *JTS* 21: 96–101

Barnes, T. D. (1978) *The Sources of the Historia Augusta*. Brussels

Bassett, S. (ed.) (1992) *Death in towns: urban responses to the dying and dead, 100–1600*. Leicester

Batty, R. (2000) 'Mela's Phoenician geography', *JRS* 90: 70–94

Bauer, H. (1988) 'Basilica Aemilia' 200–11 in *Kaiser Augustus und die verlorene Republik*. Exhibition catalogue. Berlin

Beard, M. (1980) 'The sexual status of Vestal Virgins', *JRS* 70: 12–27

    (1993) 'Looking (harder) for Roman myth: Dumézil, declamation and the problems of definition', in F. Graf (ed.), *Mythos in Mythenloser Gesellschaft. Das Paradigma Roms*, 44–64. Stuttgart and Leipzig

    (1998) 'Vita inscripta', *La Biographie antique, Entretiens de la Fondation Hardt sur l'Antiquité Classique* 44: 83–118

Beard, M., J. North and S. Price (1998) *Religions of Rome* (2 vols.). Cambridge

Becatti, G. (1969) *Scavi di Ostia VI: edificio con opus sectile fuori Porta Marina*. Rome

Beloch, [K.]J. (1886) *Die Bevölkerung der griechisch-römischen Welt* (*Historische Beiträge zur Bevölkerungslehre* 1). Leipzig

Benedict, B. (1983) *The anthropology of World's Fairs. San Francisco Panama-Pacific International Exposition*. Berkeley

Berkhofer, R. F., Jr (1995) *Beyond the Great Story: history as text and discourse*. Cambridge, MA, and London

Bernand, A. and E. Bernand (1960) *Les inscriptions du Colosse de Memnon*. Paris.

Bertier, J. (1996) 'La médicine des enfants à l'époque imperiale', in *ANRW* 11.37.3: 2147–227

Bieber, M. (1977) *Ancient copies: contributions to the history of Greek and Roman art*. New York

Bignamini, I. and A. Wilton (1996) *Grand tour: the lure of Italy in the eighteenth century*. London

Biraben, J.-N. (1975) *Les hommes et la peste en France et dans les pays européens et méditerranéens, 1: La peste dans l'histoire*. Paris and The Hague

Bird, H. W. (1984) *Sextus Aurelius Victor: a historiographical study*. Liverpool

Birley, A. R. (1970) 'Africana in the Historia Augusta', *Bonner Historia Augusta Colloquium* 1968/1969: 79–90

    (1988) *The African emperor: Septimius Severus*, updated, rewritten, expanded and reillustrated edition. London

    (1996) 'Antinous', in S. Hornblower and A. Spawforth (eds.), *OCD*[3], 106. Oxford and New York

Blake, M. E. (1936) 'Roman mosaics of the second century in Italy', *MAAR* 13: 67–214

Bloomer, W. M. (1997) *Latinity and literary society at Rome*. Philadelphia

Boëthius, A. and J. B. Ward-Perkins (1970) *Etruscan and Roman architecture*. London

Boni, C. (1913) 'Recent discoveries on the Palatine Hill, Rome', *JRS* 3: 243–52

Bonnefond-Coudry, M. (1989) *Le sénat de la république romaine de la guerre d'Hannibal à Auguste: pratiques délibératives et prise de décision*. Rome

Boren, H. C. (1969), *The Gracchi*. New York

Bovini, G. and H. Brandenburg (1967) *Repertorium der christlich-antiken Sarkophage, 1: Rom und Ostia*. Wiesbaden

Bowersock, G. (1965) *Augustus and the Greek world*, Oxford

Bowman, G. (1999) ' "Mapping history's redemption": eschatology and topography in the Itinerarium Burdigalense', in L. I. Levine (ed.), *Jerusalem: its sanctity and centrality to Judaism, Christianity and Islam*, 163–87. New York

Braudel, F. (1979) *Civilisation matérielle, économie et capitalisme, XVe–XVIIIe siècle*. 3 vols. Paris

Braund, D. (2000) 'Learning, luxury and empire: Athenaeus' Roman patron', in D. Braund and J. Wilkins (eds.), *Athenaeus and his world: reading Greek culture in the Roman empire*, 3–22. Exeter

Braund, S. Morton (1996) *Juvenal: Satires book 1*. Cambridge

Brelich, A (1938) 'Trionfo e morte', *SMSR* 14: 189–93

Brendel, O. (1979) *Prolegomena to the study of Roman art*. New Haven

Brent, A. (1995) *Hippolytus and the Roman Church in the third century*. Leiden

Brilliant, R. (1999) ' "Let the trumpets roar!" The Roman triumph', in B. Bergmann and C. Kondoleon (eds.), *The art of ancient spectacle* (Studies in the History of Art 56), 221–9. Washington

Brind'Amour, P. (1983) *Le calendrier romain: recherches chronologiques*. Ottawa

Brown, P. (1981) *The cult of the saints*. London

   (1982) 'Dalla "Plebs Romana" alla "Plebs Dei": aspetti della cristianizzazione di Roma', in P. Brown, L. C. Ruggini and M. Mazza, *Governanti e intellettuali: popolo di Dio I–IV secolo*, 123–45. Turin

   (1995) Review of T. Mathews, *The clash of gods, Art Bulletin* 77: 499–502

   (1999) 'Images as a substitute for writing', in E. Chrysos and I. Wood (eds.), *East and west: modes of communication*, 15–34. Leiden

Brunt, P. A. (1971) *Italian manpower, 225 BC – AD 14*. Oxford

   (1980) 'Free labour and public works at Rome', *JRS* 70: 81–100

Bruun, C. (1991) *The water supply of ancient Rome*, Helsinki

Burke, P. F., Jr (1996) 'Malaria in the Greco-Roman world: a historical and epidemiological survey', in *ANRW* 11.37.3: 2252–81

Cabrol, F. and H. Leclerq (eds.) (1934), *Dictionnaire d'archéologie chrétienne et de la liturgie* 11. Paris

Caldelli, M. L. (1993) *L'agon Capitolinus. Storia et protagonistici dall'istituzione domiziana al IV secolo*. Rome

Cameron, Alan (1970) *Claudian: poetry and propaganda at the court of Honorius*. Oxford

   (1986) 'Pagan ivories' in F. Paschoud (ed.), *Colloque Genevois sur Symmaque*, 41–72. Paris

   (1999) 'The last pagans of Rome', in Harris (1999c) 109–21

Carandini, A. (1985) *Settefinestre: una villa schiavistica nell'Etruria romana*. 3 vols. Modena

   (1988) *Schiavi in Italia: gli strumenti pensanti dei romani fra tarda Repubblica e medio impero*. Rome

Carandini, A. and S. Settis (1979), *Schiavi e padroni nell'Etruria romana: la villa di Settefinestre dallo scavo alla mostra.* Bari

Carrott, R. G. (1978) *The Egyptian revival: its sources, monuments and meaning 1808–1858.* Berkeley, Los Angeles and London

Casal, L. A. (1990) 'Horae', *LIMC* v.i: 510–38

Casson, L. (1978) 'Unemployment, the building trade and Suetonius *Vesp.* 18', *BASP* 15: 43–5

(2001) *Libraries in the ancient world.* New Haven

Ceausescu, P. (1976) 'Altera Roma: histoire d'une folie politique', *Historia* 25: 79–108

Chambers, I. (1994) *Migrancy, culture, identity.* London and New York

Charles-Gaffiot, J. and H. Lavagne (1999) *Hadrien: trésors d'une villa impériale.* Milan

Chavasse, A. (1993) *La liturgie de la ville de Rome du Ve au VIIIe siècle: une liturgie conditionnée par l'organisation de la vie in urbe et extra muros.* Rome

Christenson, D. (2000) *Plautus, Amphitruo.* Cambridge

Claridge, A. (1998) *Rome: an Oxford archaeological guide.* Oxford

Clark, G. (1999) 'Victricius of Rouen: praising the saints', *JECS* 7: 365–400

Clarke, J. R. (1998) *Looking at lovemaking: constructions of sexuality in Roman art 100 BC – AD 250.* Berkeley, Los Angeles and London

Clarke, K. (1999) *Between geography and history: Hellenistic constructions of the Roman world*, Oxford

Cloud, D. (1989) 'The client–patron relationship: emblem and reality in Juvenal's first book', in A. Wallace-Hadrill (ed.), *Patronage in ancient society*, 205–18. London

Clover, F. M. (1986) 'Felix Karthago', *Dumbarton Oaks Papers* 40: 1–16

Coale, A. J. and P. Demeny (1983), *Regional model life tables and stable populations*, 2nd ed. New York/London

Coarelli, F. (1968) 'La Porta Trionfale e la Via dei Trionfi', *DdA* 2: 55–103

(1971–2) 'Il complesso pompeiano del Campo Marzio e la sua decorazione scultorea', *Rendiconti della pontificia Accademia di Archeologia* 44: 99–122

(1978) 'Il "grande donario" di Attalo I', 231–55 in *I Galli e l'Italia.* Rome

(1985) *Il foro Romano*, vol. ii. Rome

(1988) *Il Foro Boario dalle origini alla fine della repubblica.* Rome

Cohen, R. (1987) *The new helots: migrants in the international division of labour.* Aldershot

Collari, S. (1932) 'Rapporti fra malaria e tubercolosi dal punto di vista epidemiologico, clinico e biologico', *Rivista di Malariologia* 11: 308–35

Collins, S. T. (1909) *The interpretation of Vergil with special reference to Macrobius.* Oxford

Cornell, T. C. (1995) *The beginnings of Rome. Italy and Rome from the Bronze Age to the Punic Wars (1000 – 264 BC).* London

Coulston, J. C. N. (2000). '"Armed and belted men": the soldiery in imperial Rome', in J. Coulston and H. Dodge (eds.), *Ancient Rome. The archaeology of the Eternal City*, Oxford University School of Archaeology monograph 54, 76–118. Oxford

Crawford, M. H. (1997) 'Rome and the Greek world', *Economic History Review* 30: 42–52

(1996) 'Roman population', in *OCD³*, 1223. Oxford and New York

Cumont, F. (1942) *Recherches sur le symbolisme funéraire des Romains*. Paris

Curran, J. R. (2000) *Pagan city and Christian capital: Rome in the fourth century*. Oxford

Daltrop, G., U. Hausmann and M. Wegner (1966) *Die Flavier*. Berlin

Dassmann, E. (1975) 'Ambrosius und die Märtyrer', *JbAC* 18: 49–68

Davis, L. (1989) *The silver pigs*. London

(1990) *Shadows in bronze*. London

Deckers, J. G., G. Mietke and A. Weiland (1994) *Die Katakombe 'Commodilla'*. Vatican

Deckers, J. G., H. R. Seeliger and G. Mietke (1987) *Die Katakombe 'Santi Marcellino e Pietro'*. Vatican

DeLaine, J. (1997). *The Baths of Caracalla. A study in the design, construction and economics of large-scale building projects in imperial Rome*, *JRA* supplementary vol. 25. Portsmouth, RI

(2000) 'Building the Eternal City: the construction industry of imperial Rome', in J. Coulston and H. Dodge (eds.), *Ancient Rome. The archaeology of the Eternal City*, Oxford University School of Archaeology monograph 54, 119–41. Oxford

Delehaye, H. (1912) *Les origines du culte des martyrs*. Brussels

(1927) *Sanctus: essai sur le culte des saintes dans l'antiquité*. Brussels

(1930) 'Loca Sanctorum', *Analecta Bollandiana* 48: 5–64

(1934) *Cinq leçons sur la méthode hagiographique*. Brussels

Del Panta, L. (1989) *Malaria e regime demografico: la maremma grossetana nell'ottocento preunitario*. Messina

Delumeau, J. (1957) *Vie économique et sociale de Rome dans la seconde moitié du XVIe siècle*. Paris

de Neeve, P. W. (1984) *Peasants in peril: location and economy in Italy in the second century BC* (inaugural lecture). Amsterdam

Dennis, F. (1999) 'The Prince and I', in *London: the lives of the city*, *Granta* 6: 312–23

Desowitz, R. (1992) *The malaria capers: more tales of parasites and people, research and reality*. New York

Dobson, M. J. (1997) *Contours of death and disease in early modern England*. Cambridge

Dodge, H. (1991), 'Ancient marble studies: recent research', *JRA* 4: 28–50

(2000). ' "Greater than the pyramids": the water supply of ancient Rome', in J. Coulston and H. Dodge (eds.), *Ancient Rome. The archaeology of the Eternal City*, Oxford University School of Archaeology monograph 54, 166–209. Oxford

Dols, M. W. (1977) *The Black Death in the Middle East*. Princeton

von Domaszewski, X. (1895) *Die Religion des römischen Heeres*. Trier

Douglass, L. (1996) 'A new look at the Itinerarium Burdigalense', *JECS* 4: 313–33

Duchesne, L. (1955) *Liber Pontificalis*, vol. 1. Paris

Duncan-Jones, R. P. (1982), *The economy of the Roman Empire. Quantitative studies*, 2nd ed. Cambridge

(1996) 'The impact of the Antonine plague', *JRA* 9: 108–36

Dupont, F. (1976) 'Signification théatrale du double dans l'*Amphitryon* de Plaute', *REL* 54: 129–41

(1997) 'Recitatio and the reorganisation of the space of public discourse', in T. Habinek and A. Schiesaro (eds.), *The Roman cultural revolution*, 44–59. Cambridge

Dyson, T. (1997) 'Infant and child mortality in the Indian subcontinent, 1881–1947', in A. Bideau, B. Desjardins and H. Pérez Brignoli (eds.), *Infant and child mortality in the past*, 109–34. Oxford

Earl, D. C. (1963), *Tiberius Gracchus: a study in politics*. Brussels

Eastmond, A. (1994) 'Leaf of an ivory diptych: an apotheosis', in D. Buckton (ed.), *Byzantium*, 57–8. London

Eck, W. (1984) 'Senatorial self-representation: developments in the Augustan period', in F. G. B. Millar and E. Segal (eds.), *Caesar Augustus: seven aspects*, 129–67. Oxford

(1997) 'Rome and the outside world: senatorial families and the world they lived in', in B. Rawson and P. Weaver (eds.), *The Roman family in Italy. Status, sentiment, space*, 73–99. Oxford

Edwards, C. (1993) *The politics of immorality in ancient Rome*. Cambridge

(1996) *Writing Rome: textual approaches to the city*. Cambridge

(2002) 'Acting and self-actualisation in imperial Rome: some death scenes', in P. Easterling and E. Hall (eds.), *Greek and Roman actors*, 379–95. Cambridge

Edwards, C. and M. Liversidge (1996) *Imagining Rome: British artists and Rome in the nineteenth century*. London

Eisner, M. (1986) *Zur Typologie der Grabbauten im Suburbium Roms*. Mainz

Elsner, J. (1995) *Art and the Roman viewer: the transformation of art from the pagan world to Christianity*. Cambridge

(1996) 'Image and ritual: reflections of the religious appreciation of classical art', *CQ* 46: 515–31

(1997) 'The origins of the icon: pilgrimage, religion and visual culture in the Roman East as "resistance" to the centre', in S. Alcock (ed.), *The early Roman empire in the East*, 178–99. Oxford

(1998) *Imperial Rome and Christian triumph*. Oxford

(2000a) 'From the culture of spolia to the cult of relics: the Arch of Constantine and the genesis of late-antique forms', *PBSR* 68: 149–84

(2000b) 'The Itinerarium Burdigalense: politics and salvation in the geography of Constantine's empire', *JRS* 90: 180–94

(forthcoming) 'Visualising woman in late antique Rome: the Projecta casket', in C. Entwhistle (ed.), *Buckton Festschrift*. Oxford

Elsner, J. and A. Sharrock (1991) 'Re-viewing Pygmalion', *Ramus* 20: 149–82

Elvin, M. (1973), *The pattern of the Chinese past*. Stanford

(1978), 'Chinese cities since the Sung dynasty', in Abrams and Wrigley (1978) 79–89

Evans, J. D. (1990) 'Statues of the kings and Brutus on the Capitoline', *Opuscula Romana* 18: 99–105

Fant, J. C. (1993) 'Ideology, gift and trade: a distribution model for Roman imperial marbles', in William V. Harris (ed.), *The inscribed economy. Production and distribution in the Roman Empire in the light of the instrumentum domesticum*, *JRA* supplement VI, 145–70. Ann Arbor

Fantham, E. (1996) *Roman literary culture. From Cicero to Apuleius*, Baltimore, MD

Favro, D. (1994) 'The street triumphant: the urban impact of Roman triumphal parades', in Z. Çelik, D. Favro and R. Ingersoll (eds.), *Streets: critical perspectives on public space*, 151–64. Berkeley and London

Fea, C. (1790) *Memorie di varie escavazioni fatte in Roma e nei luoghi suburbani vivente Pietro Santi Bartoli*, in *Miscellanea filologica, critica et antiquaria*, vol. 1. Rome

Feeney, D. C. (1991) *The gods in epic: poets and critics of the classical tradition*. Oxford
(1998) *Literature and religion at Rome. Cultures, contexts and beliefs*. Cambridge

Fentress, E. (ed.) (2000) *Romanization and the City. Creation, transformations and failures*, *JRA* supplement 38. Portsmouth, RI

Ferris, I. M. (2000) *Enemies of Rome: barbarians through Roman eyes*. Stroud

Ferrua, A. (1939) 'Filocalo, l'amante della bella scrittura', *La Civiltà Cattolica* 90: 34–47
(1942) *Epigrammata Damasiana*. Vatican

Février, P.-A. (1989) 'À propos de la date des peintures des catacombes romaines', *RAC* 65: 102–34

Finlay, R. (1981) 'Natural decrease in early modern cities', *P&P* 92: 169–74

Finley, M. I. (1984) *The ancient economy*, 2nd ed. London

Finney, P. C. (1994) *The invisible god*. Oxford

Fowden, G. (1993) *From empire to commonwealth*. Princeton

Frankfurter, D. (1998) *Religion in Roman Egypt*. Princeton

Frazer, J. G. (1911) *The magic art and the evolution of kings*, vol. 11 (*The Golden Bough: a study in magic and religion*, 3rd ed.). London

Frazer, M. (1989) 'Oreficerie altomedievali', in R. Conti (ed.), *Il Duomo di Monza: i tesori*, 15–54. Milan

Fredericks, S. G. (1976) 'Juvenal's fifteenth satire', *Illinois Classical Studies* 1: 174–89

Freyberg, H.-U. von (1989) *Kapitalverkehr und Handel im römischen Kaiserreich (27 v. Chr. – 235 n. Chr.)*. Freiburg i. Br.

Friedländer, L. (1928) *Roman life and manners under the early empire*, 4 vols. (translated from the 7th enlarged and revised ed. of the *Sittengeschichte Roms*). London and New York

Frier, B. W. (1999) 'Roman demography', in D. S. Potter and D. J. Mattingly (eds.), *Life, death, and entertainment in the Roman empire*, 85–109. Ann Arbor
(2001) 'More is worse: some observations on the population of the Roman empire', in Scheidel (2001b) 139–59

Furet, F. (1978) *Penser la révolution française*. Paris

Gabba, E. (1956) *Appiano e la storia delle guerre civili* (Biblioteca di cultura, 59). Florence

Gabba, E. and M. Pasquinucci (1979), *Strutture agrarie e allevamento transumante nell'Italia romana (III–I sec. a.c.)*. Pisa

Galinsky, G. K. (1966) 'Scipionic themes in Plautus' *Amphitruo*', *TAPA* 97: 203–35

Gallant, T. W. (1988) *Risk and survival in ancient Greece*. Cambridge

Galley, C. (1998) *The demography of early-modern towns: York in the sixteenth and seventeenth centuries*. Liverpool

Garcia-Bellido, M. P. (1989) 'Punic iconography on the Roman denarii of M. Praetorius Cestianus', *American Journal of Numismatics* 1: 37–49

Garnsey, P. (ed.) (1980) *Non-slave labour in the Graeco-Roman world*. Cambridge
  (1988) *Famine and food supply in the Graeco-Roman world: responses to risk and crisis*. Cambridge
  (1998) *Cities, peasants and food in classical antiquity: essays in social and economic history*, ed. with addenda by W. Scheidel. Cambridge
  (1999) *Food and society in classical antiquity*. Cambridge

Gazda, E. K. (1995) 'Roman sculpture and the ethos of emulation', *HSCP* 97: 121–56

Geller, J. J. (1931) *Famous songs and their stories*. New York

Gellner, E. (1988) *Plough, sword and book*. London

Gerke, F. (1936) *Der Sarkophag des Junius Bassus*. Berlin

Giardina, A. and Aldo Schiavone (eds.) (1981) *Società romana e produzione schiav- istica*, 3 vols. Rome/Bari

Gilles, H. M. and D. A. Warrell (1993) *Bruce-Chwatt's essential malariology*, 3rd ed. London

Gnoli, R. (1988) *Marmora romana*. Rome (1st edn 1971)

Gordon, R. (1979) 'The real and the imaginary: production and religion in the Greco-Roman world', *Art History* 2.1: 5–34
  (1990) 'Religion in the Roman Empire: the civic compromise and its limits', in M. Beard and J. North (eds.), *Pagan priests*, 235–40. London

Goudineau, C. and A. Reborg (eds.) (1991) *Les villes Augustéennes de Gaule* (Actes du Colloque international d'Autun 6–8 Juin 1985). Autun

Gowers, E. (1993) *The loaded table. Representations of food in Roman literature*. Oxford
  (1995) 'From Capitol to Cloaca: the anatomy of Rome', *JRS* 85: 23–32

Grabar, A. (1969) *Christian iconography: a study of its origins*. London

Graf, A. (1915) *Roma nella memoria e nelle immaginazioni del Medio Evo*. Turin

Green, C. M. C. (1996) 'Did the Romans hunt?', *Classical Antiquity* 15: 222–60

Greenhalgh, Paul (1988) *Ephemeral vistas: the Expositions Universelles, Great Exhi- bitions and World's Fairs, 1851–1939*. Manchester

Greenhalgh, Peter (1980) *Pompey, the Roman Alexander*. London

Greenhill, A. W. (1848) *A treatise on the small-pox and measles by Abú Becr Mohammed Ibn Zacaríyá Ar-Rázi (commonly called Rhazes)*. London

Gregorovius, F. (1907) *Roman journal* (trans. Mrs Hamilton). London

Gregory, A. (1994) ' "Powerful images": responses to portraits and the political use of images at Rome', *JRA* 7: 80–99

Grenier, J. (1989) 'La décoration statuaire du Serapeum du Canope de la Villa Adriana: essai de reconstruction et d'interpretation', *Mélanges de l'Ecole française de Rome, antiquité* 101.2: 925–1019

    (2000) 'Il "Serapeo" e il "Canopo": un "egitto" monumentale e un "mediterraneo"', in Ministero per i beni e le attività culturali, Soprintendenza archeologica per il Lazio, *Adriano: architettura e progetto*, 73–5. Milan

Griffin, M. (1986) 'Philosophy, Cato and Roman suicide', *G&R* 33: 64–77, 192–202

    (1991) 'Urbs Roma, plebs and princeps', in L. Alexander (ed.), *Images of Empire, Journal for the Study of the Old Testament* supplement 122, 19–46. Sheffield

Grmek, M. D. (1989) *Diseases in the ancient Greek world*. Baltimore and London

    (1991) 'La dénomination latine des maladies considérées comme nouvelles par les auteurs antiques', in Sabbah (1991) 195–214

Gros, P. (1985) *Mission archéologique française à Carthage. Byrsa* III, *CEFR* 41

    (1990) 'Le premier urbanisme de la Colonia Julia Carthago', *L'Afrique dans l'Occident Romain. CEFR* 134: 547–73

Gruen, E. (1990) *Studies in Greek culture and Roman policy*. Leiden

    (1992) *Culture and national identity in Republican Rome*. Ithaca

Habinek, T. (1998) *The politics of Latin literature. Writing, identity and empire in ancient Rome*. Cambridge

Halkin, L. (1948) 'La parodie d'une demande de triomphe dans l'Amphitryon de Plaute', *AC* 17: 297–304

Halstead, P. (1987) 'Traditional and ancient rural economy in Mediterranean Europe: plus ça change', *JHS* 107: 77–87

Halstead, P., and J. O'Shea (eds.) (1989) *Bad year economics. Cultural responses to risk and uncertainty*. Cambridge

Hanfmann, G. M. A. (1951) *The Season Sarcophagus in Dumbarton Oaks*. Cambridge, MA

Hannestad, N. (1986) *Roman art and imperial policy*. Aarhus

    (1999) 'How did rising Christianity cope with pagan sculpture?' in E. Chrysos and I. Wood (eds.), *East and West: modes of communication*, 173–203. Leiden

Hansen, M. (1988) *Three studies in Athenian demography*. Copenhagen

Hanson, J. (1959) *Roman theater-temples*. Princeton

Hardie, A. (1983) *Statius and the Silvae. Poets, patrons and epideixis in the Greco-Roman world*. Liverpool

Hardie, P. (1992) 'Augustan poets and the mutability of Rome', in Anton Powell (ed.), *Roman poetry and propaganda in the age of Augustus*, 59–82. Bristol

Harlesberghe, G. H. (1984) 'Le culte de Dea Caelestis', *ANRW* 11.17.4: 2203–23

Harris, W. V. (1979) *War and imperialism in republican Rome, 327–70 BC*. Oxford

    (1999a) 'Demography, geography and the source of Roman slaves', *JRS* 89: 62–75

    (1999b) 'Introduction: Rome in late antiquity', in Harris (1999c) 9–14

    (ed.) (1999c) *The transformations of Urbs Roma in late antiquity*, *JRA* suppl. 33. Portsmouth, RI

Harvey, P. (1981) 'Historical allusions in Plautus and the date of the Amphitruo', *Athenaeum*: 59: 480–9

Häuber, C. and F. X. Schültz (1999) 'The multi-disciplinary, multimedia geographical information system applied to archaeology, GIS[A] FORTVNA. The basics of development', *Proceedings of the XVth international congress of classical archaeology, Amsterdam, July 12–17 1998. Classical archaeology towards the 3rd Millennium.* Allard Pierson, series 12: 194–6

Hellemo, G. (1989) *Adventus Domini.* Leiden

Henderson, J. (1997) *Figuring out Roman nobility. Juvenal's eighth satire.* Exeter
  (1998) *A Roman life. Rutilius Gallicus on paper and in stone.* Exeter
  (2001a) 'From Megalopolis to Cosmopolis: Polybius or there and back again', in S. Goldhill (ed.), *Being Greek under Rome*, 29–49. Cambridge
  (2001b) 'Going to the dogs / Grattius <&> the Augustan subject', *PCPS* 47: 1–22

Hermansen, G. (1981) *Ostia: aspects of Roman city life.* Alberta

Hershkowitz, D. (1995) 'Pliny the poet', *G&R* 42.2: 168–81

Hinds, S. (1998) *Allusion and intertext. Dynamics of appropriation in Roman poetry.* Cambridge

Hobsbawn, E. and T. Ranger (eds.) (1983) *The invention of tradition.* Cambridge

Hodges, R. and D. Whitehouse (1983) *Mohammed, Charlemagne and the origins of Europe. Archaeology and the Pirenne thesis.* London

Hollis, A. S. (1977) *Ovid Ars Amatoria book 1.* Oxford

Hölscher, T. (1987) *Römische Bildsprache als semantisches System* (Abhandlungen der heidelberger Ak. der Wiss., phil.-hist. Kl., 1987.2). Heidelberg

Honoré, T. (1987) 'Scriptor Historiae Augustae', *JRS* 77: 156–76

Hoogma, R. P. (1959) *Der Einfluß Vergils auf die Carmina Latina epigraphica. Eine Studie mit besonderer Berücksichtigung der metrisch-technischen Grundsätze der Entlehnung.* Amsterdam.

Hopkins, D. R. (1983) *Princes and peasants: smallpox in history.* Chicago and London

Hopkins, K. (1961) 'Social mobility in the later Roman empire: the evidence of Ausonius', *CQ* 11: 239–49
  (1966) 'On the probable age structure of the Roman population', *Population Studies* 20: 245–64
  (ed.) (1971) *Hong Kong: the industrial colony: a political, social and economic survey.* Hong Kong and Oxford
  (1974) 'Demography in Roman history', *Mnemosyne* 27: 77–8
  (1978a) *Conquerors and slaves. Sociological studies in Roman history 1.* Cambridge.
  (1978b) 'Economic growth and towns in classical antiquity', in Abrams and Wrigley (1978) 35–77
  (1978c) 'Rules of evidence', *JRS* 68: 178–86
  (1980) 'Taxes and trade in the Roman Empire (200 BC – AD 400)', *JRS* 70: 101–25
  (1983a), 'Models, ships and staples', in P. Garnsey and C. R. Whittaker (eds.), *Trade and famine in classical antiquity*, 84–109. Cambridge
  (1983b), *Death and renewal. Sociological studies in Roman history 11.* Cambridge
  (1987) 'Graveyards for historians', in F. Hinard (ed.), *La mort, les morts et l'au-delà dans le monde romain*, 113–26. Caen

(1990) 'Seven missing papers' in J. Andreau and H. Bruhns (eds.), *Parenté et stratégies familiales dans l'antiquité romaine*. Actes de la table ronde des 2–4 octobre 1986, *CEFR*, 623–30. Rome

(1995/6) 'Rome, taxes, rents and trade', *Kodai* 6/7: 41–75 (repr. in W. Scheidel and S. von Reden, *The ancient economy: recent approaches*, 190–230. Edinburgh 2002)

(1999) *A world full of gods: pagans, Jews and Christians in the Roman empire*. London

Horden, P. and N. Purcell (2000) *The corrupting sea: A study of Mediterranean history*. Oxford

Hornblower, S. (1982) *Mausolus*. Oxford

Huet, V. (1999) 'Napoleon I: a new Augustus', in C. Edwards (ed.) *Roman presences: receptions of Rome in European culture 1789–1945*, 53–69. Cambridge

Hülsen, C. (1910) *Il libro di schizzi di Giuliano da Sangallo, Cod. Vat. lat. Barber. 4424*. Leipzig

(1927) 'Die basilica des Junius Bassus und die Kirche S. Andreae Cata Barbara auf dem Esquilin', in *Festschrift J. Schlosser*, 53–67. Zürich, Leipzig and Vienna

Humbert, J.-M. (1994) 'Egyptomania: a current concept from the Renaissance to Postmodernism', in J.-M. Humbert, M. Pantazzi and C. Ziegler (eds.), *Egyptomania: Egypt in western art 1730–1930*, 21–6. Ottawa

Hume, D. (1875) 'On the populousness of ancient nations', in T. H. Green and T. H. Grose (eds.), *Essays: moral, political and literary*, vol. 1, 381–443. London

Hummel, C. (1999) *Das Kind und seine Krankheiten in der griechischen Medizin: von Aretaios bis Johannes Aktuarios (1. bis 14. Jahrhundert)*. Frankfurt

Hunt, E. (1982) *Holy Land pilgrimage in the later Roman Empire* AD 312–460. Oxford

Hunt L. (1984) *Politics, culture and class in the French Revolution*. Berkeley

Hunter, R. (1987) 'Middle comedy and the Amphitruo of Plautus', *Dioniso* 57: 281–98

Hurst, H. R. (1985) 'Fouilles britanniques au Port circulaire, et quelques idées sur le développement de Carthage romaine', *Cahiers des Etudes Anciennes* 17: 143–56

(1993) 'Cartagine, la Nuova Alessandria', *Storia di Roma* 3.2: 327–37

(1999) *The Sanctuary of Tanit at Carthage in the Roman period: a re-interpretation*. *JRA*, supplement 301. Portsmouth, RI

Huskinson, J. (1974) 'Some pagan figures and their significance in early Christian art', *PBSR* 42: 68–97

(1982) *Concordia Apostolorum: Christian propaganda at Rome in the fourth and fifth centuries*. Oxford

Huttunen, P. (1974) *The social strata in the imperial city of Rome. A quantitative study of the social representation in the epitaphs published in the Corpus Inscriptionum Latinarum vol.* VI. Oulu

Iacopi, I. (1997) *La decorazione pittorica dell'Aula Isiaca*. Milan

Ihm, C. (1960) *Die Programme der christlichen Apsismalerei vom vierten Jahrhundert bis zur Mitte des achten Jahrhunderts*. Wiesbaden

Jensen, R. M. (2000) *Understanding early Christian art*. London

Johne, K. P., J. Köhn and V. Weber (1983) *Die Kolonen in Italien und den westlichen Provinzen des römischen Reiches*. Berlin

Jones, A. H. M. (1964) *The later Roman empire*. Oxford

Jones, A. H. M., J. R. Martindale and J. Morris (1971) *The prosopography of the later Roman empire* I *(AD 260–395)*. Cambridge

Jongman, W. (1988) *The economy and society of Pompeii*. Amsterdam

(1990) 'Het Romeins imperialisme en de verstedelijking van Italië', *Leidschrift* VII.I: 43–58

(1998) 'De betovering van Moses Finley', *Lampas* 31: 336–50

(2000a) 'Slavernij en verstedelijking. De transformatie van Italië in de tweede en eerste eeuw v. Chr.', *Lampas* 30: 254–68

(2000b) 'Hunger and power. Theories, models and methods in Roman economic history', in Herman Bongenaar (ed.), *Interdependency of institutions and private entrepreneurs. Proceedings of the second MOS symposium, Leiden 1998*, MOS Studies 2, 259–84. Istanbul

(2000c) 'Wool and the textile industry of Roman Italy: a working hypothesis', in E. Lo Cascio (ed.), *Mercati permanenti e mercati periodici nel mondo romano. Atti degli Incontri Capresi di storia dell'economia antica (Capri 13–15 ottobre 1997)*, 187–97. Bari

(2001) 'Roma II. Bevölkerung und Wirtschaft der Stadt Rom', in H. Cancik and H. Schneider (eds.), *Der neue Pauly. Enzyklopädie der Antike* X, 1077–83. Stuttgart/Weimar

(forthcoming a) 'The loss of innocence: Pompeian economy and society between past and present', in P. Foss and J. Dobbins (eds.), *Pompeii and the settlements under Vesuvius*. London

(forthcoming b) 'A golden age. Death, money supply and social succession in the Roman Empire', in E. Lo Cascio (ed.), *Credito e moneta nel mondo Romano*. Bari

Jongman, W. and R. Dekker (1988) 'Public intervention in the food supply in pre-industrial Europe,' in P. Halstead and J. O'Shea (eds.), *Bad year economics: cultural responses to risk and uncertainty*, 114–26. Cambridge

Jongste, P. F. B. (1995) *Het gebruik van marmer in de romeinse samenleving*. Leiden

Kiilerich, B. (1993) *Late fourth century classicism in the plastic arts: studies in the so-called Theodosian renaissance*. Odense

Kinney, D. (1994a) 'The iconography of the Ivory Diptych Nichomachorum-Symmachorum', *JbAC* 37: 64–96

(1994b) Review of T. Mathews, *The clash of gods*, *Studies in Iconography* 16: 237–42

(1997) 'Spolia, damnatio and renovatio memoriae', *MAAR* 42: 117–48

Kiss, Z. (1984) *Etudes sur le portrait impérial romain en Egypte*. Warsaw

Klein, R. (1972) *Der Streit um der Victorienaltar*. Darmstadt

Kleiner, D. E. E. (1981) 'Second-century mythological portraiture: Mars and Venus', *Latomus* 40: 512–44

(1992) *Roman sculpture*. New Haven

Kolb, F. (1995) *Rom: Geschichte der Stadt in der Antike*. Munich

Kolendo, J. (1980) *L'Agricoltura nell'Italia romana: tecniche agrarie e progresso economico della tarda Repubblica al Principato*. Rome

Krautheimer, R. (1980) *Rome: profile of a city*. Princeton
(1983) *Three Christian capitals*. Berkeley and Los Angeles

Krautheimer, R., S. Corbet and W. Frankl (1970) *Corpus Basilicarum Christianarum Romae*, vol. IV. Vatican

Künzl, E (1988) *Der römische Triumph: Siegesfeiern in antiken Rom*. Munich

Kuttner, A. (1993) 'Some new grounds for narrative: Marcus Antonius' base (the "Ara Domitii Ahenobarbi") and republican biographies', in P. Holliday (ed.), *Narrative and event in ancient art*, 198–229. Cambridge

Lahusen, G. (1983) *Untersuchungen zur Ehrenstatue in Rom: literarische und epigraphische Zeugnisse*. Rome

Laird, A. (1993) 'Sounding out ecphrasis: art and text in Catullus 64', *JRS* 83: 18–30

Lancel, S. (1995) *Carthage: a history*. Oxford

Lanciani, R. A. (1897) *The ruins and excavations of ancient Rome: a companion book for students and travellers*. London

Landers, J. (1993), *Death and the metropolis. Studies in the demographic history of London 1670–1830*. Cambridge

Landers, J. and Mouzas, A. (1988) 'Burial seasonality and causes of death in London 1670–1819', *Population Studies* 42: 59–83

Landwehr, C. (1985) *Die antiken Gipsabgüsse aus Baiae: griechische Bronzestatuen in Abgüssen römischer Zeit*. Berlin

Laqueur, R (1909) 'Über das Wesen des römischen Triumphs', *Hermes* 44: 215–36

La Rocca, E. (1985) *Amazzonomachia: le sculture frontonali del tempio di Apollo Sosiano*. Rome

Laurence, R. (1997) 'Writing the Roman metropolis', in H. Parkin (ed.), *Roman urbanism: beyond the consumer city*, 1–20. London and New York

Lawrence, M. (1961) 'Three pagan themes in Christian art', in M. Meiss (ed.), *De artibus opuscula XL: essays in honor of Erwin Panofsky*, vol. 1, 323–34. New York

Leclant, M. (1958) 'Reflets de l'Egypte dans la littérature latine d'après quelques publications récentes', *REL* 36: 81–5

Le Glay, M. (1961) *Saturne Africain, Monuments*, vol. 1. Paris
(1966) *Saturne Africain, Histoire*. Paris

Lepelley, C. (1981) *Les Cités de l'Afrique romaine au bas-empire*, vol. II. Paris

Levi, A. C. (1952) *Barbarians on Roman imperial coins and sculpture*. American Numismatic Society. Numismatic Notes and Monographs 123

Ling, R. (1991) *Roman painting*. Cambridge

Lipinsky, A. (1960) 'Der Theodolinden Schatz im Dom zur Monza', *Das Münster* 13: 146–73

Littman, R. J. and M. L. Littman (1973) 'Galen and the Antonine Plague', *AJP* 94: 243–53

Lo Cascio, E. (1997) 'Le procedure di recensus dalla tarda repubblica al tardo antico e il calcolo della popolazione di Roma', in *La Rome impériale: démographie et logistique. Actes de la table ronde (Rome, 25 mars 1994)*, 3–76. Rome
  (2001) 'Recruitment and the size of the Roman population from the third to the first century BCE', in Scheidel (2001b) 111–37
  (forthcoming) 'Did the population of imperial Rome reproduce itself?'
Loriot, X. and D. Nony (1997) *La Crise de l'Empire romain 235–285*. Paris
Lunadoro, G. (1664) *Relatione della corte di Roma*. Rome
MacDonald, W. L. and J. A. Pinto (1995) *Hadrian's villa and its legacy*. New Haven and London
MacKendrick, P. (1975) *The Dacian stones speak*. Chapel Hill
McLynn, N. (1994) *Ambrose of Milan*. Berkeley and Los Angeles
MacMullen, R. (1974) *Roman social relations 50 BC to AD 284*. New Haven and London
Malamud, M. (forthcoming) *Rome and imperial America: architecture, spectacle and the performance of empire*
Malbon, E. S. (1990) *The iconography of the sarcophagus of Junius Bassus*. Princeton
Manchester, K. (1986) 'Tuberculosis and leprosy in antiquity: an interpretation', *MASCA Journal* 4: 22–30
  (1992a) 'Leprosy: the origin and development of the disease in antiquity', in D. Gourevitch (ed.), *Maladie et maladies: histoire et conceptualisation. Mélanges en l'honneur de Mirko Grmek*, 31–49. Geneva
  (1992b) 'The palaeopathology of urban infections', in Bassett (1992) 8–14
Mango, C. (1990) 'Constantine's mausoleum and the cult of relics', *Byzantinische Zeitschrift* 83: 51–62
Marasco, G. (1998) 'Erodiano e la Crisi dell'Impero', *ANRW* 11.34.4: 2837–927
Marchiafava, E. and A. Bignami (1894) *On summer–autumn malarial fevers*. London
Marganne, M.-H. (1991) 'L'Egypte médicale de Pline l'Ancien', in Sabbah (1991) 155–71
Markus, R. (1990) *The end of ancient Christianity*. Cambridge
Marshall, A. J. (1976) 'Library resources and creative writing at Rome', *Phoenix* 30: 252–64
Marvin, M. (1993) 'Copying in Roman sculpture: the replica series', in E. D'Ambra (ed.), *Roman art in context*, 161–88. Englewood Cliffs, NJ
  (1997) 'Roman sculptural reproductions', in A. Hughes and E. Ranfft (eds.), *Sculpture and its reproductions*, 7–29. London
Mathews, T. (1993) *The clash of gods*. Princeton
Matthews, J. (1975) *Western aristocracies and the imperial court, AD 364–425*. Oxford
  (1986) 'Ammianus and the eternity of Rome', in C. Holdsworth and T. P. Wiseman (eds.), *The inheritance of historiography AD 350–900*, Exeter Studies in History 12, 17–29. Exeter
Mazzarino, S. (1951) *Aspetti sociali del iv secolo*. Rome

Merati, A. (1963) *Il tesoro del Duomo di Monza*. Monza
Meyboom, P. G. P. (1995) *The Nile mosaic of Palestrina: early evidence of Egyptian religion in Italy*. Leiden and New York
Meyer, H. (1991) *Antinoos. Die archäologischen Denkmäler unter Einbeziehung des numismatischen und epigraphischen Materials sowie der literarischen Nachrichten*. Munich
Middleton, J. H. (1892) *The remains of ancient Rome*. London
Mielsch, H. and H. von Hesberg (1995) *Die heidnische Nekropole unter St Peter in Rom*. Rome
Miles, M. (1985) *Image as insight*. Boston
Miller, P. C. (1998) ' "Differential networks": relics and other fragments in late antiquity', *JECS* 6: 113–38
Millett, M. (1990) *The romanization of Britain: an essay in archaeological interpretation*. Cambridge
Moatti, C. (1998) *La Mémoire perdue. Recherches sur l'administration romaine*, CEFR 243, Rome
Mommsen, T. (1859) 'Die ludi magni und Romani', *RhM* 14: 79–87 (repr. in *Römische Forschungen* 11: 42–57. Berlin, 1879)
    (1882) *Chronica Minora Saec. iv, v, vi, vii*, vol. 1. Berlin (= *MGH: Auctorum Antiquissimorum* 9)
    (1887) *Römisches Staatsrecht*, vol. 1 (3rd ed.). Leipzig
Morey, C. R. (1959) *The gold-glass collection of the Vatican Library with additional catalogues of other gold glass collections*. Vatican
Morley, N. (1996) *Metropolis and hinterland: the city of Rome and the Italian economy 200 BC – AD 200*. Cambridge
Morris, I. (1994) 'The Athenian economy twenty years after *The ancient economy*', *Classical Philology* 89: 351–66
    (1999) 'Foreword' in updated edition of M. I. Finley, *The ancient economy*. Berkeley/Los Angeles/London
Muhlberger, S. (1990) *The fifth-century chroniclers, Prosper, Hydatius and the Gallic Chronicler of 452*. Leeds
Müller, H. W. (1969) *Der Isiskult im antiken Benevent und Katalog der Skulpturen aus den Ägyptischen Heiligtümern im Museo del Sannio*. Berlin
Mundle, I. (1961) 'Dea Caelestis in der Religionspolitik des Septimius Severus und der Julia Domna', *Historia* 10: 228–37
Murray, C. (1981) *Rebirth and afterlife*. Oxford
Musée de la civilisation gallo-romaine (1998) *La fascination de l'antique, 1700–1770: Rome découverte, Rome inventée*. Lyon
Neuerburg, N. (1969) 'Greek and Roman pyramids', *Archaeology* 22.2: 106–15
Nicolai, V. F., F. Bisconti and D. Mazzoleri (1998) *Le catacombe cristiane di Roma*. Regensburg
Nicolet, C. (1980) *The world of the citizen in republican Rome*. London
    (1991) *Space, geography and politics in the early Roman empire* (trs. Helene Leclerc). Ann Arbor
Noy, D. (2000) *Foreigners at Rome: citizens and strangers*. London

O'Connor, D. (1969) *Peter in Rome*. London

O'Gorman, E. C. (1993) 'No place like Rome: identity and difference in the Germania of Tacitus', *Ramus* 22: 135–54

Omran, A. R. (1971) 'The epidemiologic transition: a theory of the epidemiology of population change', *Milbank Memorial Fund Quarterly* 49: 509–38

Osborne, R. (1994) 'Looking on – Greek style. Does the sculpted girl speak to women too?', in I. Morris (ed.), *Classical Greece: ancient histories and modern ideologies*, 81–96. Cambridge

(1998) 'Sculpted men of Athens: masculinity and power in the field of vision', in L. Foxhall and J. Salmon (eds.), *Thinking men: masculinity and self-representation in the classical tradition*, 23–42. London

Packer, J. (1997) *The Forum of Trajan: a study of the monuments*. Berkeley

Paine, R. R. and G. R. Storey (1997) 'Latin funerary inscriptions: (yet) another attempt at demographic analysis', in *Preatti, XI international congress of Greek and Latin epigraphy*, 847–54. Rome

Pampana, E. (1963) *A textbook of malaria eradication*. Oxford

Pape, M. (1975) *Griechische Kunstwerke aus Kriegsbeute und ihre öffentliche Aufstellung in Rom* (PhD diss.). Hamburg

Parkin, T. G. (1992) *Demography and Roman society*. Baltimore and London

Patterson, J. R. (1992) 'Patronage, collegia and burial in imperial Rome', in Bassett (1992) 15–27

(1999) 'Via Ostiensis', in E. M. Steinby, *Lexicon topographicum urbis Romae*, vol. v, 143. Rome

(2000a) 'On the margins of the city of Rome', in V. M. Hope and E. Marshall (eds.), *Death and disease in the ancient city*, 85–103. London and New York

(2000b) *Political life in the city of Rome*. Bristol

Peebles, B. (1936) 'La Meta Romuli', *Atti della Pontificia Accademia Romana di archeologia. Rendiconti* 12: 21–63

Pera, R. (1979) 'Probabili significati della scritta INDULGENTIA AUGG IN CARTHAGINEM ed INDULGENTIA AUGG IN ITALIAM su alcune monete di Settimio Severo e Caracalla', *Rivista Italiana di Numismatica e Scienze Affini* 81: 103–14

Pergola, P. (1999) *La catacombe Romane: storia e tipografia*. Rome

Perrenoud, A. (1979) *La population de Genève du seizième au début du dix-neuvième siècle: étude démographique, 1: structures et mouvements*. Geneva and Paris

Pfanner, M. (1980) 'Codex Coburgensis Nr 88: Die Entdeckung der Porta Triumphalis', *MOAI(R)* 87: 327–34

Picard, Ch. G. (1954) *Les Religions de l'Afrique antique*. Paris

(1959) 'Pertinax et les Prophètes de Caelestis', *Revue de l'Histoire des Religions* 55: 41–62

Pietri, C. (1976) *Roma christiana*, vol. 1. Rome

(1983) 'Liturgie, culture et societé: l'exemple de Rome à la fin de l'antiquité (IVe–Ve siècles)', *Concilium* 182: 65–77

(1986) 'Damase, Evêque de Rome', in *Saecularia Damasiana*, 31–58. Vatican

Piranesi, G. B. (c. 1748) *Vedute di Roma*. Rome

Platner, S. B. and T. Ashby (1929) *A topographical dictionary of ancient Rome.* London

Poeschke, J., ed. (1996) *Antike Spolien in der Architektur des Mittelalters und der Renaissance.* Munich

Poggio Bracciolini, G. F. (1723) *De varietate fortunae.* Paris.

Pollitt, J. J. (1978) 'The impact of Greek art on Rome', *TAPA* 108: 155–74
 (1983) *The art of Rome, c. 753 BC – AD 337.* Cambridge
 (1986) *Art in the Hellenistic age.* Cambridge

Pompei: l'informatica al servizio di una città antica (1998). Rome

Pooley, C. and J. Turnball (1998) *Migration and mobility in Britain since the eighteenth century.* London

Postan, M. M. (1975) *The medieval economy and society.* Harmondsworth

Potter, T. W. (1979), *The changing landscape of southern Etruria.* London

Purcell, N. (1987) 'Tomb and suburb', in H. von Hesberg and P. Zanker (eds.), *Römische Gräberstraßen: Selbstdarstellung, Status, Standard*, 25–41. Munich
 (1994) 'The city of Rome and the plebs urbana in the late Republic', in *CAH* IX, 2nd ed., 644–88. Cambridge
 (1999) 'The populace of Rome in late antiquity: problems of description and historical classification', in Harris (1999c) 135–61
 (2000) 'Rome and Italy', in *CAH* XI, 2nd ed., 405–43

Raban, J. (1974) *Soft city.* London

Rakob, F. (2000) 'The making of Augustan Carthage', in Fentress (2000) 73–82

Rapport, N. and A. Dawson (eds.), (1998) *Migrants of identity: perceptions of home in a world of movement.* Oxford and New York

Rathbone, D. W. (1981) 'The development of agriculture in the "Ager Cosanus" during the Roman Republic: problems of evidence and interpretation', *JRS* 71: 10–23
 (1983) 'The slave mode of production in Italy', *JRS* 73: 160–8
 (1990) Review of Carandini (1988), *JRS* 80: 195–6

Rawson, E. (1975) 'Caesar's heritage: Hellenistic kings and their Roman equals', *JRS* 65: 148–59
 (1985) *Intellectual life in the late Roman Republic.* London

Raymond, A. (1972) 'Les grandes épidémies de peste au Caire aux XVII et XVIII siècles', *Bulletin d'Etudes Orientales* 25: 203–10

Reekmans, L. (1989) 'L'implantation monumentale Chrétienne dans le paysage urbain de Rome de 300 à 850', *Actes de XIe congrès internationale d'archéologie Chrétienne* 2, 861–915. Rome

Rey, E. and G. Sormani (1881) 'Statistica delle cause di morte', in *Monografia della città di Roma e della Campagna Romana*, vol. I, 121–48. Rome

Reynolds, J. (1981) 'New evidence for the imperial cult in Julio-Claudian Aphrodisias', *ZPE* 43: 317–27
 (1986) 'Further information on imperial cult at Aphrodisias', in *Festschrift D. M. Pippidi = Studii Clasice* 24: 109–17

Richardson, J. S. (1975) 'The triumph, the praetors and the senate in the early second century BC', *JRS* 65: 50–63

Richardson, L. (1992) *A new topographical dictionary of ancient Rome*. Baltimore and London

Rickman, G. (1980) *The corn supply of ancient Rome*. Oxford

(1991) 'Problems of transport and development of ports', in A. Giovannini (ed.), *Nourrir la Plèbe: Actes du colloque . . . en hommage à Denis van Berchem*, 103–15. Basel

Ridgway, B. S. (1984) *Roman copies of Greek sculpture: the problem of the originals*. Ann Arbor

Ridley, R. T. (1992) 'The praetor and the pyramid: the tomb of Gaius Cestius in history, archaeology and literature', *Bolletino di Archeologia* 13: 1–29

Riggsby, A. M. (1995) 'Pliny on Cicero and oratory: self-fashioning in the public eye', *AJPh* 116.1: 123–35

Ringrose, D. R. (1983) *Madrid and the Spanish economy (1560–1850)*. Berkeley

Rives, J. (1995) *Religion and authority in Roman Carthage from Augustus to Constantine*. Oxford

(1999) 'The Decree of Decius and the religion of empire', *JRS* 89: 135–54

Rizzo, G. E. (1936) *Monumenti della pittura antica scoperti in Italia, sez. III: la pittura Ellenistico-Romana, Roma, fasc. II: Le pitture della Aula Isiaca di Caligola*. Rome

Roullet, A. (1972) *The Egyptian and Egyptianizing monuments of imperial Rome*. Leiden

Royden, H. L. (1988) *The magistrates of the Roman professional collegia in Italy. From the first to the third century* A D. Pisa

Russell, J. C. (1985) *The control of late ancient and medieval population*. Philadelphia

De Ruyt, F. (1936) 'Etudes de symbolisme funéraire', *Bulletin de l'Institut Historique Belge de Rome* 17: 143–85

Rydell, R. W. (1984) *All the world's a fair: visions of empire at American international expositions, 1876–1916*. Chicago

Rydell, R. W. and N. E. Gwinn (eds.) (1994) *Fair representations: world's fairs and the modern world*. Amsterdam

Sabbah, G. (ed.) (1991) *Le latin médical: la constitution d'un langage scientifique. Réalités et langage de la médecine dans le monde romain*. St-Etienne

Sablayrolles, R. (1999) 'Fastigium equestre. Les grandes préfectures équestres', in S. Demougin, H. Devijver and M.-Th. Raepsart-Charlier (eds.), *L'ordre équestre. Historie d'une aristocratie* (IIe siècle av. J.C. – IIIe ap. J.-C.), *CEFR* 129, 351–89. Rome

Saïd, E. W. (1993) *Culture and imperialism*. London

Sakamoto-Momiyama, M. (1977) *Seasonality in human mortality: a medico-geographical study*. Tokyo

Sallares, R. (1991) *The ecology of the ancient Greek world*. London

(1999) 'Malattie e demografia nel Lazio e in Toscana nell'antichità', in D. Vera (ed.), *Demografia, sistemi agrari, regimi alimentari nel mondo antico*, 131–88. Bari

(2002) *Malaria and Rome: a history of malaria in ancient Italy*. Oxford

Saller, R. P. (1983) 'Martial on patronage and literature', *CQ* 33: 246–57

(1994), *Patriarchy, property and death in the Roman family*. Cambridge

Salzman, M. R. (1990) *On Roman time: the codex-calendar of 354 and the rhythms of urban life in late antiquity*. Berkeley and Los Angeles

(1999) 'The christianization of sacred time and sacred space', in Harris (1999c) 123–34

Santini, C. (1991) *Silius Italicus and his view of the past*. Amsterdam

Saxer, V. (1989) 'L'utilisation par la liturgie de l'éspace urbain et suburbain: l'exemple de Rome dans l'antiquité et le haut moyen âge', *Actes du XIe congrès international d'archéologie Chrétienne* 2, 917–1033. Rome

Scheid, J. (1986) 'Le flamine de Jupiter, les Vestales et le général triomphant', in C. Malamoud and J.-P. Vernant (eds.), *Corps des dieux* (Le Temps de la réflexion 7), 213–30. Paris

(1993) 'The Priest' in A. Giardina (ed.), *The Romans*, 55–84. Chicago

Scheidel, W. (1994) 'Libitina's bitter gains: seasonal mortality and endemic disease in the ancient city of Rome', *Ancient Society* 25: 151–75

(1996a) *Measuring sex, age and death in the Roman empire: explorations in ancient demography*, *JRA* supplement ser. 21. Ann Arbor

(1996b) 'Finances, figures and fiction', *CQ* 46: 222–38

(1997) 'Quantifying the sources of slaves in the early Roman Empire', *JRS* 87: 156–69

(1999) 'Emperors, aristocrats and the Grim Reaper: towards a demographic profile of the Roman élite', *CQ* 49: 254–81

(2001a) *Death on the Nile: disease and the demography of Roman Egypt*. Leiden

(ed.) (2001b) *Debating Roman demography*. Leiden

(2001c) 'Progress and problems in Roman demography', in Scheidel (2001b) 1–81

Schiavoni, C. and E. Sonnino (1982) 'Aspects généraux de l'évolution démographique à Rome: 1598–1824', *Annales de Démographie Historique* 91–109

Schlatter, F. (1992) 'Interpreting the mosaic of Santa Pudenziana', *VC* 46: 276–95

Schneider, R. (1986) *Bunte Barbaren: Orientalstatuen aus farbigem Marmor in der römischen Räpresentationskunst*. Worms

Schofield, M. (1991) *The stoic idea of the city*. Cambridge

Schtaerman, E. M. (1969) *Die Blütezeit der Sklavenwirtschaft in der römischen Republik*. Wiesbaden

Schumacher, W. N. (1958) 'Zum Sarkophag eines christlichen Konsuls', *MDAI(R)* 65: 99–120

(1987) 'Die Konstantinischen Exedra-Basiliken', in Deckers et al. (1987) 132–86

Scobie, A. (1986) 'Slums, sanitation and mortality in the Roman world', *Klio* 68: 399–433

Scott, I. J. (1975) *Piranesi*. London

Seager, R. (1979) *Pompey: a political biography*. Oxford

Seeliger, H. R. (1987) 'Die Geschichte der Katakombe "inter duos lauros"', in Deckers et al. (1987) 67–70

Sepulcri, A. (1903) 'I papiri della basilica di Monza e le reliquie inviate da Roma', *Archivio Storico Lombardo* 19: 241–62

Sharrock, A. (1994) *Seduction and repetition in Ars amatoria II*. Oxford

Shaw, B. D. (1996) 'Seasons of death: aspects of mortality in imperial Rome', *JRS* 86: 100–38

Shelley, P. B. (1964) *Letters* (ed. F. Jones). London

Shelton, K. (1981) *The Esquiline Treasure*. London

Sidebottom, H. (1998) 'Herodian's historical methods and understanding of history', *ANRW* 11.34.4: 2775–836

Simon, E. (1992) 'The Diptych of the Symmachi and the Nicomachi: an interpretation', *G&R* 39: 56–65

Sivan, H. (1993) *Ausonius of Bordeaux: genesis of a Gallic aristocracy*. London

Smelik, K. A. D. and E. A. Hemelrijk (1984) 'Who knows what monsters demented Egypt worships? Opinions on animal worship in antiquity as part of the ancient conception of Egypt', *ANRW* 11.17.4: 1852–2000

Smith, R. R. R. (1988) '*Simulacra gentium*: the ethne from the Sebasteion at Aphrodisias', *JRS* 78: 50–77

Snyder, G. F. (1985) *Ante pacem*. Macon

Solin, H. (1971) *Beiträge zur Kenntniss der griechischen Personennamen in Rom*. Helsinki

Spielmann, I. (1906) *St Louis International Exhibition 1904: the British section*. London

Spivey, N. (1995) 'Bionic statues', in A. Powell (ed.), *The Greek world*, 442–59. London

Spurr, M. S. (1986) *Arable cultivation in Roman Italy c. 200 B C – c. A D 100*. London

Stahl, W. H. (1952) *Commentary on the Dream of Scipio*. New York

Stambaugh, J. E. (1988) *The ancient Roman city*. Baltimore

Stanley, F. H., Jr (1990) 'Geographical mobility in Roman Lusitania: an epigraphical perspective', *ZPE* 82: 249–69

Stein, P. (1930) *Die Senatssitzungen der ciceronischen Zeit (68–43)*. Münster

Steinby, E. M. (1993–9) *Lexicon topographicum urbis Romae*. Rome

Stevens Curl, J. (1994) *Egyptomania. The Egyptian revival: a recurring theme in the history of taste*. Manchester and New York

Stewart, Andrew (1997) *Art, desire and the body in ancient Greece*. Cambridge

Sullivan, J. W. (1994) 'Saints Peter and Paul: some ironic aspects of their imaging', *Art History* 17: 59–80

Swain, S. C. R. (1996) *Hellenism and empire. Language, classicism, and power in the Greek world, A D 50–250*. Oxford

Syme, R. (1939). *The Roman revolution*. Oxford

 (1971). *Emperors and biography. Studies in the Historia Augusta*. Oxford

Talbert, R. J. A. (1984) *The senate of imperial Rome*. Princeton

Tanner, J. (2000) 'Portraits, power and patronage in the late Roman republic', *JRS* 90: 18–37

Thompson, L. A. (1989) *Romans and blacks*. London

Toutain, J. (1920) *Les Cultes païens dans l'empire romain*, vol. III. Paris

Toynbee, J. M. C. (1934) *The Hadrianic school*. Cambridge

Toynbee, J. and J. Ward-Perkins (1956) *The shrine of St Peter, and the Vatican excavations*. London

Treggiari, S. (1980) 'Urban labour at Rome', in Garnsey (1980) 48–64

Trillmich, W. and P. Zanker (eds.) (1990) *Stadtbild und Ideologie. Die Monumentalisierung hispanischer Städte zwischen Republik und Kaiserzeit.* Munich

Urlichs, C. (1871) *Codex urbis Romae topographicus.* Würzburg

Van Dam, R. (1993) *Saints and their miracles in late antique Gaul.* Princeton

Van Hear, N. (1998) *New diasporas: the mass exodus, dispersal and regrouping of migrant communities.* London

Veblen, T. (1926) *The theory of the leisure class: an economic history of institutions.* New York

Vermeule, C. C. (1977) *Greek sculpture and Roman taste: the purpose and setting of Greco-Roman art in Italy and the Greek imperial east.* Ann Arbor

Verschuur, G. L. (1996) *Impact! The threat of comets and asteroids.* New York and Oxford

Versnel, H. S. (1970) *Triumphus: an inquiry into the origin, development and meaning of the Roman triumph.* Leiden

Visconti, C. L. (1887) 'Trovamenti di oggetti d'arte e di antichità figurata', *Bollettino della commissione archeologica comunale di Roma* 15: 132–6

Visconti, C. L. and V. Vespignani (1877) 'Delle scoperte avvenute per la demolizione delle torri della Porta Flaminia', *Bollettino della commissione archeologica comunale di Roma* 4: 184–252

Vitali, L., ed. (1966) *Il Tesoro del Duomo di Monza.* Milan

de Vos, M. (1980) *L'egittomania in pitture e mosaici romano-campani della prima età imperiale.* Leiden

(1996) 'Iseum Metellinum', in E. M. Steinby, *Lexicon topographicum urbis Romae*, vol. III, 110–12. Rome

Vout, C. (2000) 'Objects of desire: eroticised political discourse in imperial Rome' (PhD diss.). Cambridge

de Vries, J. (1984) *European urbanization 1500–1800.* London

Waelkens, M. (1985) 'The provenance of the statues of Dacian prisoners in Trajan's forum at Rome', *AJA* 89: 641–53

Waetzoldt, S. (1964) *Die Kopien des 17 Jahrhunderts nach Mosaiken und Wandmalereien in Rom.* Vienna and Munich

Wallace-Hadrill, A. (1983) *Suetonius. The scholar and his caesars.* London

(1987) 'Time for Augustus: Ovid, Augustus and the Fasti', in M. Whitby, P. Hardie and M. Whitby (eds.), *Homo Viator. Classical essays for John Bramble*, 221–30. Bristol

(1989) 'Rome's cultural revolution', *JRS* 79: 157–64

(1990) 'Roman arches and Greek honours: the language of power at Rome', *PCPS* 36: 143–81

(1998) 'To be Roman, go Greek: thoughts on hellenisation at Rome', in M. Austin, J. Harries and C. Smith (eds.), *Modus operandi: essays in honour of G. Rickman*, 79–91. London

Walter, H. (1993) *Les barbares de l'occident romain.* Paris

Ward-Perkins, B. (1984) *From classical antiquity to the middle ages: urban public building in northern and central Italy AD 300–850.* Oxford

Warren, L. B. (1970) 'Roman triumphs and Etruscan kings: the changing face of the triumph', *JRS* 60: 49–66

Waywell, G. B. (1978) *The free-standing sculptures of the Mausoleum at Halicarnassus in The British Museum: a catalogue.* London

Weingarten, S. (1999)'Was the pilgrim from Bordeaux a woman?', *JECS* 7: 291–7

Weingärtner, D. G. (1969) *Die Ägyptenreise des Germanicus (Papyrologische Texte und Abhandlungen* 11). Bonn

Weinstock, S. (1971) *Divus Julius.* Oxford

Weitzmann, K. (1979) *Age of spirituality: late antique and early Christian art, third to seventh century; catalogue of the exhibition at the Metropolitan Museum of Art, November 19, 1977 through February 12, 1978.* Princeton

White, H. (1978) *Tropics of discourse: essays in cultural criticism.* Baltimore

White, P. (1975) 'The friends of Martial, Statius and Pliny, and the dispersal of patronage', *HSCP* 79: 265–300

  (1978) 'Amicitia and the profession of poetry in early imperial Rome', *JRS* 68: 74–92

  (1982) 'Positions for poets in early imperial Rome', in B. K. Gold (ed.), *Literary and artistic patronage in ancient Rome,* 50–66. Austin, TX

Whitehouse, H. (1977) 'Wall painting in the Museo Nazionale, Naples', *PBSR* 45 (new series, vol. 32): 52–64

Whittaker, C. R. (1964) 'The revolt of Papirius Dionysius AD 190', *Historia* 12.3: 348–69

  (1969) *Herodian, with an English translation.* Cambridge, MA

  (1988) 'Trade and the aristocracy in the Roman empire', *Opus* 4: 49–75 (repr. in *Land, city and trade in the Roman empire.* Aldershot and Brookfield 1993)

  (1993) 'The poor in the city of Rome', in *Land, city and trade in the Roman Empire,* vol. VII, 1–25. Aldershot

  (2000) 'Africa', in A. K. Bowman, P. Garnsey, D. Rathbone (eds.), *The Cambridge Ancient History,* vol. XI *The High Empire, AD 70–192,* 514–43. Cambridge

Wild, R. A. (1984) 'The known Isis-Sarapis sanctuaries of the Roman period', *ANRW* II.17.4: 1739–1851

Wilken, R. (1992) *The land called holy: Palestine in Christian history and thought.* New Haven,

Winkler, M. M. (1983) *The persona in three satires of Juvenal.* Hildesheim

Wisch, B. and S. S. Munshower (1990) *Art and pageantry in the renaissance and baroque.* University Park, PA

Wiseman, T. P. (1985) 'Competition and cooperation', in T. P. Wiseman (ed.), *Roman political life 90 BC – AD 69,* 3–19. Exeter

Witt, R. E. (1971) *Isis in the Graeco-Roman world.* London

Wood, I. (1999) 'Images as a substitute for writing: a reply', in E. Chrysos and I. Wood (eds.), *East and west: modes of communication,* 35–46. Leiden

Woodman, A. J. (1988) *Rhetoric in classical historiography: four studies.* London and Sydney

Woolf, G. D. (1998) *Becoming Roman: the origins of provincial civilisation in Gaul.* Cambridge

  (2000) 'Urbanization and its discontents in early Roman Gaul', in Fentress (2000) 115–31

Wright, D. (1998) 'The persistence of pagan art and patronage in fifth century Rome', in I. Sevcenko and I. Hutter (eds.), *AETOS: studies in honour of C. Mango*, 354–69. Stuttgart

Wrigley, E. A. (1978) 'A simple model of London's importance in changing English society and economy 1650–1750', in Abrams and Wrigley (1978) 215–43

Wyke, M. (1992) 'Augustan Cleopatras: female power and poetic authority', in A. Powell (ed.), *Roman poetry and propaganda in the age of Augustus*, 98–140. London

Yates, R. D. S. (2001) 'Cosmos, central authority, and communities in the early Chinese empire,' in S. E. Alcock, T. N. D'Altroy, K. D. Morrison and C. M. Sinopoli (eds.), *Empires. Perspectives from archaeology and history*, 351–68. Cambridge

Zanker, P. (1970) 'Das Trajansforum in Rom', *Archäologischer Anzeiger* 85: 499–544
　(1979) 'Zur Funktion und Bedeutung griechischer Skulptur in der Römerzeit', in *Le classicisme à Rome aux Iers siècles avant et après J.-C.* (Entretiens Hardt 25), 283–314. Geneva
　(1988) *The power of images in the age of Augustus*. Michigan
　(1995) *Die Maske des Sokrates. Das Bild des Intellektuellen in der antiken Kunst*. Munich
　(1997) 'In search of the Roman viewer', in D. Buitron-Oliver (ed.), *The interpretation of architectural sculpture in Greece and Rome*, 187–91. Washington

Zecchini, G. (1983) 'Il santuario della Dea Caelestis e l'Historia Augusta', *Contributi dell'Instituto di storia antica, Universita cattolica del Sacro Cuore* 9: 150–67
　(1990) 'C. Iulio Cesare e il galata moriente', in M. Sordi (ed.), *Dulce et decorum est pro patria mori: la morte in combattimento nell'antichità*, 247–59. Milan

Zetzel, J. E. G. (1982) 'The poetics of patronage in the late first century BCE', in B. K. Gold (ed.), *Literary and artistic patronage in ancient Rome*, 87–102. Austin, TX

Ziegler, C. (1994) 'From one Egyptomania to another: the legacy of Roman antiquity', in J.-M. Humbert, M. Pantazzi and C. Ziegler (eds.), *Egyptomania. Egypt in western art 1730–1930*, 15–20. Ottawa

Zurbrigg, S. (1994) 'Re-thinking the "human factor" in malaria mortality: the case of Punjab, 1868–1940', *Parasitologia* 36: 121–35

Index

51022954R00149

Made in the USA
Lexington, KY
08 April 2016